GLOBAL CORRUPTION

LAW, THEORY AND PRACTICE

GLOBAL CORRUPTION
LAW, THEORY AND PRACTICE

VOLUME-1

Havard Yıldız
Sadiq Hasan

Kruger Brentt
Publishers
2024

Kruger Brentt Publishers UK. LTD.
Company Number 9728962
Regd. Office: 68 St Margarets Road, Edgware, Middlesex HA8 9UU

ISBN: 978-1-78-715-136-9

For information on all our publications visit our website at http://krugerbrentt.com/

PREFACE

Corruption has become a significant issue in the world today, affecting the social, economic, and political aspects of life. It is a global problem that is not limited to any specific country or region. Corruption takes many forms, from bribery to embezzlement and money laundering. In this essay, we will explore the laws, theories, and practices related to global corruption. Corruption is a criminal offense in most countries. The laws that deal with corruption differ from one country to another. However, most countries have enacted laws that prohibit corrupt practices. These laws define what constitutes corrupt practices and provide penalties for those who engage in them. The United Nations Convention against Corruption (UNCAC) is a global legal framework that provides a basis for countries to combat corruption. The convention provides guidelines on how countries can prevent and combat corruption in various sectors, including public administration, finance, and law enforcement. Several theories attempt to explain the causes of corruption. One of the most popular theories is the principal-agent theory. According to this theory, corruption occurs when there is a misalignment of interests between the principal and agent. The principal is the person who entrusts another person (the agent) to carry out a task on their behalf. In the case of corruption, the agent uses their power to serve their interests rather than those of the principal.

Another theory that explains corruption is the cultural theory. According to this theory, corruption is a product of cultural values and norms. In societies where corruption is tolerated, it becomes a norm, and people engage in it without feeling guilty. The cultural theory explains why corruption is prevalent in some countries and not in others. Combating corruption is not an easy task. It requires the cooperation of various stakeholders, including the government, civil society, and the private sector. Governments have a responsibility to ensure that laws are enacted and enforced to prevent and punish corrupt practices. Civil society plays a crucial role in monitoring government activities and advocating for transparency and accountability. The private sector also has a responsibility to prevent corruption by implementing strong ethical and compliance programs. Global corruption is a complex issue that requires a multi-faceted approach to combat it. Laws, theories, and practices are essential in the fight against corruption. The legal framework provides a basis for countries to enact and enforce laws that prohibit corrupt practices. The theories of corruption help to explain the causes of corruption and provide insights into how to prevent it. The practice of combating corruption requires the cooperation of various stakeholders, including the government, civil society, and the private sector. By working together, we can create a world that is free from corruption.

Havard Yıldız

Sadiq Hasan

CONTENTS

VOLUME–2

CHAPTER-1

CORRUPTION IN CONTEXT: SOCIAL, ECONOMIC AND POLITICAL DIMENSIONS

WHY CORRUPTION MATTERS: THE ADVERSE EFFECTS OF CORRUPTION

A CASE ILLUSTRATION OF THE IMPACT OF CORRUPTION

The TV report noted below investigates the cancellation of World Bank funding ($1.2 billion loan) for a major bridge proposal (worth nearly $3 billion) in Bangladesh. The bridge is critical to both the economic growth of the country and the safety of hundreds of thousands of poor Bangladesh citizens who cross the Padma River daily in crowded, unsafe boats.1 The World Bank cancelled funding for the bridge project because very senior politicians and officials in the Bangladesh government allegedly solicited bribes from bidding companies. SNC-Lavalin allegedly agreed to pay those bribes in order to get the engineering contract (worth $50 million) to supervise the bridge construction. SNC-Lavalin is one of the five

Background on the Padma Bridge Corruption Scandal

When allegations of bribery concerning the awarding of the engineering contract to SNC- Lavalin arose, the World Bank (WB) instituted an investigation by an external evaluation panel in the Fall of 2012. According to the report of the WB Panel, there was evidence that in late March of 2011 two members of the Bangladesh Bridge Project Evaluation Committee (BPEC) unlawfully informed senior SNC-Lavalin officers in Bangladesh that SNC-Lavalin was currently second behind another firm, Halcrow, in the bidding process, but that no final recommendation had been made. In addition to BPEC's recommendation, the awarding of the engineering contract would also have to be approved by Minister Syed Abul Hossain of the Bangladesh government. SNC-Lavalin officers allegedly took several steps to improve the company's ranking on BPEC's list. Mohammad Ismail, Director of an SNC-Lavalin subsidiary in Bangladesh was the main representative in the bidding process, along with SNC-Lavalin local consultant Md Mostafa. Ismail and Mostafa dealt directly with Zulfiquar Bhuiyan, the Secretary of the Bridge Authority and also a member of BPEC, and Minister Hossain. Bhuiyan indicated that he and the Minister expected to have a face-to-face meeting with a top SNC-Lavalin executive to "seal the project." Ramesh Shah was Vice-President of SNC-Lavalin International Inc. (SLII) and reported to Kevin Wallace who was Senior Vice- President of SLII and the senior SNC-Lavalin executive assigned to the Padma Bridge project. SLII was a relatively small subsidiary or division of the SNC-Lavalin Group of companies. Its head office was located in Oakville, Ontario.

In May 2011, Ramesh Shah and Kevin Wallace flew to Bangladesh for a face-to-face meeting with Buiyan and Minister Hossain. The meeting was facilitated by an influential government Minister, Abul Hasan Chowdhury, whom the prosecution alleges was also an agent of SNC- Lavalin. After the meeting, Ramesh Shah wrote in his notebook, "PADMA PCC...4% Min...1% Secretary." "PCC" was SNC-Lavalin's internal notation for "project consultancy or commercial costs" which apparently was used in SLII's accounts to refer to bribery payments. "Min" presumably referred to Minister Hossain and "Secretary" presumably referred to Secretary Buiyan. Two weeks later, SNC-Lavalin International Inc. was awarded the contract.

As noted, the World Bank "suspended" its funding for Padma Bridge in 2012 pending an external evaluation of alleged corruption by a WB Investigative Panel. After completing its initial evaluation, the WB panel recommended corruption charges be laid against several persons, including Minister Hossain. Bangladesh's Anti-Corruption Commission (ACC) laid conspiracy to bribe charges against seven persons, but they adamantly refused to include Minister Hossain. The World Bank threatened to cancel the Padma Bridge loan agreement due to this refusal to conduct a "full and fair" corruption inquiry of all suspects. In January 2013, before a formal cancellation occurred, Bangladesh "withdrew" its formal request to the World Bank for funding of the bridge.

The bridge was scheduled for completion in 2014. According to Bangladesh news sources, work on the bridge began in 2015 using domestic financing and apparently a $2 billion investment from China. The government of Bangladesh initially claimed the bridge would be complete by 2018. In January of 2016, the Executive Committee of National Economic Council (ECNEC) approved a third revision to the Padma Bridge project raising the total project cost to more than Tk 80 billion (roughly US $1.02 billion) over budget. The Bangladesh Bridge Authority claimed that the increased budget is due to delayed implementation and associated factors including rising costs for construction materials, consultancy services, and land, as well as recruiting more people to speed up the process.2 Independent sources have suggested that the climbing costs were also at least in part due to further bribery and corruption, and that in order to fund the project the Bangladeshi government had to divert resources from essential services like health care.3 Meanwhile, a hundred or more citizens continue to die yearly crossing the river on overcrowded and unsafe boats.

The World Bank alerted the RCMP to evidence of possible corruption it had uncovered. After investigating, the RCMP initially laid bribery charges against two top SLII executives, Mohammed Ismail and Ramesh Shah. They are both Canadian citizens. Then, in September 2013, the RCMP laid bribery charges against three more persons: Wallace and Bhuiyan, both Canadian citizens, and former Minister Abul Hassan Chowdhury, who is a Bangladeshi national. A preferred indictment was filed on October 28, 2013, alleging one count of bribery by all five men committed between December 1, 2009 and September 1, 2011, contrary to s. 3(1)(b) of the Corruption of Foreign Public Officials Act. Chowdhury brought an action to stay the proceedings against him on the grounds that there was no jurisdiction to prosecute him, a Bangladeshi citizen who had never been in Canada, and whose alleged unlawful conduct occurred in Bangladesh. Canada has no extradition treaty with Bangladesh and had not attempted to have Bangladesh surrender Chowdhury for prosecution in Canada. Chowdhury was successful in his court challenge and the charges against him were stayed: Chowdhury v The Queen. Charges against Mohammed Ismail were subsequently dropped, and the remaining three continued to await trial on the bribery charge.

In an important pre-trial issue in World Bank Group v Wallace, the Supreme Court of Canada unanimously ruled that the World Bank does not have to disclose its investigative reports and similar matters to the four accused.6 Any other result would have hampered the investigation and would have been a significant blow to future cooperation from agencies such as the World Bank.

Based on the evidence of alleged corruption collected by the World Bank, SNC-Lavalin Group Inc. and the World Bank signed a Negotiated Resolution Agreement in which SNC- Lavalin International Inc. (SLII) and over 100 SNC-Lavalin Group Inc. affiliates have been debarred from bidding on World Bank funded projects for 10 years. The remainder of SNC- Lavalin Group Inc. will also be debarred if SNC-Lavalin does not comply with the terms of the settlement in regard to improving their internal compliance program. It is hard to determine what portion of total SNC-Lavalin work is likely to be affected by the World Bank debarment, although by some estimates it is thought to be less than two percent.

Meanwhile the Bangladesh ACC continued to investigate the charge of conspiracy to bribe by seven persons: three Bangladesh officials (including the Prime Minister's nephew, Ferdous, Zaber and Bhuiyan), three SNC officials (Wallace,

Shah and Mohammed Ismail), and SNC's local agent Mostafa. Remarkably, the ACC, in its final report in September 2014, concluded that there was not sufficient evidence to proceed with a charge of conspiracy to bribe against any of these men. The ACC also reported that Ministers Hossain and Chowdhury had no involvement in the alleged bribery scheme [See Chapter 6 at Section 3.2 for further discussion of the Bangladesh ACC]. The ACC report was then filed with the Bangladesh court and on October 30, 2014, the Court acquitted all seven persons of conspiracy to bribe.

World Bank Group v Wallace, 2016 SCC 15. The World Bank received emails from tipsters suggesting that there had been corruption in regard to the bridge supervision contract. The World Bank did its investigation and found evidence of corruption. After debarring SNC-Lavalin Group Inc. from bidding on World Bank-sponsored projects for 10 years, the World Bank shared the tipsters' emails, its own investigative reports and other documents with the RCMP. The RCMP used that information to obtain a warrant to intercept private communication (a wiretap warrant) and a search warrant to obtain certain documents from SNC-Lavalin offices. After the conspiracy to corrupt charge was laid, the accused person brought an application before an Ontario Superior Court trial judge to quash the wiretap authorization and thereby exclude from trial the evidence collected by wiretap. As part of the wiretap challenge, the accused sought an order requiring production to them of certain World Bank investigative documents. The trial judge concluded that certain World Bank documents were "likely relevant" to the accused's right to a fair trial and therefore ordered those documents be produced for review before the court. The SCC quashed the production order on two grounds. First, the World Bank was granted immunity from such disclosure under the Articles of Agreement setting up the World Bank, Articles which Canada and some 185 countries have agreed to. Second, even if the World Bank did not have immunity, the documents sought did not pass the "likely relevant" test, and therefore a court could not lawfully order their disclosure.

Criticism of the World Bank

It should be noted that some commentators are highly critical of the World Bank's lending practices. For example, Paul Sarlo[7] argues that the World Bank facilitates large scale corruption by making huge development loans to notoriously corrupt governments without imposing a regime of due diligence to ensure the loan is used for the intended project.[8] This lack of due diligence opens the door to theft of 20-40% of loans by corrupt leaders or through the companies they hire to complete the project. Ultimately it is the citizens of the corrupt borrowing country who pay, since they are responsible for full repayment of the loan with interest even if part of the loan is stolen.

A Shocking Conclusion

On January 6, 2017 the trial judge, Justice Nordheimer, threw out all the wiretap evidence in the case on the basis, amongst others, that the information provided in the Information to Obtain (ITO) was nothing more than "speculation, gossip and rumour".9 If that was true, what does that say about the experience and competence of the senior RCMP officers who sought the wiretap, and of any prosecutor who may have assisted in obtaining it?10 If the trial judge's overall characterization of the ITO was incorrect, why didn't the Public Prosecution Service of Canada (PPSC) appeal that decision? Barely one month later, on February 10, 2017, the Crown elected to call no witnesses at the trial on the grounds that "we 7 Paul Sarlo, "The Global Financial Crisis and the Transnational Anti-Corruption Regime: A Call for Regulation of the World Bank's Lending Practices" (2014) 45 Geo J Intl L 1293.

For example, the World Bank lent Indonesia $30 billion during the thirty-year rule of notoriously corrupt General Suharto. The International Monetary Fund has been subject to similar criticism related to irresponsible lending. For example, a portion of an IMF loan to Russia was used by Boris Yeltsin for his re-election campaign in 1996: Clare Fletcher and Daniela Herrmann, The Internationalisation of Corruption (Burlington, VT: Ashgate, 2012) at 68.

"The fact that a particular investigation may be difficult, does not lower the standard that must be met in order to obtain a Part VI authorization. Reduced to its essentials, the information provided in the ITO was nothing more than speculation, gossip, and rumour. Nothing that could fairly be referred to as direct factual evidence, to support the rumour and speculation, was provided or investigated. The information provided by the tipsters was hearsay (or worse) added to other hearsay." (R v Wallace, 2017 ONSC 132 at para 71).

For more details concerning allegations of SNC-Lavalin's involvement in corruption of Bangladeshi public officials, World Bank's investigation and subsequent withdrawal from funding the project, and RCMP investigation into this matter, see World Bank, "World Bank Statement on Padma Bridge" (29 June 2012), online: <http://www.worldbank.org/en/news/press- release/2012/06/29/world-bank-statement-padma-bridge, and World Bank> and World Bank Group v Wallace, [2016] 1 SCR 207, 2016 SCC 15. had no reasonable prospect of conviction based on the evidence". If the wiretap evidence was as legally suspect as Justice Nordheimer found, why didn't the PPSC pursue the other available evidence before the trial began that would have supported the continuation of the prosecution, including the possibility of a plea agreement or a non-prosecution agreement with one of the original conspirators in exchange for their cooperation and testimony? It is in the public interest to ask whether the RCMP officers and prosecutors were up to the task of investigating and prosecuting this foreign bribery case? An inquiry and subsequent public explanation of why this important CFPOA case fell apart will be helpful for future investigations and prosecutions and may help reduce the damage done to Canada's reputation.

Corruption is "public enemy no. 1" in the developing world, according to World Bank President Jim Yong Kim, and "every dollar that a corrupt official or corrupt business person puts in his or her pockets is a dollar stolen from a pregnant woman who needs healthcare, or from a girl or boy who deserves an education, or from communities that need water, roads and schools." Recently, it has been estimated that as much as $1 trillion annually is siphoned off from developing countries by corruption, tax evasion and other large financial crimes. The World Bank has estimated that as much as $40 billion in foreign aid to the world's poorest countries has been lost to corruption in recent years. And 3.6 million people die from inadequate health care and living conditions each year in part because corruption has stolen away development aid. UN Development Programme Administrator Helen Clark stated that "corruption can stand in the way of people getting basic services," while UK Prime Minister David Cameron said "don't let anyone keep corruption out of how we tackle poverty." In 2008, the US Assistant Attorney General warned that "corruption is not a gentleman's agreement where no one gets hurt. People do get hurt. And the people who are hurt the most are often residents of the poorest countries on earth."

The remainder of Section 1 will look at the nature, causes and consequences of corruption that have motivated such strong condemnation of corruption by world leaders.

Four Concerns about Corruption

The Organization for Economic and Cooperative Development (OECD) prepared a Background Brief in 2013 entitled "The Rationale for Fighting Corruption" as part of the organization's CleanGovBiz: Integrity in Practice Initiative.12 The initiative seeks to involve civil society and the private sector in anti-corruption strategies. The brief provides an overview of the reasons why everyone should be concerned about corruption. The text of this brief is set out below:

BEGINNING OF EXCERPT

The Rationale for FigWhting Corruption

The costs of corruption for economic, political and social development are becoming increasingly evident. But many of the most convincing arguments in support of the fight against corruption are little known to the public and remain unused in political debates. This brief provides evidence that reveals the true cost and to explain why governments and business must prioritise the fight against corruption.

What is Corruption?

Corruption is the abuse of public or private office for personal gain. It includes acts of bribery, embezzlement, nepotism or state capture. It is often associated with and reinforced by other illegal practices, such as bid rigging, fraud or money laundering. [Transparency International describes corruption as "the abuse of entrusted power for private gain."]

What does Corruption Look Like?

It could be a multinational company that pays a bribe to win the public contract to build the local highway, despite proposing a sub-standard offer. It could be the politician redirecting public investments to his hometown rather than to the region most in need. It could be the public official embezzling funds for school renovations to build his private villa. It could be the manager recruiting an ill-suited friend for a high-level position. Or, it could be the local official demanding bribes from ordinary citizens to get access to a new water pipe. At the end of the day, those hurt most by corruption are the world's weakest and most vulnerable.

Why Fight Corruption?

Corruption is one of the main obstacles to sustainable economic, political and social development, for developing, emerging and developed economies alike.

Overall, corruption reduces efficiency and increases inequality. Estimates show that the cost of corruption equals more than 5% of global GDP (US$ 2.6 trillion, World Economic Forum) with over US$ 1 trillion paid in bribes each year (World Bank). It is not only a question of ethics; we simply cannot afford such waste.

1. Corruption increases the cost of doing business

First, bribes and drawn-out negotiations to bargain them add additional costs to a transaction. Second, corruption brings with it the risk of prosecution, important penalties, blacklisting and reputational damage. Third, engaging in bribery creates business uncertainty, as such behaviour does not necessarily guarantee business to a company; there can always be another competing company willing to offer a higher bribe to tilt the business in its favour.

On the macro level, corruption distorts market mechanisms, like fair competition and deters domestic and foreign investments, thus stifling growth and future business opportunities for all stakeholders. IMF research has shown that investment in corrupt countries is almost 5% less than in countries that are relatively corruption-free. The World Economic Forum estimates that corruption increases the cost of doing business by up to 10% on average. Siemens, the German engineering giant, had to pay penalties of US$ 1.6 billion in 2008 to settle charges that it routinely engaged in bribery around the world. A significant negative impact of corruption on a country's capital productivity has been proven.

2. Corruption leads to waste or the inefficient use of public resources

As a result of corruption, investments are not allocated to sectors and programmes which present the best value for money or where needs are highest, but to those which offer the best prospects for personal enrichment of corrupt politicians. Thus resources go into big infrastructure projects or military procurement where kickbacks are high, to the detriment of sectors like education and health care. Moreover, public tenders are assigned to the highest bribe payer, neglecting better qualified companies not willing to bribe, which undermines the quality of the projects carried out. In some instances public funds are simply diverted from their intended use, embezzled and exploited for private enrichment. Corruption also slows down bureaucratic processes, as inefficient bureaucracies offer more leverage for corrupt public officials: the longer the queue for a service, the higher the incentive for citizens to bribe to get what they want. Finally, nepotism - in both private and public organisations - brings incompetent people into power, weakening performance and governance.

Several studies provide evidence of the negative correlation between corruption and the quality of government investments, services and regulations. For example, child mortality rates in countries with high levels of corruption are about one third higher than in countries with low corruption, infant mortality rates are almost twice as high and student dropout rates are five times as high (Gupta et al. 2011). Numbers on the monetary loss due to corruption vary, but are alarming. The African Union (2002) estimates that 25% of the GDP of African states, amounting to US$148 billion, is lost to corruption every year. The US health care programmes Medicare and Medicaid estimate that 5% to 10% of their annual budget is wasted as a result of corruption.

3. Corruption excludes poor people from public services and perpetuates poverty

The poor generally lack privileged access to decision makers, which is necessary in corrupt societies to obtain certain goods and services. Resources and benefits are thus exchanged among the rich and well connected, excluding the less privileged. Moreover, the poor bear the largest burden [proportionate to their income] of higher tariffs in public services imposed by the costs of corruption... They might also be completely excluded from basic services like health care or education, if they cannot afford to pay bribes which are requested illegally. The embezzlement or diversion of public funds further reduces the government's resources available for development and poverty reduction spending.

The significant impact of corruption on income inequality and the negative effect of corruption on income growth for the poorest 20% of a country have been proven empirically (Gupta et al. 2002). The World Bank (Baker 2005) estimates that each year US$ 20 to US$ 40 billion, corresponding to 20% to 40% of official development assistance, is stolen through high-level corruption from public budgets in developing countries and hidden overseas. Transparency International (Global Corruption Report 2006) found that about 35% of births in rural areas in Azerbaijan take place at home, because poor people cannot afford to pay the high charges for care in facilities where care was supposed to be free.

4. Corruption corrodes public trust, undermines the rule of law and ultimately delegitimizes the state

Rules and regulations are circumvented by bribes, public budget control is undermined by illicit money flows and political critics and the media are silenced through bribes levering out democratic systems of checks and balances. Corruption in political processes like elections or party financing undermines the rule of the people and thus the very foundation of democracy. If basic public services are not delivered to citizens due to corruption, the state eventually loses its credibility and legitimacy.

As a result, disappointed citizens might turn away from the state, retreat from political processes, migrate – or – stand up against what they perceive to be the corrupt political and economic elites. The global uprisings from the Arab world to India, Brazil and occupy Wall Street are proving that business as usual can no longer be an option for a number of countries. [footnotes omitted]

END OF EXCERPT

Four Other Related Concerns about Corruption

In addition to the four concerns described above, several other concerns are worthy of specific note, namely corruption's impact on (i) human rights, (ii) gender equality, (iii) global security and (iv) climate change and environmental degradation.

Human Rights and Corruption

In Corruption: Economic Analysis and International Law, Arnone and Borlini elaborate on the impact of corruption on the rule of law and human rights:

Massive corrupt dynamics, indeed, weaken the basic foundations both of the representative mechanisms underlying the separation of powers and of human rights. ... Since corruption generates discrimination and inequality, this relationship [between human rights and government corruption] ... bears on civil and political rights. For instance, it strengthens the misappropriation of property in violation of legal rights ... it likely leads to the rise of monopolies which either wipe out or gravely vitiate freedom to trade. Corruption strikes at economic and social rights as well: the commissioning by a public entity of useless or overpriced goods or services, and the choice of poorly performing undertakings through perverted public procurement mechanisms are mere examples of how corruption can endanger the second generation of human rights.

The relationship between fundamental HR and corruption could not be expressed more vividly than in the words of the UN High Commissioner for Human Rights, Navy Pillay: “Let us be clear. Corruption kills. The money stolen is enough to feed the world’s hungry every night, many of them children; corruption denies them their right to food, and in some cases, their right to life” ... The departure point and organizational principle of the 2004 [UN Development Program’s] analyst study is that “Corruption affects the poor disproportionately, due to their powerlessness to change the status quo and inability to pay bribes, creating inequalities that violate their human rights.”

In their article “The International Legal Framework Against Corruption: Achievements and Challenges,” Jan Wouters et al. note the increasing tendency to frame corruption as a human rights issue.

To help understand the link between corruption and human rights, the International Council on Human Rights Policy divides corruption-based human rights violations into direct, indirect and remote violations. For example, bribing a judge directly violates the right to a fair trial, while embezzling public funds needed for social programs indirectly violates economic and social rights. Many commentators hope this focus on human rights will create new human rights-based remedies and assist in anti-corruption efforts.

The coupling of corruption and human rights remains an increasingly popular trend. In April 2015 in Doha, at the 13th United Nations Congress on Crime Prevention and International Justice, Dean and Executive Secretary of the International Anti-Corruption Academy, Martin Kreutner, stated, “All the universal goals run the risk of being severely undermined by corruption. ... Corruption is the antithesis vis-à-vis human rights, the venom vis-à-vis the rule of law, the poison for prosperity and development and the reverse of equity and equality.”

While recognizing the important connection between corruption and human rights, recently some authors have further analyzed the potential dangers and limitations of confining discussions of corruption to the language of human rights.

Recent publications have also taken a closer look at the connection between corruption and human rights in particular geographic areas. In particular, Anne Peters in her Working

BEGINNING OF EXCERPT

An entirely different set of questions concerns the proceedings in which such a human rights violation might be claimed and whether the change in perspective

– away from a primarily criminal law approach to anti-corruption toward human rights – is practical in terms of legal policy and valuable in terms of legal ethics.

Opportunity for moral and practical strengthening of the anti-corruption agenda

Proponents of endowing the anti-corruption instruments with a human rights approach believe that this will upgrade these instruments in political and moral terms and thus ensure improved implementation of anti-corruption measures. The classical argument is "empowerment". The human rights approach can elucidate the rights of persons affected by corruption, such as the rights to safe drinking water and free primary education, and show them how, for instance, the misappropriation of public funds in those areas interferes with their enjoyment of the goods to which they are entitled. In that way, affected persons would be empowered to denounce corruption to which they otherwise would be helplessly exposed.

The UN Human Rights Council believes that the greatest advantages consist, firstly, in shifting the existing criminal law focus of the anti-corruption instrument away from individual perpetrators toward the systemic responsibility of the State and, secondly, in an improvement of the status of victims.

A weakness of the purely criminal law approach to anti-corruption is becoming apparent especially in China, where the broad and indeterminate criminal offences can easily be abused to eliminate or at least discredit political opponents. The human rights perspective shifts the focus away from repression toward prevention and thus also away from the abusive initiation of criminal proceedings.

Finally, the shift from criminal law to human rights changes the intensity and burden of proof. While a public servant accused of bribery or criminal breach of trust enjoys the presumption of innocence, the human rights approach requires States to exonerate themselves before the treaty bodies when accused of deficient anti-corruption measures. For instance, a State must demonstrate that while it is willing to allot sufficient means to an authority, it is unable to do so due to a lack of resources. The follow-up question would be whether statistical evidence or the mere observation of the luxurious lifestyle of high-ranking politicians would be sufficient to corroborate the misappropriation of public funds that is presumed by the practice of the CESCR and also by the UN Convention against Corruption. Article 20 UNCAC calls upon States parties to "consider" establishing "illicit enrichment" as a criminal offence. Under such a criminal law provision, a significant increase in the assets of a public official that he or she cannot reasonably explain in relation to his or her lawful income could be punished. Such an implicit presumption of guilt is problematic in terms of the rule of law.

Practical recommendations

The practical strategy implied by this change in perspective would be mutual mainstreaming. Human rights mainstreaming of anti-corruption efforts would mean that the realization of human rights would be one of the anti-corruption goals from the outset. In legal practice, this would imply an interpretation of all criminal offences relating to corruption in a way that takes into account human rights. On a complementary basis, anti-corruption mainstreaming of all human rights procedures should be implemented.

The implementation of this recommendation would include the following: In the work of the human rights treaty bodies, the guidelines for all country reports and for all country-specific concluding observations of the committees as well as the mandates of the human rights special rapporteurs should include corruption as a checkpoint that must be addressed. Not only human rights NGOs, but also specialized anti- corruption NGOs should be allowed to participate in the Universal Periodic Review as well as in treaty-specific monitoring. One might also conceive of a "General Com- ment on Corruption and Human Rights" that would apply to all treaties. Finally, an anti-corruption mandate could be included in the international standards for the national human rights institutions.

The practical benefit of the change in perspective is diminished, however, in that the international mechanisms are themselves weak when it comes to enforcing human rights. The options for individual complaints at the international level are limited - but some openings do exist, for example individual communications to various Human Rights Treaty Bodies. Of course, it should not be forgotten that the domestic institutions are the primary enforcers of international human rights. If a domestic court were to condemn organs of the State for a violation of human rights through corruption, this would be a comparatively strong sanction. In many States, however, this is not to be expected, due to corruption in the justice system. This means that "empowerment" through human rights remains more symbolic than practical.

Risk of moral weakening

The strength of taking a human rights approach to anti-corruption instruments is simultaneously its weakness, however. This is because of the ambivalent attitude of the Global South toward "Western" human rights. Their critique of the idea of human rights overlaps with fundamental objections to the international anti-corruption agenda.

This fundamental critique is clothed in the language of cultural relativism, ideology, or economics. According to the critique, the anti-corruption strategy is merely the imposition of a particular "Western" model of the State in numerous respects: A liberal State governed by the rule of law is required as a regulatory framework for a free market. This demand is based on a neoliberal agenda that wants to push back an interventionist, heavily bureaucratized model of the State.

The critique accuses the "rule of law" of serving primarily the economic interests of property owners and of capital.

Secondly, according to this critique, the conception of corruption as an evil is based on the picture of a State that performs public duties by way of public officials who are hired on the basis of merit and who act according to legal rules that formally apply to all. But this disqualifies communities based on family and clan relationships, which are sustained by exchanging gifts and providing group members with official posts. The values of reciprocity and loyalty underlying these communities are not acknowledged, but rather are replaced with Western meritocratic thinking and formal equal treatment. The allegation of legal and cultural imperialism and of the dictate of Western capital is further nourished by the human rights approach to anti-corruption strategies. According to that view, both sets of international instruments are merely two variants of imperialism.

However, economic and anthropological research relativizes this fundamental critique of anti-corruption strategies and thus the danger that they might be weakened by imbuing them with a human rights approach. The allegation that both anti- corruption and human rights are hegemonic or US-dominated strategies and/or strategies driven by global capital sounds more like an attempt to justify the behaviour of elites whose power and sinecures are threatened by anti-corruption and by the demand for respect of human rights. Individuals affected in many different regions of the world and cultures have demonstrated on Tahrir Square or the Maidan, in Caracas or Mexico City, for freedom and fair prices of bread and against the corruption of the elites.

Conclusion and outlook

Shift in the prerogative of interpretation

In terms of communication theory, the change in perspective proposed here is a kind of "framing", i.e., a new framework for interpretation associated with a new prerogative of interpretation. It is important in this regard that this prerogative of interpretation shifts in institutional terms as well: away from the World Bank and toward the UN Human Rights Council. Potentially, this new discursive power also entails a new power to act.

In legal terms, the connection between anti-corruption law and human rights protection proposed here can be construed as a systemic integration of two subareas of international law. Or, the human rights approach to anti-corruption instruments can be seen as their constitutionalization. Some international lawyers complain that the latter smacks of "human rightism", or of a "hubris" of international human rights protection. But this alleged hubris can also be seen in more positive terms as the legitimate reinstitution of the human being as the normative reference point for all law, including international law.

Devaluation of the Global South?

We have seen that the determination of a concrete violation of human rights by a concrete corrupt act is easier in the domain of petty corruption. In the domain of grand corruption, such as bribery of government ministers by foreign investors or the diversion of funds from the public budget, the connection between corrupt conduct and human rights violations of concrete victims is much harder to make. Now Western democracies suffer less from petty corruption than from grand corruption, including what is provocatively termed "legal corruption" in the form of non- transparent election financing and the resulting vested interests of politics, or in the form of a toleration of the smooth transition of public officials to lucrative jobs in the private sector, in which the insider knowledge gained in office can be put to use in the new company ("revolving door" phenomenon).

Because the reconceptualization in terms of human rights focuses primarily on petty corruption, it casts a spotlight on the Global South. But it would be exaggerated to say that this spotlight constitutes a devaluation of non-Western societies and thus represents a paternalistic, civilizing mission of the West against the rest of the world. The change in perspective does not downplay or excuse grand corruption, including "legal" corruption in the Western world. It is merely less able to capture it, because grand corruption has a different, less individualized structure of wrongfulness.

The State, public office, and universalizability

Until well into the 19th century, patronage and the purchase of public offices were largely considered legal and legitimate components of governance even in Europe. The awareness that these forms of exercising and influencing political power and administration were illegitimate and to be combated could only emerge with the development of the modern State – a State in which an impartial bureaucracy is called upon to apply the law equally and in which all public officials are required to act in the public interest, not in the interest of their family or ethnic group.

In a patrimonial State in which the political and administrative positions are primarily intended to generate income ("rent seeking"), the idea of corruption has no place. In that sense – as already indicated at the outset – the modern State governed by the rule of law and the concept of corruption are inextricably linked. This also explains why anti-corruption is difficult in regions of the world where this understanding of the State and the associated institutional safeguards are weak.

But – to use an example – is it really the same from the perspective of a motorist whether the sum of money he or she has to pay at a road block in order to pursue his or her course represents a bribe to a corrupt traffic police officer – as in many African States – or a motorway toll – as in France for example?

In both cases, the motorist's freedom of movement is limited by him being forced to pay. The difference is that the motorway toll is based on a law that serves the public interest, namely maintenance of the motorway network, and at the same time applies equally to everyone (with reasonable differences based on type of vehicle, number of persons, or other relevant criteria). In contrast, the bribe is not based on a fee schedule defined in a political or at least orderly administrative procedure – but it may under certain circumstances help feed the police officer's family. The difference between a bribe and a State fee is thus based solely on the legitimacy and legality of the institutions and procedures in which they are defined, collected, and used.

Augustine's insight that States not governed by law and justice are nothing but large bands of thieves has lost none of its validity after more than 1,000 years. Only if this insight proves to be universally applicable can a global anti-corruption strategy be successful. And the "individualized" conception of corruption – namely the insight that corruption interferes with the rights of each individual citizen – can make a greater contribution to this universalization than the invocation of an anonymous general interest and an abstract conception of public office. [footnotes omitted]

END OF EXCERPT

Gender Equality and Corruption

Corruption affects women differently than men and carries implications for gender equality. According to the UNDP report Corruption, Accountability and Gender: Understanding the Connections, corruption "exacerbates gender-based asymmetries in empowerment, access to resources and enjoyment of rights."19 Reasons for corruption's disproportionate effects include the fact that women make up most of the global poor, who suffer most from corruption, and the fact that women have lower levels of literacy and education, which can adversely affect their knowledge of their rights. The report summarizes the effects of corruption on women as follows:

The data suggests that 'petty' or 'retail' corruption (when basic public services are sold instead of provided by right) affects poor women in particular and that the currency of corruption is frequently sexualized – women and girls are often asked to pay bribes in the form of sexual favours. Women's disempowerment and their dependence on public service delivery mechanisms for access to essential services (e.g., health, water and education) increases their vulnerability to the consequences of corruption- related service delivery deficits. In addition, women's limited access to public officials and low income levels diminishes their ability to pay bribes, further restricting their access to basic services. Therefore, corruption disproportionately affects poor women because their low levels of economic and political empowerment constrain their ability to change the status quo or to hold states accountable to deliver services that are their right.

The report provides more specific examples of the ways women and girls experience corruption in various countries and settings. For example, in many countries, women and girls bear water-gathering responsibilities—corruption prevents the construction of more convenient water infrastructure. In the arena of education, women and girls might face sexual extortion in order to be graded fairly or pay for school, as illustrated in Botswana. The report also describes the disproportionate impact of corruption on women entrepreneurs, who often lack the resources to make bribe payments for licenses and permits to start a business. Other corruption-related issues for women include increased vulnerability to sexual violence in the context of police and judicial corruption and blocked access to maternity hospitals when staff members demand bribes.

Global Security and Corruption

In her book Thieves of State, Sarah Chayes argues that corruption fuels threats to international security. She ties endemic corruption by elites to national and international revolution and violence in the Arab world, Nigeria, Ukraine and various historical settings. Chayes draws attention to Al-Qaeda's assertions that the main rationale behind the 9/11 attacks was George

W. Bush's cozy relationship with kleptocratic Arab heads of state. To demonstrate a pattern of association between corruption and destructive, terroristic acts, she compares the example of contemporary jihadists to Dutch Protestants who ransacked property of the corrupt Catholic Church during the Reformation. Similar to these early Protestants, the jihadists "articulate their struggle, at least in part, as a reaction to the kleptocratic practices of local rulers."Chayes also cites other threats to global security fueled by corruption, such as uprisings leading to government collapse in countries like Syria, the ease of trafficking in conflict minerals and other illegal goods in corrupt countries like Zimbabwe, and unreliable military regimes.

Although Chayes' first-hand experience leads to the conclusion that terrorism is, in part, a reaction to corrupt regimes in certain countries, other empirical research undermines the idea that corruption is a motivating factor for terrorism in general. Research by Teets and Chenoweth suggests that "[c]orruption does not motivate terrorism because of grievances against corrupt states, but rather it facilitates terrorism...corruption lowers the barriers to terrorist attacks, probably because obtaining illicit materials to conduct attacks is more difficult in less corrupt or transparent countries." Matthew Simpson's research, described in an article titled "Terrorism and Corruption: Alternatives for Goal Attainment Within Political Opportunity Structures," also "cast[s] doubt on the notion that terrorist violence is the expression of grievances developed in response to perceived corruption within the political process." Rather, Simpon's research indicates that organizations turn to terrorism when other extralegal avenues, like corruption, are blocked; "[i]n instances where the particular path of corruption could not be employed to gain political influence, these organizations used alternative strategies – terrorism being high on the list – to fill the gap." However, Simpson recognizes that more research is required to determine when the relationship between corruption control and terrorism might vary due to other factors like inequality and development.

In Corruption: Global Security and World Order, Rotberg and Greenhill further explore the connection between corruption, trafficking and global security:

The durable ties between corrupt regimes and transnational crime and transnational trafficking pose major global security problems because of the ability of criminal organizations to subvert stability and growth in poor countries, by their skill at sapping such impoverished places of revenue and legitimate modernization, by their undermining the fabric of weak and fragile societies, and by their negative reinforcement of the least favorable kinds of leadership in developing countries. ... these unholy partnerships ... by facilitating the spread of small arms and light weapons make civil wars possible and lethal.

Adding to the issue of global security, Matthew Bunn describes the link between corruption and nuclear proliferation, pointing out that "[c]orruption has been a critical enabling element of the nuclear weapons programs in Pakistan, Iraq, Libya, and Iran." Bunn explains that countries aspiring to a nuclear program are limited in their choice of means to obtain materials, and if these means are insufficient, "illicit contributions from foreign sources motivated by cash will be central to a nuclear program's success."

For an exploration of the need for anti-corruption measures and good governance to promote sustainable peace in post-conflict nations, see Bertram Spector, Negotiating Peace and Confronting Corruption: Challenges for Post-Conflict Societies (US Institute of Peace Press, 2011). Spector argues that negotiated cease-fires and other short-term measures are not enough to establish long-lasting peace; rather, good governance is needed to end the corruption that fuels conflict in the first place.

Climate Change, Environmental Degradation and Corruption

Corruption in the area of climate change holds the potential to cause wide-ranging effects. Corrupt avoidance of climate change standards can sap projects of their effectiveness in mitigating climate change, leading to adverse consequences for future generations. The resultant failure or reduced success of mechanisms designed to mitigate the impacts of climate change will also disproportionately affect vulnerable, poor populations, who are expected to bear the brunt of the effects of climate change.

Enforcement of heightened climate change standards will require good governance at both international and national levels. As stated by Transparency International (TI) in Global Corruption Report: Climate Change, "[a] robust system of climate governance – meaning the processes and relationships at the international, national, corporate and local levels to address the causes and effects of climate change – will be essential for ensuring that the enormous political, social and financial investments by both the public sector and the private sector made in climate change mitigation and adaptation are properly and equitably managed, so that responses to climate change are successful."

TI explains why climate change initiatives are uniquely vulnerable to corruption. Responses to climate change will involve massive amounts of money (investment in mitigation efforts is expected to reach almost US$700 billion by 2020), which will "flow through new and untested financial markets and mechanisms," creating fertile ground for corruption.32 Many climate issues are complex, new and uncertain, yet require speedy solutions, which also increases the risk of corruption, for example by leaving "regulatory grey zones and loopholes."

In TI's book, Patrick Alley points out that rife corruption in the forestry sector has already subverted efforts to use reforestation and forest management to slow climate change.34 According to the World Bank, timber worth an estimated US$10-23 billion is illegally logged or produced from suspicious sources every year. This illegal harvesting of timber is facilitated by "deeply engrained corruption schemes" in the industry.35 The forestry sector is particularly prone to corruption because most tropical forests are on public land and therefore susceptible to control by a small group of politicians or public servants. Timber operations are also generally located in remote areas, far from scrutiny. Further, because no countries ban the importation of illegally sourced timber aside from the US, illegal timber is easy to launder on the international market.

Corruption threatens climate change action in many other ways. For example, undue influence and policy capture are current and future risks to effective climate change policy, as demonstrated by powerful energy sector lobby groups in the US. According to TI, carbon markets are also vulnerable to undue influence, which might have contributed to over- allocation of carbon permits and huge windfall profits for European power producers in 2005-2007. Carbon markets also suffer from a lack of measuring, reporting and verification of emissions. Other problems include the current lack of transparency and accountability in climate policy both internationally and nationally. For example, Shahanaz Mueller points out that, in Austria, the lack of transparency in implementation of aspirational policies has led to disappointing performance and slow progress.36 Corruption in the construction sector also poses a huge risk to future adaptation projects; "[a]daptation without oversight presents a two-fold risk of diverted funds and substandard work ... which may put populations at even more risk of climate extremes."

TI points out that the corruption spawned by climate change is not limited to familiar forms of corruption, such as misappropriation of funds and bribery, but rather "transcends the established typologies of corruption." TI argues that its definition of corruption, the abuse of entrusted power for private gain, must be expanded in the context of climate change to include "the power that future generations have vested in all of us, in our stewardship role for the planet," and abuses of power such as "distortion of scientific facts, the breach of principles of fair representation and false claims about the green credentials of consumer products."

Empirical Evidence on the Relationship between Corruption, Reduced Economic Growth and Poverty

In a report entitled Corruption and Poverty: A Review of Recent Literature, Chetwynd et al. summarize the different theories and research connecting corruption with poverty. While Chetwynd's summary is now dated (2003), I believe it still accurately reflects the basic relationship between corruption and poverty. Their research reveals an indirect relationship between poverty and corruption explained by two main theories. Persons who attach themselves to the "economic model" argue that corruption negatively impacts indicia of economic growth, which exacerbates poverty. Chetwynd et al. refer to the second theory as the "governance model." Proponents of this theory argue that there is evidence that corruption negatively affects governance and poor governance negatively affects levels of poverty.

In the excerpt below, Chetwynd et al. use the terms "rent seeking" and "rent taking." "Rent- seeking" is a term used by economists to refer to instances where an individual or entity seeks to increase his/her portion of existing wealth by demanding a form of rent that generally is of no benefit to the larger society. The distinction between rent seeking and corruption is explained by Coolidge and Rose-Ackerman in "High-Level Rent Seeking and Corruption in African Regimes: Theory and Cases":

- "Rent seeking" is often used interchangeably with "corruption," and there is a large area of overlap. While corruption involves the misuse of public power for private gain, rent seeking derives from the economic concept of "rent" -- earnings in excess of all relevant costs (including a market rate of return on invested assets). Rent is equivalent to what most non-economists think of as monopoly profits. Rent seeking is then the effort to acquire access to or control over opportunities for earning rents. These efforts are not necessarily illegal, or even immoral. They include much lobbying and some forms of advertising. Some can be efficient, such as an auction of scarce and valuable assets. However, economists and public sector management specialists are concerned with what Jagdish Bhagwati termed "directly unproductive" rent seeking activities, because they waste resources and can contribute to economic inefficiency.

For example, a customs official who demands that a bribe be paid before allowing imports into the country may become preoccupied with seeking to maximize his/her ability to extract these bribes (a form of rent) from the public. This is both an instance of corruption and rent seeking as the customs official seeks to maximize his/her own wealth at the expense of work productivity and the public interest.

Excerpts from Chetwynd et al.'s report, Corruption and Poverty, are set out below:

BEGINNING OF EXCERPT

Introduction

Popular belief suggests that corruption and poverty are closely related in developing countries. Corruption in the public sector is often viewed as exacerbating conditions of poverty in countries already struggling with the strains of economic growth and democratic transition. Alternatively, countries experiencing chronic poverty are seen as natural breeding grounds for systemic corruption due to social and income inequalities and perverse economic incentives. This report summarizes recent research on the relationship between poverty and corruption to clarify the ways in which these phenomena interact. This understanding can inform USAID planning and programming in democracy and governance, as well as in poverty reduction strategies.

The development literature is rich with theoretical insights on this relationship, many of them founded on practical experience and careful observation. The World Bank's World Development Report for 2000/01: Attacking Poverty summarized current thinking on the corruption-poverty linkage as follows:

- The burden of petty corruption falls disproportionately on poor people ...For those without money and connections, petty corruption in public

> health or police services can have debilitating consequences. Corruption affects the lives of poor people through many other channels as well. It biases government spending away from socially valuable goods, such as education. It diverts public resources from infrastructure investments that could benefit poor people, such as health clinics, and tends to increase public spending on capital- intensive investments that offer more opportunities for kickbacks, such as defense contracts. It lowers the quality of infrastructure, since kickbacks are more lucrative on equipment purchases. Corruption also undermines public service delivery (World Bank, 2001: 201).

Many of these relationships have been examined using empirical research methods. Much of this literature is recent -- from the mid-1990s -- when major international donor institutions began to focus attention on corruption issues and researchers initiated cross-country measurement of the corruption phenomenon. This report integrates this literature to present the major themes that are hypothesized and tested.

This report is divided into three sections. The first section describes briefly how poverty and corruption are defined and measured in the literature. The second section presents the prominent themes that emerged from our review of the literature on corruption and poverty. Within this section, theoretical propositions are discussed, empirical research studies that support or refute them are described, and implications are drawn. The third section summarizes the major themes uncovered in our review.

Examining the Relationship Between Corruption and Poverty

This review found that few studies examine or establish a direct relationship between corruption and poverty.44 Corruption, by itself, does not produce poverty. Rather, corruption has direct consequences on economic and governance factors, intermediaries that in turn produce poverty. Thus, the relationship examined by researchers is an indirect one.

Two models emerge from the research literature. The "economic model" postulates that corruption affects poverty by first impacting economic growth factors, which, in turn, impact poverty levels. In other words, increased corruption reduces economic investment, distorts markets, hinders competition, creates inefficiencies by increasing the costs of doing business, and increases income inequalities. By undermining these key economic factors, poverty is exacerbated.

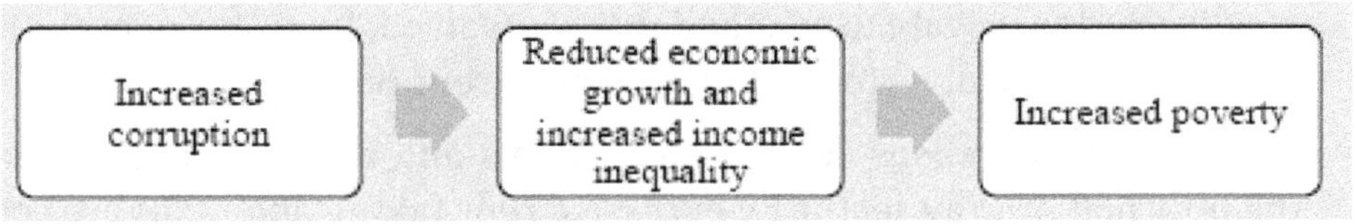

The "governance model" asserts that corruption affects poverty by first influencing governance factors, which, in turn, impact poverty levels. So, for example, corruption erodes the institutional capacity of government to deliver quality public services, diverts public investment away from major public needs into capital projects (where bribes can be sought), lowers compliance with safety and health regulations, and increases budgetary pressures on government. Through these serious challenges to governance practices and outcomes, poverty is affected.

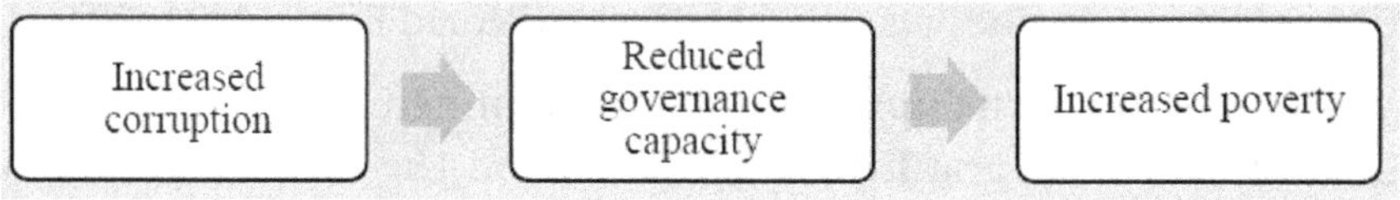

The following review of the literature is organized in relation to these models.

Economic Model

The literature shows an inverse correlation between aggregate economic growth and corruption; in general, countries with higher corruption experience less economic growth. Many of the studies reviewed for this paper address the channels through which corruption affects economic growth, for instance, through impacting investment and entrepreneurship, distorting markets, and undermining productivity. Furthermore, there is empirical evidence that corruption aggravates income inequality and is associated with slower economic growth. Finally, studies present evidence that as the rate of economic growth increases, the number of people above the poverty line tends to rise as well.

Corruption Impedes Economic Growth

The relationship between corruption and economic growth is complex. Economic theory supports the notion that corruption hinders economic growth in the following ways:

- **Corruption discourages foreign and domestic investment:** rent taking increases costs and creates uncertainty, reducing incentives to both foreign and domestic investors.
- **Corruption taxes entrepreneurship:** entrepreneurs and innovators require licenses and permits and paying bribes for these goods cuts into profit margins.
- **Corruption lowers the quality of public infrastructure:** public resources are diverted to private uses, standards are waived; funds for operations and maintenance are diverted in favor of more rent seeking activity.
- **Corruption decreases tax revenue:** firms and activities are driven into the informal or gray sector by excessive rent taking and taxes are reduced in exchange for payoffs to tax officials.

- Corruption diverts talent into rent seeking: officials who otherwise would be engaged in productive activity become pre-occupied with rent taking, in which increasing returns encourage more rent taking.
- Corruption distorts the composition of public expenditure: rent seekers will pursue those projects for which rent seeking is easiest and best disguised, diverting funding from other sectors such as education and health.

These theoretical propositions are supported by a number of empirical studies. They demonstrate that high levels of corruption are associated with low levels of investment and low levels of aggregate economic growth. For example, the results of several World Bank corruption surveys illustrate this inverse relationship between corruption and economic growth.

- Corruption discourages domestic investment. In Bulgaria, about one in four businesses in the entrepreneur sample had planned to expand (mostly through acquiring new equipment) but failed to do so, and corruption was an important factor in their change of plans. The Latvia study surveyed enterprises that had dropped planned investments. It found that the high cost of complying with regulations and the uncertainty surrounding them, including uncertainty regarding unofficial payments, were important factors for 28% of businesses foregoing new investments.
- Corruption hurts entrepreneurship especially among small businesses. Several studies reported that small businesses tend to pay the most bribes as a percentage of total revenue (especially in Bosnia, Ghana, and Slovakia). InPoland, businesses have to deal with a large number of economic activities that are licensed, making them more prone to extortion.
- Corruption decreases revenue from taxes and fees. In Bangladesh, more than 30% of urban household respondents reduced electric and/or water bills by bribing the meter reader. In several studies, respondents were so frustrated that they indicated a willingness to pay more taxes if corruption could be controlled (Cambodia, Indonesia, Romania).46

In a cross-national analysis of corruption and growth for the IMF, Tanzi and Davodi (1997) tested four hypotheses designed to explain four channels through which corruption reduces growth. Using regression analysis, results established that higher levels of corruption were associated with: (1) increasing public sector investment (but decreased productivity); (2) reduced government revenues (reducing resources for productive expenditures); (3) lower expenditures on operations and maintenance (where other studies show that high government consumption is robustly associated with lower economic growth, e.g., see Barro 1996); and (4) reduced quality of public infrastructure (as shown by indicators for road conditions, power and water losses, telecom faults and proportion of railway diesels in use). All of these findings are consistent with the observation that corruption is inversely correlated with growth in GNP.

A seminal study by Mauro (2002) used a composite of two corruption indices and multiple regression analyses with a sample of 106 countries to show that high levels of corruption are associated with lower levels of investment as a share of Gross Domestic Product (GDP) and with lower GDP growth per capita. Extrapolation of these results by the researcher suggested that if a country were to improve its corruption index from a score of six to eight on a ten-point scale, it would increase the investment rate more than 4% and annual per capita GDP growth would increase by nearly one-half percent.

Recent work by Lambsdorff (forthcoming) casts additional light on how corruption affects investment, specifically, the relationship of investment to GDP. The study categorized investment into domestic savings and net capital inflows. Regression results provided evidence that corruption negatively impacts on capital accumulation by deterring capital imports. To explore causation, Lambsdorff decomposed the corruption index into several sub-indicators that look at corruption through the lens of bureaucratic quality, civil liberty, government stability, and law and order. Only the law and order sub-indicator turned out to be important for attracting capital flows.

Another World Bank study (2000a) suggests that higher levels of corruption reduce growth through decreased investment and output. This comprehensive study looked at 22 transition countries and examined two forms of corruption – state capture and administrative corruption – and their impact on selected economic and social indicators. Data for the study were derived from the Business Environment and Enterprise Performance Survey (BEEPS).

[**Note:** The empirical data cited by Chetwynd et al. above is from the 1990s and early 2000s. Subsequent empirical research has cast doubt on the claim that high levels of corruption adversely affect economic growth in terms of GDP. In fact, corruption might increase economic growth in the short run under certain circumstances (for example, by allowing corporations to avoid meeting expensive environmental requirements). However, Toke S. Aidt argues that corruption still impedes sustainable economic growth in the long run in his article "Corruption and Sustainable Development," discussed below at page 27-28 of this book.]

Corruption Exacerbates Income Inequality

Several studies have demonstrated a relationship between corruption and income inequality. The theoretical foundations for this relationship are derived from rent theory and draw on the ideas of Rose-Ackerman (1978) and Krueger (1974), among others. Propositions include:

- Corruption may create permanent distortions from which some groups or individuals can benefit more than others.
- The distributional consequences of corruption are likely to be more severe the more persistent the corruption.
- The impact of corruption on income distribution is in part a function of government involvement in allocating and financing scarce goods and services (Gupta, Davoodi, and Alonso-Terme, 1998).

A World Bank study (2000c) of poverty following the transition to a market economy in Eastern Europe and Central Asia (ECA) produced important findings concerning income distribution and corruption. The study analyzes data on firms' perceptions of corruption and notes that more firms in ECA report that corruption is a problem than in most other geographic regions.47 The authors analyzed whether there "is any apparent link, within ECA, between corruption and measures of income inequality" (World Bank, 2000c: 169). When Gini coefficients for income per capita (measures of income inequality) were graphed against the Transparency International (TI) Corruption Perceptions Index (CPI), lower levels of corruption were seen to be statistically associated with lower levels of income inequality (simple correlation was +0.72). Similar results were obtained using different measures of corruption. The authors add that closer examination of the links between corruption and inequality show that the costs of corruption fall particularly heavily on smaller firms.

This report also examined the relationship between a particular type of corruption, state capture, and income inequality. State capture describes the situation where businesses have undue influence over the decisions of public officials. The report notes that differences in income inequality in the ECA countries are greatest in those countries where the transition has been least successful and where state capture is at its highest. In these countries, state capture has allowed large economic interests to distort the legal framework and the policy-making process in a way that defeats the development of a market economy.49 The report explores the relationship between state capture and income inequality through regressions of the Gini coefficient on measures of state capture and other variables and finds that a higher degree of state capture is correlated with higher inequality. The relationship holds even when controlling for political freedoms, location, and years under state planning (World Bank, 2000c: 172).

Gupta et al. (1998) conducted cross-national regression analysis of up to 56 countries to examine the ways that corruption could negatively impact income distribution and poverty. The study looked at the following relationships:

- **Growth :** Income inequality has been shown to be harmful to growth, so if corruption increases income inequality, it will also reduce growth and thereby exacerbate poverty.

- **Bias in tax systems :** Evasion, poor administration, and exemptions favoring the well-connected can reduce the tax base and progressivity of the tax system, increasing income inequality.
- **Poor targeting of social programs:** Extending benefits to well-to-do income groups or siphoning from poverty alleviation programs will diminish their impact on poverty and inequality (and will tend to act as a regressive tax on the poor, enhancing income inequality).

The Gupta et al. study examined these propositions through an inequality model using a Gini coefficient to measure inequality. ... The statistically significant results include:

- Higher corruption is associated with higher income inequality such that a worsening of a country's corruption index by 2.5 points on a scale of 10 corresponds to an increase in the Gini coefficient (worsening inequality) of about 4 points. Tests showed the same results for an average decrease in secondary schooling by 2.3 years, as an example of the significance of corruption.
- Even controlling for stage of economic development, corruption appears to be harmful to income inequality. Moreover, a test of directionality suggests that it is corruption that increases inequality and not the reverse.50
- Corruption tends to increase the inequality of factor ownership [i.e. the ownership of the means of production].
- Corruption increases income inequality by reducing progressivity of the tax system, that is, the impact of corruption on income inequality was shown to be higher after taxes.

In another study of 35 countries (mostly OECD countries), Karstedt hypothesized that corruption supports, stabilizes and deepens inequality. Her measures of corruption (Transparency International's CPI and Bribery Propensity Index) were tested against measures of income distribution (as well as measures of power distance between elites and other ranks, and general trust). Results showed that societies with high income inequality have high levels of corruption, while those with high levels of secondary education and a high proportion of women in government positions have decreasing levels of corruption. The relation between measures of corruption and the Gini index of income inequality was nonlinear, indicating that after countries attain a specific level of income equality, corruption tends to decrease exponentially.

How does corruption exacerbate income inequality? Evidence from diagnostic surveys of corruption in several countries suggests that corruption aggravates income inequality because lower income households pay a higher proportion of their income in bribes.

In conclusion, the literature establishes clearly that corruption impedes economic growth and augments income inequalities. How does reduced economic growth, in turn, increase poverty?

Reduced Economic Growth Rates Increase Poverty

There is evidence that the absence of economic growth (or negative growth) increases poverty. Quibria's study (2002) suggests that the burden of rapid economic retrenchment, such as seen recently in Thailand and Indonesia, hurts the poor most heavily. Similarly, in the transition countries of the former Soviet Union (FSU), the changeover to a market system was associated with a sharp initial drop in output and significantly higher levels of poverty. The expansion of poverty was initiated by the collapse of GDP, which fell by 50 percent in the FSU countries and 15 percent in Central and Eastern Europe. Poverty was found to be highly correlated with administrative corruption and corruption was empirically associated with lower economic growth rates (World Bank, 2000a).

Using a poverty model, the Gupta et al. (1998) study conducted a cross-national analysis of up to 56 countries to examine the relationship between growth and poverty. ... The authors found that higher growth is associated with poverty alleviation.

Dollar and Kraay (2002) of the World Bank Development Research Group studied a sample of 80 countries over four decades and showed that income of the lowest 20% of the population rises one for one with increases in per capita GDP. Moreover, using tests for directionality, they concluded that a 1% increase in GDP actually causes a 1% increase in the incomes of the poor.

In his comprehensive study of the so-called Asian Tigers, Quibria (2002) gives a good example of rapid economic growth (during the 1980s and 1990s) leading to a substantial decrease in those living below a poverty line of $1.25 per day.52 Further, in those countries with a more equitable distribution of income at the outset, the decrease in poverty tended to be more robust. However, even in this special case of multiple country rapid growth in a particular region, income distribution remained more or less constant over the period of growth. Similarly, Ravallion and Chen (in Easterly, 2001: 13-14) examined 65 developing countries between 1981 and 1999. They found that the number of people below the poverty line of $1 per day was reduced in countries with positive economic growth. However, they concluded that "measures of inequality show no tendency to get either better or worse with economic growth."

In conclusion, these studies show conclusively that income rises with economic growth and vice versa. It should be noted that economic growth does not necessarily lead to more equal income distribution; an increase in income may benefit the better- off rather than bringing the poor out of poverty. Income distribution seems to be an important moderating factor in the relationship between economic growth and poverty reduction.

Governance Model

The governance model postulates that increased corruption reduces governance capacity, which, in turn, increases poverty conditions. Kaufmann et al. (1999) define governance as, "the traditions and institutions by which authority in a country is exercised. This includes (1) the process by which governments are selected, monitored and replaced, (2) the capacity of the government to effectively formulate and implement sound policies, and (3) the respect of citizens and the state for the institutions that govern economic and social interactions among them."

Corruption disrupts governance practices, destabilizes governance institutions, reduces the provision of services by government, reduces respect for the rule of law, and reduces public trust in government and its institutions. Impaired governance, in turn, reduces social capital and public trust in governance institutions; this reduces the public funds available to support effective economic growth programs and reduces the capability of government to help its citizens and the poor, in particular.

Corruption Degrades Governance

Johnston (2000) suggests that serious corruption threatens democracy and governance by weakening political institutions and mass participation, and by delaying and distorting the economic development needed to sustain democracy. In a study of 83 countries, Johnston compares Transparency International's CPI with an index of political competitiveness and finds that well-institutionalized and decisive political competition is correlated with lower levels of corruption. These results were confirmed, even when controlling for GDP and examining the relationship over time.

Diagnostic surveys of corruption in Bosnia-Herzegovina, Ghana, Honduras, Indonesia and Latvia report that government institutions with the highest levels of corruption tend to provide lower quality services. The converse is also true: in Romania, the survey shows that state sector entities with better systems of public administration tend to have lower levels of corruption.

The literature shows that corruption impacts the quality of government services and infrastructure and that through these channels it has an impact on the poor. This is particularly the case in the health and education sectors. Enhanced education and healthcare services and population longevity are usually associated with higher economic growth. But under conditions of extensive corruption, when public services, such as health and basic education expenditures that especially benefit the poor, are given lower priority in favor of capital intensive programs that offer more opportunities for high-level rent taking, lower income groups lose services on which they depend. As government revenues decline through leakage brought on by corruption, public funds for poverty programs and programs to stimulate growth also become more scarce.

Gupta, Davoodi and Tiongson (2000) used regression analysis across a large sample of countries to assess an aggregate measure of education outcome and health status in a model that includes several corruption indices, per capita income, public spending on health care and education, and average years of education completed. The results supported the proposition that better health care and education outcomes are positively correlated with lower corruption. In particular, corruption is consistently correlated with higher school dropout rates and corruption is significantly correlated with higher levels of infant mortality and lower-birth weights of babies.

Mauro looked at the relationship between corruption and the composition of government spending. He found evidence that corrupt governments may display predatory behaviour in deciding how to distribute government expenditures. Specifically, his data showed corruption negatively related to education and health expenditures. ...

Gupta et al. (1998) also found that corruption can lead to reduced social spending on health and education. Countries with higher corruption tend to have lower levels of social spending, regardless of level of development. Corruption lowers tax revenues, increases government operating costs, increases government spending for wages and reduces spending on operations and maintenance, and often biases government toward spending on higher education and tertiary health care (rather than basic education and primary health care).

Impaired Governance Increases Poverty

Pioneering research on the relationship among corruption, governance and poverty has been conducted at the World Bank by the team of Kaufmann, Kraay and Zoido- Lobaton. Their studies suggest an association between good governance (with control of corruption as an important component) and poverty alleviation.

Kaufmann et al. (1999) studied the effect of governance on per capita income in 173 countries, treating "control of corruption" as one of the components of good governance. ... Analysis showed a strong positive causal relationship running from improved governance to better development outcomes as measured by per capita income.55 A one standard deviation improvement in governance raised per capita incomes 2.5 to 4 times. Analysis of updated indicators for 2000-2001 did not change these conclusions.

Kaufmann and Kraay (2002) used updated governance indicators to gain a more nuanced understanding of the role of good governance in the relationship between corruption and growth in per capita incomes.57 Using governance data for 2000/01, the authors establish empirically that for Latin American and Caribbean countries (i) better governance tends to yield higher per capita incomes, but (ii) higher per capita incomes tend to produce reduced governance capacity. The authors attribute this second finding to state capture. In short, the authors suggest that corruption (in the form of state capture) may interfere with the expected relationship between economic growth (higher per capita incomes) and better governance. The authors note that an empirical in-depth examination of the phenomenon of state capture in the Latin American and The Caribbean (LAC) region is part of the upcoming research agenda.

The effect of governance on corruption and poverty is illuminated by another World Bank study (2000a). The deterioration in governance discussed in this study was accompanied by an increase in both corruption and poverty. Thus, as seen earlier, increases in corruption tend to deteriorate governance practices, but the reverse holds true as well – reduction in governance capacity increases the opportunities for corruption.

Reduced Public Trust in Government Increases Vulnerability of the Poor

Corruption that reduces governance capacity also may inflict critical collateral damage: reduced public trust in government institutions. As trust -- an important element of social capital --declines, research has shown that vulnerability of the poor increases as their economic productivity is affected. The concept of social capital refers to social structures that enable people to work collectively for the good of the group. One of the most important and widely discussed elements of social capital is trust, both interpersonal trust and trust in institutions of government....

One of the effects of widespread corruption in government services is that it appears to contribute to disaffection and distrust, and this appears to impact particularly heavily on the poor.61 This is not surprising, because low income people are the ones who are most likely to be dependent on government services for assistance with basic needs, such as education and healthcare, and least likely to be able to pay bribes to cut through complex and unresponsive bureaucracies. Lack of trust has economic consequences: when people perceive that the social system is untrustworthy and inequitable, this can affect incentives to engage in productive activities.

Knack and Keefer (1997) tested the relationship between social capital and economic performance in 29 market economies using indicators from the World Values Surveys (WVS) on interpersonal trust. They added the WVS trust measure to investment and growth regressions and found that trust correlated highly with economic growth. Each 12 percentage point rise in trust was associated with an increase in annual income growth of about 1 percentage point. They also found that the impact of trust on growth is significantly higher for poorer countries, suggesting that interpersonal trust is more essential where legal systems and financial markets are less well developed.

In a later study, Zak and Knack (1998) found that trust is higher in nations with stronger formal institutions for enforcing contracts and reducing corruption, and in nations with less polarized populations (as measured by income or land inequality, ethnic heterogeneity, and a subjective measure of the intensity of economic discrimination). They also showed that formal institutions and polarization appear to influence growth rates in part through their impacts on trust. For example, income inequality, land inequality, discrimination and corruption are associated with significantly lower growth rates, but the association of these variables with growth dramatically weakens when trust is controlled for.

Knack (1999) also looked at the effect of social capital on income inequality. His study regressed various indicators of social capital and trust against income data by quintile and found that higher scores on property rights measures were associated with declines in income inequality. Using the WVS trust indicator, he also found that inequality declined in higher trust societies. ... Knack concludes that "social capital reduces poverty rates and improves—or at a minimum does not exacerbate—income inequality."

Conclusion

Overall, the literature reviewed in this paper demonstrates that corruption does exacerbate and promote poverty, but this pattern is complex and moderated by economic and governance factors. Table 1 summarizes the major findings of this report.

Table 1. Major Propositions Linking Corruption and Poverty

- Economic growth is associated with poverty reduction
- The burden of rapid retrenchment falls most heavily on the poor.
- Corruption is associated with low economic growth
- Corruption reduces domestic investment and foreign direct investment
- Corruption reduces public sector productivity
- Corruption distorts the composition of government expenditure, away from services directly beneficial to the poor and the growth process, e.g., education, health, and operation and maintenance
- Better health and education indicators are positively associated with lower corruption
- Corruption reduces government revenues
- Corruption lowers the quality of public infrastructure
- Corruption lowers spending on social sectors
- Corruption increases income inequality
- Corruption increases inequality of factor ownership
- Inequality slows growth
- Corruption decreases progressivity of the tax system
- Corruption acts as a regressive tax
- Low income households pay more in bribes as percent of income
- Better governance, including lower graft level, effects economic growth dramatically
- Better governance is associated with lower corruption and lower poverty levels.
- High state capture makes it difficult to reduce inequality
- Extensive, organized, well institutionalized and decisive political competition is associated with lower corruption
- Trust is a component of social capital. Higher social capital is associated with lower poverty. Corruption undermines trust (in government and other institutions) and thereby undermines social capital.

END OF EXCERPT

The 2015 OECD report, Consequences of Corruption at the Sector Level and Implications for Economic Growth and Development, explores the correlation between corruption and economic growth by focusing on four sectors that are key in promoting economic growth and development but also vulnerable to corruption: extractive industries, utilities and infrastructure, health, and education.63 The report investigates how corruption "distorts sector performance" and the consequences for economic growth and development.64 For example, in extractive industries, the report finds that corruption can siphon funds away from populations and render dependence on natural resources counterproductive for the economy. The analysis concludes that corruption in these four sectors directly affects the cost of public and private sector projects, while indirectly damaging public institutions, eroding public trust in government and increasing inequality.

In his article "Corruption and Sustainable Development," Aidt takes a new approach to analyzing the relationship between growth and corruption.65 He points out that "[m]ost of the empirical research on the consequences of corruption at the economy-wide level uses real GDP per capita," which has led to ambiguous and contradictory results regarding causal directions.66 Aidt argues that research focused on GDP is "barking up the wrong tree."67 Since "development is concerned with sustainable improvements in human welfare," Aidt instead focuses his research on the relationship between corruption and sustainable development.68 He defines sustainable development as "present economic paths that do not compromise the well-being of future generations." Aidt's research indicates that "corruption is a major obstacle to sustainable development." The following excerpt summarizes Aidt's findings on the relationship between corruption and sustainable development:

> ◉ Corruption has the potential to undermine sustainable development in many ways. ... sustainable development requires suitable investment in the economy's capital assets. A vast empirical literature strongly suggests that corruption is one reason why many societies do not make sufficient investments in their productive base. Take, for example, education, that is, investment in the stock of human capital. Since education is associated with positive externalities, the social value of these investments exceeds the private return, and public funding is justified from a social point of view, in particular for primary education. But do the funds committed always reach the schools? Expenditure tracking surveys undertaken by the World Bank in Africa suggest that the answer is no: corrupt officials manage to divert the flow of funds to other purposes, most likely to private consumption or political patronage...the macroeconomic evidence presented by Mauro (1998), Tanzi (1998) and many others shows how corruption distorts the portfolio of public spending by shifting resources away from education and towards public [sic] consumption. In short, there are good reasons to believe that corruption undermines the accumulation of human capital and may thus be a cause of unsustainable development.
>
> Another example is investment in manufactured capital. A large theoretical literature highlights different reasons why corruption reduces the incentive to invest. The basic point is that corruption, through the sale of investment licenses or simply through creation of red tape and rent-seeking, serves as a tax on investment. The macroeconomic evidence strongly confirms

that investment does not thrive in a corrupt environment. ... Tanzi and Davoodi (1998), for example, show that corruption tends to increase public investment, but that it is associated with low operation and maintenance expenditures and with poor quality of infrastructure, that is, with investments of lower quality. Moreover, Wei (2000) demonstrates that corruption acts like a tax on international investments....Along similar lines, Rose-Ackerman (1999, ch. 3), argues that corrupt politicians favor investment projects with inefficiently high capital intensity ('white elephants') because the stream of bribe income generated by such projects is front-loaded. As a consequence of this bias, too little investment is subsequently made in maintaining the capital....

The final example relates to the management of natural capital. Leite and Weidmann (2002) and many others provide macroeconomic evidence on the close association between extraction of natural resources, resource rents, and corruption. Anecdotal evidence linking the exploitation of natural resources to corruption is also abundant, ranging from kickbacks associated with logging concessions in Malaysia and Indonesia to oil concessions in Nigeria. ... The consequence of these distortions is environmental degradation. This is directly related to a vast literature on the so-called 'resource curse'. Economic logic suggests that abundance of natural resources should be beneficial for economic development. ... Yet, as first demonstrated by Sachs and Warner (1997), despite this apparent advantage, resource-rich countries tend to grow at a slower rate than other countries. One often-cited reason for this curse is that resource abundance fosters a 'rentier' economy with rampant corruption and poorly developed institutions. ... Such an environment not only encourages overuse of the natural resource base; it also crowds out investment in manufactured and human capital (Gylfason, 2001; Papyrakis and Gerlagh, 2006), misallocates talent away from innovative activities to rent-seeking (Acemoglu and Verdier, 1998) and encourages growth-harming increases in government consumption (Atkinson and Hamilton, 2003) ... the general message from this literature is that resource rents induce corruption where institutions are weak, and that corruption and weak institutions encourage overuse of natural capital. The implied net result is a significant fall in genuine investment.

These examples show that corruption can be a threat to sustainable development through the effect it has on investment in an economy's productive base. However, they also demonstrate another basic point. The effect of corruption on economic growth, defined in terms of GDP per capita, is likely to be smaller than the corresponding effect of corruption on genuine investment and sustainability, at least over the medium term. [footnotes omitted] For a detailed analysis of the effects of corruption on markets, national economies, the public sector, institutions and other aspects of economies and governance, see Marco Arnone and Leonardo S. Borlini, Corruption: Economic Analysis and International Law (Cheltenham, UK; Northampton, US: Edward Elgar Publishing, 2014).

Poverty and Corruption: A Growing Concern

Figure 1.1 Scenes from the Kibera in Nairobi. Photo by Karl Mueller. CC BY 2.0 Generic license.

The excerpts below are from Roy Cullen's readable and informative book The Poverty of Corrupt Nations.72 Mr. Cullen, a former member of the Parliament of Canada, is also a founding member of the Global Organization of Parliamentarians Against Corruption (http://gopacnetwork.org/). In his book, he finds a strong correlation between low GDP per capita and corruption (based on TI's Corruption Perceptions Index). The following excerpts illustrate some connections between corruption and poverty:

BEGINNING OF EXCERPT

Nations where corruption is rampant also tend to have a large proportion of the population living in poverty – such as the people in this shanty town – while the countries' leaders may be diverting millions from national wealth to Swiss bank accounts for their personal benefit.

[**Note:** The picture of the shanty town is not reproduced because permission could not be obtained. An alternative picture has been substituted. See Figure 1.1.]

What I will attempt to demonstrate in this book is that while bribery and corruption may have cultural connotations and roots, they are morally and economically indefensible. This book places its focus on the relationship between corruption and poverty. It has two major themes.

First, there is the need for world leaders to address the growing disparities between the rich and poor nations. How big is this gap and what are the trends? As David Landes highlights in *The Wealth and Poverty of Nations,* "The difference in income per head between the richest industrial nation, say Switzerland, and the poorest non-industrial country, Mozambique, is about 400 to 1. Two hundred and fifty years ago, this gap between richest and poorest was perhaps 5 to 1...It is estimated that in today's world, 20,000 people perish every day from extreme poverty (some argue that the figure is 50,000 daily deaths from poverty-related causes).

[**Note:** The enormous gulf globally between the rich and the poor continues to grow. For a compelling account of this income inequality and of the dangers it creates, see: Joseph Stiglitz, The Great Divide: Unequal Societies and What We Can do About Them (W.W Norton, 2015).]

Second, there is a need to deal with bribery and corruption, a growing activity that is getting completely out of hand, and one of the key factors that is slowing growth and reducing economic opportunities in the developing world.

I then argue that conventional approaches to battling poverty and corruption have not worked and need to be examined. We need to begin thinking and acting creatively to develop a new paradigm. Executing corrupt officials (25 officials have met this fate in China in the past four years) is not the answer for progressive nations with a respect for human rights and the rule of law.

The two themes mentioned above are closely interconnected. The poverty of the world's poor nations is significantly exacerbated through bribery and corruption. Later on I will describe the high degree of correlation between poverty and corruption. Not only do the problems of income distribution amongst the political elites, the working poor, and the poverty-stricken become more exaggerated, but it saps hope. Corruption also leads to political instability, donor fatigue, and the disappearance of much needed investment capital in the affected countries.

...

We know that disparities between the rich and poor nations are not a function of poverty alone. In fact, corruption is not an unknown phenomenon in the so-called developed world.... There are many underlying reasons for the wealth and income disparities. Some of these factors are not controllable, whereas corruption, with political will, can be controlled.

Quite clearly, corruption is a disease that affects every functioning aspect of governments. To better understand the correlation between corruption and good governance, researcher Tony Hahn created an Index of Public Governance (IPG). Hahn uses three levels of measurement to compute the index, drawing on data from the Freedom House's 2004 indices of political rights and civil liberties, Transparency International's 2004 Corruptions Perceptions Index, and the Economic Freedom of the World's 2004 annual report [these indices are further discussed in Section 4 of this chapter]. Each set of data represents a democratic and capitalist perspective of government based on the fundamentals that good governance ensures the ability of citizens to vote, encourages free enterprise, improves quality of life, and allows citizens to exercise their civil liberties.

Hahn's Index ranks 114 countries, revealing New Zealand at the top of the list with the highest model of good governance with a ranking of 9.45 out of 10. Following closely behind are Finland, Switzerland, Iceland, and Denmark. Also included in the top 10 are the United Kingdom, with a ranking of 9.2, and Australia and Canada, each of which have a perfect *score* in the areas of political rights and civil liberties. Surprisingly the United States missed the top 10 by one, ranking eleventh with a score of only 8.2 on economic freedom.

Most importantly, however, are the results for Africa. The first of the African countries to make the list is Botswana, which ranks 29th with a score of 7.52, with Mauritius and South Africa following closely behind. What is interesting about this, as Hahn points out, is that unemployment in Botswana is over 20 per cent and a third of the population is living with HIV/AIDS. Comparing the Index rankings with indicators of development such as life expectancy and literacy, Botswana is gravely behind South Africa and Mauritius, with a life expectancy at 33.38 years—less than half the expected age of Mauritians. Another African nation worth noting is war-torn Sierra Leone, which ranks 74th on the Index of Public Governance, ahead of both Russia (91st place) and China (99th place). Yet in comparison to indicators of development, China and Russia also greatly surpass Sierra Leone.

Hahn points to history and culture to explain why a country can have a positive ranking in the Index of Public Governance and a low incidence of development. He argues that if countries that have the foundations of good governance continue with their efforts, development will follow. This means if countries like Sierra Leone stick to the path of comparatively good governance, while countries like Russia do not, then the indicator of development should rise for Sierra Leone in comparison with Russia.

In fact, Hahn's hypothesis on the relationship between corruption and poverty appears to be supported in a correlation analysis between Hahn's IPG and GDP per capita.

However, good governance is not the only indicator of corruption—poverty plays a role as well. *Governance, Corruption, and Economic Performance* recently published by the IMF, includes studies on the impact of corruption on economic performance. Amongst the findings are the following:

- social indicators (e.g. child mortality rate, school drop-out rates) are worse where corruption is high;
- countries with higher corruption tend to have lower per capita income, a higher incidence of poverty and greater income inequality;
- tax revenue is lower in more corrupt countries;
- transition economies that have made more progress on structural reform tend to be less corrupt; and
- decentralization of taxation and spending improves governance.

...

Corruption and Society

In a December 2005 document, "Controlling Corruption: A Handbook for Arab Politicians," a number of negative impacts of corruption on society were identified...

- Substitutes personal gain for public good;
- Prevents or makes it more difficult for governments to implement laws and policies;
- Changes the image of politicians and encourages people to go into politics for the wrong reasons;
- Undermines public trust in politicians and in political institutions and processes;
- Erodes international confidence in the government;
- Encourages cynicism and discourages political participation;
- Can contribute to political instability, provoke coups d'état, and lead to civil wars;
- Perverts the conduct and results of elections, where they exist;
- Keeps the poor politically marginalized;
- Consolidates political power and reduces political competition;
- Delays and distorts political development and sustains political activity based on patronage, clienteles and money;
- Limits political access to the advantage of the rich;
- Reduces the transparency of political decision-making.

...

For politicians in Mexico, when it comes to dealing with the drug lords, the choices are very clear—take the money and run and turn a blind eye; or have you and your family face the consequences of violence turned against you. It becomes even more difficult for a politician attempting to fight the drug lords when the police themselves are corrupt, and when judges are also bribed. It takes a brave politician to buck this trend.

Corruption is not only related to regular crime, however; the downing of a Russian passenger airliner in August 2004 by terrorists highlights how corruption and terrorism can be linked. It is alleged that the terrorist who blew up one of the planes was initially denied boarding the aircraft because of some irregularities with her documentation. However, a bribe approximating US $50 was paid—allowing her to board the aircraft and eventually blow it up, causing the death of 46 people.

In conclusion, corruption has enormous implications for developing countries. It undermines democratic processes, carries with it a huge economic cost, and corruption can lead to political unrest. But corruption also impacts countries with more developed economies and it is this to aspect that we now turn our attention.

...

Developed countries are not immune from corruption—it is more a question of order of magnitude, and the level of damage that corruption can cause in the respective jurisdictions. Many or all the negative consequences associated with corruption for developing countries apply to the more developed economies. There are, however, some additional and unique considerations for the industrialized world. There is an economic cost of bribery that is reflected in a higher cost of doing business in corrupt countries. This limits levels of foreign direct investment by developed countries in developing and emerging economies. Corruption in developing countries has undoubtedly changed world migration patterns as people flee their home countries out of disgust and/or the desire to improve the quality of their lives. They may flee their country of birth if they are being persecuted for exposing corrupt practices, or when bribery has caused greater health, safety, and environmental risks. [footnotes omitted]

END OF EXCERPT

THE MANY FACES OF CORRUPTION

No Universal Definition of Corruption

Corruption is not a singular concept; it comes in many forms and occurs in both hidden and open places. It is truly a global phenomenon; no country is corruption free. Although global in its nature, there is no global consensus on a universal definition of corruption. The definition and public perception of what behaviour constitutes corruption will vary to some extent depending on the social, political and economic structure of each society. For example, the line between lawful gift-giving and unlawful bribery can be difficult to pinpoint. Some countries have more prevalent social, political and economic customs of gift-giving. In many Asian countries, for example, gift-giving is, or until recently has been, part of a complex socio-economic custom. In China, that custom is called guanxi.74 The line between gifts and bribes can also change over time within a country. Indeed, over the past 50-75 years, this has taken place rapidly in many countries with the unrelenting march of the market economy into so-called "developing countries."75 Graycar and Jancsics in "Gift Giving and Corruption" provide a very useful four-part typology to distinguish between gifts and bribes in the public administration context.

Although cultural difference may affect the nature, extent and kinds of "corruption" in different states, this absence of universal agreement does not mean there is no consensus at all on the meaning of corruption. The UN *Convention Against Corruption* does not define the word corruption. Instead, it adopts the pragmatic approach of describing a number of specific behaviours that parties to the Convention must criminalize as corrupt, and other specific behaviours that state parties should at least *consider* criminalizing. Thus, in a legal sense, corruption is the type of behaviour that a state has defined as corrupt. Chapter 2 of this book is devoted to an examination of the forms of conduct that have been defined as crimes of bribery or corruption.

"Corruption" is best seen as a broad, generic concept. Transparency International's definition of corruption best captures this generic flavour: "corruption is the abuse of entrusted power for private gain." The essence of corruption is the combination of three elements: abuse, entrusted power and private gain. The abuse of entrusted power must be more than accidental or negligent; it must be intentional or knowing. TI's definition includes abuse of power by public officials (sometimes called public corruption) as well as abuse of entrusted power by private citizens in business (also called private corruption).77 Private corruption is often dealt with through offences like theft, embezzlement, or the offering and accepting of secret commissions. When describing corruption, adjectives are often used to indicate the context or form of the corruption in question, such as:

- grand corruption and petty corruption
- public or private corruption
- domestic or local corruption versus foreign corruption
- systemic versus occasional corruption
- supply-side corruption (i.e. offering or giving bribes) versus demand-side corruption (i.e. requesting or receiving bribes), which are also sometimes

called active corruption (for the briber) and passive corruption (for the bribed official)

- administrative corruption versus state capture[78]
- political corruption as a species of public corruption, including some forms of financial contributions to political parties and election campaigns, patronage, cronyism and various forms of vote buying
- books and records offences which are accounting offences designed to hide the giving or accepting of bribes

Graycar and Prenzler, in their very readable primer on corruption, Understanding and Preventing Corruption, further suggest that corruption should be examined in the context of four components: types, activities, sectors, and places (TASP).[79] They describe the nature and meaning of each of these components. For example, types of corruption include bribery, abuse of discretion, trading in influence and patronage. Corruption can take place through a variety of activities, including the making of public appointments, the procurement of public goods, the delivery of public services and the regulation and auditing of administrative tasks and obligations. Corruption can occur in any sector of society including construction, extractive industries, municipal governance, immigration, education, health care, sports (especially at the international level), and law enforcement. And finally, corruption can take place internationally, nationally, regionally, and locally, in workplaces, governments, and corporate offices.

Another analytic tool for describing corruption is the 4 W's—who, what, where and why. The "who" describes the various actors (e.g., political leaders, government employees, corporate agents, and executives) involved in corruption events, and the "what" describes the size (petty or grand), the frequency (rare or common) and the type of corruption offences being committed (e.g., bribery of a government official to obtain a government procurement contract or influence peddling in appointments to administrative boards and tribunals). The "where" describes both the place (national or international) and the sector (public works, law enforcement, etc.). Finally, the "why" deals with the purposes or motives for engaging in corruption (including financial need, the need for acceptance and friendship, competition, and the desire to succeed, promotion of perceived efficiency, greed, etc.).

In a more global sense, the 2014 OECD Foreign Bribery Report provides a glimpse into the prevalence and characteristics of the corruption of foreign public officials.[80] The Report examines enforcement actions (207 bribery schemes) against 263 individuals and 164 entities for the offence of bribery of foreign public officials in international business transactions. The vast majority of the enforcement actions took place in the US (62%) and Germany (12.5%), with a sprinkling of enforcement actions in Korea (5%), the UK (2.8%), Canada (1.9%) and other countries. The sanctioned offences occurred all over the world. According to the report, the majority of bribes (or at least the majority of bribes targeted by law enforcement officials) came from large companies with more than 250 employees. Senior management were involved in over 50% of cases. 80% of bribes were directed towards officials of state-owned enterprises, followed by heads of state (6.97%), ministers (4%) and defence officials (3%). The values of the bribes were only available in 224 cases, but totaled $3.1 billion in those cases. At least 71% of bribes involved an intermediary such as an agent, corporate vehicle, lawyer or family member. Interestingly, almost half of the cases involved the bribery of officials in countries with high or very high human development scores, casting doubt on the idea that most bribery of public officials occurs in developing countries. In terms of sectors, 57% of cases involved bribes to secure public procurement contracts.

The above description reveals some of the many faces of corruption. Recognition of corruption's many forms and an accurate description of those various forms is essential to finding appropriate responses and mechanisms in fighting corruption. The most effective anti-corruption mechanisms are varied and multi-faceted. They vary with the type of corruption being targeted and the social, political and economic context in which that corruption occurs. There are no "one size fits all" solutions to corruption. Remedies must be tailor-made and evaluated on an ongoing basis.

Imposing Western Definitions of Corruption Globally

Some commentators claim that the developed Western countries have imposed their conception of corruption on the rest of the world via international anti-corruption instruments.81 These instruments are heavily focused on the Western economic priorities of fostering international trade and leveling the playing field for competing businesses. As a result, the international conventions focus on economic corruption of foreign officials rather than more subtle yet venomous forms of political corruption, such as corrupt party and campaign financing, cronyism or vote-buying (see Chapter 13 of this book).

The history of UNCAC and the OECD Convention (outlined in more detail in Section 6 below) explains why those conventions focus primarily on the grand corruption of political leaders in foreign states when securing lucrative contracts as opposed to political corruption. The concern over grand corruption in foreign countries is relatively recent. The history of that concern is recounted in Section 6 of this chapter. In short, the Watergate investigation led to the revelation of large, illegal presidential campaign contributions by prominent corporations through offshore subsidiaries. Further, the investigation revealed a systemic practice of corporate bribery of foreign public officials. Public outrage led to the enactment of the 1977 US Foreign Corrupt Practices Act, which made it an offence for US corporations to bribe foreign officials in order to obtain contracts abroad. Surprisingly, bribery of foreign officials was not an offence in any other country. Bribes paid in a foreign country to a foreign official were viewed as a matter for that foreign country. Indeed, bribes to foreign officials were tax deductible as an expense of doing business. Not surprisingly, American companies complained loudly that the FCPA put them at a serious competitive disadvantage in obtaining foreign government contracts, since other industrial countries were continuing to bribe foreign officials. Rather than reverse course and decriminalize bribery of foreign public officials, the American government undertook an intense international campaign to bring the major economic countries of the world into line with the American position. The US succeeded with the coming into force of the OECD Anti-Bribery Convention in 1999, followed by the broader UNCAC in 2005.

As this history demonstrates, the international conventions on corruption were born from American concerns about loss of international business and the absence of fair competition.

Few commentators argue that grand corruption of foreign public officials should not be criminalized. However, there is merit to the observation that the international conventions focus too exclusively on Western concerns regarding economic trade. One could argue that Western countries display a double standard by roundly denouncing foreign economic bribery while failing to promote global standards regarding political corruption.

The Prevalence of Corruption

Section 4 of this chapter discusses the different methods for measuring the prevalence of corruption nationally and globally. But one doesn't need sophisticated measuring devices to know that corruption is rampant world-wide. One need only peruse the news over the past year or two to see the variety of people, places and activities involved in corruption. This section sets out briefly some of these corruption scandals. For example, nine US Navy officers were recently charged with accepting cash, hotel expenses and the services of prostitutes in exchange for providing classified US Navy information to a defence contractor in Singapore.82 In May 2015, 31 executives at a Chinese mobile carrier were punished for creating a "small coffer" by inflating conference expenses and secretly keeping client gifts. The "small coffer" funds were then used for lavish entertainments. In May 2015, BHP Billiton, a mining giant, agreed to pay $25 million to settle charges laid by the US Securities Exchange Commission after BHP paid for government officials from various countries to attend the 2008 Olympics in Beijing. The officials were connected to pending contract negotiations or regulatory issues involving BHP.84

Malawi's "cashgate" has been unfolding since 2013, when investigations into the siphoning of millions of dollars by civil servants began. In a recent development, two top Malawian army officers were arrested for their involvement in the siphoning of $40 million under the guise of ordering new military uniforms that never materialized.85 In June 2015, a Beijing traffic police officer stood trial for $174,000 worth of art in exchange for favouring one company in a bid for an undersea gas pipeline contract. In June 2015, five senior executives of construction companies were arrested in relation to alleged kickbacks and overbilling schemes between contractors and officials at Petrobras. Petrobras is also pursuing civil lawsuits against engineering and construction firms to recover funds tied to corruption.

The former CEO of Petrobras, along with five other executives, resigned in February 2015, and two million people protested across Brazil in response to the scandal in March 2015. More protests against corruption at Petrobras took place in August 2015, with many protestors calling for President Dilma Rousseff to step down. In late August 2015, the speaker of the lower house of congress, Eduardo Cunha, was charged with corruption for allegedly accepting $5 million in bribes in connection with the construction of two Petrobras drilling ships. In September 2015, the former presidential chief-of-staff was charged with corruption due to his alleged involvement in kickback schemes at Petrobras. Prosecutors also allege that bribe money connected to the Petrobras scandal has made its way to the ruling party's campaign coffers.93 As of March 2016, the government of Brazil charged 179 people with criminal offences in relation to the scandal and had secured 93 convictions.94 In May of 2016, President Rouseff was suspended from her position as President in order to face an impeachment trial. In August 2016, by a 61 to 20 vote of the Senate, Rousseff was convicted of manipulating the federal budget in order to conceal the country's financial problems, impeached, and removed from office.

Since Brazil's new president, Michel Temer, and his conservative government have come into power, another scandal came to light. Brazilian police launched an investigation into fraudulent investments made by large pension funds of state-run companies whose board members were appointed by politicians. The pension funds implicated in the investigation controlled 280 billion reals (approximately US$87 billion) in assets in 2015, and the fraud scheme was valued at approximately 8 billion reals (approximately US$2.5 billion). Many of the politicians under investigation are those who were already under investigation in connection with the Petrobras scandal.96 Eight of the ten cases upon which the investigation is based involved allegedly fraudulent or reckless investments made by the companies' equity investment divisions.97 Forty senior financiers and executives were ordered to temporarily step down from their positions, abstain from capital market activity, and forfeit their passports. The most noteworthy of such executives is the chief executive of JBS, the world's largest beef exporter.

And nearly the whole world knows about the corruption charges laid against senior FIFA officials by the US.100 FIFA officials were indicted based on allegations that they took part in accepting bribes and kickbacks over the course of 24 years. The officials were alleged to have accepted bribes in relation to past bidding processes for hosting rights and in the awarding of broadcasting and marketing rights for various tournaments. The US trial date was tentatively set to begin in February, 2017. Former FIFA President Sepp Blatter, resigned just four days after his re-election in June 2015 because of the allegations of corruption. Blatter, who is not facing charges in the US, said that he will defend FIFA in the US trial.101 In March 2016, FIFA filed a victim statement and request for restitution. In the restitution claim, FIFA argues that its organization as a whole was not corrupt, but rather only its leaders were. As such, it claims that some of the $290 million seized or frozen by US prosecutors should be used to compensate the victims of the corruption: FIFA and its member associations.102 In October of 2016, former Costa Rican soccer federation president and member-elect to FIFA's In Switzerland, authorities are probing the possibility of corruption in the bidding process for the upcoming World Cups in Qatar (2022) and Russia (2018). According to Domenico Scala, the chairman of FIFA's compliance and audit committee, Qatar and Russia could be denied the opportunity to host the World cup if evidence of bribery in the bidding process comes to light. In June, 2015, Switzerland announced they were investigating 53 "suspicious activity reports" in respect to the possible laundering of bribes in connection to the hosting of the Russia and Qatar World Cups. Sepp Blatter, who is a Swiss citizen, is involved in this investigation. By September 2015, Swiss Attorney General, Michael Lauber, stated that 121 suspicious banking transactions were being investigated. Since then, a spokesman for the Attorney General's office has stated that the number of incidents under investigation had surpassed 200. Swiss officials have estimated that the case will not proceed to trial until at least the end of 2020.104 Former UEFA President Michel Platini was initially expected to succeed Blatter as President of FIFA, but that was prevented as he is under investigation by Swiss authorities in regard to a $200,000 payment he received from Sepp Blatter in 2011.105 Gianni Infantino, former General Secretary of UEFA, took over for Blatter as President of FIFA since his election in February 2016.

And elsewhere, the Panama Papers prompted widespread shock and concern about tax evasion, laundering of proceeds of corruption, and other secretive financial dealings facilitated by offshore accounts and shell companies. In 2014, Bastian Obermayer, a journalist with the German newspaper Suddeutsche Zeitung, received an anonymous telephone call. Shortly thereafter, Bastian Obermayer and his colleague Frederik Obermaier received the 11.5 million documents that are now known as the Panama Papers.107 The leaked documents came from the Panamanian law firm Mossack Fonseca, which specializes in secretive offshore banking for the wealthy.108 The International Consortium of Investigative Journalists (ICIJ) managed a team of 370 journalists from roughly 100 media organizations across 70 countries, which finally published the first coverage of the Panama Papers in April of 2016.109 Of course, not all offshore accounts are used for illegal activities, but because of their secrecy they are often used for money laundering, hiding the proceeds of bribery, and tax evasion.110 Evidence in the Panama Papers of legal, but perhaps immoral, tax avoidance has prompted backlash against the some of the world's most powerful and wealthy individuals and companies. Internationally, the revelations in the Panama Papers instigated proposals for tax reform and calls for sanctions against countries that operate as tax havens.

The Panama Papers contain information about a multitude of politicians such as Ukrainian President Petro Poroshenko and King Salman of Saudi Arabia. Russian President Vladimir Putin's associates and family members of Chinese President Xi Jinping are also mentioned.111 On April 5, 2016, Sigmunder David Gunnlaugsson stepped down from his position as Prime Minister of Iceland in response to protests following the release of the Panama Papers. The documents showed that Gunnlaugsson's wife owned an offshore company that held millions of dollars in debt from collapsed Icelandic banks.112 Shortly after he took over as President of FIFA, Gianni Infantino became the subject of an investigation by the Swiss Federal Police because the Panama Papers included a contract signed years earlier by Infantino when he was at UEFA. The contract suggests that Infantino may have sold broadcast rights below market price only to have them sold later at a far higher price.113 While serving as Prime Minister of the United Kingdom, David Cameron came under scrutiny because the Panama Papers revealed that his late father owned an offshore investment fund called Blairmore Holdings. While he initially denied having profited from the investments, on April 7, 2016, Cameron admitted that he had sold shares in the company for more than £30,000 shortly before becoming Prime Minister. Although there is no suggestion that the fund facilitated any illegal activity, Cameron's lack of transparency was criticized.114 The Papers further revealed that three of Pakistani Prime Minister Nawaz Sharif's children owned offshore assets not included on his family's wealth statement.115 On November 3, 2016, the highest court of Pakistan appointed a commission to investigate Sharif's finances after months of disagreement between Pakistan government and opposition party as to the terms of reference for the commission.116 The Panama Papers also revealed that entrepreneurs and corrupt public officials in several African countries such as Nigeria, Algeria, and Sierra Leone used shell companies to hide profits from the sale of natural resources and to hide bribes paid in order to gain access to the resources.

In other financial news, the US corruption case against Och-Ziff Capital Management, a major hedge fund company, was settled in September 2016. The corruption perpetrated by the hedge fund involved payments of bribes totaling over $100 million to officials in Congo, Libya, Chad, Niger, and Guinea to gain influence and obtain mining assets. In the terms of the settlement, Och-Ziff, which manages $39 billion, agreed to pay $412 million in criminal and civil penalties. This payment was one of the largest that has been approved under the United States' Foreign Corrupt Practices Act.118 And, in January 2017, the SEC filed a civil complaint against two former executives of Och-Zifff in respect to the abovementioned bribery schemes.

Significant controversy has also surrounded the 1MDB affair. 1MDB is a Malaysian state investment firm launched in 2009, the same year that Najib Razak became Prime Minister of Malaysia. The fund was supposed to be used to increase economic development in the country. By 2014, the company was over US$11 billion in debt. In 2015, information surfaced about a suspicious $700 million payment into Najib's bank accounts made in 2013. This information led to investigations into 1MDB in at least six countries. Najib claimed that the transfer was a legal donation from a Saudi benefactor.

On July 20, 2016, the United States Department of Justice filed lawsuits alleging that between 2009 and 2015 over $3.5 billion had been taken from the fund by officials of 1MDB and their associates.121 The lawsuits outline three separate phases of the theft. The first $1 billion was allegedly obtained fraudulently through a fictitious joint venture between 1MDB and PetroSaudi.

The following two phases focus on $2.7 billion in funds that Goldman Sachs raised and diverted into a Swiss offshore company and a Singapore bank account.122 The proceedings commenced by the US Justice Department sought to seize over $1 billion in assets including luxury properties, art by Van Gogh and Monet, and a jet. The money from 1MDB was also reportedly used to finance production of the film "Wolf of Wall Street." The production company that made the movie was cofounded by Najib Razak's stepson, Riza Aziz. Among the several individuals mentioned in the lawsuit is a high-ranking Malaysian official who is called "Malaysian Official 1" and identified as a relative of Riza Aziz.123 This individual is presumed to be Prime Minister Najib Razak.124 The US proceedings that started in July of 2016 only concern seizure of assets. Criminal charges against the individuals involved may follow.125 As of December 2016, US authorities were investigating Goldman Sachs' role in the scandal. Goldman has maintained that it believed the funds were used to buy legitimate assets for 1MDB.

Authorities in Switzerland and Singapore undertook separate investigations into the 1MDB scandal. On July 21, 2016, Singapore authorities reported having frozen or seized approximately $175 million in its investigations into transactions linked to 1MDB. They also announced forthcoming proceedings against three large Singapore banks for their inadequate attempts to prevent money-laundering.127 In Switzerland, authorities launched an investigation into whether or not Swiss banks were used to misappropriate funds diverted from 1MDB. In October of 2016, Switzerland's Office of the Attorney General announced that a Ponzi scheme may have concealed the alleged fraud.

Although not strictly a case of corruption, the recent scandal involving Volkswagen's fraudulent avoidance of state emission standards is noteworthy. In September 2015, the US Environmental Protection Agency learned that Volkswagen sold innocent Americans cars equipped with special software that would automatically cheat emissions tests.129 In June 2016, Volkswagen agreed to spend approximately $14.7 billion in order to resolve federal and state civil allegations. However, the US Department of Justice stated that the settlement would not eliminate the possibility of Volkswagen being held criminally liable for its actions.130 Indeed, on January 11, 2017, Volkswagen AG agreed to plead guilty to three felony counts and agreed to pay a $2.8 billion criminal penalty. In addition, a grand jury indicted six VW executives and employees for their roles in the emission standards fraud.

DRIVERS OF CORRUPTION

Sorting out the causes of corruption is a complicated task. In their book Corruption: Economic Analysis and International Law, Arnone and Borlini note that "[a]ny attempt to isolate and distinguish causes [of corruption] from effects suffers from the limitations imposed by the presence of multi-directional causal chains."132 For example, although bad governance has been shown to contribute to corruption, corruption can also contribute to bad governance.

Some factors that enable or drive corruption can, however, be articulated. A good starting point is Arnone and Borlini's observation that discretion and conflict of interest are the breeding grounds for corruption. Bad governance can strengthen the presence of these "preconditions." If lack of accountability is added to the mix, particularly where officials have "monopoly power over discretionary decisions," opportunities for corruption will be rife.133 Complex and opaque systems of rules tend to foster this lack of accountability, along with insufficient stigma and enforcement surrounding corruption offences.

In a study for the World Bank entitled Drivers of Corruption, Soreide enumerates other, more specific drivers of corruption.134 She begins by describing factors which increase opportunities for "grabbing" by public officials. When officials have the power to control the supply of scarce goods or services, opportunities to create shortages and demand high payments will increase. This is particularly problematic if citizens cannot choose between officials. Soreide maintains that facilitation of financial secrecy and secret ownership also drives corruption, along with information imbalances between principals and agents. For example, principals might not be informed regarding corruption in foreign markets, leaving openings for agents to exploit this ignorance by promoting bribery and pocketing a portion of the proceeds. Soreide also points out that revenues from natural resource exports and development aid are vulnerable to grabbing. In the context of aid development, both donor and recipient countries contribute to misuse of aid funds:

- The more urgent the development needs, the more the aid-offering entity pays, and the weaker the recipient government's incentives to perform better, because better performance will eventually cut the level of aid received. The desire to offer financial and other forms of support is particularly strong in emergency situations and in the most-fragile states...Such sets of circumstances are vulnerable to theft and corruption because oversight systems are weak and funds pour in from many sources, continuing as long as the needs are dire.

Many authors have pointed at incentive problems of donor agencies, and there are a number of examples where representatives of donor agencies have been involved in illegal transactions or activities that violate their organization's rules and the recipient country's legislation. Although donor agencies are aware of the potentially troubling impact of such cases on the legitimacy of their operations, they, like other bureaucracies, have encountered difficulties eradicating the challenges completely and handling revealed cases of fraud and corruption effectively. ... Jansen [2014] explains a donor-government's disincentive to react partly as a trade-off between the cost of exercising control and the ease of referring to recipient responsibilities. Among the factors is the low propensity among donor representatives to procure independent reviews and audits of aid-financed projects and programs. Sometimes these are driven by the need to seize opportunities for new projects....this tendency is intensified by heavy workloads and "pipeline problems"; that is, when funds have to be allocated within the timeframe of a financial year regardless of the status of preparatory work or controls. [footnotes omitted]

Soreide moves on to consider the factors that encourage people to exploit opportunities for corruption. Included are lack of sanction for individuals or organizations, widespread tolerance, condonement by management, lack of protection for whistleblowers and the failure of political systems and their accountability safeguards.

Many writers have sought to explain the bad governance/corruption phenomenon in Africa. Blundo has argued that the colonial legacy was instrumental in creating a climate of corruption: here the new elite simply copied the example from their former colonial masters,138 although Atyittey argues against this thesis going as far as to accuse Africans of 'carping' about colonial exploitation.139 Others have linked bad governance with the development of opportunities for corruption. For example, Collier attributes this to four factors: overregulation of private activity; expanded public sector employment; expanded public procurement; and weakened scrutiny.

To these may be added issues such as increased access to development aid, privatization programmes, and the ability to launder the proceeds of corruption through the international financial system quickly and efficiently.

Allen has argued that the constitutional models adopted by the Anglophone and Francophone African states at independence concentrated undue political power in the hands of the Executive and that this resulted in weak accountability mechanisms.142 This power was then enhanced and further entrenched by the establishment of a one-party system in many states and often largely retained despite a return to multi-party democracy and the making of new constitutions.143 This argument is taken up by Raditlhokwa who blames the spread of corruption almost solely on a crisis of leadership, accusing African leaders of a lack of self-discipline144 and a resultant 'crisis

Hatchard also explains some motives behind the corrupt acts of public officials. First on the list is financial gain, followed by the belief that corruption will not be prosecuted. Next, Hatchard describes the "[p]ressure to carry out or condone the activity" when lower-level officials are threatened or bribed into assisting the corrupt acts of higher level officials.147 The presence of traditional gift-giving practices can also motivate corrupt practices, along with the standard business practice of "[b]ona fide payments to public officials, such as gifts or hospitality, provided by a company in order to promote its image."148 The desire to circumvent inefficient bureaucracy, through facilitation payments, for example, also motivates corruption.

PERCEPTIONS AND MEASUREMENTS OF CORRUPTION

As pointed out by Graycar and Prenzler, measuring corruption can guide remedial measures and provide "an indicator of how well a society is performing in terms of a government's contract with its citizens."149 However, measuring corruption is challenging due to the lack of a uniform definition and the covert nature of corruption. A variety of methods deal with these problems in different ways. Measurements might address the level of risk of corruption, or the extent of actual corruption using various indicators, or the cost of corruption. Measurement might require creative techniques; for example, to reveal the amount of aid funding that had been skimmed in road-building projects in Indonesia, Benjamin Olken dug up chunks of road and measured the difference between funding and amounts of materials actually used. Because of the inevitable uncertainty involved in any one measurement method, Graycar and Prenzler recommend that measurements "triangulate as many indicators as possible."

Commonly-Cited Indexes of Corruption

Transparency International's Indexes

Transparency International is the world's largest anti-corruption NGO. TI has been very influential in raising the profile of the problem of corruption, in part through its research and surveys regarding the prevalence of corruption-related activities worldwide. The three main indexes and surveys published by TI are the Corruption Perceptions Index (the "CPI"), the Global Corruption Barometer (the "GCB") and the Bribe Payers Index (the "BPI").

The Corruption Perceptions Index

The CPI is the most commonly cited corruption index worldwide. As its title indicates, the CPI measures perceptions rather than actual rates of corruption. The index is an aggregate of a variety of different data sources. It reports on levels of public sector corruption, as perceived by businesspersons and country experts who deal with the country in question. Despite some limitations, it is generally acknowledged as a reliable, though not precise, indicator of public sector corruption levels. The CPI is published annually and its release gets significant media attention. The 2017 edition includes information on 180 countries and territories. Denmark and New Zealand, closely followed by Finland and Norway, topped the list with the lowest levels of perceived corruption, while Somalia, South Sudan, Syria and Afghanistan had the highest perceived corruption levels.

The Global Corruption Barometer

The GCB measures both lived experiences with corruption and perceptions on corruption amongst the general public. According to TI, it is the world's largest survey on public opinion on corruption. The 2013 edition included responses from citizens in 107 countries. It asked respondents questions regarding both their experiences with corruption in major public services and their perceptions on items such as the effectiveness of government efforts to control corruption and corruption trends and rates. The GCB is published every few years. The survey indicates that more than one in four people worldwide (25%) report having paid a bribe to a major public institution. This increases to more than three out of every four people (75%) in countries such as Sierra Leone and Liberia. In comparison, only one percent of people in countries such as Japan, Denmark and Finland report having done so.

Over the course of 2015-2017, Transparency International has been releasing the 2015/2016 edition of the Global Corruption Barometer, which is now being presented in the context of five regional surveys covering Sub-Saharan Africa, the Middle East and North Africa, Asia Pacific, and Americas.153 The first four regional surveys have already been made available.154 They show, in particular, that in Europe and Central Asia bribery rates vary considerably between the countries of the region. For instance, while 0% of households in the United Kingdom reported paying a bribe when accessing basic services, this figure was as high as 42% in Moldova and 50% in Tajikistan.

The Bribe Payers Index

The BPI is based on a TI survey of business executives in thirty of the countries around the world that are most heavily involved in receiving imports and foreign investment. The index is not published on a regular schedule. The 2011 survey focuses on the supply side of bribery and measures perceptions on how often foreign companies from the largest economies engage in bribery while conducting business abroad versus at home. This edition focused on firms in 28 countries and of the countries surveyed, Chinese and Russian companies were perceived as the most likely to engage in bribery while doing business abroad while firms from the Netherlands and Switzerland were perceived as the least likely to do so. The results are also categorized by sector. The public works construction sector was perceived as the industry sector most likely to involve bribes.

The World Bank's Worldwide Governance Indicators Project

The Worldwide Governance Indicators project (WGI) reports on six indicators of good governance, one of which is control of corruption. The WGI is an aggregate of data from a large number of surveys conducted between 1996 and 2015, and includes data on more than 200 countries and territories. The WGI may be used to compare data over time or between countries. The Control of Corruption Indicator measures perceptions of the extent to which public power is exercised for private gain.

In August 2013, the Hertie School of Governance released a report titled "Global Comparative Trend Analysis Report."158 The report, using data from the World Bank's control of corruption indicator, compares control of corruption scores among eight world regions in the period between 1996 and 2011. The regions of North America, Western Europe and Oceania were consistently ranked as the leading regions in controlling corruption. Few countries showed significant change in their control of corruption scores over the fifteen- year period.

Freedom House Publications

Freedom House is a US-based watchdog organization committed to promoting democracy and political and civil liberties globally. It publishes a number of research reports and publications relating to indicators of good democratic governance. Two major publications which deal specifically with corruption are Nations in Transit and Countries at the Crossroads.

Nations in Transit

Nations in Transit is an annually published report that studies the reforms taking place within 29 of the former communist countries of Europe and Eurasia. The report covers seven categories relating to democratic change, one of which is corruption. Its corruption index reflects "public perceptions of corruption, the business interests of top policymakers, laws on financial disclosure and conflict of interest, and the efficacy of anti-corruption initiatives."

Countries at the Crossroads

Countries at the Crossroads, published between 2004 and 2012, was an annual publication examining government performance in 70 countries at a crossroads in determining their political future. Its anticorruption and transparency section included four measurements:

1. Environment to protect against corruption (bureaucratic regulations and red tape, state activity in economy, revenue collection, separation of public and private interests, and financial disclosure);
2. Anticorruption framework and enforcement (anticorruption framework and processes, anticorruption bodies, prosecution);
3. Citizen protections against corruption (media coverage; whistleblower protection; redress for victims, and corruption in education); and
4. Governmental transparency (general transparency, legal right to information, budget-making process, expenditure accounting, government procurement, and distribution of foreign assistance).

TRACE Matrix

TRACE International is a non-profit business association, founded in 2001 by in-house anti- bribery compliance experts, that provides its members with anti-bribery compliance support. TRACE Incorporated offers risk-based due diligence, anti-bribery training and advisory services to both members and non-members.161 In collaboration with the RAND Corporation, TRACE International developed the TRACE Matrix, a global business bribery risk index for compliance professionals, which scores 199 countries in four domains – business interactions with the government, anti-bribery laws and enforcement, government and civil service transparency, and capacity for civil society oversight. Published since 2014, a new edition is released every two years.

The World Justice Project Rule of Law Index

The World Justice Project (WJP) is a US-based independent and multidisciplinary organization that seeks to advance the rule of law globally. Its overall Rule of Law Index assesses performance of governments on the basis of 44 indicators organized in eight categories, including absence of corruption in the executive branch, the judiciary, the military and police, and the legislature.164 The 2016 edition of the WJP Rule of Law Index, which covers 113 countries and territories, places Denmark, Singapore, Norway, Finland and Sweden on top of the list in the "absence of corruption" category.

Some Limitations Associated with Corruption Indexes Based on Perceptions

Although the indexes included above are useful in understanding the prevalence of corruption around the globe, most do not include objective measures of corruption. There is little empirical data measuring corruption. The empirical research that does exist is not well- developed and is generally small in scope. This is because quantifying actual rates of corruption on a large scale is difficult. Objective measures, such as the number of bribery prosecutions, are not reliable indicators; a large number of prosecutions may simply reflect a well-resourced and effective policing system and judiciary rather than a comparatively high prevalence of bribery. Because of the limitations of objective measurements, TI views perceptions of public sector corruption as the most reliable method of comparing levels of corruption across countries.

Despite the convenience and widespread use of perception measurements, indexes such as TI's CPI have also received significant criticisms. There is no guarantee that perceptions of corruption accurately reflect actual rates, and some commentators suggest that perceptions of corruption are not well-correlated with reality. The CPI in particular has been criticized for being western-centric, as it focuses on the perceptions of western business people rather than local lived experiences with corruption (although TI's Global Corruption Barometer does measure the latter).

Comparing perceptions across countries can also be difficult, as people from different regions may have different understandings about what constitutes corruption. For example, some election financing and lobbying activities in Western countries are designed to influence public officials in subtle, implicit ways—and in that sense, are corrupt—yet these practices are not legally defined as corruption.

Perception measurements raise the issue of how corruption is defined. Definitions of corruption are not universally agreed upon and different definitions may produce differing results. Some definitions include many types of corruption while others focus primarily on bribery. The common focus on corruption in public institutions has also been criticized as being western-centric. Corruption is often portrayed as a trans-cultural disease. However, it is important to consider the different cultural contexts in which it exists.

The authors of the major indexes generally caution that results are not definitive indicators of actual corruption and should not be used to allocate development aid or develop country- specific corruption responses. However, with an understanding of their limitations, these index measurements can provide important information about corruption trends around the globe.

For a detailed, multidisciplinary and cross-sectoral examination of corruption research and practice, see Graycar and Smith's *Handbook of Global Research and Practice in Corruption* (Cheltenham, UK: Edward Elgar Publishing, 2011). Chapter 3 (Heinrich and Hodess, "Measuring Corruption") provides an overview of recent developments and trends in measuring corruption. Chapter 4 (Recanatini, "Assessing Corruption at the Country Level") analyzes an alternative approach to measuring corruption, promoted by practitioners at the World Bank, that assesses a country's governance structures and institutions from various perspectives, which are briefly discussed in Section 4.1(ii) above.

MORE ISSUES ON MEASURING AND UNDERSTANDING CORRUPTION

In his article "Eight Questions about Corruption," Jakob Svensson reviews literature and data on eight topics involved in understanding corruption.167 For non-economists and non- statisticians, the data and analysis in Svensson's article are sometimes dense. What follows is a brief summary of Svensson's review. Although based on available data as of 2005, more recent data does not significantly alter the main observations in the article.

What is Corruption?

Svensson notes that the most common definition of public corruption is the misuse of public office for private gain. He also notes that no "definition of corruption is completely clear- cut." The data in his article focuses on public corruption.

Which Countries Are Most Corrupt?

Svensson notes that measuring corruption across countries is challenging because of the secretive nature of corruption and the variety of forms it takes. Svensson then discusses different corruption measurement scales, including:

- The corruption indicator in the International Country Risk Guide, which measures the likelihood of bribe requests,
- TI's Corruption Perception Index,
- Kaufmann, Kraay and Mastruzzi's Control of Corruption index (2003),
- The EBRD-World Bank Business Environment and Enterprise Performance Survey,172 and
- The International Crime Victim Surveys, run by UNODC.

Svensson then lists the countries in the bottom ten percent according to each measurement tool.

What are the Common Characteristics of Countries with High Corruption?

Based on the corruption ranking results, Svensson states:

- All of the countries with the highest levels of corruption are developing or transition countries. Strikingly, many are governed, or have recently been governed, by socialist governments. With few exceptions, the most corrupt countries have low income levels. Of the countries assigned an openness score by Sachs and Warner (1995), all of the most corrupt economies are considered closed economies, except Indonesia. [footnotes omitted]

Svensson's analysis also shows that richer countries generally have lower corruption. However, corruption levels vary widely across countries even controlling for income. For example, he notes that Argentina, Russia and Venezuela are ranked as relatively corrupt given their level of income. On the other hand, rankings of countries in sub-Saharan Africa often match the expected levels of corruption given their GDP. Svensson notes that levels of income are a stronger predictor of levels of corruption when combined with levels of schooling, forms of governance and freedom of the press.

Rose-Ackerman and Bonnie Palifka also argue that states emerging from conflict are especially susceptible to corruption, making reconstruction challenging.176 Ackerman and Palifka observe that these postconflict states have many of the factors that create incentive to engage in corruption: widespread destruction, weak controls, lack of trust in law enforcement, poverty, and a poorly functioning judiciary.

What is the Magnitude of Corruption?

Svensson (2005) points out that subjective rankings of countries as more or less corrupt do not quantify the magnitude of corruption. He outlines some past attempts to measure magnitude at the micro level. For example, to determine the magnitude of corruption involved in public education grants in Uganda, Reinikka and Svensson (2004) compared the value of disbursements to each school district with survey data on actual receipts of money and equipment by schools.178 Price comparisons can also be used to infer the magnitude of corruption. For example, Hsieh and Moretti (2006) analyzed the difference between the official selling price and estimated market price of Iraqi oil to infer the presence of underpricing and kickbacks for the regime.179

Do Higher Wages for Bureaucrats Reduce Corruption?

Svensson (2005) then reviews empirical research on the impact of certain corruption control measures on actual corruption levels. First, Svensson looks at the relationship between higher wages for public servants and corruption. After summarizing several studies, Svensson concludes:

- Thus, wage incentives can reduce bribery, but only under certain conditions. This strategy requires a well-functioning enforcement apparatus; the bribe being offered (or demanded) must not be a function of the official's wage; and the cost of paying higher wages must not be too high. In many poor developing countries where corruption is institutionalized, these requirements appear unlikely to hold.

Can Competition Reduce Corruption?

Svensson (2005) also analyzes data related to the relationship between competition and corruption:

- Another common approach to control corruption is to increase competition among firms. One argument is that as firms' profits are driven down by competitive pressure, there are no excess profits from which to pay bribes (Ades and Di Tella, 1999). In reality, however, the connections between competition, profits and corruption are complex and not always analytically clear.

For further discussion of this point, see Taylor's article.

According to Svensson, some evidence shows that deregulation does not reduce corruption by increasing competition, but rather by reducing the discretion and power of public officials. Svensson concludes:

- A variety of evidence suggests that increased competition, due to deregulation and simplification of rules and laws, is negatively correlated with corruption. But it can be a difficult task to strike the right balance between enacting and designing beneficial rules and laws to constrain private misconduct while also limiting the possibilities that such laws open the door for public corruption (Djankov, Glaeser, La Porta, Lopez-de-Silanes and Shleifer, 2003).

Why Have There Been So Few (Recent) Successful Attempts to Fight Corruption?

Svensson notes that many anti-corruption programs provide resources to existing enforcement institutions. However, these institutions are often corrupt themselves. Svensson states that, "[t]o date, little evidence exists that devoting additional resources to the existing legal and financial government monitoring institutions will reduce corruption." Although Hong Kong and Singapore are considered exceptions, both countries also implemented other wide-ranging reforms in their anti-corruption efforts.

Svensson then lists some alternative approaches to combating corruption, such as turning to private or citizen enforcement, providing citizens with access to information and delegating work to private firms. The issue of designing more effective anti-corruption institutions and practices is further addressed in Section 10 of this chapter.

Does Corruption Adversely Affect Growth?

Finally, Svensson analyzes findings on the link between corruption and economic growth, pointing out that, "in most theories that link corruption to slower economic growth, the corrupt action by itself does not impose the largest social cost. Instead, the primary social loss of corruption comes from propping up of inefficient firms and the allocation of talent, technology and capital away from their socially most productive uses (Murphy, Shleifer and Vishny, 1991, 1993)."185 Svensson also describes the potentially adverse effects of corruption on firm growth and the allocation of entrepreneurial skills, as well as impacts on social welfare and, by extension, human capital. For more on the relationship between corruption and economic growth, see Section 1.4 of this chapter.

Svensson's Conclusion

Svensson notes that the answers to his eight questions are not clear-cut and he reminds readers of how little we know about many issues concerning corruption. In Svensson's opinion, there are three areas of particular importance requiring more study:

- First and most urgently, scant evidence exists on how to combat corruption. Because traditional approaches to improve governance have produced rather disappointing results, experimentation and evaluation of new tools to enhance accountability should be at the forefront of research on corruption.

Second, the differential effect of corruption is an important area for research. For example, China has been able to grow fast while being ranked among the most corrupt countries. Is corruption less harmful in China? Or would China have grown even faster if corruption was lower? These types of questions have received some attention, but more work along what context and type of corruption matters is likely to be fruitful.

Finally, the link between the macro literature on how institutions provide a more-or-less fertile breeding ground for corruption and the micro literature on how much corruption actually occurs in specific contexts is weak. As more forms of corruption and techniques to quantify them at the micro level are developed, it should be possible to reduce this mismatch between macro and micro evidence on corruption.

For a concise article on the relationship between governance and corruption, and the difficulties of measuring both, see Daniel Kaufmann, "Back to Basics: 10 Myths About Governance and Corruption" (2005) 42:3 Finance and Development. See also Clare Fletcher

HISTORICAL DEVELOPMENT OF INTERNATIONAL CORRUPTION LAWS

Early History from Antiquity to the OECD Convention in 1997

In Martin's 1999 article "The Development of International Bribery Law", the author details the development of anti-bribery laws in the west up to the 1997 signing of the OECD Convention on Combating Bribery of Foreign Public Officials in International Business Transactions (the "OECD Anti-Bribery Convention").187 The OECD Convention was ratified by Canada in December, 1998 and came into force in February, 1999. The OECD Anti-Bribery Convention paved the way for further international actions to combat corruption, including the more expansive United Nations Convention Against Corruption (UNCAC), which entered into force in 2005.

[Tim Martin is an international advisor and governance counsel from Calgary, Alberta, Canada. He can be reached at tim@timmartin.ca.]

BEGINNING OF EXCERPT

Corruption was not a problem at the beginning of history. Rather than use bribes, people made "offerings" to their gods and leaders in the hope of receiving favors. In a sense, such reciprocities provided a social glue that allowed cultures and civilizations to develop. But with civilization came religious and civil institutions that needed rules of fairness and good governance to ensure the loyalty and trust of the populace. Kings and pharaohs had to demonstrate that the rule of law was above the influence of greasy palms. Thus began the distinction between gifts and bribes.

After presenting the Ten Commandments to Moses on Mount Sinai, God instructed the Israelites not to take *shohadh*, which is loosely translated from Hebrew as "offering."

You shall not take shohadh, which makes the clear-eyed blind and the words of the just crooked. (Exodus 23:1-3, 6-8)

Given that the Old Testament was breaking new ground, it was only natural that this distinction started a bit ambiguously. However, even after several millennia of lawyers trying to define bribery, a certain amount of haze shrouds the issue.

There are records of bribes and bribery laws from ancient times. Archaeologists have recently found an Assyrian archive which is 3400 years old that listed the names of "employees accepting bribes." An Egyptian pharaoh, Horemheb (1342-1314 BC), issued the first recorded law of a secular penalty for bribetaking. The Edict of Horemheb proclaimed that any judge who took a reward from one litigant and failed to hear the adversary was guilty of a "crime against justice" and subject to capital punishment. His threat apparently did not stop the practice of bribing the judiciary from spreading beyond Egypt.

The Greek historian Pausanius relates that before beginning each Olympic Games, all the umpires, athletes, their relatives and trainers swore over boars' flesh that they would uphold Olympic rules intended to prevent corrupt activity. Similar to present times, not everyone played by the rules. Pausanius recorded in his *Description of Greece* (5.21.5) that Calippus of Athens bought off fellow competitors with bribes, as did many other contestants. This practice continued unabated until the Roman Emperor Theodosius eventually abolished the Olympic Games in 394 AD because of rampant corruption and brutality.

As for the Romans' view of bribery, Shakespeare may have captured it best when Brutus said to Cassius in Julius Caesar:

Remember March; the ides of March remember. Did not great Julius bleed for justice sake!

What villain touch'd his body that did stab And not for justice? What, shall one of us, That struck the foremost man of all this world But for supporting robbers – shall we now Contaminate our fingers with base bribes And sell the mighty space of our large honours For so much trash as may be grasped thus?

I had rather be a dog and bay the moon Than such a Roman.

Act 4, Scene 3, lines 19-30

People's view of corruption has evolved and become more negative as the institutions of government have developed. Instead of being ambivalent about the giving of gifts to officials in a position of public trust, modern society has enacted and prosecuted laws that make such payments illegal. Over time, a bribe has come to mean "an inducement improperly influencing the performance of a public function meant to be gratuitously exercised." (For an illuminating history of bribes, please refer to J. T. Noonan, BRIBES (1984).) [See also Douglas Thompson's LLM thesis.[188]] Even though it is usually opposed on moral grounds, bribery has become a legal concept analyzed and prosecuted by lawyers. Thus in understanding how the world has grappled with corruption, one must consider the history of bribery laws.

For King and Country (And a little bit for me, too)

Francis Bacon was one of the most brilliant lawyers, judges, and philosophers in English history. He was also one of its most corrupt Lord Chancellors. Bacon was first Solicitor General, then Attorney General, and finally, in 1618, Lord Chancellor. Even though he was an extremely capable jurist who honestly and fairly dispensed justice, he was too detached and philosophical to take notice of the bribes flowing to his servants who used his good office to benefit themselves. Caught up in the byzantine politics of the court of King James I, Bacon was accused of accepting bribes to affect cases in the Court of Chancery. His enemies in Parliament impeached him with twenty-three charges of bribery and corruption. Bacon first replied with a qualified admission of guilt. The House immediately rejected his submission, whereupon Bacon caved in: "I do plainly and ingenuously confess that I am guilty of corruption, and do renounce all defence."

Sir John Trevor was probably the most corrupt Speaker in the history of Parliament. The East India Company was rumored to have bribed him to exert influence over laws affecting it. He also apparently accepted a large payment from the City of London Corporation. Indeed, a House Committee investigation discovered a written record of the City's instructions and an endorsement of the payment to Trevor. The Members of Parliament drew up a resolution in 1694 which convicted the Speaker of a "high crime and misdemeanour." Ironically, it was the responsibility of Sir John, as the Commons Speaker, to put the motion to the House, which he did in a shameless way. The motion was overwhelmingly acclaimed and Sir John slunk out of the House of Parliament. He did not return but rather sent a sicknote to the House who responded by expelling the Speaker. (These and other stories can be found in Matthew Parris, GREAT PARLIAMENTARY SCANDALS (1995).)

The English common law first dealt with foreign bribery in the trial of Warren Hastings who went to India at eighteen as a clerk of the East India Company and quickly rose through the ranks until he was appointed the British Governor of Bengal in 1772. During his tenure as Governor, he amassed a great fortune that could not be accounted for by his salary alone. Edmund Burke, a member of the House of Commons, accused the Company of great abuses in India and gradually those accusations focused on Hastings, who allegedly received large bribes while Governor. As a result of his investigations, Burke and his fellow Parliamentarians drafted Articles of Impeachment against Hastings that asserted various abuses of authority constituting "high crimes and misdemeanours" including "Corruption, Peculation and Extortion." After winning the support of the House of Commons, the impeachment trial of Hastings commenced in the House of Lords in 1787. See Peter J. Marshall, THE IMPEACHMENT OF WARREN HASTINGS (1965).

The leading case of the time (1725) concerned Thomas Earl of Macclesfield, a Lord Chancellor who was accused of selling jobs in Chancery. In that case, the House of Lords held that the sale of an office which related "to the administrations of justice" was not an offense at common law. This was reflected in the definition of bribery provided by Blackstone in his COMMENTARIES ON THE LAWS OF ENGLAND of 1765. A bribe was a crime committed by "a judge or other person concerned in the administration of justice." The definition was thus restricted to acts involving a judicial decree or its execution. By 1769 the law had expanded to make the offering of money for a government office a crime. In this environment, Hastings launched his defence which consisted of showing that he had not offered any money himself as bribes and that any presents he had received were not for himself but for the Company. To be on the safe side, he also launched personal attacks on Burke throughout the trial. Hastings' strategy was successful and resulted in the Lords deciding on April 23, 1795, after seven years of deliberation that he was not guilty. It would take another 180 years before anyone would again try to prosecute an act of foreign bribery. However, the next attempt would be in America rather than England.

New Law in the New World

America has a long tradition of being concerned about corruption. Public offices have been bought, judges were monetarily influenced, and the nation's infrastructure was sometimes built on the back of bribes. But America is a country where government is expected to be for the benefit of the people. Public officials and their decisions were not to be bought and sold by a few wealthy individuals or corporations. Bribes were seen as immoral and against the founding principles of the United States of America. Something had to be done about corruption and lawmakers were more than willing to fill the breach. A multitude of approaches was thus pursued to address the problem.

The U.S. Founding Fathers clearly had corruption on their minds when they drafted the Constitution. Their first concern was Executive Branch corruption but they expanded the concept to include the Judiciary. The mechanism they built into the Constitution to remedy this problem was impeachment. The Constitutional Convention of 1787 first specified that the grounds for impeachment would be

"Treason, Bribery, or Corruption." They later dropped "Corruption" as superfluous but added "other high crimes and misdemeanours" using the language from the Hastings trial in Parliament. This amendment supposedly provided Congress sufficient flexibility in the future to prosecute corrupt judges and Presidents. Unfortunately, the Constitution did not provide that Congressional members were subject to impeachment based upon the argument of James Madison that it was harder to corrupt a multitude than an individual. How wrong he proved to be! Bribing Congressmen became a national pastime. Eventually, Congress passed An Act to Prevent Frauds upon the Treasury of the United States in 1853 which made it illegal to bribe a member of Congress. It was not used much (possibly because of its misleading title). Indeed, during the first 150 years of the American Republic, no high ranking government leader was convicted for bribery. The Teapot Dome Scandal in the 1920s changed this complacency.

Albert Fall, Secretary of the Interior, arranged for the awarding of leases to two oil companies in 1922 in the Navy's oil reserves at Teapot Dome, Wyoming, and Elk Hill, California. After receiving many complaints, the Public Lands Committee of the Senate investigated and thereafter declared that the procurement of the leases had been "essentially corrupt." Apparently, Edward Doheny of Pan-American Petroleum made Secretary Fall a cash loan of $100,000 delivered in "a little black bag" on which neither principal nor interest was collected, and the alibi of Harry Sinclair of Mammoth Oil Company was that he bought an interest in Fall's ranch. The Supreme Court unanimously cancelled the leases as "corruptly secured" and the oil companies were forced to pay back over $47 million. All three were tried for conspiracy to defraud the United States but were acquitted. However, former Secretary Fall was convicted of bribery even though he argued that if the oilmen were innocent of giving a bribe, he could not be guilty of taking one. Fall was eventually sentenced to a fine equal to the bribe and served one year in jail. See Burl Noggle, TEAPOT DOME: OIL AND POLITICS IN THE 1920'S (1962).

American legislators continued putting in place a plethora of laws that comprehensively extended the criminal law of bribery to almost every class and occupation imaginable. There was the Anti-Racketeering Act of 1934 and the Hobbs Act of 1946. This preoccupation with bribery continued unabated until the Nixon administration in 1970 produced the most comprehensive federal statute ever designed against bribery – the Racketeering Influenced and Corrupt Organization Act (or RICO). This statute was enacted in response to the growth of organized crime but its greatest effect was to make bribery a federal offense and to give broad powers to district attorneys to prosecute anyone engaged in a "pattern" of bribes.

There was also a long history of laws meant to stop the abuses of campaign financing. President Teddy Roosevelt first pushed for the enactment of the

Tillman Act of 1907 after the president of Standard Oil claimed that he had given the Republican Party $125,000 in cash which had never been returned. The law prohibited corporate directors from using stockholders' money for political purposes and was meant to be "an effective method of stopping the evils aimed at in corrupt practice acts." This phrase had been popular for some time. The English Parliament had enacted a Corrupt Practices Act in 1883. The U.S. Congress enacted the Federal Corrupt Practices Act of 1910, which required the reporting of all contributions to national elections. This statute was amended several times, but its enforcement was infrequent, resulting in ambivalence about campaign contributions. The situation did not change until 1972 when the Federal Corrupt Practices Act was repealed and the Federal Election Campaign Act was enacted, resulting in taxpayers being permitted to deduct contributions to presidential campaigns. The government in effect had legalized payments to campaigning politicians rather than encourage potential bribes.

Throughout this period, all of the industrialized countries and most of the developing world had their own laws which made the bribery of public officials illegal. England had the Public Bodies Corrupt Act of 1889 and the Prevention of Corruption Acts of 1906 and 1916. Countries such as Canada, Denmark, France, Germany, Italy, the Netherlands, Spain, and Switzerland had prohibited the bribery of public officials under their respective Criminal Codes for many years. Some, such as France, as early as 1810. But similar to the United States, all these laws addressed the bribery of domestic officials, i.e., judges, politicians, and government officials within the country's boundaries. No one ever contemplated looking beyond their own borders. All that changed as a result of some unrelated but extraordinary events investigated by several committees of the U.S. Senate.

A Leap into Foreign Waters

In 1972 the Democratic National Committee headquarters located at the Watergate complex in Washington, D.C., was burglarized. The Senate formed a select committee the next year to investigate the burglary and found that many U.S. corporations had made illegal contributions to Richard Nixon's Committee to Re-Elect the President. The result was that fifteen prominent corporations pleaded guilty to making illegal campaign contributions and were fined. One of the corporations, Gulf Oil, provided an amazing report to the Senate committee that detailed an elaborate overseas network to siphon political bribes back to the States and to other countries. Gulf had apparently distributed more than $5 million to influential politicians from overseas bank accounts over the years. See THE GREAT OIL SPILL (1976).

On February 3, 1975, Eli Black, the Chairman of United Brands Corporation, jumped to his death from a New York skyscraper. The Securities and Exchange Commission (SEC) investigated and discovered that his corporation, the largest

American banana producer, had paid $2.5 million to senior politicians in the Honduras. The SEC successfully sued the company for securities fraud since the payments were not reported in the financial accounts of United Brands. During the same period, a military coup ousted the President of the Honduras. As a result of the United Brands' investigation and concerns around the Gulf Oil report, the SEC sent a questionnaire to U.S. companies and asked them to reveal any "questionable payments" made by them abroad. Based upon this survey, the SEC published a report showing that over 400 U.S. companies, including 117 of the Fortune 500, had made "questionable payments" totalling more than 300 million dollars.

In June 1975, Senator Frank Church and his Subcommittee on Multinational Corporations were investigating a recent price rise of Arab oil and had called upon Northrop Corporation, a major supplier of aircraft to Saudi Arabia, to provide evidence. Northrop admitted paying bribes through a Saudi agent, Adnan Khashoggi, using the "Lockheed model." After hearing this statement and seeing the questionnaire from the SEC, the auditors of Lockheed Aircraft Corporation decided that they would only certify the company's accounts if Lockheed's corporate officers signed statements that all payments to consultants were in accordance with contracts and properly recorded. As it turned out, Lockheed had been engaged in a massive program of overseas bribes to government officials who bought their planes. Its officers refused to sign the statements. It quickly became public knowledge that Lockheed was going into its stockholders' meeting with unaudited financial statements. This caught the attention of Senator William Proxmire, Chairman of the Senate Banking Committee, who immediately convened an investigation into Lockheed. The day before the Senate Committee began its hearing, the company's treasurer shot himself dead. Undeterred, the Senate Banking Committee opened its investigation on August 25, 1975. The Committee found that Lockheed had paid hundreds of millions of dollars through consultants to government officials in Saudi Arabia, Japan, Italy, and the Netherlands. When asked if he had paid a one million dollar bribe to Prince Bernhard of the Netherlands, the president of Lockheed, A. Carl Kotchian, replied:

I think, sir, that as my understanding of a bribe is a quid pro quo for a specific item in return. I would characterize this more as a gift. But I don't want to quibble with you, sir.

It appeared that even a sophisticated jet-setting business executive was unable to distinguish a gift from a bribe.

Upon further examination, the Banking Committee found that as many as nine different American laws were criminally violated by a bribe paid abroad, including the Internal Revenue Code, the Foreign Assistance Act, the Bank Secrecy Act, the Travel Act, and RICO. However, these statutes had only been peripherally violated.

To the great chagrin of the Committee, no specific law explicitly prohibited an American from paying a bribe overseas. Something had to be done to prevent the abuses perpetrated by Lockheed, Gulf Oil, and others so inclined. Senator Proxmire's Committee thus recommended that a new law be enacted to prevent overseas bribery based on their reasoning that (1) foreign governments friendly to the United States had come under "intense pressure from their own people," (2) the "image of American Democracy" had been "tarnished," (3) confidence in the financial integrity of American corporations had been impaired, and (4) the efficient functioning of capital markets had been hampered.

After very little debate in either the House or Senate, both Houses unanimously approved the Committee's bill on December 7, 1977, and President Carter subsequently signed it into law on December 19, 1977. The Foreign Corrupt Practices Act (FCPA) was thus born. This law was the first of its kind in the world. A new era of global bribery prevention had begun. The United States, like no other country before it, had decided to make the payment of bribes to foreign officials illegal and imposed rigorous record keeping requirements on U.S. companies and their overseas subsidiaries to ensure that bribes could not be hidden. However, when the dust settled and the United States surveyed the global landscape, it found itself standing alone.

All For One and One For All

American companies immediately recognized that they were at a disadvantage to their foreign competitors. They would thereafter constantly claim that they lost overseas contracts because they could not pay the bribes that foreign companies allegedly did. (This view has been reinforced in some recent studies. *See* U.S. Department of Commerce, UNCLASSIFIED SUMMARY OF FOREIGN COMPETITIVE PRACTICES REPORT (Oct. 12, 1995); James R. Hines, Jr., FORBIDDEN PAYMENT: FOREIGN BRIBERY AND AMERICAN BUSINESS AFTER 1977 (Nat'l Bureau of Econ. Res. Working Paper No. 5266, 1995). The American government believed that its companies were competing on an unlevel playing field and therefore began seeking multilateral co- operation on global bribery.

The United States has advocated changes in the bribery laws of other countries in two primary areas. The first is to criminalize the bribery of foreign officials. This reflects the debate held in the U.S. Senate when it approved the FCPA in 1977. At that time, Congress chose the stringent approach of criminalization over the option of only requiring public disclosure of foreign payments on the grounds that it was too lenient. The second area is the elimination of the tax deductibility of bribes. The U.S. government was concerned that other governments such as France and Germany allowed their corporations to deduct such payments against their income tax and thus tacitly approved the practice.

The first attempt to change international bribery law on a multilateral basis was at the United Nations (U.N.) and was wholly unsuccessful. The U. N. Economic and Social Council completed a draft agreement known as the International Agreement on Illicit Payments in 1979. This draft document outlawed all bribes to public officials, including the "grease" payments exempted under the FCPA. The Council of the General Assembly took no action to convene a conference to conclude and formalize it, despite strong efforts to do so by the United States.

Having failed at the United Nations, the U.S. moved to another forum, the Organization for Economic Cooperation and Development (OECD). The American government lobbied the OECD in 1981 to implement an illicit payments agreement. However, several countries expressed the view that differences among their legal systems would make such an agreement difficult to implement. Another attempt was made at the insistence of Congress when they amended the FCPA in 1988. Nothing resulted from either of these efforts. *See* U.S. Department of State, ILLICIT PAYMENTS: PAST AND PRESENT U.S. INITIATIVES.

The multilateral approach of the U.S. government was shelved at that point. There were a variety of unilateral attempts to extend the territoriality of the FCPA even farther beyond U.S. borders. Senator Russ Feingold introduced Bill 576 in 1995 which would have prohibited certain U.S. trade assistance agencies from aiding U.S. subsidiaries of foreign corporations, unless the director of the agency certified to Congress that the corporation maintained a company-wide policy prohibiting the bribery of public officials. Senator Hank Brown drafted a more far-reaching bill, the Foreign Business Corruption Act of 1996, to pressure foreign companies and countries. It provided for private rights of action with awards up to three times damages, allowed retaliatory actions against corrupt foreign governments on the basis of unfair trade barriers, and gave any U.S. person the right to bring action in a U.S. court against a foreign concern which violated a law of a foreign country that was substantially similar to U.S. legislation.

Neither of these bills advanced. One of the primary reasons was that the Clinton administration had decided in late 1993 to renew a multilateral effort. Since the Cold War had ended, the U.S. focused its attention on global economics and the problem of foreign bribes was given high priority in this new war. The American government carefully considered the supply and demand sides of the corruption equation in forging its strategy. It primarily focused on the supply side (or active part of bribery) and the multilateral organization that received most of its attention was the OECD.

The OECD Convention

In May 1994, a majority of the OECD countries agreed upon a suite of recommendations entitled OECD RECOMMENDATIONS ON BRIBERY IN INTERNATIONAL BUSINESS

TRANSACTIONS. However, it was not binding and was well below the objectives set by the United States. No specific measures were recommended; rather, it offered a broad list of "meaningful steps." Subsequently, after intensive lobbying by the United States and after overcoming the resistance of some European countries (especially France), the OECD Council on April 11, 1996, approved a recommendation to eliminate the tax deductibility of bribes among its member states. At the next OECD meeting in May 1997, the American government pushed for a resolution committing governments to outlaw foreign bribery in their domestic legislation by the end of 1998 and to establish a monitoring system to ensure that it was being enforced. In opposition, France and Germany, with the support of Japan and Spain, maintained that "you need an international convention for criminalizing corruption, because the legal framework in each country is different. The U.S. and its supporters viewed this as a stalling tactic since such treaties take many years to negotiate and ratify.

After much negotiation, a compromise was struck. The ministers endorsed the REVISED REC-OMMENDATION ON COMBATTING BRIBERY IN INTERNATIONAL BUSINESS TRANSACTIONS. They recommended that member countries would submit criminalization proposals to their legislative bodies by April 1, 1998, and seek their enactment by the end of 1998. The ministers also decided to open negotiations promptly on a convention to be completed by the end of 1997, with a view to its entry into force as soon as possible within 1998, and urged the prompt implementation of the 1996 recommendation on the tax deductibility of such bribes.

After six months of intensive discussions, all twenty-nine member countries of the OECD and five non-member countries agreed to sign the CONVENTION ON COMBATTING BRIBERY OF FOREIGN PUBLIC OFFICIALS IN INTERNATIONAL BUSINESS TRANSACTIONS (the OECD Convention) in Paris on December 17, 1997, reprinted at 37 I.L.M. 1 (1998). This Convention provided the framework under which all the signatory governments undertook to prohibit and act against the bribery of foreign public officials on an equivalent basis without requiring uniformity or changes in the fundamental principles of each government's legal system. The OECD Convention entered into force on the 60th day following the date upon which 5 of the 10 countries with the largest shares of OECD exports, representing at least 60% of the combined total exports of those 10 countries, deposited their instruments of acceptance, approval, or ratification. Such ratification had to occur by December 31, 1998, to be binding upon all signatory countries. Canada's deposit of its instrument on December 17, 1998, met the pass mark and resulted in the OECD Convention's entering into force on February 15, 1999. At the time of writing, fourteen countries had deposited their instruments of ratification and the remaining signatory countries have publicly stated that they will complete their ratification process during 1999 [as of 2016, 41 countries have adopted the Convention].

The Convention has a clearly defined scope. It provides that each government "shall establish that it is a criminal offence under its law for any person intentionally to offer, promise or give any undue pecuniary or other advantage, whether directly or through intermediaries to a foreign public official, for that official or for a third party, in order that the official act or refrain from acting in relation to the performance of official duties, in order to obtain or retain business or other improper advantage in the conduct of international business." The Convention makes it an offence for nationals of signatory countries to give a bribe to a foreign public official. In other words, it is directed against offences committed by the bribegiver and not the public official receiving the bribe.

Signatory countries have undertaken to make the bribery of a foreign public official punishable by effective, proportionate, and dissuasive criminal penalties. A foreign public official includes persons elected or appointed to hold legislative, administrative, or judicial office of a foreign country. It also covers Public Agencies, Public Enterprises, and Public International Organizations. Despite intense lobbying by the U.S., it is not an offence to make payments to political parties or officials of those parties.

The Convention provides that the bribe and its proceeds are subject to seizure and confiscation. Where more than one government has jurisdiction, they are required to consult with a view to determining the most appropriate jurisdiction for prosecution. Bribery of a foreign public official is considered an extraditable offence amongst the signatory governments. All parties to the Convention have undertaken to cooperate in carrying out a program of systematic follow-up to monitor and promote the full implementation of the Convention. The OECD has recently set up a Centre for Anti- Corruption Compliance to provide information and training on anti-corruption laws. This Centre provides one of the most comprehensive websites available on foreign corruption: [updated link: http://www.oecd.org/daf/anti-bribery/]. [See also the UNODC anti-corruption website TRACK at http://www.track.unodc.org/.] The commentaries on the Convention state that it is not an offense if the advantage was permitted or required by the written law or regulation of the foreign public official's country. Also, making small "facilitation" payments is not an offense since they are not payments made "to obtain or retain business or other improper advantage."

Without question, the OECD Convention is the most significant international treaty on foreign bribery up to this time [1999]. However, it is but one piece of the American strategy. At the urging of the U.S., the G-7 countries supported the recommendations of the OECD when they met in Lyon, France, in July 1996. The

United Nations General Assembly also approved a resolution on "Action Against Corruption" in January 1997 and the Council of the European Union adopted a Framework Convention Against Corruption in May 1997. The U.S. has also worked closely with non-governmental organizations such as the International Chamber of Commerce (ICC) and Transparency International (TI).

In March 1996, the ICC approved and published its Rules of Conduct on bribery in international business transactions. These rules prohibit extortion and bribery for any purpose, not just to obtain or retain business, making them more stringent than the previous ICC Code published in 1977. The rules now cover extortion and bribery in judicial proceedings, tax matters, and environmental and other regulatory cases, as well as in legislative proceedings. (The ICC's website on extortion and bribery is [updated link: http://www.iccwbo.org/Advocacy-Codes-and-Rules/Document- centre/2004/ICC-Rules-of-Conduct-and-Recommendations-to-Combat-Extortion- and-Bribery-(2005-Edition)/]).

Transparency International was founded in May 1993 with its headquarters in Germany. It is a not-for-profit, non-governmental organization that attempts to counter corruption in international business transactions. It does this through international and national coalitions which encourage governments to establish and implement effective law, policies, and anti-corruption programs. Each year, TI publishes a corruption [perception] index which lists [global perceptions on] the most and least corrupt countries in the world. It has also established a program called "Islands of Integrity" which attempts to arrange, in welldefined markets, a pact among competitors to stop corruption simultaneously, by entering into an Anti- Bribery Pact. (For further details on TI, see its homepage at [updated link: http://www.transparency.org]).

The United States has not forgotten the demand side (or passive part) of bribery. It pursued the corruption agenda at both the Organization of American States (OAS) and the Asia-Pacific Economic (APEC) Forum. Its greatest success to date has been at the OAS. In a meeting held in Caracas, Venezuela, in March 1996, the OAS adopted an Inter-American Convention Against Corruption. Once again, the United States led the implementation of this convention, with strong support from several South American countries, including Venezuela. Colombia opposed the treaty's extradition provisions and Uruguay objected to the bank secrecy provisions. However, it was eventually signed by twenty-five OAS members and has been ratified by sixteen member states at this time [as of 2015, 33 OAS members have signed on].

The OAS Convention provides that each country shall prohibit and punish the offering or granting, directly or indirectly, by its nationals, residents, or businesses, to a government official of another state, of any article of monetary value or other benefit in connection with any economic or commercial transaction in exchange for any act or omission in the performance of that official's public functions. Such offenses shall be an extraditable offense in any extradition treaty existing between or among the countries. Countries shall also provide each other the broadest possible measure of assistance in the identification, tracing, freezing, seizure, and forfeiture of property or proceeds obtained, derived from, or used in the commission of any offence established in accordance with the convention. (The OAS website on corruption can be found at [updated link: http://www.oas.org/juridico/english/fightcur.html]).

The U.S. government lobbied the APEC Forums that met in Manila in 1996 and Vancouver in 1997 to approve recommendations similar to those adopted by the OECD. Several Asian members of the APEC Forum publicly stated their misgivings about the U.S. proposal, citing cultural differences amongst the member economies. Nothing happened with this proposal, and it was quietly dropped.

The Clinton administration also pushed the corruption agenda in the multilateral organizations that govern world trade and dispense development funds, in particular, the World Trade Organization (WTO), the World Bank, and the International Monetary Fund (IMF). At the WTO's Singapore conference in December 1996, the United States, with support from Canada, the European Union, Japan, and nine other countries, proposed new public procurement rules that would criminalize bribes and require more transparency in the awarding of government contracts. As expected, resistance to the proposal arose from a variety of developing countries. A group led by Malaysia and including Indonesia, Thailand, Brunei, the Philippines, Bahrain, Zimbabwe, Cuba, Egypt, and Uganda argued that due regard be given to the national policies of each country.

...

In 1996, the World Bank initiated a policy that required it to investigate complaints of corruption and if it found sufficient grounds, allowed it to blacklist companies and governments that participated in bribery. Under this policy, evidence of corruption could result in the cancellation of World Bank financing in a country and in the prevention of a bribing company from participating in contracts financed by the World Bank. The World Bank has made a clear public statement of its position in a report published in September 1997 entitled Helping Countries Combat Corruption: The Role of the World Bank. The report states that bribes are one of the primary elements of corruption used to obtain government contracts and services and that poorly regulated financial systems permeated with fraud "can undermine savings and deter foreign investment. They also make a country vulnerable to financial crises and macroeconomic instability."

The World Bank has begun to act against countries where it has found corruption in its projects. The bank stopped funding development projects in Nigeria and Zaire, and it has launched strict reforms to improve the monitoring of its money. The World Bank also suspended a $76 million loan to Kenya for energy development because it could not ensure that contracts would be awarded fairly and openly. Developing countries have to take these actions seriously since the World Bank finances about 40,000 contracts worth $25 billion each year. (Further details on the World Bank's anticorruption program can be found at [updated link: http://www.worldbank.org/en/topic/governance/brief/anti-corruption].)

[In the last five years, the World Bank funded on average $40 billion worth of projects a year; the World Bank has also significantly increased the number of debarments in that same period—from 2009-2013 there have been 492 debarments.189]

On a similar basis, the IMF has denounced corruption in developing countries. As part of its monetary policy, it has urged countries wanting to borrow from the IMF to institute anticorruption reforms. The IMF has also acted closely with the World Bank against corrupt regimes. In August 1997, the IMF suspended a $220 million loan to Kenya because of a scandal in the gold and diamond export trade. The next month, the IMF put a $120 million loan to Cambodia on hold "because of problems in governance which concern corruption and logging." As the IMF takes a leading role in resolving the financial crises of several Southeast Asian countries, it is imposing conditions on its loans that directly address corruption and bribery. South Korea has been forced to open its markets, curtail state-owned firms and crony capitalism, and make its financial systems more transparent. Thailand and Malaysia had to accept the same recipe and Indonesia was required to close sixteen loss-making banks, including one owned by former President Suharto's son. [Basically, the IMF maintains that good governance is the key to economic success and that it promotes good governance by engaging in surveillance of its member countries' economic policies].

Despite such pressures, laws dealing with bribery in developing countries themselves haven't changed much. Bribery laws in third world countries are often confusing and sometimes even contradictory. They tend not to reflect local customs and practice and are often ignored. When they are applied, it is often done arbitrarily and inconsistently. The punishment under such host country laws is usually severe and consists of imprisonment or fines and occasionally death. The punishment tends to apply to individuals only and not to corporations. For an investing company, the individuals most at risk are the company's employees and representatives who work or reside in the host country.

Investing companies often face a dilemma with these laws. Whereas they try to conform to the requirements of the bribery laws of their country of residence, this may not necessarily translate into conformance with host country laws. One example is the defences or exceptions under the FCPA. Facilitating payments or reasonable business expenditures may not strictly be allowed in the host country's law even though much greater sins are publicly practiced. These laws will undoubtedly change if a WTO convention on bribery is enacted, but in a way which is presently unknown.

Don't Blame Uncle Sam!

One gets the impression that the American government has single-handedly changed corruption laws around the world, for which they can be commended (or criticized, depending on one's perspective). However, it is not the complete story. The United States has indeed been the primary catalyst in this tremendous change, but looking beyond its initiative there are a multitude of reasons that have converged to create wide and growing support for the prevention of bribery in foreign countries.

The United States has mounted a massive global campaign in every conceivable multilateral organization in the world. (The primary U.S. Government website on foreign corruption is found at [updated link: http://www.imf.org/external/np/exr/facts/gov.htm]). A lot of this campaign is motivated by self-interest, but there is also a genuine desire to make the world a better place to do business. The U.S. government has relentlessly pursued the simple goal of having other countries' multinationals play by the same rules applicable to U.S. companies. Its strategy is clearly laid out in the 1996 Annual Report to Congress of the Trade Promotion Coordinating Committee. One of the Report's more novel ideas was the establishment of a hotline at the U.S. Department of Commerce for reporting bribery allegations. (This recommendation has not been implemented to the gratitude of scurrilous bribers around the world!)

There is a dawning realization that bribes eliminate competition, create inefficiencies, and ultimately cost countries and their consumers money. One only has to look at a list of the most corrupt countries and see that it is very similar to the list of the least developed countries in the world. It has been demonstrated that countries with high corruption have less investment and lower growth rates in their economy. See generally Paulo Mauro, WHY WORRY ABOUT CORRUPTION? (1997). The result has been growing support in international trade and development organizations for policies aimed directly at eliminating corruption.

END OF EXCERPT

In their book Handbook of Global Research and Practice in Corruption, Graycar and Smith note some reasons why corruption has increasingly been seen as a significant global concern:

- International trade has been a feature of human behavior for millennia. But in recent centuries new transport mechanisms and new technologies have made for economic interdependence. Compounded by digital technologies which move money around the world at the speed of light, and global business moguls who seek advantage opportunistically and capriciously, corruption takes on a new dimension. Political instability has also taken on a cross-national dimension, and it is often fuelled by, and in turn fuels corruption.

International Corruption Instruments Culminating in UNCAC (2005)

Webb in "The United Nations Convention Against Corruption" describes the major international anti-corruption instruments developed between 1997 and the enactment of UNCAC.191 The brief summaries below of the major international instruments developed between 1996 and 2005 are derived from Webb's article.

The Organization of American States Inter-American Convention Against Corruption (1996)

The Organization of American States Inter-American Convention Against Corruption (OAS Convention) was signed by 22 countries in 1996, including the US. Canada signed the convention in 1999 and 33 countries have now signed on. The OAS Convention was the first binding international instrument on corruption. Venezuela led the group of Latin-American countries that lobbied for its creation. The United States was also a strong supporter of the Convention. The OAS Convention has a broader scope than the OECD Anti-Bribery Convention. Besides criminalizing the bribery of foreign officials, the OAS Convention requires that signatory states also criminalize the acceptance or solicitation of bribes. It therefore addresses both active bribery (the giving of a bribe) as well as passive bribery (the receiving of a bribe). Since the OAS Convention prohibits any bribe paid in relation to "any act or omission in the performance of that official's public function" (Article VIII, OAS Convention), it is broader than the equivalent OECD Anti-Bribery Convention provision, which only criminalizes bribery when it relates to a business transaction or contract. In addition, the OAS Convention encourages signatory states to criminalize other acts of corruption not strictly covered under anti-bribery laws, such as the misuse of confidential information by public officials.

As Webb notes, the OAS Convention's greatest weakness is its lack of a strong enforcement mechanism. In 2001 the Conference of State Parties established a peer review system to monitor implementation of the Convention. Under this system a

Committee of Experts selects a state for review and then prepares a preliminary report on that country's implementation of the Convention. This report is then made available for review by the subject state. The final report is then submitted to the Conference of States Parties and published. The Committee of Experts can only make recommendations for improvements and cannot recommend sanctions for states who fail to meet their international obligations under the Convention.

OECD Convention on Combating Bribery of Foreign Public Officials in International Business Transactions (1997)

As discussed in the excerpt from Martin's article, "The Development of International Bribery Law," the OECD Anti-Bribery Convention was a key development in the international fight against corruption. The Convention has now been ratified by 35 OECD member states and 7 non-member countries (Argentina, Brazil, Bulgaria, Colombia, Costa Rica, Lithuania, Russia and South Africa).192 While the OECD Convention initially seemed to come with a more rigorous review process than the OAS Convention, Webb writes that the monitoring mechanism had "mixed results."193 Implementation of the OECD Anti-Bribery Convention is monitored by the OECD Working Group on Bribery, which uses a multi-phase peer- review system to evaluate and report on state parties' implementation of the Convention. The review system has worked slowly at times and has not always been well-funded. In many countries the introduction of new anti-corruption legislation has not had a significant impact domestically. Webb concludes that "[d]espite its focused scope, widespread ratification, and well developed monitory system, it [the OECD Anti-Bribery Convention] is yet to produce significant changes on the ground."194 Some other commentators have a more positive view of the impacts of the OECD Anti-Bribery Convention. In my view, the OECD Convention's review system has prompted more government attention (and funding) for anti-corruption activities and, at least for Canada and the UK, has prompted some legislative and practice improvements. For example, in Canada, new federal money was directed towards enforcement of the Corruption of Foreign Public Officials Act (CFPOA) and amendments were made to the Act due to criticisms and suggestions from the OECD review mechanism. Pressure for the new UK Bribery Act, 2010 arose from many sources including the OECD review mechanism.

A detailed review of the activities of the OECD Working Group on Bribery can be found in their 2013 and 2014 Annual Reports.

For further background on the development of the OECD Anti-Bribery Convention and a review of its application in member countries' domestic legislation, see Davids and Schubert, "The global architecture of foreign bribery control: Applying the OECD Bribery Convention" in Graycar and Smith, (2011).

Council of Europe Criminal Law and Civil Law Conventions on Corruption (1999)

The Council of Europe Criminal Law Convention on Corruption

This multilateral instrument was adopted by the Council of Europe in 1999. The Council of Europe (COE) is a political organization composed of 45 European nations, including many from Central and Eastern Europe. The COE Criminal Law Convention on Corruption (COE Criminal Law Convention) may also be adopted by non-European states. Indeed, both Mexico and the United States are both signatories to the Convention. The Convention applies to private sector as well as public sector bribery. The Convention requires that member states prohibit active and passive bribery, but does not require that signatory states criminalize other forms of corruption. The COE Criminal law Convention also provides support mechanisms for parties fighting corruption, such as the requirement that signatory countries protect informants. In addition, although the facilitation of the tracing and seizing of assets is addressed, the Convention does not deal with the return of stolen assets exported out of the country of origin.

The Council of Europe Civil Law Convention on Corruption

The COE Civil Law Convention on Corruption (COE Civil Law Convention) is the first international instrument to address civil law legal remedies for those affected by corruption. Like the COE Criminal Law Convention, the COE Civil Law Convention may also be adopted by non-COE member states. As of May, 2013, 33 states had ratified the Convention. The COE Civil Law Convention focuses on the act of bribery and requires that signatory states provide domestic legal avenues for victims of corruption to recover damages against those who participated in acts of corruption as well as those who failed to take reasonable care to prevent corruption. The Convention addresses the protection of whistleblowers and allows courts to declare a contract invalid if its validity was "undermined by an act of corruption" (Article 8 COE Civil Law Convention). Although civil law mechanisms may allow victims of corruption to participate in the enforcement of anti-corruption laws on their own initiative, Webb notes that there are several disadvantages with addressing corruption through civil law means. Civil enforcement of anti-corruption laws could lead to a reduced ability of government agencies to control the overall anti-corruption strategy. As well, many victims of corruption may not have the means to take a civil claim to court.

Group of States against Corruption

The Group of States against Corruption (GRECO) is a monitoring organization that was established in 1999 by the Council of Europe. It monitors compliance with the Council of Europe's anti-corruption standards. All states that are party to either the

Criminal or Civil Law Conventions on Corruption are subject to GRECO's compliance monitoring. Currently, GRECO includes 48 European States, as well as the US.

A team of experts nominated by GRECO members evaluates state parties' implementation of the Council of Europe's anti-corruption conventions. Each evaluation round assesses member states on a different corruption subtopic. First, member states are evaluated and recommendations are issued on how the state could improve its compliance. Next, a compliance report that evaluates how well the country complied with the recommendations of the earlier evaluation report is completed. All evaluation and compliance reports are made public and are available on GRECO's website.

Convention of the European Union on the Fight Against Corruption Involving Officials of the European Communities or Officials of Member States (1997)

The Convention of the European Union on the Fight Against Corruption Involving Officials of the European Communities or Officials of Member States (EU Convention) builds on the 1995 Convention on the Protection of the European Communities Financial Interests and the 1996 and 1997 Protocols. The EU Convention is focused on addressing bribery of officials. It is limited to acts that are harmful to the EU's economic interests and only addresses corruption occurring within EU member nations. Following the EU Convention, the EU addressed private sector corruption in the 1998 EU Joint Action Act. The 2003 Communication on a Comprehensive EU Policy against Corruption encouraged member states to act on their multilateral anti-corruption obligations; however, it was drafted in non-binding language.

For a recent, detailed analysis of European countries which have progressed and those that have regressed in the past 15 years, see Mungiu-Pippidi, The Good, the Bad and the Ugly:

African Union Convention on Preventing and Combating Corruption (2003)

The African Union Convention on Preventing and Combating Corruption (AU Convention) is a broadly conceived, regional anti-corruption agreement. It was adopted in 2003 potentially covering 53 states. It required 15 states to ratify before coming into force and this was achieved in 2006. As of May 2013, 31 states ratified the Convention.197 While the Convention is very comprehensive and is generally phrased in mandatory language, its enforcement mechanism relies on self-reporting. State parties are required to report on their implementation of the Convention to an Advisory Board elected by the Executive Council. However there is no obligation on the part of the Advisory Board to check the veracity of the country reports. Webb states that the lack of follow-up mechanisms to monitor enforcement may allow state parties to avoid fully implementing the Convention. However, Carr takes a more optimistic view of the AU Convention. She states that the "AU Convention is progressing in the right direction and with more harmonisation on the way through international and inter-regional agreements on various strengthening measures, such as codes of conduct for public officials and protection of informants, the war [against corruption] should ease in intensity."

For an in-depth review of the AU Convention and a comparison between it and other international and domestic instruments, see Thomas R. Snider and Won Kidane, "Combating Corruption Through International Law in Africa: A Comparative Analysis" (2007) 40 Corn ILJ 691.

For further information on corruption and anti-corruption strategies in Africa see:

- John Hatchard, Combatting Corruption: Legal Approaches to Supporting Good Governance and Integrity in Africa (Cheltenham, UK; Northampton US: Edward Elgar, 2014).
- The African Development Bank Group, http://www.afdb.org
- The African Parliamentarians Network Against Corruption (APNAC), www.apnacafrica.org and
- The African Union Advisory Board on Corruption, http://www.auanticorruption.org/

United Nations Convention Against Corruption (2003)

The United Nations Convention Against Corruption (UNCAC) was adopted by the General Assembly in December, 2003 and came into force in 2005 (with 140 state signatories). As of February 2017, 183 states are parties to UNCAC.199 The term "State Parties" refers to states that have ratified or acceded to the Convention, thereby expressing their consent to be bound by the Convention; the term "signatories" refers to those states that signed the Convention before it entered into force in December 2005, thereby indicating their intent to ratify the Convention.

Webb notes that the negotiating process leading to UNCAC grew out of negotiation of the United Nations Convention Against Transnational Organized Crime (UNCTOC, 2000). As part of its strategy to curb organized crime, UNCTOC also requires that signatory states criminalize active and passive bribery relating to public officials. For a good description of the negotiations behind, and the content of, UNCTOC, see Dimitri Vlassis, "UNCTOC and its Protocols" in The Changing Face of International Criminal Law: Select Papers (International Centre for Criminal Law Reform and Criminal Justice Policy: Vancouver, 2002) at 75-103.

By December 2000, however, the United Nations General Assembly decided that a more comprehensive international agreement on anti-corruption was needed. Over seven sessions, in 2002 and 2003, the Ad Hoc Committee for the Negotiation of the Convention against Corruption negotiated the text of the Convention. The draft version of UNCAC was adopted by the General Assembly in October 2003 and was officially signed at Merida, Mexico in December 2003.

The UNCAC is broader in scope than the OECD Anti-Bribery Convention and many of the earlier, regional anti-bribery agreements. As Webb notes, the Convention addresses the following three main anti-corruption strategies:

- **Prevention:** The provisions of Chapter II of UNCAC contain preventative measures which target both the public and private sectors. These non-mandatory provisions propose the establishment of anti-corruption organizations and lay out measures for preventing corruption in the judiciary and public procurement. Member states are encouraged to involve nongovernmental organizations (NGOs) in uncovering and stopping corruption. (See UNCAC Articles 11, 9 and 6).
- **Criminalization:** Chapter III of UNCAC requires member states to criminalize a wide array of corruption activities, including bribery, embezzlement of public funds, trading in influence, concealing corruption and money laundering related to corruption. Though these measures are mandatory, the UNCAC adds qualifying clauses allowing member states some flexibility in adopting criminal legislation "in accordance with fundamental principles of domestic law" or "to the greatest extent possible within [the state's] domestic legal system" (See UNCAC Articles 23 and 31). Resistant government officials could potentially use these clauses to justify inaction.
- **International Cooperation:** Chapter IV mandates that member states cooperate in preventing, investigating and prosecuting corruption. Signatories of UNCAC agree to give mutual legal assistance through gathering and transferring evidence for court trials and extraditing accused offenders. Furthermore, member states must also support each other in tracing, freezing, seizing, and confiscating proceeds of corruption.200

The negotiation process was not without controversy. According to Webb, the topics that generated the most disagreement among negotiating parties were the provisions addressing asset recovery, private sector corruption, political corruption, and implementation of the Convention.

Asset Recovery: A key aspect of UNCAC is the fact that it addresses the recovery of state assets exported from state coffers by corrupt officials. In this regard Webb states:201

- Asset recovery therefore became a sort of 'litmus test' for the success of the negotiating process as a whole. Although there were intense debates on how to reconcile the needs of the countries seeking the return of the assets with the legal and procedural safeguards of the countries whose assistance is needed, the representatives always emphasized its importance throughout the negotiations. The high priority of the issue was bolstered by the Security Council resolution deciding that all UN member states should take steps to freeze funds removed from Iraq by the Saddam Hussein or his senior officials and immediately transfer them to the Development Fund for Iraq, and take steps to facilitate the safe return to Iraqi institutions of Iraqi cultural property that had been illegally removed. The African representative, in particular, believed that the words and spirit of this resolution should be incorporated into the UNCAC.

In the end, provisions on asset recovery formed an entire chapter of the UNCAC. The provisions have been hailed as 'ground-breaking'. But this overstates their true impact. [footnotes omitted]

Then Webb adds:

The effectiveness of the asset recovery provisions depend to a large extent on the measures for mutual legal assistance. ... Overall, even though the chapter on asset recovery is not as revolutionary as some people say, it is a significant step forward in dealing with a complex problem in international affairs. Most importantly, the Convention ties the asset recovery provisions to a wide range of corrupt acts, not just bribery.

Asset Recovery is dealt with in detail in Chapter 5.

Private Sector: Considering the economic strength of many multinational corporations, private sector corruption was also considered during the UNCAC negotiating process. The European Union was strongly in favour of including the criminalization of private sector bribery during the UNCAC negotiations. The United States was opposed as it viewed this initiative as an undesirable constraint on private sector business dealing. The final version of UNCAC only includes non-binding articles relating to the criminalization of private sector bribery and embezzlement. UNCAC does, however, require that state parties take steps to prevent private sector corruption. As well, the Convention requires state parties to ensure that individuals and other legal entities that suffered damages as a result of corruption have the right to bring civil cases against those who are responsible. Due in part to the American business community's fears of a plethora of lawsuits being brought against American companies by overseas litigants, each state has the ability to determine under what circumstances these types of claims will be permitted.

In regard to private-to-public sphere corruption, UNCAC is more comprehensive than the OECD Anti-Bribery Convention in several respects. UNCAC criminalizes the bribery of domestic officials as well as foreign officials. Also UNCAC mandates that state parties prohibit bribes from being tax deductible; in comparison, this step is only a recommendation in the OECD Anti-Bribery Convention.

Financing of Political Parties: At one point in the negotiating process Austria, France, and the Netherlands proposed an article (Article 10) that mandated signatory countries adopt regulations aimed at addressing corruption and increasing transparency in elections and campaign financing. The United States voiced strong opposition to the mandatory language of the article. This was a reversal from the American stance on the same issue during the OECD Anti-Bribery Convention negotiations 20 years earlier. Eventually a compromise was struck and the mandatory directions in Article 10 were replaced with Article 6, which only asks that states "consider" taking steps to enhance transparency in elections and campaign financing. As Webb writes, "[t]he Ad Hoc Committee ultimately had to recognize that campaign contributions are a crucial part of the election systems in many countries and it had to tread carefully in order to avoid the Convention coming into conflict with a core aspect of democratic politics."203 Despite strong public concern on this issue, the UNCAC negotiating committee failed to reach agreement on a binding article addressing corruption in campaign financing.

Implementation, Enforcement, and Monitoring: Despite stronger proposals by several delegations, the final version of UNCAC was criticized for not establishing stronger monitoring mechanisms to ensure that signatory states comply with the Convention. UNCAC established a "Conference of State Parties," meant to enable the exchange of information and cooperation among signatory states, but no formal review mechanism was agreed upon. In 2009, the Conference of State Parties agreed on a peer review process to evaluate state parties' self-assessments of compliance with the Convention. The review process comprised of two five-year cycles with a quarter of the member states reviewed each year: the first cycle (2010-2015) reviews compliance with Chapters III (Criminalization) and IV (International Cooperation) and the second cycle (2015-2020) will cover Chapters II (Preventative Measures) and V (Asset Recovery).

UNCAC has influenced global cooperation in fighting corruption. In "The United Nations Convention Against Corruption," Jousten highlights UNCAC's impact in three areas:

- As a global convention it has considerably expanded the geographical scope of cooperation,
- it provides common definitions of certain key offences, and requires (or, in some cases, at least encourages) States Parties to criminalize these acts, and

- it has standardized, and contributed to, the development of procedural forms of co-operation.

The UNODC developed materials for a university-level course on UNCAC. The course materials are available on the UNODC's webportal TRACK (Tools and Resources for Anti- Corruption Knowledge, under the section "Education": www.track.unodc.org). The "Education" section of TRACK also contains a Menu of Resources which identifies 20 anti- corruption topics and provides a list of relevant academic articles, books, reports etc., on each topic. In addition, this book is also available on UNODC's TRACK webportal: http://www.track.unodc.org/Education/Pages/ACAD.aspx.

For a discussion of the compliance challenges and impacts of UNCAC, see Ophelie Brunelle- Quaraishi, "Assessing the Relevancy and Efficacy of the United Nations Convention Against Corruption: A Comparative Analysis" (2011) 2:1 Notre Dame Intl & Comp LJ 101. See also Jan Wouters, Cedric Ryngaert and Ann Sofie Cloots, "The International Legal Framework Against Corruption: Achievements and Challenges" (June 2013) 14:1 Melb J Intl L 205.

The Meaning and Effect of International Conventions

In international law, a convention (or treaty) is a statement of principles, rules and procedures on a specific topic which is adopted by international bodies such as the United

Nations. The adoption of a convention by the UN does not automatically bind all UN members to comply with the convention. At the time a convention is adopted, a number of countries will sign (become signatories) to the convention. By becoming signatories, those countries indicate their general agreement with the principles and purposes of the convention. However, countries are only bound by a convention or treaty by ratifying it. Ratification signals that a country has laws and practices in place that are in compliance with the convention and that the country is ready to be bound by the treaty under international law.

In countries such as England, Canada and Australia, ratification is a power exercised by the Executive (i.e., the elected government and, more specifically, the cabinet). Parliamentary approval is not required, although all treaties and conventions are tabled in Parliament before ratification by Canada. In the US, ratification takes place through the combined actions of the Executive and a two-thirds vote of the Senate.

Once ratified, the particular state becomes a "party" or "state party" to the convention.

Some conventions have protocols. A protocol is an addition or a supplement to an existing convention. State parties are not automatically required to adopt protocols and for that reason protocols are often referred to as "optional protocols." In the case of the OECD Anti- Bribery Convention, there have been three subsequent instruments, called "Recommendations," which are also optional.

If states disagree on the interpretation of a convention or treaty provision, the dispute can be referred to an international tribunal or arbiter for resolution. Conventions and treaties frequently have specific provisions allowing countries to withdraw from (or denounce) the convention (e.g., Article 70 of UNCAC and Article 17 of the OECD Anti-Bribery Convention).

On the topic of enforcement of conventions and treaties, Canada's Approach to Treaty Making, a publication from Canada's Library of Parliament, states:

- Compliance with and the enforceability of international treaties is a broad topic that cannot be dealt with in any comprehensive manner in a few paragraphs. Ultimately, there are multiple forms of international treaties, multiple levels of enforceability, and multiple mechanisms for enforcement. Various bodies are available to assist with the enforcement of international treaties and conventions at the international and regional levels. For example, trade treaties may be subject to enforcement under the NAFTA or through the World Trade Organization, which have various levels of tribunals to ensure compliance with their standards. Other trade treaties are subject to enforcement by arbitral tribunals that can impose financial penalties on parties to the agreement. By contrast, human rights treaties are often subject to some form of oversight through the United Nations treaty bodies. The Concluding Observations issued with respect to country compliance under these UN treaty bodies are not legally binding, but they do carry significant moral suasion. Breaches of humanitarian law, such as war crimes and crimes against humanity, are dealt with by the International Criminal Court, which has the power to sentence individuals to imprisonment. The International Court of Justice is also charged with settling legal disputes submitted to it by states in accordance with international law generally, and with giving advisory opinions on legal questions referred to it by UN organs and specialized agencies. [Footnotes omitted]

On a practical level, enforcement of UNCAC and the OECD Convention is dependent on the implementation monitoring process which the State Parties have agreed to in each Convention.206 In accordance with Article 12 of the OECD Convention, a detailed monitoring program of each state party is done under a framework developed and conducted by its Working Group on Bribery (see 2009 Recommendation of the Council for Further Combatting Bribery of Foreign Public Officials, Recommendations XIV and XV). The Working Group's Evaluation and

Monitoring Reports for each country can be viewed on their website. Once the enforcement recommendations set out in the Country Evaluation Report are made public that country is under political and moral pressure to comply with the recommendations.

Article 63 of UNCAC leaves the issue of monitoring State Parties compliance to the Conference of State Parties who are directed to agree upon activities, procedures and methods of work to achieve the Convention's objectives, including (in Article 63(4)(e)) periodic review of the "implementation of the Convention by its State Parties." UNCAC adopted a review mechanism during the 3rd Conference of State Parties in Doha in 2009 (Resolution 3/1).

Under the review mechanism, each state party is reviewed by two peer states under the co-ordination of the UNODC Secretariat. The terms of reference, guidelines and blueprint for UNCAC reviews can be found in the 2011 UNODC publication Mechanisms for the Review of Implementation of the United Nations Convention against Corruption: Basic Documents. In short, peer reviews of all states are to begin over a four-year time frame beginning in 2010, with a country's year of review being determined by lottery. [Canada is in year 3, the UK in year 2, the US in year 1].

The two peer review countries are made up of one review country from the same region as the country being reviewed and another review country from a different region. The first step of the review is the completion and submission of a detailed self-assessment report by the country under review, followed by electronic communication; then (normally) a site visit and the writing of the review report (the executive summary is made public, but not the report itself). For more information on the progress of the UNCAC review mechanism, see the April 7, 2016 Progress Report of the Implementation of the Mandates of the Implementation Review Group." Each evaluation cycle of the Mechanism for the Review of Implementation of the United Nations Convention against Corruption lasts four years.

The Progress Report from the most recent session of the Implementation Review Group, which occurred in April of 2016, provides information on the first review cycle. At this seventh session, country pairings for the second cycle of reviews were drawn. Thirty countries are expected to be reviewed during the first year of the second cycle.

Development and Revision of National Laws Against Corruption

US and UK Anti-Corruption Laws

Following the multilateral agreements reached in the international forum, many countries have enacted or revised domestic laws to comply with their international convention obligations. As already noted, the United States' Foreign Corrupt

Practices Act (1977) was an influential example of a rigorous anti-corruption law long before the international instruments were established.

The United Kingdom's Bribery Act (2010) is the latest illustration of a strong and broad domestic anti-corruption law. Both the US and UK laws have broad extra-territorial provisions, and therefore foreign companies and persons conducting global businesses with a link to either country must comply with these two "domestic" laws. Both US and UK corruption laws will be examined throughout this book as illustrations of how other countries could comply with UNCAC and other anti-corruption conventions.

Compliance by state parties with international anti-corruption obligations remains inconsistent. The 2015 Transparency International (TI) report "Exporting Corruption? Country Enforcement of the OECD Anti-Bribery Convention Progress Report 2015" indicates that of the 39 state parties to the OECD Convention, only four (Germany, Switzerland, the UK, and the US) are actively enforcing the OECD Convention, while six countries (including Canada) have moderate enforcement, nine others have limited enforcement, and twenty have little or no enforcement.210 TI views the "Active Enforcement" ranking as a necessary step to effectively deterring companies and individuals from bribing foreign public officials.

Canada's Domestic Legislation

Canadian corruption and bribery laws will be examined in detail in subsequent chapters of this book. In short, the 1998 Corruption of Foreign Public Officials Act (CFPOA) was enacted in order to fulfill Canada's obligations under the OECD Anti-Bribery Convention. The CFPOA makes it a criminal offence in Canada for Canadian corporations or individuals to bribe or offer a bribe to a foreign official in order to win business or gain an improper advantage. In 2013, the federal government amended the CFPOA in several ways to increase its scope and effectiveness. Canada currently meets its anti-corruption international obligations under UNCAC by a combination of provisions in its Criminal Code and CFPOA.

Enforcement of the CFPOA was nearly non-existent prior to 2008-2009 since there were no police resources specifically allocated to CFPOA enforcement. Canada was criticized by many commentators and eventually by the OECD Working Group on Bribery for its non- enforcement of CFPOA provisions.

As a consequence of this criticism, the federal government funded the creation of two new RCMP foreign corruption units. Since that time there have been a few major convictions for foreign bribery, two other cases awaiting trial, and apparently 10 to 15 other cases under investigation. TI currently ranks Canada's enforcement of the OECD Convention as "Moderate," one level below the "Active Enforcement" level, which is considered the appropriate level.

DIVERGENT POLITICAL AND ECONOMIC VIEWS ON CORRUPTION

Libertarians, Cultural Ethnographers and Liberal Democrats

In her article "Corruption: Greed, Culture and the State," Rose-Ackerman argues that while lawyers view corruption mainly as a problem of law enforcement, some commentators in other disciplines contest the very concept of corruption.212 To analyze this perspective, Rose- Ackerman reviews how both free-market libertarians and cultural ethnographers have drawn on a distrust of the modern state to legitimize, excuse, and explain corruption. She further argues that these views are overly simplistic and are at times, internally inconsistent. Instead, she advocates for an approach to anti-corruption theory that acknowledges the importance of the modern state and seeks to build transparency and accountability in government institutions.

Libertarians and Corruption

Rose-Ackerman describes the libertarian view of corruption "as a symptom of an intrusive, meddling state that systematically reins in the free market and undermines entrepreneurial activity and competition... [Libertarians] argue that market actors who pay bribes to avoid complying with the rules, to lower tax bills, or to get favours, limit the harm that the state can do, and consequently enhance the benevolent operation of the free market as a locus of individual freedom."213 She suggests that libertarians prefer very little state regulation and view bribery as a technique that can be used to facilitate the efficient functioning of free markets. As an example, Rose-Ackerman submits that a libertarian would not be concerned about the illegality of using a bribe to get around a costly regulation, and instead would approve of this transaction. In support of this libertarian position, Rose-Ackerman cites Becker214 and the authors of "Economic Freedom and Corruption" who write, "The fewer resources (includes assets and regulatory power) a government controls, the fewer the opportunities for corruption."

Furthermore, Rose-Ackerman describes the extreme libertarian views of Brennan and Buchanan, who perceive state taxation and regulation as equivalent to theft. Brennan and Buchanan's view, Rose-Ackerman argues, would allow government officials to act in self- interest and extract private benefits, initiating the government's devolution into a kleptocratic monster. Rose-Ackerman critiques this libertarian view and maintains that democracies, while not always completely efficient or perfect, are the best available way to reflect the will of the people. Indeed, as long as the rules of the constitution are followed, and human rights are respected, Rose-Ackerman argues that using government inefficiency, or bad laws, as a way to justify bribery "trivializes and undermines democratic institutions."

Ethnography and Corruption

Rose-Ackerman also asserts that cultural anthropologists and ethnographers excuse the corrupt giving of gifts and favours, but do so by employing different justifications than libertarians. From the perspective of a cultural anthropologist, Rose-Ackerman argues traditions that emphasize payments, gifts or favours to friends and family are privileged over formal rules and laws. Indeed, she states "scholars in this tradition often refuse to label transactions as corrupt if they are based on affective ties, or they claim that, even if formally illegal, the practices are socially acceptable, economically beneficial, and compensate for the imperfections of government and of electoral institutions."

The author suggests that cultural anthropologists blame corruption on a mismatch between traditional practices and the development of impartial bureaucratic and democratic systems. Thus, if a society is transitioning from personal transactions to a formal set of rules and laws, cultural feelings of duty may clash with professional obligations and lead to corrupt acts. Additionally, Rose-Ackerman asserts that in some cultures, many ethnographers find the current, dominant conception of corruption is simply a part of everyday life in a citizen's social interactions with the state. In these instances, such as paying a fee to avoid taxes or bribing a judge for the "loss" of a key legal document, the social norms justify the behaviour, even though they mix economic motives and social practices. As examples of these anthropologic assertions, Rose-Ackerman relies on the work of de Sardan,219 Hasty220 and Smith221 who developed these themes in the African context. Specifically, Rose-Ackerman cites Smith's studies of Nigerian culture, where locals considered modern conceptions of corruption, which involved helping friends and family, proper moral behaviour. Furthermore, Rose-Ackerman submits that in Africa corruption is recognized and criticized by many people, even though "they themselves participate in networks that socially reproduce corruption."222 Rose-Ackerman also acknowledges a similar cultural norm of ambiguity regarding bribes to friends and family in China, termed guanzi, or as it translates "social connections."

Rose-Ackerman while sympathetic to the position of those who find their social obligations conflict with their professional ones, reasons that "while deeply embedded and self- reinforcing, ... norms must change ... if a society is ever to build a legitimate democracy."223 She further argues that the current condemnation of corruption by citizens leaves openings for potential reform.

In summary, Rose-Ackerman believes libertarians and ethnographers share very similar normative positions. She states, "both stress the way payoffs to public officials permit nonstate institutions to flourish in spite of a set of formal rules that constrain private behaviour. However, each gives a different set of institutions priority – the market for one and social ties for the other."224 In addition, Rose-Ackerman argues both groups perceive corruption as a response to a dysfunctional reality.

Grand Corruption

The main type of corruption Rose-Ackerman is concerned with is what she terms "grand corruption." In instances of grand corruption, those at the top of the state hierarchy, such as political leaders, participate in corrupt acts in return for funds. The problem with this, Rose- Ackerman argues, is that grand corruption will lead to distortions in the quality and quantity of government decisions, divert funds to public officials' private accounts and create unfair electoral advantages. Grand corruption is sometimes initiated by multinational firms, whom Rose-Ackerman contends, invoke cultural norms as their justification for giving bribes to public officials. For example, Rose-Ackerman cites the 2006 international arbitration dispute where a firm paid a two-million-dollar bribe to the President of Kenya and tried to argue that the payment was made to satisfy the local custom of harambee. The Kenya government, under new leadership argued there was no valid contract because of the bribe and the arbitration tribunal agreed with them.

Rose-Ackerman analyzes multiple justifications she believes others use to excuse grand corruption.226 First, multinational firms argue that presenting bribes is simply an attempt to be culturally sensitive. The author points out this excuse is invalid because the unfavourable terms of the contract, obtained because of the bribe, negatively affected the citizens of the nation. Thus, if the firm was being culturally sensitive they would consider the cultural needs of more than just the one public official whom they bribed. Second, Rose-Ackerman critiques the argument used by high ranking officials that a bribe is simply a tribute to their prestigious status, in line with cultural traditions--an argument which conflicts with established tradition where bribes go from higher-status to lower-status individuals.

If high ranking officials were really following traditions, Rose-Ackerman claims, they would be insulted by these bribes and reject them. Third, Rose-Ackerman states culturalists argue that grand corruption is imported from wealthy, capitalist countries where businesses have profit-maximization as their goal. In other words, the bribes and corruption only occur because of this western influence. In her assessment this argument is too simple because both parties, including the political leaders, must agree to make a corrupt deal and some are willing to use the excuse of culture to justify self-gain. Thus, Rose-Ackerman assets "one needs to be cautious in accepting at face value assertions that seemingly corrupt transactions reflect entrenched cultural practices acceptable to most people."

Democratic Legitimacy and the Control of Corruption

The author asserts that a democratic state may exercise coercive power in making decisions, which may have a greater cost on some individuals over others, as long as the state publicly justifies its exercise of power. Furthermore, Rose-Ackerman recognizes that a democracy does not mean unanimous consent or a lack of policymaking delegation. Broadly speaking, Rose-Ackerman believes a properly functioning democracy is a legitimate way to organize society. However, Rose-Ackerman argues if elected officials or bureaucrats engage in self- interested behaviour, such as corruption, this undermines the state's claim to legitimacy. She acknowledges that in situations where public power is bound up with paternalistic obligations, it may be difficult to separate corrupt dealings with local practices. Nevertheless, Rose-Ackerman argues if corruption is allowed to take place in government, state agents will likely rewrite rules to increase their self-gain and will create a feedback loop that weakens the legitimacy of the government. Furthermore, Rose-Ackerman argues that "tensions between the democratic welfare state and the private market and between that state and a country's traditional cultural practices are all but inevitable."

Therefore, Rose-Ackerman suggests that anti-corruption policy can take three paths: first, to accept the presence of cultural norms and channel them into less destructive paths; second, to bypass cultural norms by substituting institutions that require other skills and values; or third, to transform these cultural norms. She also cautions that aggressive approaches to anti-corruption may destroy the goodwill and loyalty of citizens. Rose-Ackerman acknowledges there is no easy solution to the critiques of anti-corruption efforts, but provides eight potential areas of reform.

- Simple Transparency is Necessary
    - There must be the publication of and easy access to all laws, statutes, regulations, legal guidelines and practice manuals. Moreover, there should be an independent external audit body, which oversees government spending.
- External Oversight of Government Activity is Essential
    - Removing press restrictions and sponsoring training in investigative journalism is one solution to provide external monitoring of government action. This area of reform is tied to the first suggestion, as civilians must have access to information before they can review it and issue complaints.
- Transparent and Competitive Processes for Large-Scale Procurement Should Exist

  - This measure is specifically aimed at countering grand corruption, but she recognizes there will be an occasional need for sole-source procurement. In these instances, she advises the government be transparent with their negotiations and attempt to obtain a high quality result at a good price.
- The State Should Enforce Bribery Laws Against Major Offenders both Inside and Outside of Government
  - This may entail, making special efforts to apprehend organized crime involved in corruption.
- Creation of a Complaint Mechanism Process to Report Bribes
  - There should be a way for individuals and businesses to report bribes and have their claims dealt with in a timely manner.
- Reforms Should Be Made to Improve Government Function and Reduce Corruption
  - Rules and regulations should be studied to identify where reforms or repeals may be necessary to reduce corruption.
- The Working Conditions of Civil Servants and the Judiciary Should be Improved
  - Improving the pay, working conditions and recruitment process of civil servants, coupled with increased internal monitoring, should help reduce the likelihood of corruption.
- Electoral Law May Need Reform
  - In areas where politicians are found to be corrupt, electoral law and its enforcement may need to be reformed.

In conclusion, Rose-Ackerman acknowledges that while international treaties and civil society initiatives aimed at curbing global corruption are a step in the right direction, their effects do not have the same "bite as hard law" and are only a complement to much needed domestic reform. In addition, she urges moving away from simplistic claims such as corruption is necessary because of a dysfunctional government, and instead, argues for realistic domestic reforms, such as increasing the effectiveness of public services and ensuring conflicts are resolved fairly, in order to reduce corruption.

The Three Authority Systems: Traditional, Patrimonial and Rational-Legal

In his article "Corruption in the Broad Sweep of History," Marcus Felson uses Max Weber's three categories of historical authority systems to conceptualize corruption and place it within its political and economic context.

BEGINNING OF EXCERPT

Corruption is a product of the interplay between (a) primary human imperatives and (b) an economic and social system trying to control and channel those imperatives. Primary human imperatives include both looking after one's personal interests and meeting social commitments to friends and relatives. A strong tension is inherent between these primary human imperatives and the larger economic and social system. That tension is strongest with the modern form of economic organization. Hence corruption, despite its ancient presence, becomes especially relevant in a modern world. Although corruption becomes especially an issue as developing nations move towards a modern world, we should not assume that the tension will go away once they are developed.

Those aware of Max Weber (1947 [1904]) will immediately recognize the origins of the current argument in his description and analysis of the broad sweep of economic and social history. Weber was perhaps the greatest historical theorist of economic and social life. On the one hand, he gathered vast detail as he studied and described each society. On the other hand, Weber summarized those details within a very general analytical framework. Each society has a prevalent authority system that governs its behavior, and that authority system is central for understanding it. Weber synthesized information about the broad sweep of economic and social history with three authority systems: (a) traditional, (b) patrimonial, and (c) rational-legal. This chapter explains his general categories, then shows why they help us to understand and conceptualize corruption.

Within a traditional system, individuals are constrained by the rules and mores of society, but those constraints do not stand between primary human imperatives and productivity. Thus a traditional hunting and gathering society follows the teachings of the past and the social ties of kinship, whether or not these lead to greater efficiency. Traditional systems often apply in agrarian societies with small village life, and are not oriented towards a modern society. However, traditional systems may persist into the modern era. A prime example of a traditional system is the interplay of the Hindu religion and the economy in India. Each economic role is largely defined by caste and hence by tradition, within minimal economic flexibility and little regard to efficiency. Within a traditional system, many economic behaviours that we might regard as corrupt from an outside viewpoint are actually part of the rules. Thus assigning jobs by caste and village is intrinsic to the way of life, and should not be viewed as corrupt behavior as a matter of personal deviance, except when those collective obligations are circumvented.

The patrimonial system is very distinct from the traditional system because of its reliance on personal rule. In this system the ruler does not distinguish between personal and public life, treating state resources and decisions as his personal affair. The agents of the ruler act in his name and on his behalf. It is still possible for those agents to be corrupt only in the sense that they cheat the ruler of his due. If the ruler's agents mistreat the citizens, they are acting within the rules of the system—so long as they send the proceeds back to the ruler and do not take more than their allotted share. This is quite evident in the history of tax farmers whose job was to demand tribute and payments from the provinces. They would be perceived as corrupt to us today, but they were not corrupt in terms of their system, unless they hid the proceeds from the ruler in their own selfish interest. Examples of patrimony range from Roman emperors to President Ferdinand Marcos in the Philippines and Colonel Khadaffi in Libya—reflecting extension of authority beyond a local area. This leads us to as whether such power has been established by force or by normative authority or some combination. But regardless of the answer to that question, extracting resources from the population is intrinsic to the system, not a violation of it.

The rational-legal system of economic and social organization has an entirely different set of expectations from the traditional and patrimonial systems. The rational-legal system is closely related to Weber's textbook concept of 'formal organization' and bureaucracy—a word he uses in positive terms. Under this system, all persons follow rules and fit into formal roles that are separate from the personal, family, and friendship interests of their incumbents. The rulers and role incumbents are substitutable, so that a formal organization persists over time, pursuing goals beyond the individual. This impersonality includes hiring based on competence and certification, and promotion based on ability and productivity. The role incumbents must follow rules, and must be oriented towards goal achievement beyond themselves. They are also supposed to treat each client equally, according to the rules, ignoring personal ties and predilections. Thus modern life conflicts fundamentally with primary human imperatives. Bureaucracy in Weber's terms is like a machine, since it separates personal interests (including family and friend commitments) from interests, facilitating the latter. Yet this form of economic and social organization only emerged in the past 200 years or less in Europe, and in most of the world did not begin to spread until after 1950. In many parts of the world, the rational-legal form is only beginning to emerge. The distinction between persons and positions is difficult to accept fully in any era, which helps explain why it was so late to arrive.

Of course, Weber's concept of rational formal organization is an ideal type. It describes the official position of many modern societies; but that does not mean that everybody follows those rules all of the time. Indeed, a rational-legal system creates a fundamental tension in society, because it is only natural for each person to take care of oneself and one's family and friends, even in in violation of general rules and roles. Thus the rational-legal system is almost directly in conflict with primary human imperatives—which do not go away simply because society no longer welcomes them as much as before. Indeed, corruption has much greater potential in the rational legal system than in the traditional or patrimonial systems of economic and social organization. The levels of corruption possible in a rational-legal system far exceed anything possible in the traditional system, which provides more local controls and hardly expects people to abandon their personal ties while engaging in productive work. The corruption in a modern system also exceeds the corruption of the patrimonial system, within which one must cheat the ruler in order to be corrupt, but the ruler and his agents extracting from everybody else is part and parcel of that economic and social system.

The corruption potential of a rational-legal system is dramatically greater mainly because that system conflicts with basic human tendencies. If human beings are both selfish and social, then the modern form conflicts with each. It conflicts with the selfish tendencies because each individual has something to gain from evading less pleasant role assignments or taking resources beyond entitlement. It conflicts with social tendencies because each individual feels commitment to friends, family and those with less social distance and wants to help them more than strangers. Hence treating everybody alike under the rules is unnatural for real people.

Given its conflict with human selfishness and human sociability, the rational-legal system should have died an early death. Yet it survives and spreads for a simple reason: this strange and hardly human form of social and economic organization is extremely productive in material terms. It makes more cars. It processes more customers and clients. It shortens lines and puts a chicken in every pot. And so the least human of social and economic systems is also the most productive. Thus our selfish and social interests are torn between the immediate gains from violating the rules and the more general gains from following them. The best individual solution is to break the rules yourself but get everybody else to follow them, yielding a productive society as a whole that you can then exploit. However, if too many people do that then the productivity of the whole system declines and the rational-legal system becomes a figment of the imagination.

Imaginary rational-legal systems are all too common. In a way the real lesson of the 2000 Presidential election and the case of Gore vs Bush in Florida is the corruption and mismanagement of state and local governments in the United States. In Weber's terms, each occupational role is assigned to a specialist, with overlapping roles minimized. Those familiar with corruption issues will immediately recognize this as a flaw, for the lack of overlap makes it easier for one person to corrupt the system and avoid discovery. In contrast, overlapping makes it possible for someone else to check, or more generally for the people to check one another.

Weber relied too much on the power of the normative system to keep each incumbent performing properly. Here we turn to another great theorist, James Madison (1787), whose famous Federalist Paper Number 10 explained the need for a system of checks and balances. Although Madison was considering legislative matters, his general principle was that individuals are corruptible (in the broad sense), but that their selfish and personal interests can be used to counter one another.

The theory of checks and balances may be the essential general theory of corruption control. In both government and business, checks and balances are employed to protect responsible decisions and actions. Rival political parties, parliamentary question periods, a free press, regulatory agencies, free competition in the marketplace, overlapping roles, auditors and accountants—each of these is a special example of the general rule that checks and balances are needed to prevent personal and social interests from impairing efficiency and productivity. Thus Madison sought to reconcile primary human imperatives with the requirement that everyone has a fair shake.

Modern corruption has to do with positions, and modern organization creates lots of positions demanding that people suppress their selfish interests. In the era of traditional and patrimonial authority, corruption was limited and modern corruption did not exist (although a more primitive and limited form of corruption did apply, even then). When organization is poorly designed and managed, we can expect corruption as a result; but we can also expect various organizational goals to be poorly achieved. In fighting corruption, we must always remember what we are asking of people: to set aside personal interest and personal ties and to follow rules for the greater impersonal good. But we must also understand that we can never completely win the war against corruption, nor can we give it up. We can never win it because primary human imperatives always outweigh impersonal goals. We can never give up the struggle because our modern prosperity depends on containing these personal and social goals while on the job. But if we don't contain it, it grows and takes over. Like housekeeping, no vacuum sweeper works permanently but the failure to vacuum lets a home get dirtier and dirtier.

Yet corruption cannot be controlled by assuming that people can be trained in ethics alone, since it is impossible to talk people out of being people. But it is possible to train people to supervise one another and hence to provide a system of checks and balances. Such a system works best when criminalization and punishment work only at the extreme, when the system operates on a normal basis without getting to that point. Control depends on designing more secure systems, efficient supervision, and effective checks and balances. As technology takes new forms, it brings new opportunities for corruption and hence demands new checking and balancing. With the march of technology, more and more value is intangible—contained in electronic data that are not easily watched with the naked eye. But systems can be designed to keep track of electronic data, too, thus interfering with the opportunities for corruption. As society becomes more complex in technology, corrupt practices can more easily escape notice, at least for a while. But in time we learn to use technology to reduce the complexity of supervision and thence to create methods for managing, checking, and balancing so that formal organization keeps personal and social needs under a reasonable degree of containment. An organization must find simplicity and accountability to avoid corruption. That means overcoming organizational and technical complexity with new forms of simple checks and balances. When that is achieved, modern society can achieve simple monitoring while requiring complex conspiring, and corruption will diminish. Developing nations face the same principles but at an earlier stage, with formal organization replacing family and patrimonial systems in places not yet ready for that to happen. But, of course, no place is fully ready to give up its personal and social tendencies, and so the work of reducing corruption is never complete.

END OF EXCERPT

Felson's contention that the rational-legal system holds the greatest potential for corruption is reflected in empirical data. In their article "Democracy and Corruption: a Complex Relationship," Shrabani Saha et al. use sophisticated econometric models to show the rise in corruption in countries that have transitioned from autocratic regimes to electoral democracies (the ultimate rational-legal system). The authors conclude that electoral democracy and political rights alone are insufficient to reduce corruption; in fact, electoral democracy alone aggravates widespread corruption because there are less checks and balances against corruption in an electoral democracy than in an autocratic regime. Effective democratic institutions, such as an independent judiciary, free press, strong rule of law in the economic system and distribution of social benefits and respect for civil rights, are crucial to reducing corruption. These institutions deter corruption by increasing the probability that corrupt acts will be detected and punished.

For a counterpoint to "economistic" understandings of corruption, see Barry Hindess, "Good government and corruption" in Peter Larmour and Nick Wolanin, eds, Corruption and Anti-Corruption (Canberra: Asia Pacific Press, 2001). Hindess argues that a narrow focus on economic corruption obscures other, more general forms of corruption in government. By ignoring these other forms of corruption, we fail to see the damaging effects of party politics, police corruption and other insidious problems of political life in western democracies.

For an analysis of how unethical, yet technically, legal quid pro quos are institutionalized in professional environments, and how this institutionalized corruption affects the independence of politics and professions, see Garry C Gray, "Insider Accounts of Institutional Corruption: Examining the Social Organization of Unethical Behaviour" (2013) 53 Brit J Criminol 533.

A SOCIOLOGICAL PERSPECTIVE ON INSTITUTIONAL CORRUPTION

As conventional wisdom would have it, corruption and illegality go hand in hand. Tacitus' famed words, Corruptissima re publica plurimae leges, often translated as 'the more corrupt the state, the more numerous the laws,' evokes multiple meanings, but one rendering elucidates on the expansiveness of corruption beyond the law.233 Bribery and other direct quid pro quo conflict of interest exchanges involving public officials and fiduciaries are well recognized as indictable offences in many countries, but corruption also operates on an invisible level, embedded within the social norms and institutional practices of professional environments. This form of corruption can be referred to as institutional corruption. Conceptually it requires that we go beyond the focus on illegal behaviour to also include unethical and professional activities that violate public trust. Institutional corruption therefore requires a shift in focus towards examining "influences that implicitly or purposively serve to distort the independence of a professional in a position of public trust."

In summarizing an account from a confidential interview that I conducted with a consultant for a multilateral development institution who was also a tenured professor, we can observe distinctions between traditional corruption and institutional corruption.235 Over more than a decade, Anthony had taken on consulting assignments that required him to evaluate projects being considered for grant funding from a multi-lateral donor.236 On more than one occasion while abroad on assignment, he had been offered bribes in return for writing favorable reports. He said these bribes could involve very large sums of money. In one case the bribe was perhaps five percent of the grant total, amounting to more than double the annual salary that he was earning as a tenured professor. Anthony acknowledged that these overtly illegal and at times threatening experiences fit the traditional conceptualization of corruption.

Following this discussion I asked Anthony if he had experienced other kinds of conflicts, namely situations that caused him to wrestle with what to do in his work for the multilateral donor. Anthony recounted a situation where his research findings and recommendations in a commissioned report did not fit with the ideological perspective held by his manager at the multilateral development institution. After some careful consideration he felt he could not compromise, because of the impact the alternative could potentially have for the country in question. Anthony recalled having a lengthy conversation over the phone with that manager and being asked to change the report. He refused, and acknowledged in that phone call that his contract was coming up for renewal and that he knew this disagreement could affect it. He saw this possible consequence as an expected, even logical outcome given the norms of consulting. There was nothing illegal about the situation, but the 'corrupting' effect of the earlier bribery examples and the threat of reduced hours is the same: both were influences intended to alter the outcomes of Anthony's reports.

Looking back on that exchange, Anthony is convinced that he would have been offered more consulting hours in the subsequent year had he submitted a report that fit with his manager's desired outcome. He also questioned what he would have done had he not held a tenured professorship, and if consulting had been his primary mode of employment. He was convinced that his professorship had structurally enabled him to stand behind his report. In this case, he was able to resist institutional corruption, but acknowledges that he still felt pressured to 'go along, to get along'.

The concept of public trust is an important element of institutional corruption theory. If Anthony was not a university professor, but instead was a full-time consultant who depended on the availability of future consulting opportunities, should we be less trusting of Anthony's ability to remain independent? Would the possibility of missing out on future consulting opportunities lead to subtle forms of dependency within Anthony's social and professional networks? If so, then what other subtle improper influences may exist in professional environments that could compromise the independence of professionals in positions of public trust?

From Bribery to Political Corruption

While the United States, since the enactment of the FCPA in 1977, has been a driving force behind global attempts to regulate quid-pro-quo corruption and in particular, bribery, (c.f., the OECD Anti-Bribery Convention in 1999 and the UNCAC in 2005), it has been reluctant to impose similar regulations on political corruption. During the UNCAC negotiations, the United States resisted proposals from Austria, France, and the Netherlands to impose mandatory regulations that would address issues of corruption in campaign finance. While campaign finance reform, and the issue of money in politics, is a contentious policy issue in the United States237 it also provides a good example of the value of an institutional corruption approach.238

Political Corruption: The Case of Jack Abramoff

Prior to being convicted of fraud and being sent to prison, Jack Abramoff was one of the most influential lobbyists in the United States.239 Upon release from prison,

Abramoff now spends his time exposing the role that institutional corruption plays in political decision- making and campaign financing. During one public interview, Abramoff told the interviewer the following: "We know a bribe is when you show up with a stack of cash and say, 'Here's $10,000 in cash, and can you do this for me?' But if I show up with 10 $1,000 campaign contributions and say the same thing, that's not a bribe in Washington. Outside of Washington, everybody gets this... but inside Washington, that's the way it's done... We have institutionalized corruption in Washington. It's perfectly accepted, and it's acceptable to virtually everybody, and that's where things need to change."

The role of money in politics, in particular through campaign finances, is attracting increased international attention. For instance, in response to major corruption scandals in Brazil, the Supreme Court of Brazil declared on September 17, 2015, that corporate donations to election campaigns are unconstitutional.241 And, in the United States, several US politicians seeking the party nomination for leader of the Democratic Party, including Hillary Clinton, Bernie Sanders, and Lawrence Lessig, campaigned for the November 2016 election with campaign finance reform as a major component of their election platform. There is a growing narrative developing in the United Sates that politicians are becoming less dependent upon the people they represent and more dependent on those who support their campaign finance initiatives.

However, rather than leading to direct quid-pro-quo corruption, the growing dependency on funders of campaigns in the United States is contributing to more subtle forms of institutionalized corruption through relational forms of dependency corruption. By creating situations where politicians become dependent on funders, it is suggested that integrity and independence are compromised. In turn, this leads to situations where self-censoring behaviour (such as deciding which policies or amendments to pursue, or alternatively, vote against) can begin to feel normal and perhaps even justified among politicians in positions of public trust. As Lawrence Lessig notes, "knowing that there are members of Congress dependent on campaign cash, private interests exploit that dependency, by seeking special benefits from the governments ('rents') and returning the favor ever so indirectly with campaign contributions. And knowing that they are so dependent upon private support, members of Congress will work to keep their fingers in as much of private life as possible... [And] because this is 'just the way things are done', no one needs to feel guilty, or evil in this system."

Given that the corruption described here is institutional in nature and often rationalized as a normal part of politics, a sociological account of institutional corruption is timely. For instance, an analysis of the insider accounts of institutional corruption provided by Jack Abramoff after he was released from prison reveals the mechanics of how the independence of American politicians can be exploited by lobbyists. In particular, through various techniques such as campaign finance contributions, legal loopholes, and the manipulation of social networks that result in improper influences that while often legal, may lead to corrupting outcomes.

Take for instance, the revolving door metaphor, where professionals holding jobs in congressional offices move into lobbying jobs and vice versa. Abramoff shows how this can contribute to institutionalized forms of corruption given the subtle and often hidden financial incentives that exist for public representatives.243 According to Abramoff, industry lobbyists are well aware of the importance of social relationships and social networks in a revolving door system. While there are cooling-off regulations in some countries that attempt to limit government employees from immediately going through the revolving door to a lobbying job, there still remains various corrupt ways that these regulations can be skirted. According to Abramoff, lobbyists are still able to informally capture individual members of the United States Congress, as well as their staff, even without offering a formal contract of employment. Improper influences can be quite insidious Abramoff states:

As I started hiring staff, particularly chiefs of staff [to members of Congress], I would say 'hey look when do you want to leave the hill?' 'Well, I don't want to leave for two years.' 'Ok, in two years I'll hire you.' I hired them right then. The minute they knew they were coming to work for me their whole job changed. They are human beings. If you have a job and you know you are going somewhere else you are at least going to be thinking about the next job. You don't want that business to go away... When I tell people this... they don't understand that their staff becomes my staffer. For two years that staffer is not only my staffer... but is better than my staffer. Because my staffer can't find the things that person is going to find and look out for our interests more than we could... one of the real pernicious and corrupt parts of the system, and again completely legal, and unknown entirely.

According to Abramoff, he cultivated these kinds of improper influences in close to 100 of the 435 United States congressional offices. He also noted that staffers were "perfect targets for revolving-door techniques." The impact of the revolving door is that it contributes to dependencies between lobbyists and government officials (dependence corruption) whereby "public officials might be more likely to insert legal content known as riders that are favourable to lobbying clients into bills that are to be voted on by members of Congress."As Abramoff notes:

- A lobbyist trying to enact his client's wishes needs to get his amendment onto a bill likely to pass both the House and the Senate, to then be signed by the president. No bill is more likely to pass than a reform bill... so smart lobbyists always keep an eye out for reform bills. It's ironic, if not horrific,

> that this is the case. The very bills designed to limit corruption and improve our system of government sometimes serve as vehicles for special interests.

According to Abramoff, the technique of inserting corrupt riders into a reform bill is a common practice, one that is intertwined with problems of political corruption embedded in the revolving door between government and industry. While reform efforts attempt to prevent political corruption, in particular, gifts that represent an illegal and overt attempt to buy influence, they do not always capture or prevent the more subtle forms of institutional corruption. Abramoff's insider accounts reveal that political contributions to campaigns "are a significant form of indirect gifting that can accomplish the same things [as quid-pro-quo corruption] but without the legal ramifications."248 As Abramoff commented in an interview:

- You can't take a congressman to lunch for $25 and buy him a hamburger or a steak or something like that. But you can take him to a fundraising lunch and not only buy him that steak but give him $25,000 extra and call it a fundraiser. And you have all the same access and all the same interaction with that congressman.

The above insider accounts of structured and systematic corruption provided by Jack Abramoff illustrate the value of an institutional corruption approach to traditional studies of political corruption.

Conclusion

Corruption, especially corruption that is specialized and intricately woven beyond the public eye, is often legal despite its potential for harm. Far too often, the general public has no choice but to trust that professionals will both recognize and resist corrupting influences when they arise in their professional environments. However, rather than simply trust that each individual professional will "do the right thing" and maintain integrity in the face of improper and potentially corrupting influences, institutional corruption theory offers an alternative. Examine institutional practices, structures, and relationships that bear on the trustworthiness and independence of public officials and professionals, and corrupting systems can be exposed, understood, and eventually mitigated.

CORPORATE SOCIAL RESPONSIBILITY AND CORRUPTION

In his article "Enhancing the Effectiveness of the Foreign Corrupt Practices Act Through Corporate Social Responsibility," Dan Heiss states "over the last decade, combating corruption has taken a place alongside human rights, labour rights, and environmental protection as one of the major issues in corporate social responsibility (CSR)."He further argues, "...to be truly effective in reducing the level of bribery in international business, the FCPA must work to encourage corporations to be socially responsible. Thus, to reduce corruption, corporations should be encouraged to think about not just what they should not do, but also what they can do. That is, corporations need to consider what they can do to work with other businesses, home and host country governments, local communities, and civil society organizations to reduce the levels of corruption in any particular country. To assist in this process, ... the enforcement of the FCPA should be structured to support the various actors and major initiatives in the CSR field that combat corruption."

What is Corporate Social Responsibility?

Corporate social responsibility (CSR) is a broad and evolving concept.252 Its content is shaped by shifting societal expectations which are dependent in part on the industrial context in which it operates and the people who are impacted by its behaviour. The John F. Kennedy School of Government at Harvard University explains that CSR is a concept that arises from the growing expectation that businesses should embrace social accountability.253 In the same vein, the Conference Board of Canada suggests that the foundation of CSR is the notion that corporations have responsibilities to stakeholders other than their shareholders.

Industry Canada, a government department, defines CSR as "the way a company achieves a balance or integration of economic, environmental and social imperatives while at the same time addressing shareholder and stakeholder expectations."The UK Government describes CSR as "the voluntary actions that businesses can take over and above legal requirements to manage and enhance economic, environmental and societal impacts." Though definitions of CSR vary, international sources reflect consensus on the following characteristics:

- CSR involves obligations apart from the formal requirements of law, and is instead a reflection of normative standards;
- CSR involves companies demonstrating varying degrees of commitment to concepts such as corporate citizenship, sustainable development, and environmental sustainability; and,
- governments, citizens, and investors now generally expect companies to adopt some form of internal CSR business strategy.

While CSR is dynamic and still developing, it is clear that the global corporate community has adopted CSR as an important item on the business agenda.

How Did CSR Develop?

Carroll, in his article "Corporate Social Responsibility: Evolution of a Definitional Construct," suggests that our contemporary notion of CSR is the product of an American school of thought dating to the mid-twentieth century, perhaps originating with Howard R. Bowen's seminal book Social Responsibilities of the Businessman (1953).259 Bowen asked the fundamental question, "What responsibilities to society may businessmen [and business women] reasonably be expected to assume?"260 He suggested that businesspersons have a responsibility to act in accordance with society's values and best interests. Carroll notes that the Committee for Economic Development (CED), which published Social Responsibilities of Business Corporations in 1971, asserted that society expected businesses to assume greater moral responsibility and "contribute to the quality of American life."261 In 1979, Carroll outlined three dimensions of CSR: corporate responsibilities, social issues of business, and corporate actions.262 Otherwise put, corporate responsibilities lead corporations to respond to certain social issues, as determined by societal and corporate values and priorities.263 While Carroll's concept of CSR has evolved in subsequent decades, it remains foundational for contemporary CSR theory.264 Today, CSR is one of many related concepts that influence the role of businesses in society. These include corporate social performance (CSP), corporate citizenship, inclusive business, social entrepreneurship, and sustainable development. In a recent UNESCAP Report, the authors stated the following in regard to the development of the concept of corporate social responsibility:

- [T]he focus on developing new or refined concepts of CSR gradually gave way to alternative approaches such as corporate citizenship (Pinkston and Carroll, 1994), business ethics (Shapiro, 1995) and stakeholder theory (Freeman, 1984), although the core concerns of CSR were reflected in those new approaches. The CSR concept served as the basis, building block or point-of-departure for other related initiatives, many of which adopted CSR principles (Carroll, 2008).

Since entering into the twenty-first century, more focus has been given to implementation of CSR initiatives and empirical study of CSR impacts. However, some development of the CSR concept has been continuously observed. Schwartz and Carroll (2003) reduced Carroll's four categories of corporate responsibilities (i.e. economic, legal, ethical and philanthropic) to a three-domain approach, namely economic, legal and ethical. The International Labour Organization (ILO) (2007) redefined CSR as a way that enterprises consider the impact of their operations on society and CSR principles are integrated in enterprises' internal processes and interactions with stakeholders on a voluntary basis. More recently, the European Commission (2011) simplified the CSR definition as the responsibility of enterprises for their impacts on society, which indicates that enterprises should have a process in place to integrate CSR agenda into their operations and core strategies in close corporation with stakeholders. The World Business Council for Sustainable Development (WBCSD) (2012) also emphasized a balance of return on financial, natural and social capitals, particularly suggesting the integration of CSR reporting into annual report.

For further reading on the evolution of CSR, see Archie B. Carrol, "Corporate Social Responsibility: Evolution of a Definitional Construct" (1999) 38 Bus & Soc'y 268. See also From Corporate Social Responsibility to Corporate Sustainability: Moving the Agenda Forward in Asia and the Pacific, Studies in Trade and Investment No 77 (UNESCAP: 2013).

There are also critics and skeptics of the notion of corporate social responsibility: for example, in Dustin Gumpinger's article "Corporate Social Responsibility, Social Justice, and the Politics of Difference: Towards a Participatory Model of the Corporation," the author states:

- The problem is that the notion of corporate social responsibility, under the current corporate law framework, is an oxymoron. The corporation's legal mandate is to pursue its own best interests and thus to maximize the wealth of its shareholders. Hence, corporate social responsibility is illegal and impossible to the extent that it undermines a company's bottom line. Acting out of social concern can only be justified insofar as it tends to bolster the corporation's interests. It is not surprising then that critics have characterized corporate social responsibility as an "ideological movement" designed to legitimize the power of transnational corporations.

In order to foster a world in which corporate decision-makers act genuinely in the interest of individuals and groups other than shareholders, the institutional nature of the corporate form must be reconceptualised. But if corporate social responsibility is an ineffective tool for evaluating corporate decisions, actions and outcomes, where should we turn? I shall argue that, as a dominant social institution, the corporation ought to be held to the same theoretical standards as other social institutions: namely, to the standard of social justice. [Footnotes omitted] Gumpinger concludes with the following thoughts:

Historically, corporations were public purpose institutions; today, they remain legal institutions in that they rely on legislation to create and enable them. Under this legal framework, corporations have come to govern virtually every aspect of our daily lives, despite the fact that they lack the democratic accountability of governments. This fusion of power and unaccountability has given rise to claims that the corporate form is inherently unjust and should be changed.

The corporation's propensity to cause and reinforce dominations and oppression highlight the need to build democratic decision-making structures into the corporate form. To achieve this goal, corporate law theory needs to abandon its desire for political unity, which tends to exclude the perspectives of the oppressed and the disadvantaged. Rather, a theory of the firm ought to be based on a heterogeneous notion of the public which gives voice to those who are systematically excluded from corporate decision-making. Hence, corporate law ought to provide the means through which the distinct voices and perspectives of those who are oppressed and disadvantaged by the corporation may be recognized and represented. If the corporation proves unable to serve this goal in addition to its primary goal of accumulating and generating wealth then it may be time to conceptualize an institution that can.

Some Current CSR Policies and Initiatives

In order to develop an understanding of current expectations for CSR policies, it is helpful to consult commonly referenced international instruments. Though CSR is reflected in a vast array of global policies and initiatives, the following standards are referred to across the globe to aid businesses forming internal CSR strategies:

- International Organization for Standardization ("ISO") 26000: Provides guidance on how businesses and organizations can operate in a socially responsible way and helps to clarify the concept of social responsibility. See www.iso.org/iso/home/standards/iso26000. Other ISO standards, such as ISO 9000 on corporate quality management and ISO 14001 on environmental management are also relevant in the CSR context.
- Global Reporting Initiative G4 Guidelines ("GRI G4"): Promotes corporate transparency by providing guidance on how to disclose information and what types of information should be disclosed. Anti-corruption is addressed as an aspect of the "society" reporting category. See https://www.globalreporting.org/resourcelibrary/GRIG4-Part1-Reporting- Principles-and-Standard-Disclosures.pdf.
- Transparency International's Business Principles for Countering Bribery (TI Principles): Provides a framework for companies to develop comprehensive anti- bribery programs. See http://www.transparency.org/whatwedo/pub/business_principles_for_countering_bri bery.
- The World Economic Forum Partnering Against Corruption Principles for Countering Bribery (PACI Principles) is derived from the TI Principles. See http://www3.weforum.org/docs/WEF_PACI_Principles_2009.pdf.
    - The TI and PACI Principles are discussed and critiqued in Adeyeye's book Corporate Social Responsibility of Multinational Corporations in Developing Countries: Perspectives on Anti-Corruption.
- The UN Global Compact: Is the largest global corporate citizenship initiative. It proposes ten principles of responsible and sustainable corporate conduct. See https://www.unglobalcompact.org/what-is-gc/mission/principles.

By way of illustration, the UN Global Compact asks companies to embrace, support and enact, within their sphere of influence, a set of core values in the areas of human rights, labour standards, the environment, and anti-corruption. These core values are expressed in the form of ten principles set out below:

Human Rights

- Principle 1: Businesses should support and respect the protection of internationally proclaimed human rights; and
- Principle 2: make sure that they are not complicit in human rights abuses.

Labour

- Principle 3: Businesses should uphold the freedom of association and the effective recognition of the right to collective bargaining;
- Principle 4: the elimination of all forms of forced and compulsory labour;
- Principle 5: the effective abolition of child labour; and
- Principle 6: the elimination of discrimination in respect of employment and occupation.

Environment

- Principle 7: Businesses should support a precautionary approach to environmental challenges;
- Principle 8: undertake initiatives to promote greater environmental responsibility; and
- Principle 9: encourage the development and diffusion of environmentally friendly technologies.

Anti-Corruption

- Principle 10: Businesses should work against corruption in all its forms, including extortion and bribery.

In regard to the 10th Principle, the UN Global Compact website, amongst other things, provides the following commentary:

BEGINNING OF EXCERPT

Why should companies care?

There are many reasons why the elimination of corruption has become a priority within the business community. Confidence and trust in business among investors, customers, employees and the public have been eroded by recent waves of business ethics scandals around the globe. Companies are learning the hard way that they can be held responsible for not paying enough attention to the actions of their employees, associated companies, business partners and agents.

The rapid development of rules of corporate governance around the world is also prompting companies to focus on anti-corruption measures as part of their mechanisms to express corporate sustainability and to protect their reputations and the interests of their stakeholders. Their anti-corruption systems are increasingly being extended to a range of ethics and integrity issues, and a growing number of investment managers are looking to these systems as evidence that the companies undertake good and well-managed business practice.

Businesses face high ethical and business risks and potential costs when they fail to effectively combat corruption in all its forms. All companies, large and small, are vulnerable to corruption, and the potential for damage is considerable. Business can face:

- **Legal risks:** not only are most forms of corruption illegal where they occur but it is also increasingly becoming illegal in a company's home country to engage in corrupt practices in another country;
- **Reputational risks:** companies whose policies and practices fail to meet high ethical standards, or that take a relaxed attitude toward compliance with laws, are exposed to serious reputational risks. Often it is enough to be accused of malpractice for a company's reputation to be damaged even if a court subsequently determines the contrary;
- **Financial costs:** there is clear evidence that many countries lose close to $1 trillion due to fraud, corruption and shady business transactions and in certain cases, corruption can cost a country up to 17% of its GDP, according to the UN Development Programme in 2014. This undermines business performance and diverts public resources from legitimate sustainable development;
- Erosion of internal trust and confidence as unethical behaviour damages staff loyalty to the company as well as the overall ethical culture of the company.

What can companies do?

The UN Global Compact suggests that participants consider the following three elements when fighting corruption and implementing the 10th principle:

- **Internal:** As a first and basic step, introduce anti-corruption policies and programmes within their organizations and their business operations;
- **External:** Report on the work against corruption in the annual Communication on Progress; and share experiences and best practices through the submission of examples and case stories;
- **Collective Action:** Join forces with industry peers and with other stakeholders to scale up anti-corruption efforts, level the playing field and create fair competition for all. Companies can use the Anti-Corruption

Collective Action Hub to create a company profile, propose projects, find partners and on-going projects as well as resources on anti-corruption collective action;

- Sign the "Anti-corruption Call to Action", which is a call from Business to Governments to address corruption and foster effective governance for a sustainable and inclusive global economy.

END OF EXCERPT

The Need for Increased Trust in Business

Kimmel in a FCPA Blog post reports on the Edelman 2017 Trust Barometer as follows:

BEGINNING OF EXCERPT

Earlier today Edelman released the findings of its 17th annual Trust Barometer, a poll of 33,000 respondents in 28 countries. This year's results were strikingly different from their 2016 findings. In fact, trust to "do what is right" declined in all four major institutions: NGOs, Business, Media and Government.

I had the good fortune of an invitation to a pre-release webinar hosted by Edelman on January 13, enabling me to report early on the 2017 Trust Barometer findings.

As Trust Across America continues its mission to help build trust in business, the following are some of the key takeaways from the presentation:

- Only 37 percent of respondents trust the CEO as a credible spokesperson.
- CEO credibility dropped in all 28 markets, reflecting a global crisis of leadership.
- 82 percent of respondents believe "Big Pharma" needs greater regulation.
- 53 percent of respondents do not believe that financial institutions have been reined in "enough."
- The main opportunities for businesses to prove they are "doing no harm" include focus on bribery, executive compensation, tax havens, overcharging for products, and reducing costs by decreasing product quality.
- The ways business can best show they are "doing more" is through their treatment of employees, producing high quality products, listening to customers, paying their fair share of taxes, and employing ethical business practices.
- CEOs must engage in talking "with" not "at" people. They should be more spontaneous, blunt, include personal experience in dialogue, and participate in their company's social media.

- And finally, Edelman's survey results reflect a fundamental shift from the old "For the people" to the new "With the people."

What actions must big business take?

It is incumbent on Boards of Directors, CEOs and their C-Suites to:

- Acknowledge that they individually have a problem, and collectively are responsible for the growing crisis of trust in business.
- Recognize that trust is indeed a hard asset and a measurable currency, not an intangible to be taken for granted.
- Find the courage and take action to elevate trust across and among all stakeholder groups.

Through its *FACTS® Framework, Trust Across America's research focus picks up where Edelman's findings leave off. For the past eight years we have been measuring the trust "worthiness" or integrity of the largest 1,500 U.S. public companies.

We find that industry is not destiny and a handful of corporate leaders are already reaping the rewards of high trust. Edelman's 2017 findings do, however, support our call for a different "way" of doing business, and perhaps that "way" will find increasing support from big business in 2017.

END OF EXCERPT

Concluding Note

Chapter 8 of this book considers the role of the corporate lawyer in anti-corruption initiatives. Legal counsel should be prepared to provide corporate clients with guidance on developing internal policies that will ensure fulfillment of legal and ethical obligations from both an anti-corruption and CSR perspective. Chapter 8 provides guidance to corporate lawyers who want to ensure that their clients' anti-corruption policy and programs are conforming to national and international expectations for corporate behaviour.

SUCCESSES AND FAILURES IN INTERNATIONAL CONTROL OF CORRUPTION: GOOD GOVERNANCE

Ten Lessons to Be Learned in Designing Anti-Corruption Initiatives

In the 2011 report Contextual Choices in Fighting Corruption: Lessons Learned,272 prepared by the Hertie School of Governance for the Norwegian Agency for Development Cooperation (NORAD), Alina Mungiu-Pippidi et al. review the successes and failures of the international community's anti-corruption initiatives and strategies in the previous fifteen years.273 From this review, the authors extract the lessons learned to help guide future anti-corruption initiatives. It should be noted that the authors' conclusions are not necessarily agreed upon by all anti-corruption scholars and practitioners.

The excerpts below are from the Executive Summary and provide an overview of the report's findings:

BEGINNING OF EXCERPT

[xix:]

Fifteen years have passed since World Bank President James Wolfensohn called for a global fight against the 'cancer' of corruption, a call that was answered by much of the development community. Since then, awareness of the systemic nature of corruption has dramatically increased, mostly due to the advocacy efforts of NGOs such as Transparency International and the visibility of corruption rankings such as TI's CPI and the World Bank's Governance Indicators (WGI). The demand also increased for a comprehensive and integrated global legal framework to fight corruption, which was eventually met with the adoption of the UNCAC. This report is a general reflection on the impact of this global effort and is not intended as an evaluation. Its main objectives are to understand and assess the cognitive framework of the global anti- corruption effort; its relevance for the development agenda; and to offer some explanations and solutions fifteen years later.

Once it became apparent that development resources could potentially disappear in environments characterized by weak governance and corruption, anti-corruption developed into a specific approach to development assistance (good governance as means). Promoting good governance, however, also become an objective in itself (good governance as end), as donors realized that the economy of aid could not be separated from the broader country governance. Unfortunately, not much significant progress has been registered globally since the World Bank began monitoring the world governance indicators, despite an unprecedented investment in good governance policies and an unprecedented rise in awareness (Kaufmann, 2009). Progress seems to be made in atypical polities, such as the United Arab Emirates, Hong Kong or Cape Verde, or remains controversial (Georgia). Countries that have evolved within the previous decade have, in fact, regressed in the fifteen years of global anti-corruption. When reviewing countries continent by continent, it is almost impossible to find a steady progression to the 'green' area which represents the top quarter of ratings, although the lower part of the scale shows better results. What we do find, however, is involution: South Africa, Argentina, Malaysia or Ukraine. Good governance is not only hard to achieve, but difficult to sustain.

[xiii-xiv:]

Why, despite unprecedented investment in anti-corruption in the last fifteen years and since the implementation of global monitoring instruments and global legislation, have so few countries managed to register progress? This new report commissioned by the Norwegian Agency for Development Cooperation (NORAD) to the Hertie School of Governance argues that conceptual flaws, imprecise measurement instruments and inadequate strategies are to blame. But it also argues that the quest for public integrity is a political one, between predatory elites in a society and its losers and fought primarily on domestic playgrounds. As such, the donor community can play only a limited part and it needs to play this part strategically in order to create results. Based on new statistical evidence, the report recommends cash-on- delivery/selectivity approaches for anti-corruption assistance [cash-on-delivery is a term used in the aid community to mean an aid scheme whereby funding is only delivered once progress on an agreed upon goal is achieved by the aid recipient]. Effective and sustainable policies for good governance need to diminish the political and material resources of corruption and build normative constraints in the form of domestic collective action. Most of the current anti-corruption strategies, on the contrary, focus on increasing legal constraints, which often fail because most interventions are localized in societies that lack the rule of law.

As governance is defined as the set of formal and informal institutions shaping "who gets what" in a given polity, the understanding of governance regimes is an indispensable step towards creating a more strategic approach to anti-corruption. Three distinct types of governance regimes are described in the report: open access or ethical universalism regimes, which exist in most of the developed world; closed access regimes, divided between neo-patrimonial (where power is monopolized by the ruler and their clique) and competitive particularistic (where several groups compete for the spoils, but spoiling the state remains the rule of the game). Free elections by themselves do not solve the problem of corruption: more democracies than autocracies feature presently among systemically corrupt countries. The widely used perception indicators, which are presumed to measure corruption, actually measure governance in general, not only illegal corruption, which is only a small part of the overall picture (hence their insensitivity to change). Governance regimes are stable: the few countries that succeeded in changing over the last few decades are presented in section 7 on page 72 [these countries include Tanzania, Albania, Indonesia, Paraguay and Georgia].

Most corruption academic literature conceptualizes anti-corruption at the individual level, as do most current theories about anti-corruption. This presumes that corruption is a deviation from an otherwise established norm of ethical universalism, where every citizen is treated equally by the state and all public resources are distributed impartially. In fact, outside the developed world, the norm is not ethical universalism, since the process of modernization leading to an impersonal state autonomous from private interest was never completed in most countries. Most anti- corruption instruments that donors favour are norm-infringing instruments from the developed context, when they should be norm-building instruments for developing contexts. There is a gross inadequacy of institutional imports from developed countries which enjoy rule of law to developing contexts, shown in section 6 (Table 13 on page 56) of the report, where statistical evidence found no impact by anti- corruption agencies, Ombudsmen-like institutions and the ratification of the United Nations Convention against Corruption (UNCAC). What is presented in most anti- corruption literature as a principal-agent problem is in fact a collective action problem, since societies reach a sub-optimal equilibrium of poor governance with an insufficient domestic agency pushing for change.

The report argues that the question "what causes corruption" is therefore absurd. Particularism exists by default, since most human societies have limited resources to share, and people tend to share them in a particular way, most notably with their closest kin and not with everyone else. Modern states are based on universal citizenship, which entails fair treatment of every citizen by the government. But there are very few states that have thus far succeeded in moving from the natural state to this ideal of modernity. The question should change from "what causes corruption" to "what makes particularism evolve into universalism". What determines a change in the equilibrium?

The classic answer offered by modernization theory is development. As societies grow richer, people become more autonomous, with normative constraints to discretionary power and corrupt allocation as the result. Even countries with a poor quality of governance grow, with examples ranging from Italy to Mexico. However, in many cases development is systematically hindered by government favouritism towards private actors and non-rational (particular) allocation, resulting in a vicious circle of captive states and poor societies. Disregarding factors that cannot be influenced by policy, the report found quite a few significant determinants of the degree of control of corruption where human agency can play an important role (see Table 12 on page 49), including the strong impact of the internet infrastructure, reduction in red tape, economic openness, civil society activity, freedom of information acts and media freedom. These are all areas where development donors can play a large role, even when disregarding individual rights and independence of the judiciary, which are more political and thus more difficult to influence. Although some of these proxies do not seem to address corruption directly, any contribution to their improvement is a clear and substantial anti-corruption aid that can be measured.

[xiv-xviii: The report concludes with a list of the ten lessons that can be learned from the fifteen years since the World Bank called for a global fight against corruption. These include:]

1. Although globalization has turned corruption into a global phenomenon, subsequently addressed by a global governance approach (anti-bribery conventions, UNCAC, the emergence of a global civil society), the battlefield where this war is lost or won remains national. Case studies of historical and contemporary achievers show that although external constraints played a large role in inducing disequilibrium in particularistic countries and triggering change, a transformation has to be reflected in a new equilibrium of power at the society level for it to be both profound and sustainable.
2. Transitions from corrupt regimes to regimes where ethical universalism is the norm are political and not technical-legal processes. There is no global success case of anti-corruption as promoted by the international anti-corruption community. Successful countries followed paths of their own. Fighting corruption in societies where particularism is the norm is similar to inducing a regime change: this requires a broad basis of participation to succeed and it is highly unrealistic to expect this to happen in such a short interval of time and with non-political instruments. The main actors should be broad national coalitions, and the main role of the international community is to support them in becoming both broad and powerful. All good governance programs should be designed to promote this political approach: audits, controls and reviews should be entrusted to 'losers' and draw on natural competition to fight favouritism and privilege granting. No country can change without domes-tic collective action which is both representative and sustainable over time. The media, political oppositions and civil society should not be seen as non-permanent guests taking part in consultations on legal drafts but as main permanent actors in the process of anti-corruption and holding decisive seats in all institutions promoting ethical universalism. Which windows of opportunities to use, what actors have more interest in changing the rules of the game and how to sequence the change depends on the diagnosis of each society and cannot be solved by a one-size-fits all solution. Chapter 2 of UNCAC, Preventive measures, can accommodate a variety of such programs. But also a number of what are seen as democracy promotion efforts (building a free media, civil society, community voice, empowerment) should in fact be considered as anti-corruption programs.

3. Lesson number three is that on this political front, the international community has often played an ambiguous and inconsistent role and has thus sabotaged its own efforts. The failure of the anti-corruption conditionality is partly grounded in the lack of understanding of particularism as a regime of governance and in consequently selecting various implausible principals as main actors to change the regime. Just as importantly, it is also partly caused by the overriding of good governance promotion by other strategic policy priorities. To minimize this in the future, good governance programs and particularly UNCAC implementation should be tied to assistance on a cash-by-delivery mechanism only, as the European Union has already suggested for its revamped North African European Neighbourhood Policy support. Diplomacy should also act in concert with aid, promoting representative anti-corruption actors in societies and avoiding the 'professionalization' of anti-corruption by limitation to a circle of 'experts'.
4. Lesson number four is that there are no silver bullets or maverick institutions in fighting corruption. We found no impact of anticorruption agencies (explained by their inadequacy in an environment without an independent judiciary and where particularism is the rule of the game, not the exception) and of Ombudsman (explained by the control of such agencies by the government or group in power). Particularly in African countries, where particularism is the norm and predatory elites are in charge, it is inadequate to transplant new institutions and try to ring-fence them against particularism (Simons 2008). We found, however, some limited impact of freedom of information acts (FOIA). The impact of FOIA and the second generation transparency tools (transparency of budgets, legislative drafts, statements of assets) which is substantiated by qualitative evaluation studies is explained by the fact that their implementation depends to a great extent on non-governmental actors.
5. Lesson number five is about the lack of significant impact (in statistical tests) by the UNCAC after five years, which should not come as a surprise in this context. After all, five years after the 1948 adoption of the Universal Declaration of Human Rights, only a handful of countries in the world were considered as fully respecting such rights. By 2010, according to Freedom House, their number had grown to 87, representing 45 percent of the world's 194 polities and 43 percent of the global population. 57 percent of the global population still lives in countries where human rights are only imperfectly observed, if at all. The advance in this interval is attributed to liberalizing autocrats, international pressures for norm adoption and implementation, but primarily to freedom fighters and the rise in demand

for freedom in each of these countries. The story of UNCAC is similar. The norm was set: many countries formally adopted ethical universalism as a norm, which simplifies the job of anti-corruption fighters. But without massive domestic demand for new rules of the game and public participation in a sustainable mechanism which would prevent the eternal reproduction of privilege and shift allocation to ethical universalism, we are unlikely to see significant progress. Strategies must be conceived accordingly: UNCAC is a collection of institutional tools, not all similarly effective or useful, of which some have the potential to become effective weapons. This is true, however, only if local actors take them up and fight the long fight with them. What the international community can do, in any event, is to push UNCAC implementation and review as a mechanism to stir collective action. UNCAC will have an impact only if the entire society contributes to a check on the government. Such a permanent check could play a far more important role than the international review of UNCAC. For example, if the country of Ruritania were to ratify UNCAC, donors should push for a national stakeholders' commission to check on implementation, including media, local communities, and anti-corruption NGOs. The review should take place on an annual basis and those in charge of implementation should report to this body and make the report public. Accountability to the entire society regarding the implementation of UNCAC is a minimal requirement in building the general accountability of governments. In this context, the ownership principle in anti-corruption must simply be interpreted as ownership by the society, not by the government. Funds for anti-corruption should also be disbursed only in consultation with such an inclusive stakeholder body and after its assessment of trend and impact.

6. Lesson number six is about the importance of civil society, for which the report finds statistical and qualitative evidence. However, the kind of civil society needed to serve as a watchdog at the community as well as national level is frequently missing in many countries. In the last ten years and due to donors funding, the world was more populated with professional 'expert' civil society than with watchdog and whistle-blowing civil society. Any country ruled by particularism is bound to have many 'losers' who are shortcut by networks of privilege. Without their collective action, there is no sustainable change in the rules of the game, and their empowerment becomes therefore the chief priority. We do see success models in South Korea and a few Eastern European countries.
7. Lesson seven is about developing indicators and measures to allow better monitoring of trends and impact of policies. The aggregate measures of

corruption, particularly the WGI Control of Corruption, which allows measuring confidence error on top of perceptions of corruption, have played a great role by setting the stage for a global competition for integrity among countries. But once it comes to the process of change itself and the impact of certain policies, they become less helpful. Section 3 of this report suggests the use of a new generation of indicators which allow us to understand what the real norm (practice) is and how it changes over time. The full reports on Brazil and Romania posted online present such indicators.

8. Lesson eight is about the fit of repressive policies to various development contexts. It is very risky to fight corruption by repressive means whenever particularism is the main allocation norm because some people will be above the law and the selection of those to be prosecuted cannot be anything but biased. The risk is that the whole judicial aspect of AC will simply become a hunt for opponents or those poorly connected who cannot bail themselves out. The case of corruption determined by scarcity in very poor countries, for example when the government is in payment arrears or severely underfunds certain sectors, deserves a completely different treatment. A repressive approach has never solved scarcity problems. Either the state should abandon the task if it is unable to fund it, or funds should be found to pay policemen, doctors, and the rest. Resorting to a more ancient system of collecting fees for services, or transferring ownership of the service to anyone who can fund it, might prove palliative. This problem cannot be fought by anticorruption measures, and should not be even considered as corruption. Unless, such policies are implemented, an investment on the part of the country and donors of raising legal constraints will fail (and this is frequently the only AC policy promoted). Investment in strong legal constraints only works in developed institutional environments.
9. Lesson number nine is that policies of drying resources for corruption are essential, along with increasing normative constraints. The long term advocated – and partly discredited – economic liberal policies of the World Bank have an important good governance component which has proved significant both in our statistics models (and of others) and in the case studies. The discredit does not come from their failure to produce growth but from the difficulty of transposing them into practice: privatizations often produce private rents, as governments embark in such policies and then try to control competition and preserve them. But the success stories are mostly the successes of liberal economic policies, particularly of red tape reduction, tax simplification and privatization.

10. The final lesson is about formalization, which plays an important role in explaining corruption. Societies become transparent, and thus modern, following a process of bargaining where individuals agree to pay taxes in exchange for certain public goods. This agreement does not exist in particularistic societies, as everyone knows that access is not equal, and this hinders their development. Societies hide from predatory rulers to defend themselves, and this is why it is important that government and society work together for more transparency. Successful policies of formalization are based on bargaining, not repression, except in the area of criminal economy (smuggling, drugs, traffic, money laundering). Formalization, understood as a process of persuasion and incentivizing of property and business registration, is an essential step in reducing informality. [footnotes omitted]

END OF EXCERPT

Heeks and Mathisen, in "Understanding Success and Failure of Anti-Corruption Initiatives," argue that anti-corruption initiatives often fail because of "design-reality gaps," which they describe as "a mismatch between the expectations built into their design as compared to on- the-ground realities in the context of their implementation. Successful initiatives find ways to minimize or close these gaps. Effective design and implementation processes enable gap closure and improve the likelihood of success."

ANOTHER CASE STUDY: BAE ENGAGES IN LARGE-SCALE CORRUPTION IN SAUDI ARABIA

In "Black Money," Frontline (PBS, 2009) available online: http://video.pbs.org/video/ 1114436938/ (55 min), Lowell Bergman investigates an $80 billion arms deal between BAE Systems, a British corporation, and Saudi Arabia. Details of the contract were not released publicly. At the same time, members of the Saudi royal family and Saudi government officials received huge personal payments and gifts from BAE. When British prosecutors began investigations, Saudi Arabia threatened to pull support for Britain's fight against terrorism. The British prosecutors backed off. The video introduces some of the major anti- corruption legal developments in international as well as British and American law. It highlights the scale with which multinational corporations have been involved in the shadowy world of international bribery.

Update: In 2010, BAE pled guilty in the US to charges of failing to keep accurate accounting records and conspiring to make false statements to the US government. Although the charges related to various cases of corruption, BAE did not, however, admit to actual bribery in the plea bargain. BAE was required to pay $400 million to the US Treasury. The company avoided further sanctions, such as debarment from public procurement in the US, because it did not plead guilty to actual corruption offences. In the same plea deal, BAE was also required to pay £30 million to the UK and Tanzania. The UK's Serious Fraud Office was investigating allegations of corruption by BAE in seven or eight other countries, but dropped the other cases after settling the Tanzania case.

In 2011, BAE was required to pay a further $79 million as a civil penalty to the US Department of State for alleged violations of the Arms Export Control Act and the International Traffic in Arms Regulations. The Department of State imposed a statutory debarment from the US public procurement process but concurrently rescinded the debarment, implying that BAE is "too big to debar."

See Chapter 7, Section 4.6 for further discussion of the BAE case.

CHAPTER-2

BRIBERY AND OTHER CORRUPTION OFFENCES

INTRODUCTION AND OVERVIEW

As noted in Chapter 1, corruption is a broad concept. In part, what counts as corruption is shaped by social, political and economic beliefs and norms in a given society. While there are legitimate disputes on whether certain forms of conduct are or should be classified as corruption, there is a core of conduct which is almost unanimously viewed as corruption. The fact that the periphery of corruption is grey does not provide any insurmountable barrier to defining and criminalizing the core of corruption.

If the concept of corruption is generally understood, in the words of Transparency International, to be "the abuse of entrusted power for private gain," it is readily apparent that there are many types of behaviour that constitute corrupt abuse of public power for private gain. For the most part, states do not treat corruption as one offence, but rather create a number of separate offences to deal with corrupt behaviour. Those separate offences can be defined narrowly to apply only to corrupt behaviour in the sense of the misuse of public power or they may be defined to apply more broadly to all persons, whether or not those persons are in positions of public power. For example:

- Theft (embezzlement) is (in general) the unlawful taking of another's property. When that taking is by a public official in respect to public funds, that conduct is corrupt. States can treat this latter corrupt behaviour as simply one example of the general offence of theft, or can create a specific crime of corruption called theft by public officials in respect to their entrusted powers.
- Fraud is (in general) the unlawful taking or use of another's property by dishonest means (i.e., lies, false pretences, omission of material information, etc.). When that fraud is committed by a public official in respect to their

public functions that conduct is corrupt. States can treat this latter conduct as simply one example of the general offence of fraud, or they can create a specific crime of fraud by public officials carrying out their public duties. Bribes offered or received in the context of public procurement and bid rigging can be treated as offences of fraud or as specific corruption offences.

- Extortion is a third example. It is (in general) a crime of theft which is committed by threatening economic or physical harm to another, unless the threatened person gives the person making the threat the money or other benefit or advantage being demanded. Once again, extortion can be committed by or in respect to a public official in the context of their public functions in which case the conduct can be criminalized under a specific crime of extortion by, or of, public officials, or it can be treated as one example of the general offence of extortion.

On the other hand, there are offences that are specifically created to deal with the corrupt behaviour of public officials in respect to their public functions. For example:

- Bribery is (in general) the asking or taking by a public official of a benefit or advantage for private gain in exchange for a misuse of the official's entrusted powers. Bribery is also a bilateral offence—it criminalizes the conduct of the public official and also the conduct of third party bribers who have offered, given or agreed to give a bribe to a public official.
- Buying or selling a public office or exercising or promising to exercise improper influence on an appointment to a public office is an offence of corruption and is a specific offence in the penal codes of many nations.

There are other offences relevant to corruption and bribery. These offences include money laundering and books and records offences, which are seen as necessary to effectively fight against the commission of large-scale bribery, as well as other economic crimes.

Rose-Ackerman notes that merely creating offences will not on its own adequately address corruption. She states:

- A narrowly focused reform may not limit corruption unless combined with greater overall governmental transparency and outside monitoring. Particular laws against bribery, extortion, and self-dealing will never be sufficient to deal with widespread corruption. Fundamental redesign of the relations between the state and society will often be the only way to control systemic corruption. Nevertheless, well-designed and enforced laws against bribery and extortion are a necessary backup to any broader reform.

As noted in Chapter 1, the United Nations Convention against Corruption (UNCAC) has been ratified by 183 countries across the globe. It is by far the most influential international anti-corruption instrument. State Parties to UNCAC are required to enact legislation criminalizing certain offences and are required to consider criminalizing other offences. In other words, UNCAC contains both mandatory and optional corruption offences and provisions. Signatories to UNCAC and members of the OECD are required to implement mandatory offences and to consider implementing optional offences. Both types of provisions are listed below.

Mandatory Offences:

1. Bribery of National Public Officials
2. Bribery of Foreign Public Officials
3. Public Embezzlement
4. Money Laundering
5. Obstruction
6. Liability of Legal Entities
7. Accomplices and Attempts
8. Conspiracy to Commit Money Laundering
9. Book and Records Offences2

The OECD Convention is restricted to criminalizing bribery of foreign public officials in the course of international business transactions. The OECD Convention does not contain offence provisions on items (1), (3) and (5) listed above from UNCAC.

As you will see in the course of reading this chapter, domestic law in the US, UK and Canada incorporates all the mandatory provisions set out above, albeit with slightly different language and scope. Appendix 1 of this chapter references the exact provisions in each country that correspond to the UNCAC provisions.

Optional Offences:

1. Foreign Official Taking a Bribe
2. Giving a Bribe for Influence Peddling
3. Accepting a Bribe for Influence Peddling
4. Abuse of Public Function to Obtain a Bribe
5. Illicit Enrichment
6. Private Sector Bribery
7. Embezzlement in the Private Sector
8. Concealing Bribery Property

Apart from the offence of illicit enrichment, these optional offences can also be found in US, UK and Canadian law.

While UNCAC and the OECD Anti-Bribery Convention include a number of corruption offences, this chapter explores the two most commonly charged offences: (1) bribery of national and foreign public officials and (2) books and records offences. The other Convention offences are listed in Appendix I at the end of this chapter. The offence of money laundering is explored in detail in Chapter 4 of this book. The remainder of this chapter involves a description of the elements of and relevant defences to bribery and books and records offences both domestically and in foreign countries under:

1. UNCAC
2. OECD Convention on Corruption of Foreign Officials
3. US law, especially the Foreign Corrupt Practices Act (FCPA)
4. UK law, especially the Bribery Act 2010 and
5. Canadian law, especially the Corruption of Foreign Public Officials Act (CFPOA).

Chapter 3 then continues with an analysis of several general criminal law principles that are relevant to defining the scope of bribery and books and records offences, namely:

1. extra-territorial jurisdiction for bribery offences
2. criminal liability of corporations and other legal entities
3. party or accomplice liability and
4. inchoate liability (attempts, conspiracy and solicitation).

An understanding of the foreign bribery laws of the US and UK is especially important for lawyers and their corporate clients in other jurisdictions because these two countries have wide extra-territorial jurisdiction provisions in their bribery statutes. Foreign persons and companies can often be prosecuted under the US or UK law. For example, a Canadian company which offers a bribe to a public official in Bangladesh can be prosecuted not only in Canada, but also in the US under the FCPA if the Canadian company's shares are listed on the New York Stock Exchange (or any other US Stock Exchange).

DOMESTIC BRIBERY

UNCAC

Offence of Bribery of a National Public Official

Article 15 of UNCAC requires State Parties to create a criminal offence in respect to bribery of its public officials. Article 15 states:

Article 15. Bribery of national public officials

Each State Party shall adopt such legislative and other measures as may be necessary to establish as criminal offences, when committed intentionally:

1. The promise, offering or giving, to a public official, directly or indirectly, of an undue advantage, for the official himself or herself or another person or entity, in order that the official act or refrain from acting in the exercise of his or her official duties;
2. The solicitation or acceptance by a public official, directly or indirectly, of an undue advantage, for the official himself or herself or another person or entity, in order that the official act or refrain from acting in the exercise of his or her official duties.

Active and Passive Bribery

Article 15(a) is sometimes referred to as active bribery of a domestic public official, while Article 15(b) is sometimes called passive bribery. "Active" bribery refers to the giving or the offering of a bribe or other form of "undue advantage" to a national public official. "Passive" bribery, though somewhat a misnomer, refers to the actions of the corrupt public official who accepts, or in some cases, actively solicits, a bribe.

Public Official

Bribery is an offence involving public officials. "Public official" is defined in Article 2(a) of UNCAC as follows:

- "Public official" shall mean: (i) any person holding a legislative, executive, administrative or judicial office of a State Party, whether appointed or elected, whether permanent or temporary, whether paid or unpaid, irrespective of that person's seniority; (ii) any other person who performs a public function including for a public agency or public enterprise, or provides a public service as defined in the domestic law of the State Party and as applied in the pertinent area of law of that State Party; (iii) any other person defined as a "public official" in the domestic law of a State Party.

As Michael Kubiciel notes in his article "Core Criminal Law Provisions in the United Nations Convention Against Corruption," the UNCAC definition of "public official" is very broad. It includes persons who do not hold official positions but perform a public function or provide a public service. This definition is more expansive than the definition prescribed by earlier multilateral conventions. The definition recognizes that even those who do not occupy official positions may still exercise influence and be subject to corruption.

Undue Advantage

Another key term in Article 15 is "undue advantage." The United Nations Office on Drugs and Crime (UNODC)'s Legislative Guide for the Implementation of the United Nations Convention against Corruption states that an "undue advantage may be something tangible or intangible, whether pecuniary or non-pecuniary."[4] As Kubiciel notes, the word "undue" is an imprecise term. According to a strict interpretation, "undue advantage" could mean all types of advantages, even small, culturally acceptable gifts. The word "undue" could also support a flexible interpretation and exclude gifts of low value that are generally socially acceptable (e.g., a cup of coffee). He warns, however, that the "line between an acceptable gift and corruption is thin."[5] A tradition of gift-giving should not necessarily be an automatic defence to a bribery charge. Kubiciel argues that states should be careful to evaluate which behaviours are actually cultural traditions, and whether even those that can be characterized as cultural traditions are nonetheless harmful to public confidence in the state. Some countries deal with the issue by passing laws or regulations requiring all public officials to report (and sometimes surrender) to an appropriate authority a) the receipt of any gift/advantage, or b) the receipt of a gift/advantage over a specified monetary value.

Offering, Promising or Giving

Article 15(a) criminalizes the "offering, promising or giving" of an undue advantage. Therefore, the unilateral offer of a bribe, irrespective of whether the offer was accepted, must be criminalized by State Parties.

Soliciting or Accepting

Similarly, a request for a bribe, whether or not a bribe is agreed to or is actually given is to be criminalized (Article 15(b)). Kubiciel argues that the prohibition of an "acceptance" of an "undue advantage" (Article 15(b)) should be interpreted to mean that an offence is committed even if the public official acquiesces to the offer of a bribe, but subsequently returns the bribe or does not follow through on performance of the corrupt agreement. The latter circumstances would be, however, relevant to determining an appropriate sentence for the public official. It also raises the issue of whether voluntary withdrawal from the bribery scheme might be accepted as a defence as it is in the law of attempts in some countries.

Intention

Article 15 clearly states that the prohibited conduct in that article must be committed intentionally. The phrase in subparagraphs (a) and (b) "in order to act or refrain from acting in the exercise of his or her official duties" requires that "some link must be established between the offer or advantage and inducing the official to act or refrain from acting in the course of his or her official duties."6 In instances where the accused offers a bribe that is not accepted, the accused must have intended to offer the advantage and must also have intended to influence the behaviour of the recipient in the future. Kubiciel notes that this phrase does not expressly prohibit instances where an undue advantage is offered or received by an official after the official has acted or refrained from acting in the exercise of his or her official duties. It could be argued that such conduct does constitute "indirectly" giving an undue advantage if the parties know or reasonably suspect that an undue advantage will be given after the fact. Alternatively, if courts do not adopt that interpretation of "indirectly," State Parties could consider implementing legislation that criminalizes this type of behaviour.

Defences

There are no special defences for domestic bribery under UNCAC. Of course, the absence of any elements of the offences in Articles 15 to 25 will constitute a defence.

- Article 28 of UNCAC deals with knowledge, intent and purpose as elements of an offence. The provision states that "[k]nowledge, intent or purpose required as an element of an offence established in accordance with this Convention may be inferred from objective factual circumstances." Absence of these objective factual circumstances is a defence if the knowledge, intent or purpose is not proven in another way. The UNCAC Commentary provides that "national drafters should see that their evidentiary provisions enable such inference with respect to the mental state of an offender, rather than requiring direct evidence, such as a confession, before the mental state is deemed proven."

The issue of whether facilitation payments are prohibited by UNCAC is discussed in Section 4 below.

Limitation Periods

Article 29 of UNCAC sets out its requirements in respect to limitation periods. Article 29 states:

- Each State Party shall, where appropriate, establish under its domestic law a long statute of limitations period in which to commence proceedings for any offence established in accordance with this Convention and establish a longer statute of limitations period or provide for the suspension of the statute of limitations where the alleged offender has evaded the administration of justice.

The Legislative Guide notes "the concern underlying this provision is to strike a balance between the interests of swift justice, closure and fairness to victims and defendants and the recognition that corruption offences often take a long time to be discovered and established."7 This justifies the wording of Article 29, which requires States to "introduce long periods for all offences established in accordance with the Convention and longer periods for alleged offenders that have evaded the administration of justice."

The provisions under UNCAC with regard to limitation periods parallel those under the OECD Convention, but with the additional option of suspending the limitation period when the offender is found to have been evading the administration of justice. The Legislative Guide suggests two ways that State Parties may implement Article 29.

The first is to review the length of time provided for by existing statutes of limitations. The second is to review the way in which limitation periods are calculated. The Legislative Guide notes that "Article 29 does not require States parties without statutes of limitation to introduce them."9

Sanctions

UNCAC has very little in the way of requirements or guidance for sanctions and sentencing in regard to corrupt conduct. It does not specify any maximum or minimum sentences for corruption offences. Instead, Article 12(1) of UNCAC provides that "each State Party shall take measures, in accordance with... its domestic law... to provide effective, proportionate and dissuasive civil, administrative or criminal penalties" for violation of corruption prevention standards and offences involving the private sector.

And Article 30(1) provides that "each State Party shall make the commission of [corruption] offences ... liable to sanctions that take into account the gravity of that offence." As an ancillary consequence, Article 30(7) indicates that State Parties should consider disqualification of persons convicted of corruption from holding public office for a period of time.

OECD Convention

As the name of the Convention implies, the OECD Convention on Combatting Corruption of Foreign Public Officials in International Business Transactions only deals with bribery of foreign public officials, not domestic public officials.10 Thus the OECD Convention is not relevant to this section on domestic bribery.

US Law

Offense of Bribery of a National Public Official

Domestic bribery is criminalized under both state and federal criminal law. Federal law (18 USC., chapter 11) sets out a number of offenses dealing with bribery, graft and conflict of interest. The principal federal section prohibiting both active and passive bribery is section 201 of 18 USC. Section 201(b)(1) which criminalizes any person who "directly or indirectly, corruptly gives, offers or promises anything of value" to (or for the benefit of) any public official (or person nominated or selected to be a public official) with intent to influence any official act or the commission of any act of fraud by that official on the US, or to induce a public official to violate that official's lawful duties. Section 201(b)(2) creates similar offenses for a public official to "corruptly demand, seek, receive, accept or agree to receive or accept anything of value" in return for improper influence or use of his or her public powers and duties. Section 201(a) defines "public official," "person selected as a public official" and "official act." The above offenses are similar to bribery offenses in most countries. The conduct (actus reus) elements which need to be proven are: (1) the offering/giving or seeking/receiving of "anything of value" to or by (2) a current or selected public official (3) for improper influence of an official act or duty. The mental element (mens rea) is doing so "corruptly with intent to influence an official act or duty." The expression "anything of value" is very wide and can include many things other than money. Also, there is no minimum economic value (or dollar figure) placed on a thing of value. A prosecutor who offers an accomplice immunity or leniency is offering a thing of value, but that is not bribery because the offer is not for a corrupt purpose. "Public official" is also defined widely. The expression "an official act" is defined in § 201(a) as follows:

- (3) the term "official act" means any decision or action on any question, matter, cause, suit, proceeding or controversy, which may at any time be pending, or which may by law be brought before any public official, in such official's official capacity, or in such official's place of trust or profit.

In R v McDonnell,11 the US Supreme Court interpreted the meaning of "official act." The Court held that the prosecutor must "identify a 'question, matter, cause, suit, proceeding or controversy' that 'may at any time be pending' or 'may by law be brought' before a public official" and then prove the public official made a decision or took action on that issue or agreed to do so.12 The action taken must involve formal exercise of governmental power similar in nature to a lawsuit, determination before an agency or hearing before a committee.13 In this regard, a typical meeting, call or event will not be an "official act." The Court was critical of the prosecution's expansive definition of "official act" noting that "White House counsel who worked in every administration from that of President Reagan to President Obama warn that the Government's 'breathtaking expansion of public corruption law would likely chill federal officials' interactions with the people they serve.'"

The US Supreme Court's decision has been widely criticized and has provoked calls for reform.

In regard to the mental element—a corrupt intent to influence, or be influenced in, the commission of an official act—the US Supreme Court has held that the prosecution must establish a quid pro quo, that is "specific intent to give or receive something of value in exchange for an official act." This excludes vague expectations or generalized hope of some future benefit and in this way excludes election campaign donations if they are not made in exchange for a specific official act.

Section 201(c) creates a separate offense sometimes referred to as giving or promising "illegal gratuities." Section 201(c) involves giving or accepting a gratuity for or because of the performance of an official act. There is no need to show the official act was conducted improperly or illegally, nor any need to show a quid pro quo for the gratuity. In effect, the section provides that it is an offense to give or accept a gratuity in respect to the official's public duties. As the US Supreme Court said in Sun-Diamond Growers "[F]or bribery there must be a quid pro quo—a specific intent to give or receive something of value in exchange for an official act. An illegal gratuity, on the other hand, may constitute merely a reward for some future act that the public official will take (and may already have determined to take), or for a past act that he has already taken."18

Defenses

A person charged with a domestic bribery or illegal gratuities offense is entitled to plead any general defense that is applicable to any other crime. These defenses might include claims of entrapment or abuse of due process, but both of these defenses have requirements that will limit their availability in most bribery cases. If a person engages in bribery under physical duress, that duress will constitute a defense if the general requirements for the defense of duress exist. Likewise, necessity may be a defense, if there was no other reasonable option but to pay a bribe. For example, paying a bribe (which was more than a facilitation payment) to a customs officer who demands a bribe before allowing a shipload of perishable goods to be lawfully unloaded may well be excused on the basis of necessity (assuming there was no other reasonable option). Likewise, the general defenses of double jeopardy, res judicata and incapacity are available. Also, prosecution of the offense is barred if the prosecution violates an applicable state or federal statute of limitations.

Limitation Periods

18 USC. Chapter 11 does not set out any specific limitation periods. Accordingly, the general statute of limitations of five years for non-capital offenses applies to the

bribery offences under the US Code.20 This five-year limitation can be extended by three more years in certain circumstances (see Section 3.3.3 below).

Sanctions

According to § 202(b)(4), whoever commits the offense of bribery under § 202(b) "shall be fined under this title [a maximum of $250,000 for individuals or $500,000 for organizations] or no more than three times the monetary equivalent of the thing of value, whichever is the greater, or to imprisonment for not more than fifteen years, or to both, and may be disqualified from holding any office of honor, trust or profit under the United States."

Anyone committing the offense of illegal gratuities under § 201(c) is "fined under this title [a maximum of $250,000 for individuals or $500,000 for organizations] or imprisoned for not more than two years, or both." The actual sentences imposed for both offenses are subject to the US Federal Sentencing Guidelines.21 For a description of sentencing principles and practices applicable to corruption offenses, see Chapter 7, Section 4 of this book.

UK Law

Introduction

The Bribery Act 2010 (hereinafter referred to as the Bribery Act) came into force on July 1, 2011. It is the culmination of 10 to 12 years of study, consultation and debate.22 The Bribery Act constitutes a codification of the law of bribery in England which prior to that time was a complex amalgamation of statute and common law.23 The new Act creates four bribery offences. There are two general offences: (1) offering or giving a bribe and (2) accepting a bribe. There is also a third offence of bribing a foreign public official and a new fourth offence of failure of a "commercial organization" to prevent bribery by one of its associates.

The Bribery Act is broad in several respects. Both domestic and foreign bribery are covered in this one statute. And as will be discussed in Chapter 3, the extra-territorial reach of the Bribery Act is quite extensive. Further, apart from the offence of bribing a foreign public official, the other three offences apply to giving or taking a bribe in both the public and the private sectors. This lack of distinction between public and private or commercial bribery has been criticized by Stuart P. Green. Green advocates treating commercial bribery as a crime, but also argues that its treatment should be distinguished from that of public bribery due to the distinct "moral and political character" of public bribery. As explained by Peter Alldridge, commercial or private bribery "distort[s] the operation of a legitimate market," while public bribery creates "a market in things that should never be sold."

It is rather artificial to divide the offences under the Bribery Act into domestic and foreign offences since, with the exception of bribery of a foreign public official, the other three offences apply to both domestic and foreign activities over which the UK asserts fairly wide jurisdiction. In this section, I cover these latter three offences which apply both domestically and to certain foreign activities. The offence of bribery of a foreign official will be dealt with in Section 3.4 below.

Offences

Offence of Bribing another Person: Section 1

Section 1 of the UK Bribery Act sets out two cases or scenarios in which a person will be guilty of the offence of "bribing another person" or "active bribery." In both cases, section 1(5) specifies that it does not matter whether the bribe is made by a person directly or through a third party. Furthermore, it does not matter if the bribe is actually completed; the offer or promise is enough to make out the offence.

The offence of bribing another person in Case 1 (section 1(2)) occurs where a person "offers, promises or gives a financial or other advantage to another person," and intends that advantage to either "induce a person to perform improperly a relevant function or activity," or "reward a person for the improper performance of such a function or activity." This means the parties must intend acts beyond the offering or receiving of the bribe. Section 1(4) stipulates that it does not matter whether the person who has been bribed is the same person who is to perform (or has already performed) the activity in question.

Section 1(3) describes Case 2 as a situation where a person "offers, promises or gives a financial or other advantage to another person," and "knows or believes that the acceptance of the advantage would itself constitute the improper performance of a relevant function or activity." The receiver need not behave improperly nor even intend to do so; in this case, the receipt of the advantage is itself improper.

Note also that "person," as defined by the UK Interpretation Act 1976, extends to "a body of persons corporate or incorporate" and thus a body corporate can be liable if its "directing mind and will" was implicated in the wrongdoing.

The expression "a relevant function or activity," which is a component of the offence in all cases, is described in section 3 of the Bribery Act as:

- any function of a public nature,
- any activity connected with a business [which includes a trade or profession],
- any activity performed in the course of a person's employment, and
- any activity performed by or on behalf of a body of persons (whether corporate or unincorporate).

The activity, if one of the above, must then meet one or more of the following conditions:

- Condition A is that a person performing the function or activity is expected to perform it in good faith.
- Condition B is that a person performing the function or activity is expected to perform it impartially.
- Condition C is that a person performing the function or activity is in a position of trust by virtue of performing it.

A function or activity can be "relevant" even if it has no connection with the UK at all and is performed outside of the UK. This question of the jurisdictional reach of the UK Bribery Act is more fully examined below in Section 1.8 of Chapter 3.

Section 4 of the Bribery Act explains that a relevant function or activity is performed "improperly" if it is performed in breach of a relevant expectation or where there is a failure to perform the function in circumstances where that failure is itself a breach of a relevant expectation. Relevant expectations are described in Conditions A, B and C above. Therefore, a person exercising a relevant function will be expected to act in good faith, to perform their function impartially or to avoid breaching trust. This means that the performance of the function in Case 1, or the mere acceptance of the financial advantage in Case 2, might be improper if it demonstrates bad faith, partiality or a breach of trust.

Finally, section 5(1) states that "the test of what is expected is a test of what a reasonable person in the United Kingdom would expect in relation to the performance of the type of function or activity concerned." Section 5(2) adds that if the performance is not part of the law of the UK, then local customs and practices must be disregarded unless they are part of the written law (either legislative or judicially created) applicable to the country or territory in question. Ultimately this extends UK norms and standards to foreign sovereign nations, a position which will undoubtedly prove controversial. According to the Joint Committee on the Draft Bribery Bill, the UK Government's deliberate intention is to "encourage a change in culture in emerging markets" by eliminating local custom from a criminal court's considerations.

Offences Relating to Being Bribed: Section 2

Section 2 of the Bribery Act sets out four cases in which a person will be guilty of offences related to being bribed. The offence of "being bribed" is sometimes referred to as "passive bribery" despite the fact that section 2 also includes active conduct on the part of a government official or other person "requesting" a bribe. The offences are formulated in a rather complex way and often appear to overlap, but the drafter's intention is to ensure that the provisions will cover all the ways in which being bribed might occur. In all cases, it does not matter if the person actually receives the bribe; the offence may be made out simply by requesting or agreeing to receive the bribe.

There are four possible routes to liability:

- **Section 2(2):** The first offence is described as "Case 3" (Cases 1 and 2 are dealt with in section 1). In this scenario, the person "requests, agrees to receive or accepts a financial or other advantage intending that, in consequence, a relevant function or activity should be performed improperly" (whether by the person mentioned or another person). The key in this case is that the recipient of the bribe intends improper performance to follow as a consequence of the bribe. The improper performance may be done by the receiver or by another person.
- **Section 2(3):** In Case 4, a person is guilty where he or she "requests, agrees to receive or accepts a financial or other advantage" and "the request, agreement or acceptance itself constitutes the improper performance by the person of a relevant function or activity." In this case, the taking of the bribe in and of itself amounts to improper performance of the relevant function. As described above with regard to Case 2, for this case to be made out the request, agreement or acceptance must itself prove bad faith, partiality, or a breach of trust. For example, the offence would be made out if a civil servant requested $1000 in order to process a routine application.30
- **Section 2(4):** Case 5 deals with a person who requests, agrees to receive or accepts the bribe "as a reward for the improper performance... of a relevant function or activity." The performance can be done by the person being bribed or another person.
- **Section 2(5):** Finally, Case 6 deals with a situation where, "in anticipation of or in consequence of a person requesting, agreeing to receive or accepting a financial or other advantage, a relevant function or activity is performed improperly" (either by that person or by another person at the culpable receiver's request or with the receiver's assent or acquiescence). According to section 2(8), if a person performing the function or activity is someone other than the receiver, it "does not matter whether that performer knows or believes that the performance of the function or activity is improper."

In all cases, it does not matter whether the bribe is accepted directly by the receiver or through a third party, and it does not matter if the bribe is for the benefit of the receiver or another person.

The descriptions in Section 2.4.2(i) above pertaining to the definitions of "relevant function or activity," "improper performance" and "expectation" apply equally to section 2 offences.

In Cases 4, 5 and 6, according to section 2(7), "it does not matter whether the person knows or believes that the performance of the function or activity is improper." This section has resulted in a lack of clarity concerning the mens rea for the various cases in both sections 1 and 2. Section 2(7) seems to create a distinction between sections 1 and 2: in section 1, the "briber" must intend improper performance or improper receipt, whereas the "bribee" in section 2 can be guilty even if he or she did not know his or her performance was improper.

G.R. Sullivan has considered the varying interpretations and suggests that section 2(7) was included for the sake of certainty, in order to confirm that normative awareness of wrongfulness is not necessary for those who accept advantages.32 The goal, according to the Joint Committee on the Draft Bribery Bill, is to encourage people to "think twice" when seeking or taking an advantage. Sullivan further suggests that the same concept can be taken for granted in Cases 1-3, which would mean a briber is not required to know that the behaviour they intend to induce in the bribee is improper. Put another way, ignorance of the law is not a defence.

Commercial Organization Failing to Prevent Bribery: Section 7

Section 7 of the Bribery Act creates a new strict liability offence of failure of a commercial organization to prevent bribery. Section 7 defines the scope of this new offence in the following words:

- A relevant commercial organisation ("C") is guilty of an offence under this section if a person ("A") associated with C bribes another person intending—
  - to obtain or retain business for C, or
  - to obtain or retain an advantage in the conduct of business for C.

For more information on section 7, refer to Section 2.6.1 of Chapter 3.

Offence by Consent or Connivance of Senior Officers: Section 14

If any of the bribery offences under sections 1, 2 or 6 are committed by a body corporate or a Scottish partnership, section 14 of the Bribery Act mandates that a "senior officer" or someone purporting to act in that capacity will be personally criminally liable (as will the body corporate) if the offence was committed with the officer's consent or connivance.

Senior officer is defined in section 14(14) as a "director, manager, secretary or other similar officer." While the word "manager" is not defined and could be broadly interpreted, Nicholls et al. note that it was narrowly defined in a somewhat similar provision in R v. Boal to include only "decision-makers within the company who have the power and responsibility to decide corporate policy and strategy. It is to catch those responsible for putting proper procedures in place." I question whether the narrow Boal definition is consistent with the purpose of putting a duty on "managers" in general to not consent or connive in the commission of bribery by those under their supervision.

The words "consent and connive" are also not defined in the Bribery Act. Nicholls et al. suggest that section 14 will be satisfied by knowledge or "willful blindness" to the conduct that constitutes bribery along with remaining silent or doing nothing to prevent that conduct from occurring or continuing.36 See also Chapter 3, Section 3.4.

Finally, a "senior officer" will only be liable for a bribery offence committed by the corporation if that senior officer has a "close connection" to the UK as defined in section 12(4) of the Bribery Act.

Defences

Section 5(2) of the Bribery Act indicates that no bribery offence is committed if the payment of a financial or other advantage "is permitted or required by the written law applicable to the country or territory concerned." In some countries, the law or government policies require the appointment of a commercial agent as a condition of doing business in that country. The agent is appointed by or associated with persons in high places and demands large agent fees for little or no work.37 The agent's fees are shared with the high officials. This practice is a form of bribery, but it is not defined as corruption in such countries and is in fact legally required in those countries.

Section 13 of the Bribery Act provides a defence for persons whose conduct, which would otherwise constitute a bribery offence, is proven on a balance of probabilities to be necessary for the proper exercise of intelligence or armed services functions. Where the conduct that comprises the bribery offence is necessary for the proper exercise of any function pertaining to UK intelligence or armed services, the defence is made out. The head of the intelligence service or Defence Council must also ensure that arrangements are in place to ensure that any conduct constituting an offence will be necessary. Subsection (5) provides that where a bribe is paid by a member of the intelligence service or armed forces and they are able to rely on the section 13 defence, the receiver of that bribe is also covered by the defence. In England, legally impossible attempts are not generally recognized as crimes.

Sullivan criticizes section 13 for its potential to provide space for "what may be highly questionable conduct." Although Sullivan recognizes the utility of such a defence, he worries "it might encourage payments made in circumstances far removed from matters of vital national security," especially since the duties of the Intelligence Service include protecting the UK's economic wellbeing.

No other bribery-related defences are specifically set out in the Bribery Act, such as committing bribery under duress or by necessity. While the requirements for these defences are rather stringent, there is no reason why they should not apply if the defence requirements are present. The Ministry of Justice Guidance states explicitly that duress may be available if a bribery offence was committed to prevent loss of life, limb or liberty.40 Since duress, which includes duress by threat or by circumstances, only applies when the defendant is under threat of immediate or nearly immediate death or serious bodily harm, the defence would not cover less pressing health and safety concerns.41 As a result, Sullivan expresses concern regarding the potential of the Bribery Act to catch payments extracted through extortion, especially in light of the Act's broad jurisdiction in areas where extortionate demands are common.42 The defence of necessity has the potential to assist defendants under the Act, but is still uncertain and relatively novel in the UK. Necessity acts as a justification for the defendant's conduct in UK law, unlike duress, which is an excuse for wrongful acts committed under pressure. Necessity is based on the idea that sometimes the benefits of breaking the law outweigh the benefits of compliance. The defence is more likely to succeed for property offences, such as bribery, than offences involving the infliction of physical harm.

Other defences such as honest mistake of fact, incapacity and diplomatic immunity should also be available if the requirements for those defences are met. Immunity from the criminal law applies to foreign visiting sovereigns, foreign diplomats and members of the foreign armed forces. Entrapment is another defence available to a charge of bribery. The scope of the entrapment defence in England is set out by the House of Lords in R. v. Loosely and Attorney General's Reference (No. 3 of 2000).44 It is a non-exculpatory defence and therefore does not exonerate the accused. There is no verdict of not guilty, but rather a stay of proceedings on the basis that the investigative activities of the state were unfair and that prosecution of the offence would tarnish the integrity of the court and be an affront to the public conscience. The test for entrapment is whether the state activity goes beyond providing an opportunity to commit a crime and instead has actually instigated the offence. The details of this test are set out in Loosely. Nicholls et al. suggests that the test "is practical, secures the balance of fairness for all interests, and is 'ECHR-centric' in approach and formulation... [and] will be applicable across the range of covert investigations from a corrupt petty official... suspected of taking small bribes to long-term infiltration into commercial corruption, fraud/money laundering, or corrupt networks centered around organized crime."45 Random-virtue testing (offering a person an opportunity to commit a crime in circumstances in which there is no reasonable suspicion that the person intended to engage in the commission of a crime) is not permitted. Entrapment and integrity testing are also discussed in Chapter 6, Section 4.6.3.

(i) Section 7 – Adequate Procedures Defence

The "adequate procedures" defence applies to section 7 of the Bribery Act. Section 7(2) states that a full defence to the charge is available if the commercial organization can prove on a balance of probabilities that it had adequate procedures in place and followed those procedures at the time the bribery occurred in order to prevent associated persons from engaging in bribery. As is more fully argued by Stephen Gentle, this defence has proven to be contentious.

Section 9 requires the Secretary of State to publish guidance for commercial organizations regarding the "adequate procedures" that companies should implement to prevent persons associated with the company from bribing.

After much debate, lobbying and consultation, the Secretary of State for Justice (head of the Ministry of Justice) on March 30, 2011 issued the Bribery Act 2010 Guidance (Guidance, or UK Guidance where required for clarity). On the same day, the Serious Fraud Office (SFO) and the Crown Prosecution Service (CPS) published their Bribery Act 2010: Joint Prosecution Guidance of the Director of the SFO and the DPP (Joint Guidance) to ensure consistency between police and prosecutors and to indicate that police and prosecutors will have careful regard for the Guidance issued by the Secretary of State.

The Guidance is organized around six principles for establishing adequate procedures to prevent corruption. After each principle is set out, the Guidance provides commentary on the meaning and scope of each principle. The six principles are as follows:

- Principle 1: Proportionate procedures

A commercial organisation's procedures to prevent bribery by persons associated with it are proportionate to the bribery risks it faces and to the nature, scale and complexity of the commercial organisation's activities.

- Principle 2: Top-level commitment

The top-level management of a commercial organisation (be it a board of directors, the owners or any other equivalent body or person) are committed to preventing bribery by persons associated with it. They foster a culture within the organisation in which bribery is never acceptable.

- Principle 3: Risk assessment

The commercial organisation assesses the nature and extent of its exposure to potential external and internal risks of bribery on its behalf by persons associated with it. The assessment is periodic, informed and documented.

- Principle 4: Due diligence

The commercial organisation applies due diligence procedures, taking a proportionate and risk based approach, in respect of persons who perform or will perform services for or on behalf of the organisation, in order to mitigate identified bribery risks.

- Principle 5: Communication (including training)

The commercial organisation seeks to ensure that its bribery prevention policies and procedures are embedded and understood throughout the organisation through internal and external communication, including training that is proportionate to the risks it faces.

- Principle 6: Monitoring and Review

The commercial organisation monitors and reviews procedures designed to prevent bribery by persons associated with it and makes improvements where necessary.

Appendix A of the Guidance is composed of eleven case studies for further illustration and clarification of the six principles for "adequate procedures." For example, case study 1 focuses on the problem of facilitation payments and discusses what a company can do when faced with demands for them.

Transparency International UK has also provided guidance on the Bribery Act. It produced a 100-page Guidance on Adequate Procedures and an 80-page Adequate Procedures Checklist, as well as publications on Due Diligence, Diagnosing Bribery Risk and Assessment of Corruption in (Ten) Key Sectors. These guidance documents are designed to assist companies to comply with the Bribery Act by providing clear, practical advice on good practice anti-bribery systems that in Transparency International's opinion constitute "adequate procedures" for compliance with the Bribery Act. Other useful documents, policies and recommended anti- bribery strategies exist and are outlined by Nicholls et al.

Limitation Periods

In accordance with general principles of UK criminal law, the offences in the UK Bribery Act are not subject to any limitation periods in respect to laying charges. Applicable human rights legislation mandates that once charges have been laid, defendants are entitled to receive a public hearing within a "reasonable time" — see for example the UK Human Rights Act 1998 and the European Convention on Human Rights, Article 6(1).

Sanctions

Section 11 describes the penalties for all of the above offences. It states:

- An individual guilty of an offence under section 1, 2 or 6 is liable—
    - on summary conviction, to imprisonment for a term not exceeding 12 months, or to a fine not exceeding the statutory maximum, or to both,
    - on conviction on indictment, to imprisonment for a term not exceeding 10 years, or to a fine, or to both.

- Any other person guilty of an offence under section 1, 2 or 6 is liable—
    - on summary conviction, to a fine not exceeding the statutory maximum,
    - on conviction on indictment, to a fine.
- A person guilty of an offence under section 7 is liable on conviction on indictment to a fine.
- The reference in subsection (1)(a) to 12 months is to be read—
    - in its application to England and Wales in relation to an offence committed before the commencement of section 154(1) of the Criminal Justice Act 2003, and
    - in its application to Northern Ireland, as a reference to 6 months.

The statutory maximum fine is £5000 in England and Wales or £10,000 in Scotland, if the conviction is summary. If convicted on indictment, the amount of the fine is unlimited under the Act. Companies convicted of bribery are also liable to exclusion from obtaining future public contracts in the EU (Article 57 of Directive 2014/24/EU of the European Parliament and of the Council on public procurement (repealing Directive 2004/18/EC)).

A section 7 offence can only be tried on indictment, and thus an organization convicted of a section 7 offence is subject to an unlimited fine, provided that fine is fair and proportionate in the circumstances of each case.

For a detailed description of sentencing principles and practices applicable to corruption offences, see Chapter 7, Section 5 of this book.

Canadian Law

Offences

The Canadian Criminal Code contains eight specific offences relating to corruption and bribery committed in Canada:

- s. 119 Bribery of Judges or Members of Parliament or Provincial Legislative Assemblies
- s. 120 Bribery of Police Officers or other Law Enforcement Officers
- s. 121 Bribery/Corruption of Government Officials [Influence Peddling]
- s. 122 Fraud or Breach of Trust by a Public Official
- s. 123 Municipal Corruption
- s. 124 Selling or Purchasing a Public Office
- s. 125 Influencing or Negotiating Appointments to Public Offices
- s. 426 Giving or Receiving Secret Commissions

The offences are in part overlapping, so the same conduct can sometimes constitute an offence under more than one provision. The offences apply to both individuals and corporations. The offences concerning bribery of judges, politicians and police officers (sections 119-120) are considered to be the most serious offences and are punishable by a maximum of 14 years imprisonment. The other bribery and corruption offences (sections 121-125 and 426) are punishable by a maximum of 5 years imprisonment.

These offences are largely unchanged since their incorporation into Canada's first criminal code in 1892. Several of these offences are loosely related to the common law offence of misconduct in public office. Canada abolished common law offences in 1955 and therefore the common law offence of misconduct in public office is of no force or effect in Canada.51 However, this common law offence recently underwent a major resurgence in some common law jurisdictions52 such as Hong Kong, Victoria and New South Wales in Australia, and the UK, even after the enactment of the UK's Bribery Act 2010.53

The following description of domestic bribery and corruption offences in Canada is taken from G. Ferguson, "Legislative and Enforcement Framework for Corruption and Bribery Offences in Canada," a paper presented at the First ASEM Prosecutors General Conference (as part of the Canada-China Procuratorate Reform Cooperation Program) in Shenzhen, China, December 9-12, 2005. This paper has been updated to December 2016.

BEGINNING OF EXCERPT

Bribery of Judges, Members of Parliament or Provincial Legislative Assemblies

Section 119 of the Criminal Code creates offences which apply both to the person who accepts or obtains a bribe and to the person who offers the bribe. Anyone committing this offence is guilty of an indictable offence and liable to imprisonment for a term not exceeding fourteen years.

Elements of the Offence: With regard to the person accepting or obtaining the bribe, the following elements constitute the full offence:

- The accused must be the holder of a judicial office, or be a member of Parliament or the legislature of a province;
- The accused must accept or obtain, agree to accept or attempt to obtain any money, valuable consideration, office, place or employment for himself or herself or another person;54
- This must be done corruptly, and must relate to anything done or omitted or to be done or omitted by the accused in the accused's official capacity.

The offence for the person offering the bribe is essentially the mirror-image of that outlined above: the accused must corruptly give or offer any money, valuable consideration, office, place or employment to the holder of a judicial office or a member of Parliament or of the legislature of a province. The bribe must relate to anything done or omitted by that person in their official capacity, and may be for that person or any other person.

With respect to ministerial officers, the distinction between political and non-political officers has no significance, and includes ministers of the Crown.

"Corruptly"

As noted, the only specifically required mental element is that the accused act corruptly. "Corruptly" does not mean "wickedly" or "dishonestly"; rather, it refers to an act performed in bad faith, designed wholly or partially for the purpose of bringing about the effect forbidden by this section.56 The accused's conduct need not amount to a bribe to perform a specific act, or a reward for its accomplishment.57

"Official Capacity"

Provided the accused corruptly received money for influence "in his official capacity," the use to be made of the money is irrelevant.58 It is not necessary that the corrupt act of a Member of Parliament relate to their legislative duties; rather, it may be connected to their participation in an administrative act of government.59 Similarly, a cabinet minister, in absence of contrary evidence, acts in their official capacity as a member of the legislature when taking ministerial actions connected with the administration of the ministry.

In a highly publicized trial, Senator Michael Duffy was charged with 31 counts relating to allegations of breach of trust, fraudulent practices and accepting a bribe, and was ultimately acquitted on all charges. A charge under section 119(a) of the Criminal Code involved allegations that Senator Duffy improperly claimed residency expenses and repaid $90,000 using money received from Nigel Wright, Chief of Staff to then Prime Minister Harper, that the $90,000 was a corruptly received bribe. Justice Vaillancourt found that Senator Duffy did not accept the funds voluntarily but was forced to accept them so the government could manage a political fiasco. Therefore, the acceptance of funds was not done corruptly. Justice Vaillancourt found the charge would have otherwise been stayed as a result of an officially induced error.

Bribery of Police Officers or other Law Enforcement Officers

Section 120 of the Criminal Code creates offences similar to those outlined in section 119, but in relation to a different group of public officers: police officers, justices, and others involved in the administration of criminal law.

Elements of the Offence: As in section 119, the offence can be committed in two general ways. First, the accused must be a justice, police commissioner, peace officer, public officer or officer of a juvenile court, or be employed in the administration of criminal law. The accused must corruptly accept or obtain, agree to accept, or attempt to obtain for himself or herself or any other person, any money, valuable consideration, office, place or employment.

The offence may also be committed where the accused corruptly gives or offers any money, valuable consideration, office, place or employment to a justice, police commissioner, peace officer, public officer or officer of a juvenile court, or a person employed in the administration of justice. There must be an intention that the person bribed will interfere with the administration of justice, procure or facilitate the commission of an offence or protect from detection or punishment a person who has committed or who intends to commit the offence. Importantly, the individual bribing the officer must know or believe the person accepting the bribe is in fact an officer, or the requisite intent is not made out.

Anyone committing this offence is guilty of an indictable offence and liable to imprisonment for a term not exceeding fourteen years.

Bribery/Corruption of Government Officials [Influence Peddling]

Section 121 of the Criminal Code outlines seven different offences relating to fraud on the government, each briefly discussed below. The commission of any of these offences is an indictable offence punishable by imprisonment for a term not exceeding five years. Care must be taken in interpreting whether section 121 includes municipal corruption, since section 118 states that "government" means federal or provincial government, and therefore does not include municipal governments. However, the definitions of "office" and "official" have been interpreted widely to include municipal offices and officials. In any event, section 123 criminalizes municipal corruption.

Giving or Accepting a Benefit

Section 121(1)(a) provides that it is an offence for a government official63 to demand, accept, or offer to accept from any person a loan, reward, advantage or benefit of any kind as consideration in respect to the government official's duties.64 It also creates a reciprocal offence where a person gives, offers or agrees to give or offer to an official or any member of the official's family, or to anyone for the benefit of the official, an item of the same description.

In either case, the action may be performed directly or indirectly, and must be done as consideration for cooperation, assistance, exercise of influence, or an act or omission. This action must be in connection with the transaction of business with, or any other matter of business relating to, the government or a claim against Her Majesty or any other benefit that Her Majesty is entitled to bestow. It is legally irrelevant whether or not, in fact, the official is able to cooperate, render assistance, exercise influence or do or omit to do what is proposed, as the case may be. There is no requirement that the official be acting in their official capacity when contravening this section.

R v Cogger clarified the mens rea element of this offence: the accused must intentionally commit the prohibited act with knowledge of the circumstances that are necessary elements of the offence.

Where the accused is an official, they must be aware that they are an official; they must intentionally demand or accept a loan, reward, advantage or benefit of any kind for themself or another person; and they must know that the reward is in consideration for their cooperation, assistance or exercise of influence in connection with the business transaction or in relation to the government. However, it is irrelevant that accused did not know their act constituted a crime or that they did not intend to accept a bribe by their definition of that term. Furthermore, willful blindness is a sufficient substitute for knowledge.

Commissions or Rewards

Section 121(1)(b) of the Criminal Code provides that it is an offence for anyone having dealings of any kind with the government to pay a commission or reward to or confer an advantage or benefit of any kind with respect to those dealings on an employee or official of the government with which the accused deals, or any member of their family, or anyone whose involvement will benefit the employee or official. Although no mental element is specified, the jurisprudence suggests that the accused must intend to confer a benefit with respect to the dealings with the government. It is an offence if a gift is given for an ulterior purpose, even if no return is ultimately given and even if there is no acceptance by the official.

Officials and Employees

Pursuant to section 121(1)(c) of the Criminal Code, it is an offence for an official or employee of the government75 to demand, accept or offer or agree to accept a commission, reward, advantage or benefit76 from a person who has dealings with the government. This may be accomplished directly or indirectly by the accused, or through a member of the accused's family, or through anyone for the benefit of the accused.

Although no mental element is specified, R v Greenwood79 held that the offence is committed where the employee makes a conscious decision to accept a gift, knowing at the time of receipt that the giver has dealings with the government.

There is no requirement that the accused actually intended to exercise some undue influence in the giver's favour.

Influence Peddling/Pretending to Have Influence

Section 121(1)(d) of the Criminal Code relates to offers of influence in return for a benefit. In order to establish the elements of the offence, it must be shown that the accused had or pretended to have influence with the government or an official, and demanded, accepted or offered or agreed to accept a reward, advantage or benefit of any kind for himself or herself or another person. This acceptance must be in consideration for cooperation, assistance, exercise of influence or an act or omission in connection with the transaction of business with, or any matter of business relating to, the government, a claim against Her Majesty or any benefit that Her Majesty is authorized or is entitled to bestow, or the appointment of any person, including the accused, to office. No mental element is specified, but as a true crime, there is a presumption of mens rea which can be established by proof of intent, recklessness, or wilful blindness.

The Supreme Court of Canada in R v Giguere80 emphasized that this subsection is limited to persons who have (or pretend to have) a significant nexus with government. "Influence" involves being able to actually affect a decision (or pretending to be able to do so), such as influencing the awarding of a contract.

The element that "the transaction of business with or any matter of business relating to the government" was considered in R v Carson81 .... The accused, Carson, worked as a Senior Advisor to former Prime Minister Stephen Harper in the years 2006-2009. In 2010-2011, Carson attempted to influence the department of Indian and Northern Affairs Canada [INAC] to purchase water treatment products from a company called H20, in part to try to benefit a romantic partner. Carson admitted he had influence with the Government at the time of the alleged offence and used this influence to benefit his partner. Justice Warkentin found that INAC did not have power to purchase systems; that decision was left to individual First Nation communities. Therefore, the accused's conduct did not involve a matter of business relating to the government and the accused was acquitted. In a comment on the case, Steve Coughlan suggests, properly in my mind, that a conviction for attempting to commit the offence should have been entered instead.

A majority of the Court of Appeal set aside the acquittal and entered a verdict of guilty. The majority stated Section 121 (1) provides that it matters not "whether or not, in fact, the official is able to cooperate, render assistance, exercise influence, or do or omit to do what is proposed." Accepting a benefit in exchange for exercising influence on government officials in order "to push through their water treatment products to First Nation Bands" is a "matter of business related to the government."

On further appeal, a majority of the Supreme Court of Canada dismissed Mr. Carson's appeal, stating:

- In my view, the offence under s. 121(1)(d) requires that the promised influence be in fact connected to a matter of business that relates to government. Furthermore, a matter of business relates to the government if it depends on or could be facilitated by the government, given its mandate. The phrase "any matter of business relating to the government" therefore includes publicly funded commercial transactions for which the government could impose or amend terms and conditions that would favour one vendor over others. Governments are not static entities – legislation, policies, and structures delimiting the scope of government activity evolve constantly. "Any matter of business relating to the government" must not be considered strictly with reference to existing government operational and funding structures.

Providing Reward

Section 121(1)(e) of the Criminal Code provides that it is an offence for anyone to give, offer or agree to give or offer a reward, advantage or benefit of any kind to a minister of the government or an official in consideration for cooperation, assistance, exercise of influence or an act or omission. This conduct must be in connection with the transaction of business with, or any matter of business relating to, the government, a claim against Her Majesty or any benefit that Her Majesty is authorized or is entitled to bestow, or the appointment of any person, including the accused, to office. No mental element is specified, but the normal presumption that mens rea (intent, recklessness or wilful blindness) is required for a true crime should apply to this offence.

Tender of Contract

Section 121(1)(f) of the Criminal Code relates to tenders to obtain contracts with the government. The offence may be committed in two ways. First, it is an offence for anyone, having made a tender to obtain a contract with the government, to give, offer or agree to give or offer a reward, advantage or benefit of any kind to another person. That person must be someone who has made a tender, or a member of their family, or another person where that person's involvement will benefit someone who has made a tender. This must be done as consideration for the withdrawal of the other person's tender.

The offence is also committed where the accused demands, accepts, or offers or agrees to accept a reward, advantage or benefit of any kind from another person as consideration for the withdrawal of the accused's tender.

No mental element is specified for either way of committing the offence, but once again mens rea will be presumed.

Contractor with Government Contributing to an Election Campaign

Section 121(2) of the *Criminal Code* provides that it is an offence for anyone, in order to obtain or retain a contract with the government, or as a term of any such contract, whether express or implied, to directly or indirectly subscribe or give, or agree to subscribe or give, to any person valuable consideration for one of two purposes:

- promoting the election of a candidate or a class or party of candidates to Parliament or the legislature of a province; or
- to influence or affect in any way the result of an election conducted for the purpose of electing persons to serve in Parliament or the legislature of the province.

Consequently, the required mental element of the offence is to act with the purpose of effecting one of the two objectives listed above. If the accused acts pursuant to a term of a contract with the government, no further mental element is required. Otherwise, the accused must also act "in order to" obtain or retain a contract with the government.

Section 121(1)(f) and 121(2) are public procurement offences, but they do not appear to be used. Instead, public procurement offences are prosecuted as frauds under the Criminal Code or as bid-rigging under section 47 of the federal Competition Act.

Breach of Trust by Public Officer

Section 122 is specifically directed at fraud or breach of trust committed by public officials. It is punishable by a maximum of five years imprisonment. The term "official" is defined in section 118 and was interpreted in R v Sheets85 to include:

- ... a position of duty, trust or authority, esp. in the public service or in some corporation, society or the like' (cf. The New Century Dictionary) or 'a position to which certain duties are attached, esp. a place of trust, authority or service under constituted authority' (cf. The Shorter Oxford Dictionary).

The Supreme Court of Canada in R v Boulanger87 reviewed the common law authorities relating to misfeasance in public office in order to clarify the elements of the section 122 offence. Chief Justice McLachlin for the court concluded at para 58 that the Crown must prove the following elements:

1. The accused was an official;
2. The accused was acting in connection with the duties of his or her office;
3. The accused breached the standard of responsibility and conduct demanded of him or her by the nature of the office;

4. The conduct of the accused represented a serious and marked departure from the standards expected of an individual in the accused's position of public trust;
5. The accused acted with the intention to use his or her public office for a purpose other than the public good, for example, for a dishonest, partial, corrupt, or oppressive purpose.

The court's interpretation ultimately infuses section 122 with a subjective mens rea, adding that mere mistakes or errors of judgment do not suffice.

In R v Vandenbussche, (1979) 50 CCC (2d) 15, the Ontario Court of Justice held that a municipal officer, although performing his official duties in an appropriate manner, was guilty of breach of trust because he still accepted benefits and rewards for his work. Using the language in Boulanger, this would constitute a breach of the standard of responsibility required of the officer. As the court succinctly put it, "Need I elaborate further on the erosion of public trust which would ensue if the proper duties of a municipal official were offered for sale on the block in the marketplace?" In R v Ellis, 2013 ONCA 739, the Court upheld a conviction for breach of trust where an Immigration and Refugee Board adjudicator strongly implied that he would change his preliminary negative decision on the applicant's refugee status to a positive decision if she entered into an intimate relationship with him.

In R v Cosh, 2015 NSCA 76, the Court examined the meaning of "official", defined in section 118 within the context of section 122 of the Criminal Code. The accused worked as a paramedic for a private company that contracted its services with the government. After becoming addicted to narcotics, he stole morphine and falsified records to cover up his theft. He pled guilty to fraud, theft and unlawful possession of morphine but disputed the breach of trust charge. The Court held that as a paramedic employed by a private company, the accused was not an "official" within the meaning of sections 118 and 122 of the Criminal Code and upheld the accused's acquittal on this count.

Municipal Corruption

Section 123 of the Criminal Code creates two offences relating to municipal corruption, each of which will be discussed in turn. Both offences are indictable and subject to imprisonment for a term not exceeding five years.

Loan/Reward/Advantage accepted by Municipal Officer

Section 123(1) provides that it is an offence for a municipal official92 to demand, accept, or offer, or agree to accept, a loan, reward, advantage or benefit of any kind from any person. Conversely, it is an offence for anyone to give, offer, or agree to give or offer, a loan, reward, advantage or benefit to any kind of municipal official.

In either case, the act must be done as consideration for the official performing one of four acts:

- abstaining from voting at a meeting of the municipal council or a committee thereof;
- voting in favour of or against a measure, motion or resolution;
- aiding in procuring or preventing the adoption of a measure, motion or resolution; or
- performing or failing to perform an official act.

No mental element is specified, but mens rea will be presumed.

Influence a Municipal Officer

Section 123 of the Criminal Code provides that it is an offence to influence or attempt to influence a municipal official to perform one of the four acts listed above by:

- suppression of the truth, in the case of a person who is under a duty to disclose the truth;
- threats or deceit; or
- by any unlawful means.

No mental element is specified; therefore, subjective mens rea will be presumed (which includes intent, recklessness or willful blindness).

Selling or Purchasing a Public Office

Section 124 targets conduct that goes beyond purchasing the influence of an officer or municipal official, and instead seeks to purchase the "office" itself.95 The section criminalizes both the sale of an appointment or resignation from office or the receipt of a reward from such a sale, as well as the purchase or giving of a reward to secure such an appointment or resignation. This offence is punishable by a maximum of five years' imprisonment.

Influencing or Negotiating Appointments to Public Offices

Closely related to the above two offences is the offence of influencing or negotiating appointments to public offices. It involves the giving or receiving of bribes in order to cooperate, assist, exercise influence, solicit, recommend or negotiate with respect to the appointment or resignation of any person from office. It also prohibits keeping without lawful authority "a place for transacting or negotiating any business relating to (i) the filling of vacancies in offices, (ii) the sale or purchase of officers, or (iii) appointments to or resignations from offices."

The acts of the accused should include something of a corrupt nature, as discussed above.

The offence is punishable by indictment. If convicted, a person is liable to imprisonment for a maximum of 5 years.

Section 425.1 – Threats and Retaliations Against Employees

Section 425.1, enacted in 2004, makes it an offence for an employer or a person acting on behalf of an employer to "take a disciplinary measure against, demote, terminate or otherwise adversely affect the employment of an employee" who has provided or is going to provide information with respect to any offence committed or going to be committed by the employer (or an officer, employee, or corporate director of the employer). The information has to be reported or will be reported to a person whose duties include the enforcement of federal or provincial law. The purpose of the section is essentially to encourage employees to assist the state in the suppression of unlawful conduct and to protect employees who do report information about offences from being disciplined for doing so.

The offence is punishable by indictment with a maximum of five years' imprisonment or by summary conviction (punishable under section 787).

Offering or Accepting Secret Commissions

Section 426 of the Criminal Code under Part X dealing with "fraudulent transactions" makes it an offence [punishable by a maximum of 5 years imprisonment] for an agent or employee98 to corruptly (i.e. secretly) offer, give or accept a reward, advantage or benefit in respect to the affairs or business of his/her principal (the principal can be either a government or a private company or business). Thus this corruption offence can relate solely to the private sphere, with no government official involved. In that sense, it is sometimes referred to as private corruption as opposed to public corruption.

The elements of the offence are summarized in R v Kelly (1992), 73 CCC (3d) 385 (SCC), at p. 406 as follows:

- There are then three elements to the actus reus of the offence set out in 426(1)(a)(ii) as they apply to an accused agent/ taker with regard to the acceptance of a commission:
  - the existence of an agency relationship;
  - the accepting by an agent of a benefit as consideration for doing or forbearing to do any act in relation to the affairs of the agent's principal, and
  - the failure by the agent to make adequate and timely disclosure of the source, amount and nature of the benefit.

The requisite mens rea must be established for each element of the actus reus. Pursuant to s. 426(1)(a)(ii), an accused agent/ taker:

- must be aware of the agency relationship;
- must knowingly accept the benefit as consideration for an act to be undertaken in relation to the affairs of the principal, and
- must be aware of the extent of the disclosure to the principal or lack thereof.

If the accused was aware that some disclosure was made then it will be for the court to determine whether, in all the circumstances of the particular case, it was in fact adequate and timely.

The word "corruptly" in the context of secret commissions means "secretly" or "without the requisite disclosure". There is no "corrupt bargain" requirement. Thus, it is possible to convict a taker of a reward or benefit despite the innocence of the giver of the reward or benefit. Non-disclosure will be established for the purposes of the section if the Crown demonstrates that adequate and timely disclosure of the source, amount and nature of the benefit has not been made by the agent to the principal.

The offence is made out by the acceptance of the benefit; that acceptance need not actually influence the agent in the manner he or she conducted affairs with the principal. The offence is established where the agent has, by accepting the benefit in secret, placed his or herself in a position of a conflict of interest, without informing the principal.99 Furthermore, the agent need not actually have a specific principal at the time the offer was made.

Section 426(2) elaborates that "every one commits an offence who is knowingly privy to the commission of an offence under subsection (1)". As the British Columbia Court of Appeal pointed out in R v Tran, the word "privy" in section 462(2) criminalizes conduct by "persons who through their own acts, participate in the prohibited conduct".

END OF EXCERPT

Defences

An accused charged with one of the above mentioned bribery or corruption offences is entitled to the same general defences as persons charged with other offences. This includes mistake of fact, officially induced error, incapacity due to mental disorder, duress, necessity, entrapment, diplomatic immunity and res judicata.102 The scope and requirements of these defences can be found in a standard Canadian criminal law textbook.103

Limitation Periods

Where an offence is punishable by indictment in Canada, there is no limitation period. This also applies where the offence is a hybrid offence and the Crown chooses to proceed indictably. Where the offence is punishable on summary conviction, or the Crown chooses to proceed summarily, the information must be laid within 6 months of the date of the offence (see section 786 of the Criminal Code). All the corruption offences in the Criminal Code are classified as indictable offences (except 425.1), and therefore there are no limitations on when a charge for corruption/bribery may be laid. Once a charge is laid, the accused is entitled to a "trial within a reasonable time" under section 11(b) of the Canadian Charter of Rights and Freedoms. In R v Jordan, 2016 SCC 27, the Supreme Court of Canada established a new framework for s. 11(b) delay.104

Sanctions

The Criminal Code classifies offences as indictable (i.e., major offence) or summary conviction (i.e., less serious offence). All corruption offences in the Criminal Code are classified as indictable offences (except section 425.1, which can be indictable or summary conviction at the prosecution's discretion). Indictable offences are further classified into varying degrees of seriousness based upon the maximum punishment available for each offence (life, 14, 10, 5 or 2 years imprisonment). The maximum punishment is set at a very high level and is designed to deal with the "worst imaginable case" for that type of offence. The Criminal Code does not include any minimum punishment for corruption offences, nor does it indicate an average or common punishment for the particular offence involved. Thus individual judges have a lot of discretion in determining an appropriate penalty for each case.

For a description of sentencing principles and practices applicable to corruption offences, see Chapter 7, Section 6 of this book.

BRIBERY OF FOREIGN PUBLIC OFFICIALS

UNCAC

Offences

Article 16 of UNCAC requires each State Party to create a criminal offence in respect to bribery of foreign public officials. Article 16 states:

Article 16. Bribery of foreign public officials and officials of public international organizations

1. Each State Party shall adopt such legislative and other measures as may be necessary to establish as a criminal offence, when committed intentionally, the promise, offering or giving to a foreign public official or an official of a public international organization, directly or indirectly, of an undue advantage, for the official himself or herself or another person or entity, in order that the official act or refrain from acting in the exercise of his

or her official duties, in order to obtain or retain business or other undue advantage in relation to the conduct of international business.

2. Each State Party shall consider adopting such legislative and other measures as may be necessary to establish as a criminal offence, when committed intentionally, the solicitation or acceptance by a foreign public official or an official of a public international organization, directly or indirectly, of an undue advantage, for the official himself or herself or another person or entity, in order that the official act or refrain from acting in the exercise of his or her official duties.

Foreign Public Official

Like the definition provided for "public official," the meaning of "foreign public official" is broad and focuses on function and influence rather than official status. "Foreign pubic official" is defined in Article 2(b) as meaning: "any person holding a legislative, executive, administrative or judicial office of a foreign country, whether appointed or elected; and any person exercising a public function for a foreign country, including for a public agency or public enterprise."

Officials of IPOs

In addition to prohibiting bribery of foreign public officials, the bribery of officials of international public organizations is also prohibited. An "official of a public international organization" refers to international civil servants or other persons authorized to act on behalf of public international organizations (Article 2(c)). This would include organizations such as the World Bank or International Monetary Fund. Article 16(1) also applies to corruption in the context of international aid.

Active and Passive Bribery

While Article 16(1) requires criminalization of active bribery of foreign public officials, Article 16(2) only requires a State to consider criminalization of passive bribery (i.e., solicitation or acceptance of a bribe by foreign public officials). In other words, Article 16(2) does not require States to criminalize the corrupt behaviour of foreign public officials. Such conduct by foreign public officials is, or should be, a criminal offence of bribery under that public official's own state law, as required by Article 15(b) of UNCAC. However, a State's failure to enact legislation reflecting Article 16(2) would result in that State being unable to prosecute a foreign public official for passive bribery. For example, because Canada has not enacted provisions reflecting Article 16(2), Canada is unable to prosecute foreign public officials for soliciting or accepting bribes and can only prosecute Canadian legal entities for bribing foreign public officials. Prosecution of foreign public officials must be left, if at all, to the foreign public officials' State.

For Business or other Undue Advantage

Kubiciel notes another significant difference between Articles 15 and 16: namely, Article 16(1) only prohibits acts of bribery intended to "obtain or retain business or other undue advantage in relation to the conduct of international business." Article 15(a) and (b) has no similar clause. Similarly, Article 1 of the OECD Convention only requires State Parties to criminalize the offering or giving of bribes "in order to obtain or retain business or other improper advantage in the conduct of international business." For example, a Canadian citizen who bribes a police officer in Mexico to avoid being charged with drunk driving in Mexico is not subject to prosecution for bribing a foreign public official under Canada's CFPOA.

Undue Advantage

Kubiciel also highlights the vagueness of the term "undue advantage" which appears in both Articles 15 and 16 of UNCAC (as well as Article 1 of the OECD Anti-Bribery Convention). Kubiciel states:

> ◉ The interpretation of the term "undue advantage" is even more complicated when national courts and law enforcement agencies have to evaluate whether an advantage offered or granted abroad is undue or not. Generally speaking, courts can apply the standards of their own legal order, so that they are not bound to the perceptions abroad. Thus, local traditions or the tolerance by foreign authorities are no excuse per se for offering or giving advantages to foreign public officials or officials of international organizations. However, advantages whose acceptance is permitted or even required by the foreign law are not criminalized by Article 16. [Footnotes omitted]

Defences

The defences available for bribery of a foreign public official are the same as those for bribery of a domestic public official, already discussed at Section 2.1.2 above.

Limitation Periods

The limitation periods for bribery of a foreign public official are the same for bribery of a domestic public official, already discussed at Section 2.1.3 above.

Sanctions

The sanction provisions in UNCAC for foreign bribery are the same as the sanctions for domestic bribery, discussed at Section 2.1.4 above.

OECD Convention

Offences

Article 1(1) of the OECD Convention requires that state parties make it a criminal offence under domestic law for:

- Any person intentionally to offer, promise or give any undue pecuniary or other advantage, whether directly or through intermediaries, to a foreign public official, for that official or for a third party, in order that the official act or refrain from acting in relation to the performance of official duties, in order to obtain or retain business or other improper advantage in the conduct of international business.

Active but Not Passive Bribery

Like UNCAC, the OECD Convention requires state parties to criminalize active bribery, but not passive bribery, and also requires that the bribe be in relation to "the conduct of international business." The OECD Convention does not require states to consider the criminalization of passive bribery like Article 16(2) of UNCAC.

Liability for Accomplices, Attempts and Conspiracy

Article 1(2) mandates that "complicity in, including incitement, aiding and abetting, or authorisation of an act of bribery of a foreign public official shall be a criminal offence." The OECD Commentary clarifies that a foreign company that pays a bribe while bidding for a foreign contract is still committing the offence of bribery even if that company obtained the contract because they presented the best proposal rather than because of the bribe. In addition, Article 1 requires state parties to ensure that "[a]ttempt and conspiracy to bribe a foreign public official shall be criminal offences to the same extent as attempt and conspiracy to bribe a public official" is an offence domestically. Inchoate offences and party liability are further explored later in Sections 3 and 4 of Chapter 3.

Definitions of Foreign Public Official and Official Duties

Article 1 also sets out the following definitions (paragraph 4):

- "foreign public official" means any person holding a legislative, administrative or judicial office of a foreign country, whether appointed or elected; any person exercising a public function for a foreign country, including for a public agency or public enterprise; and any official or agent of a public international organisation;
- "foreign country" includes all levels and subdivisions of government, from national to local;
- "act or refrain from acting in relation to the performance of official duties" includes any use of the public official's position, whether or not within the official's authorized competence.

State Flexibility in Enacting OECD Convention Provisions

Pacini, Swingen and Rogers discuss the impact of the OECD Convention in their article "The Role of the OECD and EU Conventions in Combating Bribery of Foreign

Public Officials."107 They note that, unlike some earlier criminal law conventions, the OECD Convention is not "self-executing." This means that the prohibitions contained within the provision are not automatically part of domestic law. It is up to signatory nations to incorporate the elements of the prohibition of the bribery of foreign public officials into domestic law. The goal is "functional equivalency" (Commentaries on the Convention on Combating Bribery of Foreign Public Officials in International Business Transactions "OECD Commentary," para (2). In effect, Pacini et al. state that the Convention allows state parties "to pass legislation at different ends of a rather broad spectrum."

Defences

As already noted, Article 1 of the OECD Convention requires State Parties to the Convention to make it "a criminal offence for any person intentionally to offer, promise or give an undue pecuniary or other advantage... to a foreign public official... in order to obtain or retain... advantage in the conduct of international business." The Convention deals with "bribes" and leaves punishment of the foreign public official who requests or receives a bribe to the general corruption laws of the foreign state. Obviously failure to prove the elements of Article 1 constitutes a defence. The briber must (1) act "intentionally," (2) the person being bribed must meet the broad definition of "foreign public official" defined in Article 1, paragraph 4, (3) the "bribe" must constitute "an undue pecuniary or other advantage and the advantage must be offered "in the conduct of international business."

The Conduct of International Business

On its face, bribery by an NGO or a private company for charitable rather than business purposes may not be covered by Article 1. However, a brief on the OECD Convention (prepared by the OECD) notes that "bribes that benefit a foreign public official's family or political party, or another third party (e.g., a charity or company in which the official has an interest) – are also illegal."109 Any uncertainty around the scope of Article 1 does not of course prevent countries from prohibiting bribes to more effectively pursue charitable purposes. Several countries, such as Canada, the US and the UK have done so in their domestic law. Canada updated its CFPOA in 2013 to include the "charitable sector" (see Section 3.5.1 of this chapter). Previously, the word "business" was limited by section 2 of the CFPOA to for-profit endeavours. The post-2013 definition of "business" is not limited in this way and applies to bribery by NGOs and other non-profit organizations.

In the US, the provisions of the FCPA are broader than those set out in Article 1 of the OECD Convention. According to the FCPA guidance released by the US Department of Justice and Securities Exchange Commission, "[i]n general, the FCPA prohibits offering to pay, paying, promising to pay, or authorizing the payment of money or anything of value to a foreign official in order to influence any act or decision of the foreign official in his or her official capacity or to secure any other improper advantage in order to obtain or retain business."110 The Guide goes on to note that "[t]he FCPA does not prohibit charitable contributions or prevent corporations from acting as good corporate citizens. Companies, however, cannot

In the UK, the Bribery Act also provides a slightly more encompassing definition than that provided in Article 1 of the OECD Convention. Section 6 of the Bribery Act deals with bribery of foreign public officials. The person doing the bribing must intend to obtain or retain "business" or "an advantage in the conduct of business". This is quite similar to the wording used in Article 1 of the OECD Convention. However, under UK law the term "business" includes "what is done in the course of a trade or profession". This broad definition of business suggests that it may include the activities of a charitable organization or an NGO.

Further, in its Guidance document, the UK Ministry of Justice addresses the meaning of "carrying on a business" (in the context of section 7, which deals with the failure of commercial organizations to prevent bribery) as follows:

- As regards bodies incorporated, or partnerships formed, in the UK, despite the fact that there are many ways in which a body corporate or a partnership can pursue business objectives, the Government expects that whether such a body or partnership can be said to be carrying on a business will be answered by applying a common sense approach. So long as the organisation in question is incorporated (by whatever means), or is a partnership, it does not matter if it pursues primarily charitable or educational aims or purely public functions. It will be caught if it engages in commercial activities, irrespective of the purpose for which profits are made.

This excerpt suggests that charities and other NGO non-profit organizations are considered to be engaging in "business". If a charity is considered a "business" for the purpose of section 7 of the Act, it follows that the charity's activities are considered to be "business" for the purpose of section 6 of the Act, given the presumption of consistent usage of terms in legislation.

Undue Advantage

Article 1 also refers to "undue... advantage." Does the word "undue" permit facilitation payments? Facilitation payments are relatively small bribes paid to induce a foreign official to do something (such as issue a licence) that the official is already mandated to do. In order for a payment to be properly classified as a facilitation payment, "[t]he condition must be that these transfers really are of a minor nature not exceeding the social norm pertaining to them in the society in question."The OECD Convention does not clearly permit or forbid facilitation payments. The FCPA does not prohibit facilitation payments, but the UK Bribery Act does prohibit them. The 2013 amendments of the Canadian CFPOA also propose to prohibit facilitation payments, but the new provision was not proclaimed in force until October 31, 2017. The issue of facilitation payments is more fully analyzed in Section 4 of this chapter.

There are no special or specific defences under the OECD Convention for bribery of foreign public officials. The general assumption is that this offence will be subject to the same defences that apply to other such crimes in the State Party's criminal law.

Limitation Periods

Article 6 of the OECD Convention addresses statutes of limitations. It states:

- Any statute of limitations applicable to the offence of bribery of a foreign public official shall allow an adequate period of time for the investigation and prosecution of this offence.

The meaning of an "adequate" period of time is not clear. The OECD has not provided any further guidance to signatories regarding Article 6 in the Convention itself or in the Commentaries. There is some discussion of its meaning elsewhere.

The UK and Canada have no statutory limitation periods for their bribery and corruption offences. For a discussion of US statutory limitation periods, see Section 3.3.3 below.

Sanctions

The OECD Convention has very few provisions on sentences and sanctions for corruption of foreign public officials. Article 3 of the OECD Convention is entitled "Sanctions." Paragraph 1 requires bribery of foreign officials to "be punishable by effective, proportionate and dissuasive criminal penalties comparable to the penalties for corruption of domestic officials."

Paragraph 2 requires State Parties which do not recognize "corporate criminal liability" to ensure that legal persons are "subject to effective, proportionate and dissuasive non-criminal sanctions, including monetary sanctions for bribery of foreign public officials."

Paragraph 3 and 4 of Article 3 also provide as follows:

1. Each Party shall take such measures as may be necessary to provide that the bribe and the proceeds of the bribery of a foreign public official, or property the value of which corresponds to that of such proceeds, are subject to seizure and confiscation or that monetary sanctions of comparable effect are applicable.

2. Each Party shall consider the imposition of additional civil or administrative sanctions upon a person subject to sanctions for the bribery of a foreign public official.

US Law

The United States Foreign Corrupt Practices Act (FCPA) represents the first attempt by a State to criminalize the bribery of foreign public officials. First enacted in 1977, it is significant in scope and application and has led to numerous high profile prosecutions. The very broad jurisdictional reach of the FCPA will be analyzed in Chapter 3, Section 1.7. For now, suffice it to say, it applies not only to American citizens and corporations, but to all foreign corporations doing business (widely defined) in the US or traded on a US stock exchange. The FCPA has often served as a model for other countries wishing to implement similar legislation. It was amended in 1998 in order to conform to the requirements of the OECD Convention.

For an in-depth guide to the FCPA, see Tarun, The Foreign Corrupt Practices Handbook: A Practical Guide for Multinational General Counsel, Transactional Lawyers and White Collar Criminal Practitioners (Handbook); see also: A Resource Guide to the U.S. Foreign Corrupt Practices Act (Resource Guide) and Koehler, The Foreign Corrupt Practices Act in a New Era.

Offense of Bribing a Foreign Official

The following brief comments on § 78dd-1 are based on Tarun's Handbook and the Resource Guide (both cited above).

Provision

Section 78dd-1 of the FCPA prohibits the bribing of foreign officials or political parties. As highlighted in Tarun's Handbook, the FCPA's bribery offense contains five elements:

1. A payment, offer, authorization, or promise to pay money or anything of value, directly or through a third party;
2. To (a) any foreign official, (b) any foreign political party or party official, (c) any candidate for foreign political office, (d) any official of a public international organization, or (e) any other person while "knowing" that the payment or promise to pay will be passed on to one of the above;
3. Using an instrumentality of interstate commerce (such as telephone, telex, email, or the mail) by any person (whether US or foreign) or an act outside the United States by a domestic concern or US person, or an act in the United States by a foreign person in furtherance of the offer, payment, or promise to pay;

4. For the corrupt purpose of (a) influencing an official act or decision of that person, (b) inducing that person to do or omit doing any act in violation of his or her lawful duty, (c) securing an improper advantage, or (d) inducing that person to use his influence with a foreign government to affect or influence any government act or decision;
5. In order to assist the company in obtaining or retaining business for or with any person or directing business to any person.

It is important to note that the FCPA criminalizes active bribery (the person offering the bribe), but does not address passive bribery (the person receiving the bribe), and the scope of the offense is restricted to bribes made for the purpose of "obtaining or retaining business," which parallels the provisions of UNCAC and the OECD Convention. The FCPA also does not criminalize commercial bribery, although accounting offenses may catch commercial bribery. Deferred prosecution agreements also might require companies to refrain from commercial bribery.

Authorization

Authorization can be explicit or implicit. In some circumstances, acquiescence might be sufficient to indicate authorization.

Anything of Value

The phrase "anything of value" is interpreted broadly by the SEC and includes both tangible and intangible benefits. The thing of value will often be less direct than cash. There is no minimum threshold amount, but the SEC will generally only target small payments or gifts if they form part of a larger pattern of bribery.

Foreign Official

Under the FCPA, "foreign official" is defined as an officer or employee of "a foreign government or any department, agency or instrumentality thereof, or of a public international organization," or any person working for or on behalf of any of those entities. Foreign governments are not included in the provisions. As a result, when the Iraqi government received kickbacks during the UN Oil-for-Food program, the DOJ was obliged to turn to the accounting offenses to charge the companies involved.

According to Koehler in his book, The Foreign Corrupt Practices Act in a New Era, the definition of "foreign official" is in dispute, but enforcement agencies tend to interpret the phrase broadly.123 This means that "FCPA scrutiny can arise from business interactions with a variety of individuals, not just bona fide foreign government officials."124 According to Deming, "[a] critical factor in determining whether someone is a foreign public official is whether the individual occupies a position of public trust with official responsibilities."

Whether a state-owned enterprise is an "instrumentality" is particularly open to dispute. According to the Resource Guide, to determine whether an entity is an "instrumentality," an entity's ownership, control, status and function should be considered. Generally, an entity will not be included in the definition of "instrumentality" if foreign government ownership is less than 50%, unless the government has special shareholder status.

Public international organizations include the World Bank, International Monetary Fund, World Trade Organization, OECD, Red Cross and African Union.

Knowledge

Payments or offers cannot be made through third parties if the defendant knows the payment or offer will be passed on as a bribe. Actual knowledge is not required. Although carelessness or foolishness is not sufficient, knowledge includes wilful blindness towards or awareness of a high probability that the payment will be used to bribe a foreign official. This means companies must be alert to "red flags," such as close relations between a third party and a foreign public official or a request by the third party to make payments to offshore bank accounts.

Application

The anti-bribery provisions of the FCPA apply to three categories of legal entities and all officers, directors, employees, agents and shareholders thereof:

- "issuers": any company listed on a US stock exchange
- "domestic concerns": any citizen, national, or resident of the US or any company that is organized under the laws of the US
- "persons or entities acting within the territory of the US": any foreign national or non-issuer who engages in any act in furtherance of corruption while in the territory of the US.

As already noted, the jurisdictional reach of the FCPA will be dealt with in greater depth in Section 1.7 of Chapter 3.

Business Purpose Test

For a bribe to constitute an offence under the FCPA, the prosecution must show that the defendant bribed a foreign official intending the official to act in a manner which would assist the defendant in "obtaining or retaining business." Though this wording appears restrictive on its face, US courts have given a broad interpretation to "obtaining and retaining." For example, in US v. Kay (2004), the Fifth Circuit Court of Appeals held that bribes paid to obtain favorable tax treatment—which reduced a company's customs duties and sales taxes on imports—could constitute "obtaining and retaining business" within the meaning of the FCPA.130 The court ruled that avoidance of taxes can provide a company with an improper advantage over its competitors, which necessarily allows the company a greater probability of obtaining and retaining business.

Bribes in the conduct of business or to gain a business advantage also satisfy the business purpose test. Other examples of prohibited actions include bribe payments to reduce or eliminate customs duties, to obtain government action to prevent competitors from entering a market, to influence the adjudication of lawsuits or enforcement actions, or to circumvent a licensing or permit requirement. As the Resource Guide puts it:

In short, while the FCPA does not cover every type of bribe paid around the world for every purpose, it does apply broadly to bribes paid to help obtain or retain business, which can include payments made to secure a wide variety of unfair business advantages.

It should also be noted that UNCAC has expanded the definition of "international business" to include the provision of international aid. This means that nonprofit organizations "should be presumed to be fully subject to the anti-bribery provisions."

Corrupt and Willful Intent

To violate the FCPA, a bribe must be made "corruptly," which focuses on the intention of the defendant; there must be an "evil motive" or intent to wrongfully influence the recipient. Under the FCPA, it is not necessary that a bribe succeed in its purpose (i.e., actually influence a foreign official to act corruptly). If the prosecution can prove that the defendant intended to induce the foreign official to misuse his or her position of power, then the burden of proof is met, regardless of the foreign official's actual conduct or the effect on the defendant's business. Practically speaking, however, even though there is no legal requirement that the defendant benefit from the corrupt bribe, the DOJ is less likely to take enforcement action where the defendant has not personally benefitted.

The prosecution must also prove that the defendant acted "willfully." This is generally construed by courts to mean an act committed "deliberately and with the intent to do something that the law forbids, that is, with a bad purpose to disobey or disregard the law." It is not necessary that the defendant knew the specific law that he or she was breaking (i.e., that their conduct violated the FCPA), but merely that the defendant knew that his or her actions were unlawful. It should be noted, however, that proof of willfulness is not required to establish corporate or civil liability.

Intent is often a difficult element for the prosecution to prove beyond a reasonable doubt in relation to bribery offences. Tarun points out that the search for intent "will frequently turn on the transparency of a payment or relationship, direct or indirect, with a foreign government official. While some transactions or relationships will be fully concealed and thus likely corroborative of a corrupt plan or scheme, others will reveal a confounding mixture of visibility and secrecy that can defeat a conclusion of evil motive beyond a reasonable doubt." Tarun also notes that related accounting offenses are often "telltale" indications of corrupt intent.

Gifts, Entertainment and Charitable Contributions

Gifts are often used to foster cordial business relationships and promote products, especially in countries where gift-giving is culturally mandated, such as China. If a gift is given with no corrupt intent, the FCPA will not apply. However, gifts and charitable donations often disguise bribes and the line between proper and improper gifts is fuzzy, creating a compliance minefield for companies. The Resource Guide states that larger, more extravagant gifts are more likely to indicate corrupt motives, although small gifts might be part of a larger pattern of bribery. For example, in SEC v Veraz Networks, Inc (2010), the SEC settled with Veraz for violations relating to improper gifts. According to Tarun, "[t]he Veraz gift allegations – down to the detail of giving flowers for an executive's wife – represent an extreme SEC charging example and would not by themselves have likely resulted in an enforcement action. Still, the case demonstrates that the SEC will charge even minor gift abuses if they are part of a scheme."138 Not everyone agrees with the SEC and DOJ's line- drawing; for example, the recent decision to fine BHP Billiton $25 million for hosting foreign officials at the 2008 Olympics, despite the absence of evidence of any specific quid pro quo, has been criticized for going too far.

According to the Resource Guide, the "hallmarks of appropriate gift-giving" are transparency, proper recording, a purpose of showing esteem or gratitude and permissibility under local law. The DOJ has approved charitable donations, but will consider whether companies carry out proper due diligence and implement control measures to ensure that donations are unrelated to business purposes and used properly.

Defenses

In 1988, Congress added two affirmative defenses to the FCPA. In order to defend against a charge of foreign bribery, the defendant must prove either that:

- the payment was lawful under the written laws of the foreign country, or
- the payment was a reasonable and bona fide expenditure, such as travel and lodging expenses, incurred by a foreign official and was directly related either to
    - the promotion, demonstration or explanation of products or services, or (ii) the execution or performance of a contract (for example, this

could include travel and expenses incurred for training or meetings, or to visit company facilities or operations).

The fact that an act would not be prosecuted in a foreign country is not enough to invoke the local law defense. The payment itself must be lawful under foreign law. Because no foreign countries permit bribery in their written laws, the local law defense is "largely meaningless," according to Koehler.143 However, Tarun points out that the defense could be useful in the context of political campaign contributions.

The reasonable and bona fide expenditure defense can absolve a company of liability for providing gifts, travel, hospitality and entertainment for foreign officials. However, if carried too far, these expenditures can become improper and lead to FCPA scrutiny. For example, the defense will not cover side trips to tourist destinations with the sole purpose of personal entertainment.

In addition, situations of extortion or duress afford a defense by negating "corrupt intent." That being said, "economic coercion" does not amount to extortion. In other words, the argument that the bribe was required in order to gain entry into the market or to obtain a contract will fail – see United States v Kozeny. In addition, if extortion payments are not recorded properly, the SEC may pursue accounting offenses.146 See Tarun for a list of potential defenses to bribery and accounting offenses under the FCPA.147 See also the discussion of other criminal law defenses in Section 2.3.2.

The case of James Giffen provides an example of a unique defense, nick-named the "spy defense." Giffen was charged with violating the FCPA after he allegedly used $84 million from US oil companies to bribe Kazakhstan's president and various officials. However, the prosecution failed. Giffen claimed he was an informant for the CIA and argued that the US government was supporting his actions all along. The court agreed, and New York judge William Pauley called Giffen a "hero" for advancing US strategic interests in Central Asia.

Limitation Periods for Bribery of a Foreign Official

According to the Resource Guide, the FCPA does not specify a statute of limitations and accordingly the general five-year limitation period set out in 18 USC § 3282 ("Offences not capital") applies.

However, as the Resource Guide points out, there are several ways to extend the limitation period. For example, if the case is one of conspiracy, the prosecution need only prove that one act in furtherance of the conspiracy occurred during the limitations period. Thus, the prosecution may be able to "reach" bribery or accounting offenses occurring prior to the five year limitation if the offenses contributed to the conspiracy.

The limitation period can also be extended if the company or individual is cooperative and enters into a tolling agreement that voluntarily extends the limitation (i.e., waives the right to claim the litigation should be dismissed due to expiration of the limitation period). Koehler points out that, in practice, enforcement actions against corporations usually involve conduct outside the scope of the limitations period, since corporations are given the choice of extending the limitation or being charged by the DOJ. Koehler criticizes this tactic, pointing out that enforcement agencies face no time pressure, which means "the gray cloud of FCPA scrutiny often hangs over a company far too long."

Finally, if the government is seeking evidence from foreign countries, the prosecutor may apply for a court order suspending the statute of limitations for up to three years.

Sanctions

For violation of the anti-bribery provisions, corporations and other business entities are liable to a fine of up to $2 million while individuals (including officers, directors, stockholders and agents of companies) are subject to a fine of up to $100,000 and imprisonment for a maximum of 5 years.

However, the Alternative Fines Act 18 USC § 3571(d) provides for the imposition of higher fines at the court's discretion. The increased fine can be up to twice the benefit that the defendant obtained in making the bribe. The same Act specifies that the maximum fine for an individual charged under the FCPA is $250,000 (see § 3571(e)). Actual penalties are determined by reference to the US Sentencing Guidelines (§ 1A1.1 (2011). Chapter 7, Section 4 contains a detailed discussion of US sentencing practices.

Facilitation Payments

The FCPA contains a narrow exemption in § 78dd-1(b) for "facilitating or expediting payment[s]... made in furtherance of a 'routine governmental action' that involves non- discretionary acts. According to the Resource Guide, such governmental actions could include processing visas, providing police protection and mail service and the supply of utilities. It would not include such actions as the decision to award or continue business with a party, or any act within the official's discretion that would constitute the misuse of the official's office. The general focus is on the purpose of the payment rather than its value. The Resource Guide recommends companies discourage facilitating payments despite their legality under the FCPA, since they may still violate local laws in the country where the company is operating, and other countries' foreign bribery laws may not contain a similar exception (such as the UK). As a result, American individuals and companies may find they still face sanctions in other countries despite the FCPA's facilitation payment exception.

Finally, facilitation payments must be properly recorded in the issuer's books and records. A discussion of the FCPA's facilitation payments exemption and its pros and cons is provided in Section 4.

UK Law

For a detailed analysis of the UK Bribery Act offences see: Nicholls et al, Corruption and Misuse of Public Office.152 For a comparison of the FCPA and the UK Bribery Act, see: Nicholas Cropp, "The Bribery Act 2010: (4) A Comparison with the FCPA: Nuance v Nous" [2011] Crim L Rev 122.

Offences

As noted above in Section 2.4.2, the UK Bribery Act addresses both foreign and domestic bribery and applies to individuals and other legal entities. In addition to its general anti- bribery prohibitions, the Bribery Act also contains a discrete offence in section 6 that applies to bribery of foreign public officials. The reach of sections 1, 2 and 7 is very broad, subject only to jurisdictional constraints. As a result, it is difficult to envisage conduct falling within the foreign bribery offence that would not already be covered by the other offences. Sullivan posits that the primary role for the offence of bribing foreign public officials is to "flag clearly that the United Kingdom is compliant with its treaty obligations to combat the bribery of public officials."

Section 6 criminalizes the giving or promising of an advantage to a foreign public official in order to gain or retain business or a business advantage. Importantly, the offence only covers "active bribery" and not the acceptance of bribes. The briber must know the receiver is a public official and must intend to influence the official in the performance of his or her functions as a public official. Unlike section 1, the briber need not intend to influence the recipient to act improperly. This is very different from the FCPA, which requires corrupt intent. Under section 6, the intention to influence the foreign official in and of itself makes out the offence, regardless of whether the briber knows their conduct is improper or unlawful. This means that a reasonable belief in a legal obligation to confer an advantage does not provide a defence.154 Cropp criticizes this minimal mens rea requirement and illustrates its absurdity by describing trivial, de minimis scenarios that meet all the requirements of a section 6 offence. Although the Director of Public Prosecutions and the SFO are unlikely to allow prosecution of such de minimis allegations, Cropp argues that prosecutorial discretion should not be the only check on "overbreadth of application." According to Cropp, businesses should not have to depend on the whims of the prosecutor to avoid liability, but rather should be able to determine what conduct will result in prosecution from the Act itself. He further notes that this "unusual reliance on official discretion ... raises serious concerns about the extent to which the Act will be applied consistently and transparently."

A bribe can be made directly or through a third party, and can be received by the foreign public official or by another person at the official's request or with their assent. Because the official must have assented or acquiesced to the bribe, section 6 captures less peripheral and preliminary conduct than the FCPA. Instead, the UK regime relies on inchoate offences to capture such conduct.

"Foreign public officials" are defined in subsection (5) as individuals who hold legislative, administrative, or judicial positions, as well as individuals who are not part of government, but still exercise a public function on behalf of a country, public enterprise or international organization. The definition does not include political parties or political candidates.

Corporate hospitality presents a challenge for companies trying to comply with the foreign bribery provisions, especially in light of the absence of a corrupt intent requirement in section 6. Corporate hospitality is a legitimate part of doing business, but can easily cross the line to bribery. The Ministry of Justice Guidance states that the Bribery Act does not intend to criminalize "[b]ona fide hospitality and promotional, or other business expenditure which seeks to improve the image of a commercial organization, better to present products and services or to establish cordial relations." The Guidance also states that "some reasonable hospitality for the individual and his or her partner, such as fine dining and attendance at a baseball match" are unlikely to trigger section 6. According to the Guidance, the more lavish the expenditure, the stronger the inference that the expenditure is intended to influence the official.

Defences

If the foreign public official is permitted or required by the written law applicable to that official to be influenced by an offer, promise, or gift, then the offence is not made out (see section 6(3)(b)). The official must be specifically entitled to accept the payment or offer; the silence of local law on the matter is not sufficient to ground the defence. Section 6(7) addresses this defence in more detail. It clarifies that where the public official's relevant function would be subject to the law of the UK, the law of the UK is applicable. If the performance of the official's actions would not be subjected to UK law, the written law is either the rules of the organization or the law of the country or territory for which the foreign public official is acting (including constitutional or legislative laws as well as published judicial decisions).

The Bribery Act 2010 contains no other specific defences. For a discussion of general criminal law defences, see Section 2.4.3 above.

Limitation Periods

As described in Section 2.4.4, the UK Bribery Act is not subject to any limitation periods.

Sanctions

The applicable penalties have already been discussed above at Section 2.4.5 under domestic bribery.

Facilitation Payments

The UK Bribery Act, unlike the American FCPA, does not provide an exemption for facilitation payments. However the Joint Prosecution Guidance of the Director of the Serious Fraud Office and the Director of Public Prosecutions state that whether it is in the public interest to prosecute for bribery in the case of facilitation payments will depend on a number of factors set out in the Joint Prosecution Guidance. The pros and cons of exempting facilitation payments from the scope of bribery offences is examined in some detail in Section 4 of this chapter.

Canadian Law

Offences

The Corruption of Foreign Public Officials Act (CFPOA) came into force in 1999 in order to meet Canada's obligations under the OECD Anti-Bribery Convention. Section 3(1) of the CFPOA states:

- Every person commits an offence who, in order to obtain or retain an advantage in the course of business, directly or through a third party gives, offers or agrees to give or offer a loan, reward, advantage or benefit of any kind to a foreign public official or to any person for the benefit of a foreign public official

1. as consideration for an act or omission by the official in connection with the performance of the official's duties or functions; or
2. to induce the official to use his or her position to influence any acts or decisions of the foreign state or public international organization for which the official performs duties or functions.

As pointed out by Deming, the inclusion of the words "in order to obtain or retain an advantage" indicates a quid pro quo element.160 Since no particular mens rea is specified for this crime, Canadian law presumes that the necessary mental element is subjective. There is nothing in the context of this offence to displace that presumption. Proof of negligence will not be enough; to be held liable the accused person must have committed the offence with the intention of doing so or with recklessness or willful blindness to the facts. The definition of "person" in the Criminal Code also applies to the bribery offences in section 3 of the CFPOA, by reason of section 34(2) of the Interpretation Act. The definition of "person" in section 2 of the Criminal Code includes both individuals and other organizations, including corporations.

In R v Niko Resources Ltd (2011), the court demonstrated that gifts of significant value are liable to be considered a "reward, advantage or benefit" under the CFPOA.162 Niko, an oil and gas company, gave the Bangladeshi Minister for Energy and Mineral Resources an expensive SUV and a trip to Calgary and New York in order to influence ongoing business dealings. The minister attended an oil and gas exposition in Calgary, but the trip to New York was purely to visit family. These benefits were provided after an explosion at one of Niko's gas wells in Bangladesh, which had caused bad press and legal problems for Niko. The court imposed a fine of almost $9.5 million, in spite of the relatively small value of the gifts in comparison to the size of the fine and Niko's cooperation during the investigation.

"Foreign public official" is defined in section 2 of the CFPOA as follows:

- a person who holds a legislative, administrative or judicial position of a foreign state;
- a person who performs public duties or functions for a foreign state, including a person employed by a board, commission, corporation or other body or authority that is established to perform a duty or function on behalf of the foreign state, or is performing such a duty or function; and
- an official or agent of a public international organization that is formed by two or more states or governments, or by two or more such public international organizations.

This definition does not include political party officials or political candidates.

In response to criticism from a number of commentators as well as the OECD Working Group, Canada amended the CFPOA. Bill S-14, An Act to Amend the Corruption of Foreign Public Officials Act received royal assent and subsequently came into force in June, 2013. Previously, the word "business" was limited by section 2 of the CFPOA to for-profit endeavours. This has since been replaced by a definition of "business" that is not limited in this way. Thus it also applies to bribery by NGO's and other non-profit organizations, although according to Norm Keith, RCMP investigations remain focused on for-profit businesses.164 In addition, the jurisdictional provisions under the former CFPOA were amended in 2013 and the CFPOA now applies to the acts of Canadian citizens, permanent residents and Canadian corporations while they are outside of Canadian territory. Previously, Canada's ability to prosecute those engaged in bribery of foreign officials was limited by the concept of "territoriality": in order for a person to be held liable under the CFPOA there had to be a real and substantial link between the acts which constituted the offence and Canada (discussed in detail in Chapter 3, Section 1.9). The 2013 amendments also establish accounting offences, which make it a crime to falsify accounting records for the purpose of facilitating or concealing the bribery of a foreign public official.

As noted by Deming, the secret commissions offence under section 426 of the Criminal Code may be used to supplement the CFPOA if Canada has territorial jurisdiction over the conduct at issue. The secret commissions offence covers any situation involving an agency relationship and is not limited to situations in which the recipient of a bribe is a public official. Section 426 could therefore be useful when dealing with recipients who do not meet the definition of a foreign public official or when commercial bribery is at issue.

Defences

An accused charged with an offence under the CFPOA is entitled to the same general defences as persons charged with other offences. These include mistake of fact, incapacity due to mental disorder, duress, necessity, entrapment, diplomatic immunity and res judicata.

In addition, section 3(3) states that no person is guilty of an offence under section 3(1) where the loan, reward, advantage or benefit is "permitted or required under the laws of the foreign state or public international organization for which the foreign public official performs duties or functions." Further, no person will be guilty where the benefit was "made to pay the reasonable expenses incurred in good faith by or on behalf of the foreign public official" where those expenses "are directly related to the promotion, demonstration, or explanation of the person's products and services" or to "the execution or performance of a contract between the person and the foreign state for which the official performs duties or functions." According to Canada's 2013 Written Follow-Up to the OECD Phase 3 Report, the defence of "reasonable expenses incurred in good faith" has not yet been considered by any Canadian courts.

Keith pointed out the peculiarity of the wording of the defences in section 3(3). Both defences use the words "loan, reward, advantage or benefit," but Keith argues these words "tend to imply a potential questionable or even inappropriate payment to a foreign public official."166 Keith points out that providing "personal loans, special rewards, specified advantages or other benefits" to a foreign public official will rarely "appear ethical, lawful or permitted by the laws of a foreign government," and will rarely be appropriate as reimbursement for expenses incurred by the official. As a result, Keith argues that the wording of section 3(3) is difficult for businesses to interpret.

Limitation Periods

Because the offences in the CFPOA are punishable by indictment, there are no limitation periods in respect to laying a charge after an offence is alleged to have occurred. However, since there was no offence in Canada of bribing a foreign public official prior to the enactment of the CFPOA, there can be no prosecution of such conduct which occurred prior to 1999.

Sanctions

Bribing a foreign public official under section 3(1) is an indictable offence which was punishable by a maximum of 5 years imprisonment until amendments were enacted in 2013 raising the maximum penalty to 14 years imprisonment. The accounting offences under section 4 are also indictable and punishable by imprisonment for a maximum of 14 years.

Pursuant to recent Criminal Code amendments, conditional and absolute discharges or conditional sentences served in the community are no longer available sentencing options for any offence with a 14-year maximum penalty. Accused persons may also face forfeiture of the proceeds of CFPOA offences, and Public Works and Government Services Canada will not contract with businesses convicted under the CFPOA.[168] These and other consequences of a CFPOA conviction are dealt with in Chapter 7, Sections 7 to 10 of this book.

Facilitation Payments

As part of the 2013 amendments discussed above, facilitation payments, meaning those payments made to either ensure or expedite routine acts that form part of a foreign public official's official duties or functions, will no longer be exempt from liability under the CFPOA. This provision was proclaimed in force as of October 31, 2017. The pros and cons of facilitation payments are discussed in greater detail in Section 4, below.

FACILITATION PAYMENTS AND THE OFFENCE OF BRIBERY

Facilitation or "grease" payments are relatively small bribes paid to induce a foreign public official to do something (such as issue a licence) that the official is already mandated to do. As Nicholls et al. point out, "those facing demands for such payments often feel there is no practical alternative to acceding to them."[169] In almost every case the payment will be illegal in the public official's home state. Yet such payments are a routine way of life in most of the countries listed in the bottom half or quarter of the TI Corruption Perception Index. Some of the most developed nations do not prohibit their own nationals from making these payments to public officials elsewhere. Other nations prohibit facilitation payments, but make no effort to enforce that prohibition. There is significant disagreement among international players as to whether facilitation payments should be prohibited, although the current trend is towards their prohibition.[170] UNCAC and the OECD Convention do not expressly accept or reject exempting facilitation payments from the definition of offences of bribery.

Zerbes notes that in order for a payment to be properly classified as a facilitation payment, "[t]he condition must be that these transfers really are of a *minor nature not exceeding the social norm* pertaining to them in the society in question."[171] While some facilitation payment exemptions may be focused on payments of "a minor value," under the US *FCPA* the focus is on the purpose of the payment rather than its value (see Section 3.3.5 above). In addition, the payment must not be in exchange for a breach of duty or involve a discretionary decision; its purpose may only be for the inducement of a lawful act or decision on the part of the foreign public official that does not involve an exercise of discretion.

In her review of the ways in which Canada could improve its response to corruption of foreign public officials, Skinnider states the following in regard to facilitation payments:

- A review of States' practice appears to show that the tolerance for small bribes or facilitation payments is fading. Twenty years ago, when the OECD Convention was negotiated and countries passed relevant domestic legislation, such payments were common and even legal in many countries. However, now times have changed. There is no country anywhere with a written law permitting the bribery of its own officials. The only countries that permit facilitation payments to foreign public officials are the US, Canada, Australia, New Zealand and South Korea. The Australian government has recently proposed removing the facilitation payment defence. Australian lawyers support the government's plan to ban facilitation payments, saying the changes would bring the country into line with international best practices and address the 'weakest link' in the existing legislation". Many practitioners increasing believe that US authorities have simply read the exception for facilitation payments out of the statute. Others are calling for the US to repeal the exception. [footnotes omitted]

This section on facilitation payments begins by canvassing the major arguments for and against treating facilitation payments as bribes. Following this, the treatment of facilitation payments under the major international instruments as well as under US, UK and Canadian domestic law will be examined.

Arguments for and Against Facilitation Payments

Skinnider, in her paper Corruption in Canada: Reviewing Practices from Abroad to Improve Our Response, reviews the arguments for and against not treating facilitation payments as bribery as follows:

BEGINNING OF EXCERPT

Arguments to support eliminating the defence of facilitation payments

Every bribe of a government official, regardless of size, breaks the law of at least one country.174 A lack of resources, political will or interest has meant violations are rarely prosecuted, but that is changing. Permitting the citizens of one country to violate the laws of another corrodes international standards and marginalizes the global fight against corruption. It is also a double standard. The few countries that allow for facilitation payments to be made to foreign public officials prohibit their own officials from accepting them.

Companies are concerned that paying facilitation payments could lead to costly legal complications. [In countries where facilitation payments are permitted as an exception, s]ome describe it as a very limited and complicated defence and [one that] is frequently misunderstood, thus exposing businesses operating offshore to criminal liability in circumstances where they might genuinely believe they are acting lawfully. It also can make it difficult for companies to follow the laws in their domestic jurisdiction if they are required to record such payments that are illegal in the country where it is being made. Furthermore, with countries like the UK prohibiting facilitation payments, there is an increasing risk that a multinational company with foreign subsidiaries will violate the laws of the country where the subsidiary is based. Companies with offices in more than one country expressed concern that if they do not abolish the use of small bribes altogether, they must undertake different compliance programs based not only upon the location of each office, but the citizenship of the people working there. According to TRACE, many multinational companies are taking steps to eliminate "facilitation payments".

TRACE asks why governments are not following what is already the practice of many major companies.

Prior to the passing of the 2010 UK Bribery Act, the UK Law Commission Consultation Report listed a number of arguments against exempting facilitation payments:

- Inherent difficulties in determining when a payment crosses the line (does "routine" mean "frequently" or "commonplace").
- Blurs the distinction between legal and illegal payments and floodgates argument.
- Weakens the corporation's ability to implement its anti-bribery programme.
- Sends confusing messages to employees.
- Creates a "pyramid scheme of bribery."

Another argument supporting the prohibition of facilitation payments is the accounting dilemma. A business may be required to record a facilitation payment in its accounts by one jurisdiction, but this may then formalize an illegal act which, if concealed, may amount to tax evasion in another jurisdiction. It has been observed that often companies must opt between "falsifying their records in violation of their own laws or recording the payments accurately and documenting a violation of local law".

Facilitation payments can have a negative impact on society.186 Such payments can interfere with the proper administration of government, impede good governance and result in social unrest. This may even go as far as encouraging governments to fix their employees' salaries in expectation of these payments. Security concerns have also been raised. "If you pay government officials to manage differently, you shouldn't be surprised if criminals and terrorists are doing the same." If visas can be bought, borders won't be safe.

Arguments to support retaining the defence of facilitation payments

The most cited argument is that business will "lose out" to rival foreign companies that do ... make facilitation payments. They will experience competitive disadvantages because prohibiting facilitation payments will result in an uneven playing field. Such payments are seen as a necessary and acceptable part of business [in many parts of the world]. Since other jurisdictions permit such payments, to exclude them would be detrimental to businesses and competitive enterprise. Another argument is that the laws permit only payments that are minor in nature, so it is argued that they will have minimal detrimental consequences. In response to the argument that business will "lose out" to rival foreign companies that do not make facilitation payments, the UK Trade and Investment Department argues that "UK companies may lose some business by taking this approach, but equally there will be those who choose to do business with UK companies precisely because we have a no- bribery reputation, and the costs and style of doing business are more transparent." Research conducted by the World Bank demonstrated that in fact payment of bribes results in firms spending "more, not less, management time... negotiating regulations and facing higher, not lower, costs of capital". Further it may be more difficult then to resist subsequent demands for payment. A TRACE study revealed that none of the companies that approached the issue carefully and comprehensively reported significant or prolonged disruption in their business activities.

A concern has been raised that banning facilitation payments would prove impractical and ineffective. One scholar argues that in many cultures, payment for routine governmental action is a widespread practice, engrained within social norms and local mores. Inadequate wages abroad and foreign custom make such payments necessary. As he notes "it would be far better to have a provision that is workable and can be enforced, rather than have one which looks good on the statute books but is totally unenforceable".

END OF EXCERPT

Facilitation Payments and Culture

According to Strauss, the basic rationale for anti-bribery legislation is the belief that bribery is immoral.194 In her view, the essence of bribery is that it involves a payment for an advantage that one does not deserve. This violates the principle of equality, as it allows some persons to be treated preferentially and skip ahead of others in the same queue. However, some commentators have argued that this principle of equality is not universal. Or even if it is, in many cultures facilitation payments are not viewed as violating the principle of equality. There are some that argue that imposing a ban on the payment of facilitation payments by US (or UK or Canadian) corporations in foreign countries amounts to a form of cultural imperialism. Strauss argues, however, that since facilitation payments are illegal under the written domestic laws of most countries, the normative ideal in most countries around the world is to eliminate these types of payments. As well, Strauss characterizes the legislative objective of the FCPA as improving the ethical standards of American firms, and points out that the Act neither intends to nor imposes ethical standards on foreign nations.

Bailes reviews the cultural and practical arguments in favour of permitting facilitation payments. Ultimately, he concludes that the credibility of these arguments is diminishing as new approaches to combating bribery are gaining in acceptance and use. He argues that the distinction between bribes and facilitation payments is widely accepted as "hazy." There is growing awareness that facilitation payments are not so easily separated from bribery and its accompanying debilitating economic impacts on developing and corruption- rife nations. However, the artificial separation between facilitation payments and bribery has been institutionalized within many multinational corporations.197 Within these corporations, facilitation payments are viewed as a simple cost of doing business in non-Western cultures.

Unlike Strauss, Bailes does not dismiss the cultural arguments for permitting facilitation payments. The "cultural absolutism" argument suggests that it is wrong for multinational corporations and foreign states to impose western-centric views on corruption and facilitation payments on countries where these payments are embedded within local customs. He notes that "practical attempts by multinationals to develop and prescribe codes of ethics that prescribe how their employees behave are misguided and do fall into the trap of cultural absolutism."[198] Instead, Bailes suggests a more culturally sensitive approach that allows individual actors to make judgement calls based on the specific issue and context.

He acknowledges the practical difficulties faced by multinational corporations; in some cases, it may not be possible to operate in a certain location without paying facilitation payments. However, he concludes that evolving methods of curbing bribery, such as industry-wide associations that prohibit bribery, or campaigns focused on encouraging transparency and accountability in financial reporting, have the potential to assist in overcoming these practical hurdles. As pressure mounts on investors to "set the rules of the game with regard to social, economic and environmental issues such as bribery and corruption" the "first mover disadvantage"—the disadvantage faced by the first company to take a zero tolerance approach when there are other firms willing to step in and continue making facilitation payments—is disappearing.

As Robert Barrington, the Executive Director of Transparency International UK, puts it: "When a company pays a bribe of any size, it reinforces a culture of graft which is exceptionally damaging to the economies and societies in which they are paid."

THE ECONOMIC UTILITY OF FACILITATION PAYMENTS

The real economic utility of facilitation payments is also being increasingly questioned. According to Strauss, despite the views of some economists, facilitation payments are economically inefficient. These payments distort market forces and reduce economic growth by lowering both the volume and the efficiency of investment. As well, as a form of bribery, facilitation payments facilitate the abuse of public office for private gain. This damages the government's credibility with both its own citizens and foreign investors.

The contrary view is that facilitation payments can actually be economically efficient. Some commentators argue that facilitation payments permit firms to navigate more quickly through the unnecessary and time-consuming red tape that exists in certain highly bureaucratic states. However, Strauss notes that there is evidence that tolerance of facilitation payments creates incentives for bureaucrats to purposely create delays in order to increase the bribe prices firms are willing to pay.

Evidence from a study conducted by Kaufmann and Wei for the World Bank concluded that "there is no support for the 'efficient grease' hypothesis.202 In fact, a consistent pattern is that bribery and measures of official harassment are positively correlated across firms."203 "Official harassment" refers to "management time wasted with bureaucracy, regulatory burden, and cost of capital." Therefore, while a facilitation payment may initially appear enticing to a multinational firm, it is questionable whether such a payment makes economic sense in the long term.

In her discussion regarding the phasing out of the facilitation payments exemption from the US FCPA, Strauss discusses another argument against doing so: it would enable foreign corporations based in countries that do not prohibit facilitation payments to gain an advantage over American corporations. Strauss acknowledges the validity of this argument, although she notes that the reputational costs to a country that knowingly violates international anti-bribery agreements may mitigate this effect. For instance, in 2011, China passed new anti-bribery legislation that does not provide for a facilitation payment exception. But, to date, China has not prosecuted any foreign bribery cases, whether big or small.

Others argue that in certain situations, demands for facilitation payments are truly extortionate, and if corporations from countries barring facilitation payments are unable to comply they will be prevented from doing business in many countries. However, research conducted by TRACE International, a non-profit association that provides anti-bribery training and education to multinational corporations and their associates, suggests that this situation is rare. Strauss argues that allowing firms to acquiesce to these demands only increases the frequency and price of future demands. Ultimately, the only real solution is "a truly global anti-corruption regime in which companies that do not cave to extortionate bribe demands cannot be supplanted by those that do."205 Until such a regime is truly established and enforced, however, Strauss argues that any revision to the US facilitation payments exemption should recognize the difficulties firms face when confronted with truly extortionate demands.

UNCAC and OECD Convention

Facilitation Payments and the OECD Convention

The Convention does not prohibit "small facilitation payments." However, Paragraph 6(i) of the OECD's 2009 Recommendation of the Council for Further Combating Bribery of Foreign Public Officials in International Business Transactions states that, "in view of the corrosive effect of small facilitation payments," member countries should "undertake to periodically review their policies and approach on small facilitation payments in order to effectively combat the phenomenon."206 In addition, member countries should "encourage companies to prohibit or discourage the use of small facilitation payments in internal company controls, ethics and compliance programmes or measures, recognising that such payments are generally illegal in the countries where they are made, and must in all cases be accurately accounted for in such companies' books and financial records" (para 6(ii)).

Facilitation Payments and UNCAC

There is some question as to whether facilitation payments paid to foreign public officials are prohibited under UNCAC. Article 16(1) prohibits the promising, offering or giving of an "undue advantage" to a foreign public official "in order to obtain or retain business or other advantage in relation to the conduct of international business." The phrase "other advantage in relation to the conduct of international business" is ambiguous and could encompass the advantages garnered through making facilitation payments. Kubiciel addresses the issue of facilitation payments under the OECD Convention and UNCAC as follows:

- The Commentaries on the OECD Convention suggest that these payments do not constitute advantages made to obtain or retain business or other improper advantage and, therefore, are not a criminal offence under the OECD Convention. The reason for this exemption lies in the fact that the OECD Convention primarily tackles corruption as a distortion of free competition. As small facilitation payments do not impede free trade they are not covered by the ratio legis of the OECD Convention. States which follow the interpretation of the OECD may abstain from criminalizing cases in which grease payments are paid to hasten the completion of a non- discretionary routine action. However, the wording of the UNCAC does not require such a wide exemption from criminalization. Rather, the facilitation of proceedings can be conceived as an "other advantage in relation to the conduct of international business". More importantly, the aim of the UNCAC suggests a comprehensive penalization of bribery, including grease payments: Unlike the OECD Convention, the UNCAC does not focus on corruption as an obstacle for fair and free trade. Rather, the preamble of the UNCAC stresses "the seriousness of problems and threats posed by corruption to the stability and security of societies, undermining the institutions and values of democracy, ethical values and justice and jeopardizing sustainable development and the rule of law". As facilitation payments can be a first move in a game that leads to grand corruption and since all forms of bribery can, in the long run, affect institutions and legal values, states should, as a general rule, criminalize facilitation bribes.

Many organizations, such as the UK Serious Fraud Office, maintain that UNCAC is unequivocal in its prohibition of all corrupt payments, including facilitation payments. Skinnider also interprets UNCAC as prohibiting facilitation payments. Other scholars, however, interpret the failure of UNCAC to specifically address facilitation payments as a deliberate attempt to leave the decision on whether to criminalize facilitation payments up to signatory states. Brunelle-Quraishi suggests that the lack of a specific provision on facilitation payments leads to two possible conclusions:

- The first is that by refusing to acknowledge facilitation payments' legality, the UNCAC was inherently meant to leave a measure of discretion to the Member States. The second is that there was no consensus on the matter during negotiations and a broad definition of corruption was necessary in order to ensure that as many states as possible would adhere to the UNCAC.

Indeed, as will be discussed in further detail below, the US FCPA continues to include an exemption for facilitation payments while the UK's new Bribery Act prohibits them. Canada enacted legislation in 2013 criminalizing facilitation payments, but that provision was not proclaimed in force until October 31, 2017.

US Law

As noted above, the FCPA does not prohibit firms operating under its jurisdiction from making facilitation payments to foreign public officials. The prosecution has the burden of negating this exception. However, companies may still be liable under the FCPA's accounting provisions if they make facilitation payments but fail to properly record the payments as such. Firms are often unwilling to properly record facilitation payments as they are generally prohibited under the domestic legislation of the foreign public official's home state. The FCPA provides a more detailed description of what qualifies as a facilitation payment than the OECD Convention; however, interestingly, the FCPA does not specifically require that the payment be "small."

The facilitation payment exception under the FCPA has been called "illusory" by the SEC's former Assistant Director of Enforcement due to enforcement patterns:

[T]he fact that the FCPA's twin enforcement agencies have treated certain payments as prohibited despite their possible categorization as facilitating payments does not mean federal courts would agree. But because the vast majority of enforcement actions are resolved through DPAs [deferred prosecution agreements] and NPAs [non-prosecution agreements], and other settlement devices, these cases never make it to trial. As a result, the DOJ and the SEC's narrow interpretation of the facilitating payments exception is making that exception ever more illusory, regardless of whether the federal courts – or Congress – would agree.

The following excerpt from the FCPA's Resource Guide details the SEC and US DOJ's view on what type of payments qualify for the facilitation payments exemption:

BEGINNING OF EXCERPT

What Are Facilitating or Expediting Payments?

The FCPA's bribery prohibition contains a narrow exception for "facilitating or expediting payments" made in furtherance of routine governmental action. The facilitating payments exception applies only when a payment is made to further "routine governmental action" that involves non-discretionary acts. Examples of "routine governmental action" include processing visas, providing police protection or mail service, and supplying utilities like phone service, power, and water. Routine government action does not include a decision to award new business or to continue business with a particular party. Nor does it include acts that are within an official's discretion or that would constitute misuse of an official's office. Thus, paying an official a small amount to have the power turned on at a factory might be a facilitating payment; paying an inspector to ignore the fact that the company does not have a valid permit to operate the factory would not be a facilitating payment.

Examples of "Routine Governmental Action"

An action which is ordinarily and commonly performed by a foreign official in—

- obtaining permits, licenses, or other official documents to qualify a person to do business in a foreign country;
- processing governmental papers, such as visas and work orders;
- providing police protection, mail pickup and delivery, or scheduling inspections associated with contract performance or inspections related to transit of goods across country;
- providing phone service, power and water supply, loading and unloading cargo, or protecting perishable products or commodities from deterioration; or
- actions of a similar nature.

Whether a payment falls within the exception is not dependent on the size of the payment, though size can be telling, as a large payment is more suggestive of corrupt intent to influence a non-routine governmental action. But, like the FCPA's anti- bribery provisions more generally, the facilitating payments exception focuses on the purpose of the payment rather than its value. For instance, an Oklahoma-based corporation violated the FCPA when its subsidiary paid Argentine customs officials approximately $166,000 to secure customs clearance for equipment and materials that lacked required certifications or could not be imported under local law and to pay a lower-than-applicable duty rate. The company's Venezuelan subsidiary had also paid Venezuelan customs officials approximately $7,000 to permit the importation and exportation of equipment and materials not in compliance with local regulations and to avoid a full inspection of the imported goods. In another case, three subsidiaries of a global supplier of oil drilling products and services were criminally charged with authorizing an agent to make at least 378 corrupt payments (totaling approximately $2.1 million) to Nigerian Customs Service officials for preferential treatment during the customs process, including the reduction or elimination of customs duties.

Labeling a bribe as a "facilitating payment" in a company's books and records does not make it one. A Swiss offshore drilling company, for example, recorded payments to its customs agent in the subsidiary's "facilitating payment" account, even though company personnel believed the payments were, in fact, bribes. The company was charged with violating both the FCPA's anti-bribery and accounting provisions.

Although true facilitating payments are not illegal under the FCPA, they may still violate local law in the countries where the company is operating, and the OECD's Working Group on Bribery recommends that all countries encourage companies to prohibit or discourage facilitating payments, which the United States has done regularly. In addition, other countries' foreign bribery laws, such as the United Kingdom's, may not contain an exception for facilitating payments. Individuals and companies should therefore be aware that although true facilitating payments are permissible under the FCPA, they may still subject a company or individual to sanctions. As with any expenditure, facilitating payments may still violate the FCPA if they are not properly recorded in an issuer's books and records.

Hypothetical: Facilitating Payments

Company A is a large multi-national mining company with operations in Foreign Country, where it recently identified a significant new ore deposit. It has ready buyers for the new ore but has limited capacity to get it to market. In order to increase the size and speed of its ore export, Company A will need to build a new road from its facility to the port that can accommodate larger trucks. Company A retains an agent in Foreign Country to assist it in obtaining the required permits, including an environmental permit, to build the road. The agent informs Company A's vice president for international operations that he plans to make a one-time small cash payment to a clerk in the relevant government office to ensure that the clerk files and stamps the permit applications expeditiously, as the agent has experienced delays of three months when he has not made this "grease" payment. The clerk has no discretion about whether to file and stamp the permit applications once the requisite filing fee has been paid. The vice president authorizes the payment.

A few months later, the agent tells the vice president that he has run into a problem obtaining a necessary environmental permit. It turns out that the planned road construction would adversely impact an environmentally sensitive and protected local wetland. While the problem could be overcome by rerouting the road, such rerouting would cost Company A $1 million more and would slow down construction by six months. It would also increase the transit time for the ore and reduce the number of monthly shipments. The agent tells the vice president that he is good friends with the director of Foreign Country's Department of Natural Resources and that it would only take a modest cash payment to the director and the "problem would go away." The vice president authorizes the payment, and the agent makes it. After receiving the payment, the director issues the permit, and Company A constructs its new road through the wetlands.

Was the payment to the clerk a violation of the FCPA?

No. Under these circumstances, the payment to the clerk would qualify as a facilitating payment, since it is a one-time, small payment to obtain a routine, non-discretionary governmental service that Company A is entitled to receive (i.e., the stamping and filing of the permit application). However, while the payment may qualify as an exception to the FCPA's anti-bribery provisions, it may violate other laws, both in Foreign Country and elsewhere. In addition, if the payment is not accurately recorded, it could violate the FCPA's books and records provision.

Was the payment to the director a violation of the FCPA?

Yes. The payment to the director of the Department of Natural Resources was in clear violation of the FCPA, since it was designed to corruptly influence a foreign official into improperly approving a permit. The issuance of the environmental permit was a discretionary act, and indeed, Company A should not have received it. Company A, its vice president, and the local agent may all be prosecuted for authorizing and paying the bribe. [endnotes omitted]

END OF EXCERPT

Strauss argues that as other states intensify enforcement of domestic anti-bribery laws, it is becoming increasingly likely that American corporations will face criminal charges in foreign countries for offering or making facilitation payments. Strauss finds some merit in the argument that, as the chief enforcer of anti-bribery laws, the US must maintain the facilitation payment exemption to "bridge the gap between the aspirational norm of total intolerance for bribery, and the operational code in the field that actually determines how business gets done."212 However, Strauss concludes that precisely because the US is the predominant enforcer of anti-bribery legislation, "it is even more important that its laws actually align with the aspiration norm it wishes to achieve, or the gap between norm and practice will not narrow."

UK Law

The UK Bribery Act does not contain an exception for facilitation payments. Pursuant to section 6, a person will be found guilty of bribing a foreign public official if that person promises or gives any advantage to a foreign public official with the intention of influencing that person in his or her capacity as a foreign public official. To be convicted, the offender must also intend to obtain or retain business or "an advantage in the conduct of business" (section 6(2)).

In its *Guidance* document, the Ministry of Justice addresses facilitation payments as follows:

- Small bribes paid to facilitate routine Government action – otherwise called 'facilitation payments' – could trigger either the section 6 offence or, where there is an intention to induce improper conduct, including where the acceptance of such payments is itself improper, the section 1 offence and therefore potential liability under section .

As was the case under the old law, the Bribery Act does not (unlike US foreign bribery law) provide any exemption for such payments. The 2009 Recommendation of the Organisation for Economic Co-operation and Development recognises the corrosive effect of facilitation payments and asks adhering countries to discourage companies from making such payments. Exemptions in this context create artificial distinctions that are difficult to enforce, undermine corporate anti-bribery procedures, confuse anti-bribery communication with employees and other associated persons, perpetuate an existing 'culture' of bribery and have the potential to be abused.

The Government does, however, recognise the problems that commercial organisations face in some parts of the world and in certain sectors. The eradication of facilitation payments is recognised at the national and international level as a long term objective that will require economic and social progress and sustained commitment to the rule of law in those parts of the world where the problem is most prevalent. It will also require collaboration between international bodies, governments, the anti-bribery lobby, business representative bodies and sectoral organisations. Businesses themselves also have a role to play and the guidance below offers an indication of how the problem may be addressed through the selection of bribery prevention procedures by commercial organisations.

Issues relating to the prosecution of facilitation payments in England and Wales are referred to in the guidance of the Director of the Serious Fraud Office and the Director of Public Prosecutions.

Recognizing the practical difficulties potentially faced by UK businesses operating abroad, the Government reiterated the basic principles of UK prosecution policy, including the concept of proportionality (for example, it may not be in the public interest to prosecute where the payments made were very small) and stated that the outcome in any particular case will depend on the full circumstances of that case. Nicholls et al. describe the factors prosecutors are likely to consider when deciding whether to prosecute:

- The amount of the payment
- Whether the payment was a "one-off"
- Whether the payment was solicited and, if so, whether it resulted from duress or some lesser form of extortion
- The options facing the payer
- Whether the payment was reported to the police or a superior
- The likely penalty

The Joint Prosecution Guidance from the SFO and Ministry of Justice notes that "[f]acilitation payments that are planned for or accepted as part of a standard way of conducting business may indicate the offence was premeditated," which favours prosecution. On the other hand, if the payer was in a "vulnerable position arising from the circumstances in which the payment was demanded," this militates against prosecution.

Additionally, the common law defence of duress would likely apply where individuals are faced with no alternative but to make a payment to protect against loss of life, limb, or liberty. However, the defence has not been adapted or expanded to include non-physical pressure. On the other hand, the less well recognized defence of necessity in England has no similar restriction and might therefore be a viable defence.

Despite the prosecutorial policies in place and common law defences available, individuals and businesses making facilitation payments do legally face the risk of prosecution. In fact, in 2012, the Director of the SFO issued a letter reiterating in no uncertain terms that "[f]acilitation payments are illegal under the Bribery Act 2010 regardless of their size or frequency." Predictably, the prohibition of facilitation payments in the Bribery Act has received significant criticisms from the business community, many of whom fear that it will have a negative and chilling effect on small and medium-sized UK firms engaged in the export business. In May 2013, there were reports that the British government planned to review the Bribery Act and its position on facilitation payments specifically, but no changes have been made to date. Although organizations such as Transparency International UK remain firmly in support of a zero tolerance position towards facilitation payments, it is clear that the issue remains a divisive one.

Canadian Law

Section 3(2) of Bill S-14 (2013) eliminates the exception for facilitation payments that previously existed in the CFPOA. However, unlike the other amendments to the CFPOA prescribed in Bill S-14, section 3(2) did not come into force on the date the Bill received royal assent. It was finally proclaimed in force as of October 31, 2017. The former facilitation payment exemption reads as follows:

Facilitation payments

- For the purpose of subsection (1), a payment is not a loan, reward, advantage or benefit to obtain or retain an advantage in the course of business, if it is made to expedite or secure the performance by a foreign public official of any act of a routine nature that is part of the foreign public official's duties or functions, including
    - the issuance of a permit, licence or other document to qualify a person to do business;
    - the processing of official documents, such as visas and work permits;

- the provision of services normally offered to the public, such as mail pick-up and delivery, telecommunication services and power and water supply; and
- the provision of services normally provided as required, such as police protection, loading and unloading of cargo, the protection of perishable products or commodities from deterioration or the scheduling of inspections related to contract performance or transit of goods.

Greater certainty

◉ For greater certainty, an "act of a routine nature" does not include a decision to award new business or to continue business with a particular party, including a decision on the terms of that business, or encouraging another person to make any such decision.

Although Canada now has a "books and records" provision in the CFPOA, it is questionable whether it applies to facilitation payments which occurred prior to October 31, 2017 since facilitation payments remained lawful under the CFPOA until that date. Section 4 of the CFPOA criminalizes the actions of anyone who, "for the purpose of bribing a foreign public official in order to obtain or retain an advantage in the course of business or for the purpose of hiding that bribery," misrepresents bribe payments in books and records or takes other steps to misrepresent or hide illicit bribery payments. Since section 3(4) excludes facilitation payments from the ambit of benefits given in order "to obtain or retain an advantage in the course of business," it does not appear that section 4 would apply to a misrepresented or hidden facilitation payments made prior to October 31, 2017. Note that this is in contrast to the accounting provisions in the USA under their FCPA, which require accurate records be kept by issuers irrespective of what the payments are actually for.

Eliminating Facilitation Payments

Wynn-Williams argues that the removal of the facilitation payments exemption in the CFPOA puts charities "between a rock and a hard place."223 Wynn-Williams also claims that charities will be unable to fulfill their mandates if they are unable to make facilitation payments, since such payments are frequently demanded in countries where charities are attempting to deliver humanitarian aid. For example, if a charity is trying to deliver critically needed food or medication and timely delivery of the goods is dependent on a facilitation payment to a customs official, what is the charity to do? The trouble is largely with provisions of the Income Tax Act allowing the Canada Revenue Agency to revoke charitable status to organizations which are not abiding by Canadian law and public policy. This power operates independently of the criminal law and therefore revocation could occur whether or not the charity is successfully prosecuted under the CFPOA.

The author offers a number of potential solutions, including a governmental guidance advising against the prosecution of charities (as in the UK), a tying together of the CRA and criminal law such that revocation is only allowed upon conviction (so that charities might have the opportunity to argue necessity, for example), the assignment of an Ombudsperson from whom charities could seek guidance, or, most significantly, an exemption in the CFPOA for organizations delivering humanitarian aid.

Since the facilitation payments exemption has been removed from the CFPOA, charities will have to comply like any Canadian company. Recognizing the difficulties facing businesses and charities alike, in June 2014 Transparency International UK published a practical guide for companies entitled Countering Small Bribes: Principles and Good Practice Guidance for Dealing with Small Bribes including Facilitation Payments.224 The guidance contains, among other things, a set of ten basic principles for countering small bribes, a model of negotiation steps for resisting demands for bribes and practical examples and case studies.

In the following excerpt from Skinnider's paper Corruption in Canada: Reviewing Practices from Abroad to Improve Our Response, Skinnider reviews some measures Canada could adopt in order to discourage or prohibit Canadians from paying facilitation payments to public officials abroad.225

BEGINNING OF EXCERPT

Should Canada Prohibit Facilitation Payments?

As noted, although the Fighting Foreign Corruption Act226 provided for the elimination of the facilitation payments defence by repealing s. 3(4) of the CFPOA, this provision remains unproclaimed and thus Canada remains one of the few countries to continue to permit these payments. If the defence of facilitation payments is eliminated, one helpful suggestion that has been made is to incorporate a scaled penalty system for acts of lower-level bribery.227 Even without an express scaled-down penalty system, judges in Canada have a wide discretion to select a penalty for offences like bribery where no mandatory minimum penalty is specified. The general sentencing principles state that the penalty is to be "proportionate" to the nature and scope of the harm and to the culpability of the offender. These small facilitation payments would normally result in very small penalties if facilitation payments were criminalized.228 However, the high maximum penalty of 14 years imprisonment does eliminate the use of some sentencing options such as absolute and conditional discharges and conditional sentences. This elimination of these sentencing options for minor incidents of otherwise serious offences such as bribery occurred under the Conservative government's so-called "law and order" policy. Hopefully those laws will soon be repealed. Enacting a scaled-down version (e.g. a summary conviction offence of bribery) would also necessitate a consideration of whether automatic mandatory debarment from federal procurement contracts is suitable for conviction of small scale bribery offences.

Another alternative that falls short of a total prohibition on all facilitation payments is to amend the CFPOA to provide a clear definition of facilitation payments with a monetary threshold. An American commentator has reviewed the possibilities of amending the FCPA to clarify the facilitation payment exception.229 He argues for an amendment that refines the exception's current purpose-focused paradigm and adopts a complementary, regionally tailored monetary cap. According to his proposal, facilitation payments that fall below this monetary threshold will enjoy a rebuttable presumption of legality, while those in excess will presumptively stand outside the exception's shelter. This would allow corporations, prosecutors and courts a manageable and flexible standard to analyze these payments. US Congress has considered and rejected the imposition of a cap in the past. A concern raised regarding this proposal is that a cap would create an environment for abuse.

Ways to Discourage the Use of Facilitation Payments

If the government does not see it as practical to eliminate facilitation payments at this time, they should at least follow the OECD Guidance to "encourage companies to prohibit or discourage the use of small facilitation payments in internal company controls, ethics and compliance programmes or measures, recognising that such payments are illegal in the countries where they are made, and must in all cases be accurately accounted for in such companies' book and financial records".232

A "Books and Records" Provisions in the CFPOA

One way to address the concern of facilitation payments is through a "books and records" provision, an approach enacted into the CFPOA with the 2013 amendments. A company paying a bribe to a foreign public official must accurately record such a payment in its books, and if it does not, then the company violates a "books and records' provision. Representatives from Canadian business who were interviewed by the OECD Working Group noted that it is not uncommon for companies to make a payment to expedite or secure the performance of some act by a foreign public official and that "facilitation payments" are rarely recorded in corporate books and records.233 Accountants believe these are often not recorded (despite the defence) because of concerns by a company of criminal liability. Auditors also state that they do not pay close attention to "facilitation payments" when auditing a corporation because those payments usually do not materially affect the corporation's financial statements.

With the adoption of a "books and records" offence, the Canadian law now poses the same challenges that commentators have been describing regarding the

American system for years. That is, since almost every country outlaws facilitation payments under their respective domestic bribery laws, corporations are hesitant to properly record such payments as doing so essentially is tantamount to confessing to bribes in violation of a relevant foreign law. But failing to make the proper recording also violates a books and records provision.

"Publish What You Pay" Legislation

"Publish what you pay" legislation requires companies to disclose any payments made to a foreign government, including legal payments such as taxes and facilitation payments. The NGO Publish What You Pay, which advocates for increasing transparency in the extractive sector, suggests that because "companies and developed countries profit hugely from the global extractive sector, they have a responsibility to diminish the opportunities for corruption or mismanagement".

In the United States, such a requirement for the extractive industry was introduced as part of the Dodd-Frank Act following the 2008 global financial crisis.236 In the UK, Reports on Payments to Government Regulations 2014 came into force on December 1, 2014, and apply to any company or partnership that is either a large undertaking or a public interest entity (PIE), and is engaged in extractive industries (mining, oil and gas) or logging. The ESTMA, which came into force in Canada on June 1, 2015, applies to a corporation or a partnership that is engaged in the commercial development of oil, gas or minerals, and (1) is listed on a stock exchange in Canada or (2) has a place of business in Canada, does business in Canada or has assets in Canada and, based on its consolidated financial statements, meets at least two of the following conditions for at least one of its two most recent financial years: (a) it has at least $20 million in assets, (b) it has generated at least $40 million in revenue, and (c) it employs an average of at least 250 employees. The threshold for reporting single or multiple payments made by an entity to any government in Canada or in a foreign state is set at $100,000.

Promulgation of Guidelines Defining Permissible Facilitation Payments

The FCPA Resource Guide240 explains the US DOJ's and SEC's view on what type of payments qualify for this exemption. They are detailed and helpful [and are reproduced in Section 4.5 of this chapter].

The UK Ministry of Justice has addressed the facilitation payments issue241 [See Section 4.6 of this chapter]

...

The OECD Working Group recommended that Canada "consider issuing some form of guidance in the interpretation" of the defence as there is lack of clarity as to the threshold for facilitation payments and other bribes.242 However, Canada has noted its long standing practice not to issue guidelines on the interpretation of criminal law provisions. Courts are responsible for interpreting the application of the law in individual cases. But that principle does not preclude Parliament from amending the definition of facilitation by giving it a more precise definition or authorizing an agency to issue regulations in respect to the meaning or scope of facilitation payments.

Raise Awareness for Corporate Activism and Institutional Reform

Representatives from the business sector indicated that the government of Canada has not encouraged them to prohibit or discourage the use of facilitation payments.243 More and more companies are, however, introducing institutional reform. According to TRACE, increasingly companies are adopting a zero-tolerance approach to facilitation payments. For example, the Royal Bank of Canada has banned facilitation payments.244 Some companies conclude that it is sufficient to stay on the right side of the enforcement agencies in the country in which they are headquartered. Others conclude that the US authorities are the most active internationally, so they work to comply with the US legal framework. Still others try to comply with the laws of all countries in which they operate.

END OF EXCERPT

ACCOUNTING (BOOKS AND RECORDS) OFFENCES RELATED TO CORRUPTION

5.1 UNCAC

Creating criminal offences to punish false, deceptive or incomplete accounting of the payment or receipt and use of money or other assets is seen as an essential and necessary tool in fighting the hiding of corruption payments. Article 12 of UNCAC provides:

1. Each State Party shall take measures, in accordance with the fundamental principles of its domestic law, to prevent corruption involving the private sector, enhance accounting and auditing standards in the private sector and, where appropriate, provide effective, proportionate and dissuasive civil, administrative or criminal penalties for failure to comply with such measures.
2. Measures to achieve these ends may include, inter alia:
    - Promoting cooperation between law enforcement agencies and relevant private entities;
    - Promoting the development of standards and procedures designed to safeguard the integrity of relevant private entities, including codes of conduct for the correct, honourable and proper performance of the activities of business and all relevant professions and the prevention

of conflicts of interest, and for the promotion of the use of good commercial practices among businesses and in the contractual relations of businesses with the State;

- Promoting transparency among private entities, including, where appropriate, measures regarding the identity of legal and natural persons involved in the establishment and management of corporate entities;
- Preventing the misuse of procedures regulating private entities, including procedures regarding subsidies and licences granted by public authorities for commercial activities;
- Preventing conflicts of interest by imposing restrictions, as appropriate and for a reasonable period of time, on the professional activities of former public officials or on the employment of public officials by the private sector after their resignation or retirement, where such activities or employment relate directly to the functions held or supervised by those public officials during their tenure;
- Ensuring that private enterprises, taking into account their structure and size, have sufficient internal auditing controls to assist in preventing and detecting acts of corruption and that the accounts and required financial statements of such private enterprises are subject to appropriate auditing and certification procedures.

⦿ In order to prevent corruption, each State Party shall take such measures as may be necessary, in accordance with its domestic laws and regulations regarding the maintenance of books and records, financial statement disclosures and accounting and auditing standards, to prohibit the following acts carried out for the purpose of committing any of the offences established in accordance with this Convention:

- The establishment of off-the-books accounts;
- The making of off-the-books or inadequately identified transactions;
- The recording of non-existent expenditure;
- The entry of liabilities with incorrect identification of their objects;
- The use of false documents; and
- The intentional destruction of bookkeeping documents earlier than foreseen by the law.

⦿ Each State Party shall disallow the tax deductibility of expenses that constitute bribes, the latter being one of the constituent elements of the offences established in accordance with articles 15 and 16 of this Convention and, where appropriate, other expenses incurred in furtherance of corrupt conduct.

The UNCAC Legislative Guide highlights the following features of Article 12:

- Paragraph 1 of article 12 requires that States parties take three types of measures in accordance with the fundamental principles of their law. The first is a general commitment to take measures aimed at preventing corruption involving the private sector. The second type of measure mandated by paragraph 1 aims at the enhancement of accounting and auditing standards. Such standards provide transparency, clarify the operations of private entities, support confidence in the annual and other statements of private entities, and help prevent as well as detect malpractices. The third type of measure States must take relates to the provision, where appropriate, of effective, proportionate and dissuasive civil, administrative or criminal penalties for failure to comply with the accounting and auditing standards mandated above.
- Article 12, paragraph 2, outlines in its subparagraphs a number of good practices, which have been shown to be effective in the prevention of corruption in the private sector and in the enhancement of transparency and accountability.
- Risks of corruption and vulnerability relative to many kinds of illicit abuses are higher when transactions and the organizational structure of private entities are not transparent. Where appropriate, it is important to enhance transparency with respect to the identities of persons who play important roles in the creation and management or operations of corporate entities.

OECD Convention

Article 8 of the OECD Convention stipulates that:

- In order to combat bribery of foreign public officials effectively, each Party shall take such measures as may be necessary, within the framework of its laws and regulations regarding the maintenance of books and records, financial statement disclosures, and accounting and auditing standards, to prohibit the establishment of off-the-books accounts, the making of off-the-books or inadequately identified transactions, the recording of non-existent expenditures, the entry of liabilities with incorrect identification of their object, as well as the use of false documents, by companies subject to those laws and regulations, for the purpose of bribing foreign public officials or of hiding such bribery.
- Each Party shall provide effective, proportionate and dissuasive civil, administrative or criminal penalties for such omissions and falsifications in respect of the books, records, accounts and financial statements of such companies.

The OECD Convention's implementation has immediate consequences. Commentary 29 states that "one immediate consequence of the implementation of this Convention by the Parties will be that companies which are required to issue financial statements disclosing their material contingent liabilities will need to take into account the full potential liabilities under this Convention, in particular Articles 3 and 8, as well as other losses which might flow from conviction of the company or its agents for bribery."

Pacini, Swingen and Rogers discuss the impact of the OECD Convention in their article "The Role of the OECD and EU Conventions in Combating Bribery of Foreign Public Officials." In addition to commenting on the contents of Commentary 29, they note that Article 8 has implications for auditors, who "may be liable if they have not detected bribery of a foreign public official by properly examining a company's books and records."

Commentary 29 also points out that "the accounting offences referred to in Article 8 will generally occur in the company's home country, when the bribery offence itself may have been committed in another country, and this can fill gaps in the effective reach of the Convention."

US Law

Accounting Provisions Offenses

Accounting provisions in the FCPA are designed to prohibit off-the-books accounting. Traditionally, enforcement of the provisions has been via civil actions filed by the Securities Exchange Commission.252 The standard for imposing criminal liability is set out in § 78m(b)(5), which states that no person shall "knowingly" circumvent or fail to implement a system of controls or "knowingly" falsify their records. This full mens rea of "knowingly" removes liability for inadvertent errors, while willful blindness would still satisfy the requisite intent. When prosecuted as a crime by the DOJ, the burden of proof is on the prosecutor beyond a reasonable doubt. When dealt with as a civil offense by the SEC, the burden of proof is the lower standard of balance of probabilities. In practice, most of the books and records violations are dealt with as civil offenses by the SEC.

FCPA provisions operate independently of the bribery provisions, and also amend the Securities Exchange Act, meaning the accounting provisions apply to far more situations than bribery, including accounting fraud and issuer disclosure cases. Furthermore, companies engaged in bribery may also be violating the anti-fraud and reporting provisions found in the Securities Exchange Act. The DOJ and SEC also may turn to accounting offenses when the elements of a bribery offense cannot be made out.

Only one judicial decision directly addresses the accounting provisions. However, the provisions are common in enforcement actions that never make it to trial. As pointed out by Koehler, "the [accounting] provisions, as currently enforced by enforcement agencies, are potent supplements to FCPA's more glamorous anti-bribery provisions." The enthusiastic use of accounting offenses in SEC settlements creates compliance challenges for companies.

There are two general accounting provisions in the FCPA: the books and records provision and the internal controls provision. Unlike the FCPA's anti-bribery provisions, the accounting provisions do not apply to private companies. Instead, they apply to publicly held companies that are "issuers" under the Securities Exchange Act. An issuer is a company that has a class of securities registered pursuant to § 12 of the Securities Exchange Act or that is required to file annual or other periodic reports pursuant to § 15(d) of the Securities Exchange Act (244), regardless of whether the company has foreign operations.

The reach of the accounting provisions is quite broad. As the Resource Guide emphasizes:

- Although the FCPA's accounting requirements are directed at "issuers," an issuer's books and records include those of its consolidated subsidiaries and affiliates. An issuer's responsibility thus extends to ensuring that subsidiaries or affiliates under its control, including foreign subsidiaries and joint ventures, comply with the accounting provisions.

To be strictly responsible for a subsidiary for the purposes of the accounting provisions, the issuer must own more than 50% of the subsidiary stock. Where the issuer owns 50% or less of the subsidiary, they must only use "good faith efforts" to cause the subsidiary to meet the obligations under the FCPA (§ 78m(b)(6)).

For a detailed discussion of the nature, reach and implications of the accounting provisions, see: Stuart H. Deming, "The Potent and Broad-Ranging Implications of the Accounting and Record-Keeping Provisions of the Foreign Corrupt Practices Act."

Books and Records

The books and records provision (§ 78m(b)(2)(A)) states that every issuer shall "make and keep books, records, and accounts, which, in reasonable detail, accurately and fairly reflect the transactions and dispositions of the assets of the issuer." Section 78m(b)(6) defines "reasonable detail" as a "level of detail and degree of assurance that would satisfy prudent officials in the conduct of their own affairs." The SEC Chairman's 1981 advice provided that a company should not be "enjoined for falsification of which its management, broadly defined, was not aware and reasonably should not have known."

The Resource Guide notes that "bribes are often concealed under the guise of legitimate payments." According to a Senate Report, "corporate bribery has been concealed by the falsification of corporate books and records", and the accounting provisions are designed to "remove this avenue of coverup." The books and records provision can provide an avenue for prosecution where improper payments are inaccurately recorded, even if an element of the related anti-bribery provision was not met.

Internal Controls

- The "internal controls" provision at § 78m(b)(2)(B) states that every issuer (as above) shall:
  - Devise and maintain a system of internal accounting controls sufficient to provide reasonable assurances that—
  1. transactions are executed in accordance with management's general or specific authorization;
  2. transactions are recorded as necessary (I) to permit preparation of financial statements in conformity with generally accepted accounting principles or any other criteria applicable to such statements, and (II) to maintain accountability for assets
  3. access to assets is permitted only in accordance with management's general or specific authorization; and
  4. the recorded accountability for assets is compared with the existing assets at reasonable intervals and appropriate action is taken with respect to any differences.

Again, "reasonable assurances" is defined in § 78m(b)(7) as a "level of detail and degree of assurance that would satisfy prudent officials in the conduct of their own affairs." The provision allows companies the flexibility to implement a system of controls that suits their particular needs and circumstances. Reflective of the Guidance published pursuant to section 9 of the UK Bribery Act, the Resource Guide points out that "good internal controls can prevent not only FCPA violations, but also other illegal or unethical conduct by the company, its subsidiaries, and its employees." Compliance with the provision will therefore depend on the overall reasonableness of the internal controls in the circumstances of the company, including the risks of corruption in the country and sector of operation. In SEC v World- Wide Coin, the court indicated that the costs of devising a system of internal controls should not exceed the expected benefits. The court further noted that the occurrence of improper conduct does not necessarily mean internal controls were unsatisfactory.

Koehler argues that enforcement patterns potentially conflict with the reasonableness qualifications built into the books and records and internal control provisions and promoted in the Guidance and in SEC v World-Wide Coin. For example, in a 2012 SEC enforcement action, Oracle Corporation was held liable for failing to conduct audits of its subsidiary in India, even though such audits would not have been "practical or cost-effective absent red flags suggesting improper conduct. The SEC did not allege any such red flag issues. In fact, the SEC alleged that Oracle's Indian subsidiary 'concealed' ... the conduct from Oracle." Koehler argues that such enforcement actions are edging towards strict liability, in spite of the inclusion of "reasonable detail" and "reasonable assurances" in the accounting provisions. Koehler goes on to state:

- Based on the enforcement theories, it would seem that nearly all issuers doing business in the global marketplace could, upon a thorough investigation of their entire business operations, discover conduct implicating the books and records and internal controls provisions. For instance, the SEC alleged in an FCPA enforcement action against pharmaceutical company Eli Lilly that the company violated the books and records and internal controls provisions because sales representatives at the company's China subsidiary submitted false expense reports for items such as wine, specialty foods, a jade bracelet, visits to bath houses, card games, karaoke bars, door prizes, spa treatments and cigarettes. If the SEC's position is that an issuer violates the FCPA's books and records and internal controls provisions because some employees, anywhere within its world- wide organization, submit false expense reports for such nominal and inconsequential items, then every issuer has violated and will continue to violate the FCPA. [footnotes omitted]

Defenses/Exceptions

There are two exceptions to criminal liability under the accounting provisions. The first (§ 78m(b)(4)) states that criminal liability will not be imposed where the accounting error is merely technical or insignificant. The second (§ 78m(b)(6)) discharges an issuer of their responsibility for a subsidiary's accounting violations when the issuer owns 50% or less of the subsidiary and the issuer "demonstrates good faith efforts" to encourage the subsidiary to comply with the FCPA.

However, in practice, Koehler points out that enforcement agencies have eroded this good faith defense for parent companies and essentially created strict (no fault) liability. For example, the SEC charged Dow Chemical with accounting offenses committed by its fifth-tier subsidiary, even though Dow had no knowledge of the improper conduct, and even though the SEC did not allege a lack of good faith on Dow's part.

Limitation Periods for Books and Record Offenses

The limitation periods for FCPA books and records offenses are the same as for the offense of bribery, discussed at Section 3.3.3.

Sanctions for Books and Records Offenses

§ 78ff(a) of the FCPA mandates that for violation of the accounting provisions, corporations and other business entities are liable for a fine of up to $25 million while individuals (including officers, directors, stockholders and agents of companies) are subject to a fine of up to $5 million and imprisonment for a maximum of 20 years. However, the Alternative Fines Act 18 USC. Section 3571(d) provides for the imposition of higher fines at the court's discretion. The increased fine can be up to twice the benefit obtained by the defendant in making the bribe.

Actual penalties are determined by reference to the US Sentencing Guidelines (§ 1A1.1 (2011)).

UK Law

There are no accounting offences in the UK Bribery Act. However, as pointed out by Martin, a compilation of existing UK corporate laws coupled with section 7 of the Bribery Act leads to similar requirements as those in FCPA.270 Firstly, the Companies Act 2006 requires every company in the UK to keep records that can show and explain their transactions, to accurately disclose their financial positions and to implement adequate internal controls. Secondly, the defence to section 7 requires companies have "adequate procedures" in place, which means in part that the companies will need to keep proper records and implement adequate internal controls. Finally, accounting offences facilitating corruption or the hiding of the proceeds of corruption are covered in sections 17-20 of the Theft Act, 1968.

Section 17 of the Theft Act creates the offence of false accounting. Section 17(1)(a) criminalizes the conduct of a person who intentionally and dishonestly destroys, defaces, conceals or falsifies any account, record or document made or required for any accounting purpose. The falsification, etc., must be done with a view to gain or cause loss to another, but need not actually cause loss or gain. Authorities are inconsistent regarding the meaning of "accounting purpose," but a set of financial accounts is prima facie made for an accounting purpose. The defendant is not required to know that the documents are for an accounting purpose, creating an element of strict liability. Section 17(1)(b) also criminalizes the dishonest use of false or deceptive documents with a view to gain or cause loss.

Section 17 overlaps with both forgery and fraud offences. The fraud offence is broader than section 17, since it is not restricted to documents made for accounting purposes, and also has a higher maximum sentence. As a result, the Fraud Act is sometimes used instead of the false accounting provisions.

Section 18 imposes liability on directors, managers, secretaries or other similar officers of a body corporate for an offence committed by the body corporate with their consent or connivance. The purpose of this section is to impose a positive obligation on people in management positions to prevent irregularities, if aware of them. Section 19 is intended to protect investors by making it an offence for directors to publish false prospectuses to members. Section 20 makes it an offence to dishonestly destroy, deface or conceal any valuable security, any will or other testamentary document, or any original document that is belonging to, filed in or deposited in any court of justice or government department.

Canadian Law

Before 2013, CFPOA had no accounting offences. False accounting allegations were dealt with under domestic criminal law or income tax laws in circumstances where Canada had jurisdiction over the commission of those offences.

Amendments to CFPOA in 2013 created new accounting offences. The accounting provisions must be proven beyond a reasonable doubt (unlike the similar provisions in the FCPA, which need only be proven on a balance of probabilities when used by the SEC). Section 4 of the CFPOA provides:

- 4.(1) Every person commits an offence who, for the purpose of bribing a foreign public official in order to obtain or retain an advantage in the course of business or for the purpose of hiding that bribery,
    - establishes or maintains accounts which do not appear in any of the books and records that they are required to keep in accordance with applicable accounting and auditing standards;
    - makes transactions that are not recorded in those books and records or that are inadequately identified in them;
    - records non-existent expenditures in those books and records;
    - enters liabilities with incorrect identification of their object in those books and records;
    - knowingly uses false documents; or
    - intentionally destroys accounting books and records earlier than permitted by law.
- (2) Every person who contravenes subsection (1) is guilty of an indictable offence and liable to imprisonment for a term of not more than 14 years.

Section 4 was brought into force on June 19, 2013. There have been no prosecutions under it. This section was added to the CFPOA to bring the Act into line with article 8 of the OECD Convention. Other existing Criminal Code offences support Canada's implementation of Article 8 of the OECD Convention. These include the offences of making a false pretence or statement (ss. 361 and 362), forgery and the use or possession of forged documents (ss. 366 and 368), fraud affecting public markets (s. 380(2)), falsification of books and documents (s. 397) and issuing a false prospectus (s. 400). Section 155 of the Canada Business Corporations Act, which addresses financial disclosure, may also be relevant in cases involving false accounting.

CHAPTER-3

GENERAL PRINCIPLES AFFECTING THE SCOPE OF CORRUPTION OFFENCES

JURISDICTION: TO WHAT EXTENT CAN A STATE PROSECUTE BRIBERY OFFENCES COMMITTED OUTSIDE ITS BORDERS?

Overview

In today's globalized world, bribery and other forms of corruption are often transnational. Instances of bribery may involve a number of individuals or legal entities and encompass actions in multiple states. Large corporations are often multi-national, and carrying on business in numerous states. Acts of bribery by one corporation may disadvantage other foreign firms who lose business as a result. Since anti-corruption laws and their enforcement are not consistent across states, the way in which states determine jurisdiction—to whom their anti-corruption laws apply and who can be prosecuted by their courts or tribunals— has important implications for determining how effective anti-corruption laws will be in detecting, investigating, prosecuting, and punishing corruption.

There are three general forms of jurisdiction: prescriptive, enforcement and adjudicative. These were briefly described by the Supreme Court of Canada in R v Hape:

- Prescriptive jurisdiction (also called legislative or substantive jurisdiction) is the power to make rules, issue commands or grant authorizations that are binding upon persons and entities. The legislature exercises prescriptive jurisdiction in enacting legislation. Enforcement jurisdiction is the power to use coercive means to ensure that rules are followed, commands are executed or entitlements are upheld. ... Adjudicative jurisdiction is the power of a state's courts to resolve disputes or interpret the law through decisions that carry binding force [citations omitted].

As the Supreme Court noted, these forms of jurisdiction overlap in certain cases. Even if there is prescriptive jurisdiction, there may be no enforcement jurisdiction (i.e., the power to compel extradition by reason of an extradition treaty or agreement).

The rules governing extra-territorial jurisdiction must be balanced with the concept of state sovereignty. The principles of state sovereignty, including equality and territorial integrity, are reaffirmed in Article 4 of UNCAC. A state is under an international obligation to not enforce its legislative powers within the territorial limits of another state without that state's consent. However, under international law, the limits of a state's prescriptive or legislative jurisdiction (in other words the limits of how a state may determine to whom its laws apply) are less clear. See generally the International Bar Association's Report of the Task Force on Extraterritorial Jurisdiction.2

When engaged in international business transactions, it is essential for the company and its legal advisors to be aware which countries' laws apply to its activities. In that sense, jurisdiction is the most important issue in international business transactions. Brown describes six theories that states may rely upon to assert prescriptive jurisdiction (i.e., determine to whom their law applies).3 The two most accepted of these are territoriality, whereby jurisdiction is determined on the basis of where the criminal acts occurred, and nationality (sometimes termed the active personality principle), whereby a state's jurisdiction extends to the actions of its nationals no matter where the acts constituting the offence occur. Historically, common law countries have been much more reluctant to assert jurisdiction based on nationality while civil law and socialist law countries were more likely to have embraced this theory. The third theory is universality, where a state may charge any person present in its territory under its own domestic laws no matter where the acts constituting the offence occurred. This principle was traditionally reserved for piracy and has been extended more recently to crimes universally regarded as heinous, such as war crimes. The fourth theory is the protective principle, which determines jurisdiction with reference to which state's national interests were harmed by the offending act, and the fifth theory is the passive personality principle, which determines jurisdiction based on the nationality of the crime's victim or victims. Finally, there is also the "flag" principle, which is sometimes classified under the principle of territoriality and extends a state's domestic laws to acts occurring at sea on a ship flying that state's flag.

With bribery of a foreign public official, it is common for the actual act of bribery to take place within the foreign official's home country while some preparation, or perhaps just the authorization to offer a bribe, may take place in the briber's home state. Therefore, in respect to statutes that operate based on the territoriality principle alone, a home state's jurisdiction over a briber will depend on the connection required by the home state's law between the briber's conduct and the home state. A law that requires the whole or majority of the act of bribery take place within the home state will have significantly less jurisdictional reach than a law like the US FCPA, which applies (among other ways) when any or virtually any act or communication in furtherance of a corrupt payment occurs within the US.

Territoriality may be asserted under the principles of either subjective territoriality or objective territoriality. Zerk reviews the different ways in which states may assert jurisdiction based on territoriality:

- The principle of subjective territoriality gives State X the right to take jurisdiction over a course of conduct that commenced in State X and was completed in another state. A terrorist plot that was hatched in State X and executed in State Y could fall into this category. The principle of objective territoriality gives State X the right to take jurisdiction over a course of conduct that began in another state and [was] completed in State X. A conspiracy in State Y to defraud investors in State X could give rise to jurisdiction based on this principle. A further refinement of the principle of objective territoriality appears to be gaining acceptance, in the antitrust field at least. This doctrine, known as the effects doctrine, argues that states have jurisdiction over foreign actors and conduct on the basis of "effects" (usually economic effects) produced within their own territorial boundaries, provided those effects are substantial, and a direct result of that foreign conduct. Jurisdiction taken on the basis of the effects doctrine is often classed as "extraterritorial jurisdiction" on the grounds that jurisdiction is asserted over foreign conduct. It is important, though, not to lose sight of the territorial connections that do exist (i.e. in terms of "effects") over which the regulating state arguably does have territorial jurisdiction. Nevertheless, while this doctrine has become increasingly accepted in principle as more states adopt it, its scope remains controversial, especially in relation to purely economic (as opposed to physical) effects.4

UNCAC

Article 42(1) of UNCAC requires State Parties to assert jurisdiction when an offence is committed within their territory or on board a vessel flying their flag. Article 42(3) of the Convention also requires State Parties to exercise jurisdiction when the offender is present in their territory and extradition is refused on the basis that the offender is a national. Some commentators have noted that unlike the OECD Convention, UNCAC does not appear to mandate that a state assert jurisdiction in instances where the act occurred only partially within its territory.

Article 42(2) permits states to establish jurisdiction in the following circumstances:

- Subject to Article 4 of this Convention [State Sovereignty], a State Party may also establish its jurisdiction over any such offence when:
  - The offence is committed against a national of that State Party; or
  - The offence is committed by a national of that State Party or a stateless person who has his or her habitual residence in its territory; or
  - The offence is one of those established in accordance with article 23, paragraph 1(b) (ii) [conspiracy or other forms of participation in a plan to commit money laundering offences], of this Convention and is committed outside its territory with a view to the commission of an offence established in accordance with article 23, paragraph 1 (a) (i) or (ii) or (b) (i) [money laundering offences], of this Convention within its territory; or
  - The offence is committed against the State Party.

Article 42(2) is limited by Article 4, which is meant to protect state sovereignty by discouraging the exercise of extraterritorial jurisdiction within the territory of another state if the laws of that state mandate exclusive territorial jurisdiction. Some commentators, such as Lestelle, have questioned whether UNCAC permits jurisdiction to be established on the basis of other theories of jurisdiction, such as the protective principle, which is notably absent from Article 42(2). Lestelle states:

> Despite the extensive list of extraterritorial circumstances contemplated by article 42, the limitation in article 4 denudes much of the potency from the grant. Furthermore, a final theory of extraterritorial jurisdiction, the "protective" principle, is notably absent from the list in article 42. The "protective" principle provides jurisdiction if the effect or possible effect of the offense is to occur in the forum state and for offenses that threaten the "specific national interests" of the forum state. As discussed in Part I, global efforts at combating foreign public bribery would be aided by an amendment to the UNCAC that removes the limitations of article 4 and adds the "protective" principle as a basis for jurisdiction. [footnotes omitted]

It could be argued, however, that the list of permitted bases of jurisdiction provided in Article 42(2) is non-exhaustive. Article 42(6) provides that:

- Without prejudice to norms of general international law, this Convention shall not exclude the exercise of any criminal jurisdiction established by a State Party in accordance with its domestic law.

In addition, the Legislative Guide for UNCAC, produced by UNODC, states that UNCAC does not aim to alter general international rules regarding jurisdiction and that the list of jurisdictional bases in 42(2) is not meant to be exhaustive. Rather, the purpose of Article 42 is to permit the exercise of jurisdiction in such a way that ensures that corruption offences do not go unpunished because of jurisdictional gaps. As noted above, there are differing views concerning the degree of latitude afforded to states under international law when determining the basis of criminal jurisdiction.

Lestelle argues that UNCAC should be amended to expressly allow for further extraterritorial application of domestic laws, potentially based on the protective or passive personality principles. In his view, corruption is a humanitarian concern of sufficient gravity to merit the application of laws with significant extraterritorial jurisdiction. Lestelle compares corruption to piracy, the earliest crime for which states commonly asserted jurisdiction based on the universality principle. He argues that both are "crimes against the global market," and therefore far-reaching state-level laws are necessary in order to avoid the possibility that perpetrators will be able to evade prosecution. Otherwise, Lestelle warns that some states motivated by self-interest will refrain from taking legal action against perpetrators, thus creating "safe harbour" refuges where those engaged in bribery or corruption will not be prosecuted.

OECD Convention

Article 4 of the OECD Convention addresses jurisdiction. It requires that each State Party take steps to ensure it has jurisdiction over bribery offences that occur wholly or partially within its territory. This is a narrow conception of extra-territorial jurisdiction. The word "partial" is not defined. The Commentary accompanying the Convention text states that this provision should be interpreted broadly in a way that does not require "extensive physical connection to the bribery act." In addition, a State Party with "jurisdiction to prosecute its nationals for offences committed abroad shall take such measures as may be necessary to establish its jurisdiction to do so in respect of the bribery of a foreign public official, according to the same principles" (Article 4(2)). Article 4(4) also requires states to review whether their basis for jurisdiction is sufficient to effectively fight against the bribery of foreign public officials.

At the time the OECD Convention was negotiated (during the 1990s), many common law countries (including Canada) were opposed to including a requirement that signatory states assert jurisdiction based on nationality. Article 4(4) therefore represented a compromise.10 However, since that time most of the common law OECD states have incorporated the principle of jurisdiction based on nationality into their domestic anti-bribery legislation (Canada did so in 2013).

Other International Anti-Corruption Instruments

In addition to mandating that states assert jurisdiction based on the territorial principle, The Council of Europe Criminal Law Convention, the European Union Convention on the Fight against Corruption Involving Officials of the European Communities or Officials of Member States and the African Union Convention on Preventing and Combating Corruption all require State Parties to exercise jurisdiction on the basis of nationality. Interestingly, the African Union Convention is the only multilateral anti-corruption convention to expressly provide for jurisdiction based on the protective principle (see Article 13(1)(d)).

Corporate Entities

A corporation or other collective legal entity can be subject to a state's corruption laws (1) based on territorial jurisdiction if the company commits the offence (in whole or in part) in that state or (2) based on nationality jurisdiction if the company is incorporated or otherwise legally created or registered in that state. A company from one state can commit an offence in a foreign state either as the primary offender or as a secondary party offender (i.e. aid, abet or counsel another person to commit the offence).

In countries that base corporate criminal liability on the identification (i.e., "directing minds") theory, the actions and state of mind of certain employees and officers becomes in law "the actions and state of mind" of the corporation. In those instances, the corporation is the principal offender. Alternatively, a company can be liable for a corruption offence committed in a foreign state by means of secondary party liability. If the parent company aids, abets or counsels a subsidiary company or a third party agent to commit a corruption offence, the parent company is guilty of that offence as a secondary party to that offence. For example, if SNC-Lavalin Group, the Canadian parent company, were prosecuted for corruption in the Padma Bridge case, its criminal liability would be based on the claim that it aided, abetted or encouraged its subsidiary company and its third party agent (not an employee of SNC-Lavalin) to commit the offence as principal offenders.

The requisite mental element for the parent company as an aider, abettor or counsellor can vary depending on the particular offence and the state's laws for establishing corporate criminal liability. Generally speaking, the parent company's required level of fault will be (1) subjective fault (intentionally aided), (2) strict liability (aided by failing to take reasonable steps to prevent the offence), or (3) absolute liability (no mental fault element to aid, abet or counsel the offence is required).

The ability of state parties to exercise jurisdiction over foreign corporate entities, as addressed in the UNCAC and the OECD Convention, is summarized by Zerk as follows:

- While all of the treaties either authorise or require the use of nationality jurisdiction in relation to the extraterritorial activities of their corporate nationals, they do not impose specific requirements vis-à-vis the regulation of the foreign activities of foreign companies and no treaties require the regulation of such activities directly. This will be because of the acknowledged legal limitations in relation to the regulation of foreign nationals in foreign territory. However, a number of treaty provisions are potentially relevant to the situation where a foreign subsidiary or agent is primarily responsible for a bribe. For instance, the UN Convention contains provisions relating to "accessory" or "secondary liability", under which a parent company could be held responsible for a foreign bribe on the basis that it was the "instigator" of that bribe. The OECD Convention mandates liability for complicity in the bribery of a foreign public official, including "incitement, aiding and abetting, or authorization" of such an act. The "Good Practice Guideline" annexed to a recent OECD Recommendation on implementation of the OECD Convention asks state parties to ensure that "a legal person cannot avoid responsibility by using intermediaries, including related legal persons, to offer, promise or give a bribe to a foreign public official on its behalf."

There is little guidance in the treaty provisions themselves as to the extent to which accounting controls must cover the transactions of foreign subsidiaries. However, to the extent that the treaty covers foreign bribery, it would appear to be the intention that consolidated reporting (covering the transactions of foreign subsidiaries as well as the parent company) is indeed required. [footnotes omitted]

Overview of OECD Countries Jurisdiction

The 2016 OECD Liability of Legal Persons for Foreign Bribery: A Stocktaking Report provides the following summary of the types of jurisdiction each OECD country has:

BEGINNING OF EXCERPT

Some of the key findings in relation to jurisdiction are:

- All the Parties to the Convention (except Argentina) establish some form of territorial jurisdiction over legal persons for the offence of foreign bribery. In some Parties, this jurisdiction is a collateral effect of having jurisdiction over the acts of a natural person who commits foreign bribery in its territory.

- At least 23 Parties (56%) are able, in at least some circumstances, to assert jurisdiction over foreign companies that commit foreign bribery in their territory. One country—Colombia—reported to the Secretariat that its Superintendency of Corporations cannot sanction foreign legal persons for acts committed on its territory. For the other Parties, it could not be determined from the WGB reports whether such jurisdiction exists over foreign legal persons.
- At least 23 Parties (56%) can hold a domestic legal person liable for foreign bribery committed entirely abroad. In line with the WGB's 2006 Mid-Term Study of Phase 2 Reports, the Phase 3 evaluations have indicated that some Parties still cannot assert jurisdiction over a domestic legal person for an offence committed abroad unless the Party also has jurisdiction over the natural person who actually committed the offence. In several cases, the Party may not be able to assert jurisdiction over the legal person unless the natural person who committed the act was a national (e.g. Austria, Bulgaria, Chile, Estonia, Germany, Italy, Latvia, Japan and Sweden). For 16 Parties (39%), no determination was made in the WGB reports.
- At least 8 Parties (20%) seemingly can hold a foreign legal person liable for foreign bribery committed entirely abroad, provided that some condition links the foreign legal person to the country for purpose of applying its foreign bribery offence. Mailbox companies in the Netherlands are also identified as a source of concern. The Phase 3 report for the Netherlands describes varying views within the Netherlands' legal profession about whether it has effective jurisdiction over mailbox companies. The report also states that the Netherlands' approach to "mailbox companies appears to be a potentially significant loophole in the Dutch framework" and urges it "to take all necessary measures to ensure that such companies are considered legal entities under the Dutch Criminal Code, and can be effectively prosecuted and sanctioned."

Finally, although the Convention does not create obligations for Parties to assert jurisdiction over acts of foreign legal persons for offences that take place entirely outside its territory, the WGB has identified some interesting arrangements among the Parties for asserting such jurisdiction. These include:

- **Universal jurisdiction:** According to Iceland authorities, Iceland asserts universal jurisdiction for foreign bribery offences falling under the Anti-Bribery Convention. Likewise, the Phase 3 report for Norway states: "Norway has extremely broad jurisdiction over foreign bribery offences, and could, in theory, prosecute any person committing a foreign bribery offence, regardless whether the offence was committed in Norway, and regardless whether the person involved is a Norwegian national. In practice, Norway explained that the universal jurisdiction was in fact rarely relied on, and only used in exceptional cases (twice between 1975 and 2004, and never in corruption cases). At any rate, this broad jurisdiction allows Norway to exercise both territorial and nationality jurisdiction over foreign bribery offences." Estonia reports that it might be able to exercise universal jurisdiction over bribery offenses punishable by a "binding international agreement", but in the absence of case law supporting this theory, the WGB has not been able to reach a definitive conclusion.

- **Foreign legal person conducts business in, or owns property, in the territory:** The Czech Republic can assert jurisdiction over a foreign legal person for acts committed outside of its territory when that legal person "conducts . . . activities . . . or owns property" inside the Czech Republic. Similarly, the United Kingdom can apply its Section 7 offence under the Bribery Act to any "commercial organisation" that "carries on a business, or part of a business" inside the United Kingdom. In such a case, the foreign legal person would be liable for the acts of any "associated person" even if the associated person commits the offence outside of the United Kingdom.
- **Foreign legal person committed offence for the benefit of a domestic legal person:** The Czech Republic can assert jurisdiction over a foreign legal person for acts committed outside of its territory when the "criminal act was committed for the benefit of a Czech legal person."
- **Foreign legal person is closely connected to a domestic legal person or natural person:** Greek authorities maintain that Greek law would apply to a foreign subsidiary having a "sufficient connection" with a parent company located in Greece. Israeli authorities believed that they could likely assert jurisdiction over a foreign legal person, "if the crime was committed by an Israeli citizen or resident who was the controlling owner of the legal person." [footnotes omitted]

END OF EXCERPT

In regard to the nationality requirements for legal persons, the report states the following:

- Of the 41 Convention Parties, at least 16 countries (39%) will consider any legal person incorporated or formed in accordance with their laws to have their nationality. At least eight countries (20%) will look to the legal person's headquarters or seat of operations to determine its nationality, and at least another three countries (7%) will look at either the place of incorporation or the seat. Only 1 country, Brazil, restricts the application of its nationality jurisdiction to legal persons that are both incorporated in and headquartered in the country's territory.

Finally, at least 11 countries (27%) will assert nationality jurisdiction over legal entities based on "other" factors, primarily whether the company is "registered" under the country's laws or has a "registered office" on its territory. Depending on the country, these other factors may be exclusive or operate alongside the place of incorporation or the seat of the company.

US Law

The Expansive Extraterritorial Reach of the US FCPA

The US FCPA has significant extraterritorial reach. Not only does it apply in instances where any act in furtherance of the offense occurs within the territory of the US, but it also exercises jurisdiction based on nationality. As part of its territorial jurisdiction, foreign companies that are listed on a US stock exchange are subject to the FCPA. For a detailed description of jurisdiction under the FCPA, including a discussion of due process and relevant cases, see Tarun's Foreign Corrupt Practices Handbook.14 The following excerpt from the US DOJ and SEC's Resource Guide to the Foreign Corrupt Practices Act (Resource Guide) details how these two FCPA enforcement agencies interpret the FCPA's jurisdiction:15

BEGINNING OF EXCERPT

Who Is Covered by the Anti-Bribery Provisions?

The FCPA's anti-bribery provisions apply broadly to three categories of persons and entities: (1) "issuers" and their officers, directors, employees, agents, and sharehold- ers; (2) "domestic concerns" and their officers, directors, employees, agents, and shareholders; and (3) certain persons and entities, other than issuers and domestic concerns, acting while in the territory of the United States.

Issuers—15 USC. § 78dd-1

Section 30A of the Securities Exchange Act of 1934 (the Exchange Act), which can be found at 15 USC. Section 78dd-1, contains the anti-bribery provision governing issuers. A company is an "issuer" under the FCPA if it has a class of securities registered under Section 12 of the Exchange Act or is required to file periodic and other reports with SEC under Section 15(d) of the Exchange Act. In practice, this means that any company with a class of securities listed on a national securities exchange in the United States, or any company with a class of securities quoted in the over-the-counter market in the United States and required to file periodic reports with SEC, is an issuer. A company thus need not be a US company to be an issuer. Foreign companies with American Depository Receipts that are listed on a

US exchange are also issuers. As of December 31, 2011, 965 foreign companies were registered with SEC. Officers, directors, employees, agents, or stockholders acting on behalf of an issuer (whether US or foreign nationals), and any co-conspirators, also can be prosecuted under the FCPA.

Domestic Concerns—15 USC. § 78dd-2

The FCPA also applies to "domestic concerns." A domestic concern is any individual who is a citizen, national, or resident of the United States, or any corporation, part- nership, association, joint-stock company, business trust, unincorporated organization, or sole proprietorship that is organized under the laws of the United States or its states, territories, possessions, or commonwealths or that has its principal place of business in the United States. [Note that "domestic concern" includes non-profit organizations such as aid groups.] Officers, directors, employees, agents, or stockholders acting on behalf of a domestic concern, including foreign nationals or companies, are also covered.

Territorial Jurisdiction—15 USC. § 78dd-3

The FCPA also applies to certain foreign nationals or entities that are not issuers or domestic concerns. Since 1998, the FCPA's anti-bribery provisions have applied to foreign persons and foreign non-issuer entities that, either directly or through an agent, engage in any act in furtherance of a corrupt payment (or an offer, promise, or authorization to pay) while in the territory of the United States. Also, officers, directors, employees, agents, or stockholders acting on behalf of such persons or entities may be subject to the FCPA's anti-bribery prohibitions.

[According to Deming, "[w]ith the critical role that facilities of the US play in international commerce, such as the internet, banking, and air travel, a broad interpretation of what constitutes 'while in the territory of the US' could have dramatic implications."]

What Jurisdictional Conduct Triggers the Anti-Bribery Provisions?

The FCPA's anti-bribery provisions can apply to conduct both inside and outside the United States. Issuers and domestic concerns—as well as their officers, directors, employees, agents, or stockholders—may be prosecuted for using the US mails or any means or instrumentality of interstate commerce in furtherance of a corrupt payment to a foreign official. The Act defines "interstate commerce" as "trade, commerce, transportation, or communication among the several States, or between any foreign country and any State or between any State and any place or ship outside thereof...." The term also includes the intrastate use of any interstate means of communication, or any other interstate instrumentality. Thus, placing a telephone call or sending an e- mail, text message, or fax from, to, or through the

United States involves interstate commerce—as does sending a wire transfer from or to a US bank or otherwise using the US banking system, or traveling across state borders or internationally to or from the United States.

Those who are not issuers or domestic concerns may be prosecuted under the FCPA if they directly, or through an agent, engage in any act in furtherance of a corrupt payment while in the territory of the United States, regardless of whether they utilize the US mails or a means or instrumentality of interstate commerce. Thus, for example, a foreign national who attends a meeting in the United States that furthers a foreign bribery scheme may be subject to prosecution, as may any co-conspirators, even if they did not themselves attend the meeting. A foreign national or company may also be liable under the FCPA if it aids and abets, conspires with, or acts as an agent of an issuer or domestic concern, regardless of whether the foreign national or company itself takes any action in the United States.

In addition, under the "alternative jurisdiction" provision of the FCPA enacted in 1998, US companies or persons may be subject to the anti-bribery provisions even if they act outside the United States. The 1998 amendments to the FCPA expanded the jurisdictional coverage of the Act by establishing an alternative basis for jurisdiction, that is, jurisdiction based on the nationality principle. In particular, the 1998 amendments removed the requirement that there be a use of interstate commerce (e.g., wire, email, telephone call) for acts in furtherance of a corrupt payment to a foreign official by US companies and persons occurring wholly outside of the United States. [footnotes omitted]

END OF EXCERPT

Jurisdiction of US courts under the FCPA can be limited by due process requirements. In civil cases, the defendant must have "minimum contacts" with the court's jurisdiction, and the exercise of jurisdiction must be reasonable. If a defendant's actions have no effect in the US and the defendant has negligible contact with the US, these requirements might not be met. For example, in SEC v Steffen, the defendant's role in falsified records was too "tangential," and the defendant had no geographic ties to the US. The US forum had little continuing interest in pursuing the particular defendant, who also spoke little English. As a result, the court found that exercising jurisdiction over the defendant would exceed the limits of due process.

In criminal cases, personal jurisdiction arises from a defendant's arrest in the US, voluntary appearance in court or lawful extradition to the US.

Foreign individuals or legal entities that would otherwise be outside the jurisdictional reach of the FCPA may be held criminally liable pursuant to the FCPA if they aided, abetted, counselled or induced another person or entity to commit a FCPA offense or if they conspired to violate the FCPA. The following excerpt from the Resource Guide explains the SEC's and DOJ's interpretation of the scope of secondary liability provisions of the FCPA:

BEGINNING OF EXCERPT

Additional Principles of Criminal Liability for Anti-Bribery Violations: Aiding and Abetting and Conspiracy

Under federal law, individuals or companies that aid or abet a crime, including an FCPA violation, are as guilty as if they had directly committed the offense themselves. The aiding and abetting statute provides that whoever "commits an offense against the United States or aids, abets, counsels, commands, induces or procures its commission," or "willfully causes an act to be done which if directly performed by him or another would be an offense against the United States," is punishable as a principal. Aiding and abetting is not an independent crime, and the government must prove that an underlying FCPA violation was committed.

Individuals and companies, including foreign nationals and companies, may also be liable for conspiring to violate the FCPA—i.e., for agreeing to commit an FCPA violation—even if they are not, or could not be, independently charged with a substantive FCPA violation. For instance, a foreign, non-issuer company could be convicted of conspiring with a domestic concern to violate the FCPA. Under certain circumstances, it could also be held liable for the domestic concern's substantive FCPA violations under Pinkerton v. United States, which imposes liability on a defendant for reasonably foreseeable crimes committed by a co-conspirator in furtherance of a conspiracy that the defendant joined.

A foreign company or individual may be held liable for aiding and abetting an FCPA violation or for conspiring to violate the FCPA, even if the foreign company or indi- vidual did not take any act in furtherance of the corrupt payment while in the territory of the United States. In conspiracy cases, the United States generally has jurisdiction over all the conspirators where at least one conspirator is an issuer, domestic concern, or commits a reasonably foreseeable overt act within the United States. For example, if a foreign company or individual conspires to violate the FCPA with someone who commits an overt act within the United States, the United States can prosecute the foreign company or individual for the conspiracy. The same principle applies to aiding and abetting violations. For instance, even though they took no action in the United States, Japanese and European companies were charged with conspiring with and aiding and abetting a domestic concern's FCPA violations [endnotes omitted].

[Note: While the US may claim jurisdiction over the offence, they may have difficulty prosecuting foreign persons or entities if they have no extradition treaty with the foreign state or if the foreign state rejects the US claim of jurisdiction.]

Additional Principles of Civil Liability for Anti-Bribery Violations: Aiding and Abetting and Causing

Both companies and individuals can be held civilly liable for aiding and abetting FCPA anti-bribery violations if they knowingly or recklessly provide substantial assis- tance to a violator. Similarly, in the administrative proceeding context, companies and individuals may be held liable for causing FCPA violations. This liability extends to the subsidiaries and agents of US issuers.

In one case, the US subsidiary of a Swiss freight forwarding company was held civilly liable for paying bribes on behalf of its customers in several countries. Although the US subsidiary was not an issuer for purposes of the FCPA, it was an "agent" of several US issuers. By paying bribes on behalf of its issuers' customers, the subsidiary both directly violated and aided and abetted the issuers' FCPA violations.

END OF EXCERPT

Questioning the DOJ and SEC's Broad View of Territorial Jurisdiction under the FCPA

As noted in the above excerpts, the DOJ and the SEC take a very broad view of the territorial jurisdiction of the FCPA. Some commentators refer to US jurisdiction over bribery as "potentially quasi-universal."20 It is also possible to understand the FCPA's jurisdiction over issuers as being based on the effects doctrine of territoriality, as the corrupt acts on behalf of foreign corporations listed on the US markets have the potential to negatively affect the American competitors of the offending corporations.

Hecker and Laporte address the implications of the DOJ and SEC's broad interpretation of territorial jurisdiction. They state that "[a]lthough not explicitly set forth in the joint FCPA guidance, the DOJ, in particular, through its public statements and in settled cases, has taken the position that even fleeting contact with the US territory may constitute a sufficient US nexus to assert territorial jurisdiction over foreign entities and individuals for conduct that occurred outside the United States." Laporte and Hecker also note that companies are often under pressure to settle FCPA enforcement actions and are reluctant to risk challenging the DOJ and SEC's broad interpretation of the FCPA. They cite as an example a settled action against JGC Corp., a Japanese firm charged with making corrupt payments to Nigerian public officials. In this case, the DOJ asserted that the FCPA's territorial jurisdiction was established on the basis of wire transfers routed through US bank accounts.

The DOJ and SEC's expansive interpretation of territorial jurisdiction in corruption cases is reflected by the recent assertion of jurisdiction over FIFA officials by the US, although the FCPA was not used. Since the FCPA only covers bribes to government officials, the DOJ used non-bribery charges under different legislation to reach the indicted officials, namely the Racketeer Influenced and Corrupt Organizations Act (RICO) and the Travel Act, which prohibits the use of interstate travel and commerce to further an illegal activity. This assertion of jurisdiction has been criticized in relation to the officials who barely have tangential connections to the US. The DOJ claims jurisdiction because several of the FIFA officials and marketing executives were allegedly involved in palm-greasing-related activities on American soil and some of the involved marketing companies and associations have offices in the US.

Hecker and Laporte note that there is case law to suggest that the FCPA's territorial jurisdiction is not inexhaustible. Koehler also makes this observation and criticizes the DOJ guidance (quoted above) for basing its advice on settled enforcement actions lacking in judicial scrutiny rather than case law.24 Hecker and LaPorte cite a district court decision, US v Patel,25 in which the Court rejected the DOJ's argument that the act of mailing a corrupt purchase agreement from the UK to the US was sufficient to establish a territorial nexus with the US. The Court held that, in order for the FCPA to apply to foreign entities that are not considered "issuers," the act in furtherance of a corrupt payment must have taken place within US territory. Hecker and Laporte add, however, that until more US courts consider the issue, the DOJ and SEC are unlikely to retreat from their expansive interpretation of the territorial jurisdiction of the FCPA.

Hecker and Laporte also go on to state that a number of enforcement challenges arise when attempting to prosecute foreign entities with little territorial nexus with the US under the FCPA. Although mutual legal assistance agreements and cooperation with foreign states are on the rise, there nonetheless may be prolonged delays or difficulties when attempting to extradite accused persons or to obtain evidence from abroad. As a result, the DOJ and SEC rely heavily on the cooperation of the entities under investigation. In instances where evidence must be sought in foreign countries, the five-year statute of limitations period for FCPA violations may be suspended in some circumstances for up to three years. Lengthy delays in bringing matters to court may present further challenges, as witnesses may become unavailable or their memories may grow stale and evidence may be lost or destroyed. Given the difficulties in investigation and enforcement, the authors question whether it is prudent for the US to pursue enforcement actions in cases where there is only a weak territorial link to the US.

Leibold criticizes the broad extraterritorial application of the FCPA and argues that the extension of FCPA jurisdiction to foreign non-issuers may be contrary to principles of customary international law. Leibold analyzes the discrepancy in the amount of fines paid by foreign businesses versus domestic businesses and suggests that these statistics may be explained either by the fact that foreign corporations are more corrupt than the US firms, foreign corporations do not cooperate with the US law enforcement authorities, or the SEC and DOJ are unfairly targeting foreign businesses with higher penalties for FCPA violations. Finally, given the ease with which the DOJ and the SEC can bring charges against a foreign company, and the fact that most foreign corruption charges are settled rather than litigated, the FCPA may be closer to an international anti-corruption business tax than to a domestic criminal law with limited extraterritorial application. Leibold suggests that, to minimize potential foreign policy concerns and violations of international law, the SEC and DOJ should focus the enforcement of the FCPA on cases of bribery that have a close connection or substantial effect on the United States.

Similarly, Mateo de la Torre poses the question whether vigorous enforcement of the FCPA in cases where there is only a tangential link to the United States is "a valid regulatory effort or, alternatively, an act of legal imperialism." He argues that courts should place limitations on the extraterritorial reach of the FCPA in the interest of foreign jurisdictions, businesses and foreign relations. He suggests that, in determining whether extraterritorial application of the FCPA would be unreasonable, courts may look at the list of factors enumerated in section 403 of the Restatement (Third) of Foreign Relations Law, the following six of which are of particular importance:

- the link of the activity to the territory of the regulating state;
- the connections between the regulating state and the person principally responsible for the activity to be regulated, or between that state and those whom the regulation is designed to protect;
- the existence of justified expectations that might be protected or hurt by the regulation;
- the importance of the regulation to the international political, legal, or economic system;
- the extent to which another state may have an interest in regulating the activity; and
- the likelihood of conflict with regulation by another state.

Torre concludes that successful challenges to the extraterritorial application of the FCPA in courts would allow foreign jurisdictions to develop regulatory regimes that take into account their cultural, political and economic specifics while continuing to provide cross-border assistance when necessary. Simultaneously, it would free prosecutorial resources of the SEC and DOJ that would otherwise be used in prosecuting cases with only remote connections to the United States.

UK Law

For offences under sections 1, 2 and 6 (active and passive bribery and bribing a foreign public official), the Bribery Act asserts jurisdiction based on both the territoriality principle and the nationality principle:

- Offences under this Act: territorial application
- An offence is committed under section 1, 2 or 6 in England and Wales, Scotland or Northern Ireland if any act or omission which forms part of the offence takes place in that part of the United Kingdom.
  - Subsection (3) applies if—
  1. no act or omission which forms part of an offence under section 1, 2 or 6 takes place in the United Kingdom,
  2. a person's acts or omissions done or made outside the United Kingdom would form part of such an offence if done or made in the United Kingdom, and
  3. that person has a close connection with the United Kingdom.
  - In such a case—
  1. the acts or omissions form part of the offence referred to in subsection (2)(a), and
  2. proceedings for the offence may be taken at any place in the United Kingdom.
  - For the purposes of subsection (2)(c) a person has a close connection with the United Kingdom if, and only if, the person was one of the following at the time the acts or omissions concerned were done or made—
  1. a British citizen,
  2. a British overseas territories citizen,
  3. a British National (Overseas),
  4. a British Overseas citizen,
  5. a person who under the British Nationality Act 1981 was a British subject,
  6. a British protected person within the meaning of that Act,
  7. an individual ordinarily resident in the United Kingdom,
  8. a body incorporated under the law of any part of the United Kingdom,
  9. a Scottish partnership.
  10. An offence is committed under section 7 irrespective of whether the acts or omissions which form part of the offence take place in the United Kingdom or elsewhere.

11. Where no act or omission which forms part of an offence under section 7 takes place in the United Kingdom, proceedings for the offence may be taken at any place in the United Kingdom.
12. Subsection (8) applies if, by virtue of this section, proceedings for an offence are to be taken in Scotland against a person.
13. Such proceedings may be taken—
- in any sheriff court district in which the person is apprehended or in custody, or
- in such sheriff court district as the Lord Advocate may determine.

⦿ In subsection (8) "sheriff court district" is to be read in accordance with section 307(1) of the Criminal Procedure (Scotland) Act 1995.

In summary, the Bribery Act will apply if "any act or omission which forms part of the offence" occurs within the UK (section 12(1)). In addition, the Bribery Act applies to conduct occurring wholly outside the UK by persons with a "close connection" to the UK. Section 12(4) lists those considered to have a close connection to the UK, including British citizens, British nationals living overseas and all individuals ordinarily resident in the UK. Companies incorporated under UK law are also deemed to have a close connection with the UK. Foreign subsidiaries of UK parent companies are not subject to UK jurisdiction, even if wholly owned by UK parent companies. But, if a foreign subsidiary acts as an agent for a UK company, the agent's conduct can be attributed to the parent company. Pursuant to section 14, senior officers or directors of a UK corporation who were convicted of a section 1, 2 or 6 offence are also guilty of the offence if they consented or connived in the commission of the offence.

The offence of failing to prevent bribery under section 7 of the Bribery Act has much broader extraterritorial application. As Painter explains:

⦿ Section 7 stands in stark contrast to the much narrower jurisdictional provisions of Sections 1, 2, and 6 of the Bribery Act, and it is this provision that is so striking in its extraterritoriality and scope of potential criminal liability. Three separate provisions embedded within Section 7 lead to this expansive jurisdictional reach and scope. First, the Section applies to "relevant commercial organizations". This term is defined in Section 7(5) of the Bribery Act to include both entities organized under UK law as well as entities organized under the laws of any other jurisdiction if the entity "carries on a business, or part of a business, in any part of the United Kingdom". Second, unlike the Section 1, 2, and 6 offenses that require either an act or omission in the UK or at least a "close connection", a relevant commercial organization can be exposed under Section 7 of the Act for failing to prevent bribery "irrespective of whether the acts or

> omissions which form part of the offence take place in the United Kingdom or elsewhere." Third, the predicate offenses for an organization to be criminally liable under Section 7 are triggered by the acts or omissions of a person "associated with" the relevant commercial organization. Under Section 8 of the Act, an "associated person" is a person who performs services for or on behalf of the organization. The term includes employees, agents and subsidiaries, and the capacity in which the associated person performs services does not matter. These three concepts work to create an extraordinarily broad statute.

As Lordi notes, it is likely that the words "carry on a business" are intended to capture all commercial organizations doing business in the UK, not just those with a physical office in the UK.34 In effect, section 7 appears to extend its reach to "virtually all major multinational corporations."

The Guidance document to the UK Bribery Act, produced by the Ministry of Justice, attempts to assuage concerns about the extraterritorial scope of section 7 by anticipating that a "common sense approach" will be employed when determining whether an organization carries on a business in the UK.36 According to the Guidance, the mere fact that a company is listed for trading on the London Stock Exchange would not be sufficient to bring it under the jurisdiction of section 7 of the Bribery Act without further evidence of a "demonstrable business presence" in the UK. The Guidance also states that "having a UK subsidiary will not, in itself, mean that a parent company is carrying on a business in the UK, since a subsidiary may act independently of its parent or other group companies."

Lordi is skeptical, however, as there is no existing UK case law that gives meaning to the "common sense approach." Other commentators question whether the Guidance document has capitulated to business interests that objected to the reach of the Bribery Act. According to Bonneau, the Ministry of Justice's Guidance "has created loopholes that simply do not exist on the face of the Bribery Act text, risking the resurrection of some of the most infamous problems of the old common law bribery regime." It remains to be seen how the Serious Fraud Office, the agency charged with investigating offences under the Bribery Act, and the courts will interpret the jurisdiction of the Bribery Act.

In any case, a "relevant commercial organization" is liable to be convicted of an offence if persons associated with that organization commit a bribery offence, even if the bribery is committed abroad and the persons and organization have no close connection with the UK. For example, suppose an agent of Sri Lankan nationality was working for the Sri Lankan- based branch of a company incorporated in India. The Sri Lankan agent offers a bribe to an official in Sri Lanka. Importantly, the Indian company has an active branch in the UK. Under the Bribery Act, the Indian company could be prosecuted for failure to prevent bribery. Note, however, that to be personally prosecuted, the person committing the offence requires a close connection to the UK.

Canadian Law

Until 2013, the CFPOA determined jurisdiction based exclusively on the principle of territoriality. Territoriality is the jurisdictional principle which governs most criminal offences under Canadian law (Criminal Code, section 6), including the secret commissions offence in section 426. However, Canada has asserted jurisdiction based on nationality for a few crimes, such as offences under the CFPOA (since 2013), offences involving child sex tourism and certain terrorism offences committed outside of Canada. See Criminal Code, sections 7 (3.73) (3.74) (3.75) (4.1), and (4.11).

Since the Criminal Code does not define "territorial jurisdiction," its meaning has been determined by case law. The leading case was decided 30 years ago by the Supreme Court of Canada, but its definition is now outdated in the context of bribery and other transnational offences. In Libman v The Queen (1985), the Supreme Court of Canada held that in order for a Canadian criminal statute to apply, "a significant portion of the activities constituting that offence" must take place in Canada.40 If a significant portion of the criminal conduct occurs in Canada and other parts occur in a foreign state, then Canada and that foreign state have concurrent jurisdiction (or qualified territorial jurisdiction). In Libman, the Court went on to state that there must be a "real and substantial link" between the offence and Canada. In addition, the court must be satisfied that prosecution does not offend the principle of international comity. The term "comity" refers to the principle of legal reciprocity and consideration for the interests of other states. Under this principle, a state displays civility towards other nations by respecting the validity of their laws and other executive or judicial actions.

Libman sets a fairly high test for territorial jurisdiction. While Canada requires "significant portions" of the offence to occur within Canada, the US and UK assert territorial jurisdiction if "any act or omission," which constitutes an element of the offence occurs, within their borders. Prior to the 2013 amendments adding nationality jurisdiction to CFPOA, it appears that the Libman test would have excluded Canadian prosecution of bribery by Canadian individuals or companies engaged in foreign bribery, if the conduct constituting bribery occurred largely in other countries without any significant conduct in or substantial link to Canada. As noted, such a demanding test for territorial jurisdiction is not well suited to the modern realities of global business, in which the transfer of information, contracts and money between countries can occur instantaneously.

The OECD Working Group expressed concerns that Canada's standard of a "real and substantial link" failed to comply with the OECD Convention, which mandates that even a minor territorial link should be sufficient. However, the Libman standard has been relaxed somewhat in practice. For example, in R v Karigar, the first conviction of an individual under CFPOA, the accused was a Canadian acting on behalf of a Canadian company while in India.41 Even though the actual financial element of the offence (i.e., approval or funding of the bribe) did not occur in Canada, the court found there was still a real and substantial connection because the accused was acting on behalf of a Canadian company and the unfair advantage would have flowed to that Canadian company. The substantial link seems to be that the accused was a Canadian citizen working for a Canadian company (compare with Chowdhury noted below).

Canada's failure to expressly assert jurisdiction based on nationality was repeatedly criticized by commentators prior to the 2013 amendments. In the 2011 Phase 3 Report, the OECD Working Group called CFPOA's lack of extraterritorial jurisdiction based on nationality "a serious obstacle to enforcement," and urged Canada to rectify this as a "matter of urgency." 42 Prior to the 2013 amendments, Canada responded to such criticisms by arguing that the establishment of nationality jurisdiction was not explicitly mandated under its treaty obligations.

In June 2013, the CFPOA was amended by Bill S-14 to extend the Act's prescriptive jurisdiction to Canadian citizens, permanent residents and any public body or entity formed under Canadian law. These individuals or legal persons are subject to Canadian criminal liability in respect of acts of bribing a foreign public official, irrespective of whether any part of the act constituting the offence takes place in Canada. With these amendments, a Canadian accused (such as Mr. Karigar) would clearly fall within Canada's jurisdiction.

However, the CFPOA's reach is not without limits. In Chowdhury v HMQ, the accused was a citizen and resident of Bangladesh acting as an agent for a Canadian corporation, SNC- Lavalin.43 The accused had never been to Canada. In his capacity as agent for SNC-Lavalin, he allegedly facilitated the offer of bribes to foreign officials in Bangladesh in an attempt to secure for SNC-Lavalin an engineering contract for the Padma Bridge proposal.

Chowdhury launched an application claiming Canada had no jurisdiction to prosecute him for an offence of bribery under section 3(1)(b) of the CFPOA. The application was successful, and the bribery charge against Chowdhury was stayed. The Court gave a very helpful analysis of the complexity of the various concepts of jurisdiction. As the Court noted:

- The different forms of jurisdiction often overlap in real world legal problems. In this case the interplay is between prescriptive jurisdiction and adjudicative jurisdiction. Specifically, whether Parliament's legislation concerning the bribery of foreign officials brings a foreign national, whose acts in respect of the alleged offence were undertaken wholly outside of Canada, within the jurisdiction of this court.

- The problem in this case, of course, is that the applicant is not now, nor has he ever been, within Canada. He is not a Canadian citizen. He is a citizen of Bangladesh and his actions in relation to this alleged offence were all undertaken within Bangladesh. The question is whether a charge under the CFPOA gives this court jurisdiction over the applicant.

In other words, did Parliament intend section 3(1)(b) of CFPOA to apply to non-Canadians who had never been in Canada, and whose acts of bribery (for the benefit of a Canadian company) occurred entirely in a foreign state? The Court held that Parliament did not, stating the following:

- In this regard, the general rule when interpreting a statute is that Parliament is presumed to have intended to pass legislation that will accord with the principles of international law. This point is made clear in Hape where LeBel J. said, at para:

  - It is a well-established principle of statutory interpretation that legislation will be presumed to conform to international law.

  It is, of course, open to Parliament to pass legislation that conflicts with international law but if it wishes that result, it must do so clearly and expressly.

- The decision in Hape dealt with the issue of the "extraterritorial application" of Canadian law. It noted the general prohibition in s. 6(2) of the Criminal Code that I have set out above. The court went on to find that Parliament has "clear constitutional authority" to pass legislation governing conduct by non-Canadians outside of Canada. However, in exercising that authority, the court noted certain parameters that will generally apply. LeBel J. said, at para:

- [Parliament's] ability to pass extraterritorial legislation is informed by the binding customary principles of territorial sovereign equality and non-intervention, by the comity of nations, and by the limits of international law to the extent that they are not incompatible with domestic law.

- A basic part of international law is the principle of sovereign equality. Countries generally respect each other's borders and will not attempt to adjudicate matters that occurred within the borders of another sovereign country. Similarly, countries will exercise jurisdiction over their own nationals but not over another country's nationals except, of course, where that country's nationals commit an offence within another country's borders.

- Nevertheless, there are situations where a country will reach beyond its borders to prosecute individuals who commit an offence in another country. This normally only occurs where the offence committed in the other country is committed by the first country's own nationals or where the harm arising from the criminal acts in the other country is visited upon the citizens of the first country. In the former case, the basis for jurisdiction is nationality. At common law, we recognize that Canada may have a legitimate interest in prosecuting an offence involving the actions of Canadians outside of our borders. In the latter case, the basis for jurisdiction is qualified territoriality, which extends the notion of territorial jurisdiction beyond our strict borders. Under the "objective territorial principle", Canada will have a legitimate interest in prosecuting non-Canadians for criminal actions that cause harm in Canada provided a real and substantial link between the offence and Canada is established and international comity is not offended.: Libman; Hape at para. 59; Robert J. Currie, International & Transnational Criminal Law (Toronto: Irwin Law, 2010) at pp. 63-65.
- There is a last point to be taken from Hape and that is with respect to the issue that arises here, namely, the assumption of jurisdiction over foreign nationals. The court in Hape held that it was open to Parliament to pass legislation that sought to govern conduct by non-Canadians outside of Canada. The court pointed out, however, that if Parliament chose to do so, Parliament would likely be violating international law and would also likely offend the comity of nations. Again, LeBel J. said, at para:
    - Parliament has clear constitutional authority to pass legislation governing conduct by non-Canadians outside Canada. Its ability to pass extraterritorial legislation is informed by the binding customary principles of territorial sovereign equality and non-intervention, by the comity of nations, and by the limits of international law to the extent that they are not incompatible with domestic law. By virtue of parliamentary sovereignty, it is open to Parliament to enact legislation that is inconsistent with those principles, but in so doing it would violate international law and offend the comity of nations.
- As a consequence of that reality, courts will approach the interpretation of any legislation with the presumption that Parliament did not intend to violate international law and offend the comity of nations. Thus, absent clear language compelling such an interpretation, courts will adopt an interpretation that leads to the opposite outcome.

The Court also emphasized the importance of the distinction between jurisdiction over the offence and jurisdiction over the person:

- Where adjudicative jurisdiction is asserted over an alleged offence, a court must have jurisdiction over both the offence and the person accused of the offence. The two are separate and discrete issues. As Doherty J.A. succinctly said in United States v. Kavaratzis (2006), 208 C.C.C. (3d) 139 (Ont. C.A.), at para:
    - Jurisdiction over an accused is distinct from jurisdiction over an offence. This dimension of jurisdiction is less commented upon but it is crucial to the resolution of this application.
- At the risk of being repetitive, but so that it is clear, there is a distinction between Canada extending its jurisdiction over the offence, because the offence has some extraterritorial aspects, and Canada extending its jurisdiction over a person who is outside of Canada's territorial jurisdiction. Jurisdiction over the former is governed by the "real and substantial link" test set out in *Libman*. The latter is governed by the legislative language used in the offence creating statute. This point is made by Robert J. Currie in *International & Transnational Criminal Law* where the author observes, at p. 421:
    - When Parliament wishes the courts to take extraterritorial jurisdiction over persons or conduct completely outside Canadian borders, it must instruct the courts to this effect by making it explicit or necessarily implied in the legislation. Otherwise, territorial jurisdiction — as expanded by the Libman criteria — is the default.

The Court held that neither section 3(1)(b) nor other provisions of CFPOA contained such clear language, rejecting the position that jurisdiction over the offence establishes jurisdiction over all parties to the offence and noting that jurisdiction over Chowdhury would depend on his physical presence in Canada:

- In the end result, the position of the Crown appears to be that once Canada has jurisdiction over the offence, it has jurisdiction over all of the parties to that offence. I do not accept that proposition because it conflates the question of jurisdiction over the offence with the question of jurisdiction over the person. The existing authorities make it clear that these are two separate and distinct questions. Canada can achieve an affirmative answer to the first question but that does not lead inexorably to an affirmative answer to the second question. The mere fact that the applicant is a party to the offence is not sufficient, in my view, to give Canada jurisdiction over him unless and until the applicant either physically attends in Canada or Bangladesh offers to surrender him to Canada.

- This latter point is made out in some of the cases to which I have already referred. For example, in Treacy, Lord Diplock twice alludes to the fact that the English courts could gain jurisdiction over a foreign national if that person comes into the United Kingdom. Lord Diplock said, at p. 562:
    - Nor, as the converse of this, can I see any reason in comity to prevent Parliament from rendering liable to punishment, if they subsequently come to England, persons who have done outside the United Kingdom physical acts which have had harmful consequences upon victims in England. [...] It may be under no obligation in comity to punish those acts itself, but it has no ground for complaint in international law if the state in which the harmful consequences had their effect punishes, when they do enter its territories, persons who did such acts.
- The same point is made in *Liangsiriprasert* where Lord Griffiths said, at p. 250:
    - If the inchoate crime is aimed at England with the consequent injury to English society why should the English courts not accept jurisdiction to try it if the authorities can lay hands on the offenders, either because they come within the jurisdiction or through extradition procedures?
- I accept, therefore, that if Canada was able to "lay hands" on the applicant, Canada would then have the jurisdiction to try the applicant for an offence under the CFPOA over which Canada also has jurisdiction. Until that should happen to occur, the CFPOA does not extend Canada's jurisdiction to the applicant for the purposes of prosecuting him under that statute.

Since Canada has no extradition treaty with Bangladesh, Canada cannot "lay hands" on Chowdhury. The Court also rejected the Crown's argument that Chowdhury would get away with impunity unless Canada claimed jurisdiction over him. The Court stated:

- It appears that it was the Minister's view that foreign nationals were not caught by the CFPOA, that Canada would not have jurisdiction over them and that it would be up to their host country to decide on any prosecution of them.
- The Crown submits that such an interpretation would allow the applicant to get away with his activities "with impunity". Indeed, that may well be the result but, if it is, it is because the authorities in Bangladesh will have decided not to prosecute the applicant for any involvement he had in these matters and not to surrender him to Canada for prosecution here. Those are both decisions that a sovereign country is entitled to make in respect of one

of its citizens. I can think of few greater infringements on the sovereignty of a foreign state than for Canada to say that it will pre-empt or overrule those conclusions by purporting to prosecute the applicant in this country where his own country has declined to do so.

- In addition to those considerations, the principle of international comity argues against an interpretation of s. 3 that would bring foreign nationals within its ambit. A state's sovereignty is at its peak when it is dealing with its own citizens and their actions within that state's own borders.

The 2013 amendments to CFPOA (adding nationality jurisdiction) would not give Canada jurisdiction over a person like Chowdhury.

On June 4, 2014, the RCMP charged US nationals Robert Barra and Dario Berini (former CEOs of Cryptometrics), and UK national Shailesh Govindia (an agent for Cryptometrics) with an offence under section 3 of CFPOA. Canada-wide warrants were issued for all three (extradition proceedings in US and UK are an option). Based on Chowdhury, prosecutors will no doubt argue that Canada has a legitimate interest in prosecuting these foreign nationals in Canada because the bribery scheme had its genesis in Canada.

For more on Canada's jurisdiction over transnational criminal offences, see Robert J. Currie & Dr. Joseph Rikhof, International & Transnational Criminal Law, 2nd ed (Irwin Law, 2013).

Concerns with Expanded Jurisdiction

Skinnider, in Corruption in Canada: Reviewing Practices from Abroad to Improve Our Response, reviews some of the major arguments as well as some of the concerns associated with expanding jurisdiction:

BEGINNING OF EXCERPT

The broadening of jurisdiction beyond the principle of [strict] territoriality will likely result in higher incidences of concurrent jurisdiction. This could give rise to conflicting assertions of civil or criminal jurisdiction, conflicts of laws and concerns of dual criminality and double jeopardy. Companies have raised concerns as to how they are to do business and respond to investigations and prosecutions in multiple jurisdictions that have different substantive laws, enforcement procedures, penalties and available resources. Companies have also expressed concern regarding the "legalization of compliance codes" and the multiplicity of possible compliance codes found in different States.

Some commentators counter these concerns by pointing out that the reality is there is an appalling lack of enforcement, and not to waste time worrying about multiple jurisdictional issues. However, the IBA Legal Practice Division Task Force on Extraterritorial Jurisdiction has studied this issue and calls for harmonizing guidelines to alleviate this potential challenge.48 The Task Force also calls for States to consider adopting a "soft" form of double jeopardy or ne bis in idem that takes into account not just criminal liability, but "functional equivalent" civil liability for corporations and individuals.49 The lack of harmonization of corruption statutes in terms of corporate and individual liability, penalties, major elements of offences and defences, needs to be considered in devising any double jeopardy rule.

Whether a corporation may be regarded as national differs amongst States. Some States regard a corporation as national if it has been founded according to the national law or if the corporation resides in the territory. Other States relate the question of jurisdiction to the nationality of the acting natural person, not to the nationality of the legal person. Thus, States would require that the person who has acted corruptly within the structure or in favor of the legal person is one of its citizens. However, this may cause "serious legal loopholes since in the crucial cases of corporate liability investigative agencies may not be able to identify the individual instigator or perpetrator".

Moreover States "may consider that the principle of liability of legal persons links legal consequences to the legal entity itself, hence abstracting from individual persons and their nationality". The application of nationality jurisdiction to legal persons remains untested. Whether the authorities in a parent company's country can take action against the parent company where one of its foreign subsidiaries bribes a foreign public official is a priority issue for OECD.

END OF EXCERPT

For a discussion of risks of parallel proceedings, see Chapter 6, Section 7.2 of this book.

CRIMINAL LIABILITY OF CORPORATIONS AND OTHER COLLECTIVE ENTITIES

Introduction

It is well recognized among commentators that in order to effectively combat transnational corruption, mechanisms must be in place to hold corporations and other collective entities liable when they engage in bribery. For convenience, I will generally use the expression "corporate liability," but when doing so I intend to include other legally recognized collective entities. In many cases, particularly when dealing with large, decentralized multinationals, it may be impossible for an enforcement agency to determine who made the actual decision to offer a bribe.53Often the decision to offer a bribe by a frontline employee is either supported or tolerated by the upper echelons of management. 54 In such a case, punishing only the frontline employee would not sufficiently punish the corporate culture that facilitated the wrongdoing, nor would it effectively deter other corporations from allowing this culture to persist. There is therefore a need to hold corporations liable in these instances.

For many years, both common law and civil law jurisdictions resisted the idea that a corporation could be found guilty of a "crime." This reluctance was based on the traditional notion that "crimes" required proof of "personal mental fault" (also referred to as subjective fault), which usually took the form of acting intentionally or recklessly (i.e., the accused foresees that his/her conduct may cause a criminal harm, but engages in that conduct, thereby knowingly taking the risk that the criminal harm may occur). It was thought that corporations, as non-human legal fictions, could not form personal states of mind such as intention or subjective recklessness. As industrialization spread in the 18th and 19th centuries, many new offences were created to prevent or regulate industrial activities and industrialization's harmful ancillary effects. These offences were generally considered to be regulatory or administrative offences, as opposed to criminal offences. Since they were not crimes, they did not require proof of "personal fault." They were strict or absolute liability and, therefore, corporations could be and were convicted of these types of offences.

The pressure to also hold corporations liable for criminal offences began to build in the early 20th century. Common law countries slowly adopted corporate criminal liability in the first half of the 20th century. How? Generally speaking, courts in common law countries began to hold that the "personal fault" of the "directing minds" of a corporation was deemed to also be the corporation's personal fault. The critical question then became "which officers of a corporation are that corporation's 'directing minds'?"

Civil law countries were less willing to accept the fiction that a corporation can have a guilty intent or mind. However, since the mid-20th century, many, but not all, civil law countries began to embrace corporate criminal liability (an issue further discussed in Section 2.4 below).

There are currently three main legal mechanisms for imputing criminal liability to corporations. These mechanisms are significantly different. In addition, within each mechanism there can be variations in terms of broad or narrow attribution of criminal liability to corporations. The three mechanisms are:

- strict liability (used in general for US federal laws);
- directing mind or identification doctrine (used by countries such as England and Canada and by many states in the US and Australia); and
- corporate culture (used in Australian federal laws).

Pieth and Ivory briefly summarize these three mechanisms:

- by imputing to the corporation offences committed by any corporate agent or employee – no matter what steps others in the corporation had taken to prevent and respond to the misconduct (strict vicarious liability), or if others had not done enough to prevent the wrongdoing (qualified vicarious liability);
- by identifying the corporation with its executive bodies and managers and holding the corporation liable for their acts, omissions, and states of mind of those executives (identification); and
- by treating the collective entity as capable of offending in its own right, either through the aggregated thoughts and deeds of its senior stakeholders (aggregation) or though inadequate organizational systems and cultures (corporate culture, corporate (dis)organization).

Countries such as France, Austria, Italy and Switzerland have all enacted statutes that impose corporate criminal liability. Some jurisdictions, such as Germany, do not recognize corporate criminal liability, but instead impose quasi-criminal regulatory sanctions on collective entities. Outside of Europe, countries such as Korea, Japan and China recognize at least some form of corporate criminal liability. There remain, however, some countries, such as Greece and Uruguay that do not recognize criminal or quasi-criminal sanctions for companies. 56 In these countries, it is only possible to convict the employees, agents or executives of a company, but not the company itself. For a recent overview of corporate liability in Europe see: Chance's, Corporate Liability in Europe. The OECD Working Group on Bribery's 2016 review of corporate liability of the 41 countries that are parties to the OECD Anti-Bribery Convention, is also now available.

Among countries that do recognize corporate criminal liability, there are significant variations regarding the offences for which criminal liability may be imposed and the way in which that liability is triggered. Most common law jurisdictions now accept that a corporation may be found to have mens rea through its human actors. Among civil law countries, some countries accept this proposition and impose corporate criminal liability for all crimes. Other civil law countries only accept this proposition for certain listed offences. The countries that employ this "list-based" approach generally restrict corporate criminal liability to economic and other types of offences generally associated with corporations as well as offences established pursuant to international and regional conventions. A more detailed review of the ways in which various common law and civil law countries address corporate criminal liability can be found in Pieth and Ivory's chapter "Emergence and Convergence: Corporate Criminal Liability Principles in Overview"59 and in the 2016 OECD report Liability of Legal Persons for Foreign Bribery: A Stocktaking Report.

The attribution of criminal intent or fault to corporations also raises the possibility of a due diligence or compliance defence. The possible existence of that defence in the context of bribery and anti-corruption offences in the US, UK and Canada will be discussed in further detail below.

UNCAC

UNCAC does not mandate that State Parties establish criminal sanctions for corporations involved in corruption offences. However, Article 26 does require State Parties to ensure that legal entities are liable (criminally or otherwise) for their participation in offences established under UNCAC. Article 26 states:

Article 26. Liability of legal persons

- Each State Party shall adopt such measures as may be necessary, consistent with its legal principles, to establish the liability of legal persons for participation in the offences established in accordance with this Convention.
- Subject to the legal principles of the State Party, the liability of legal persons may be criminal, civil or administrative.
- Such liability shall be without prejudice to the criminal liability of the natural persons who have committed the offences.
- Each State Party shall, in particular, ensure that legal persons held liable in accordance with this article are subject to effective, proportionate and dissuasive criminal or non-criminal sanctions, including monetary sanctions.

The Legislative Guide to UNCAC addresses corporate liability under Article 26 as follows:

- Article 26, paragraph 1, requires that States parties adopt such measures as may be necessary, consistent with their legal principles, to establish the liability of legal persons for participation in the offences established in accordance with the Convention.

  The obligation to provide for the liability of legal entities is mandatory, to the extent that this is consistent with each State's legal principles. Subject to these legal principles, the liability of legal persons may be criminal, civil or administrative (art. 26, para. 2), which is consistent with other international initiatives that acknowledge and accommodate the diversity of approaches adopted by different legal systems. Thus, there is no obligation to establish criminal liability, if that is inconsistent with a State's legal principles. In those cases, a form of civil or administrative liability will be sufficient to meet the requirement.

Article 26, paragraph 3, provides that this liability of legal entities must be established without prejudice to the criminal liability of the natural persons who have committed the offences. The liability of natural persons who perpetrated the acts, therefore, is in addition to any corporate liability and must not be affected in any way by the latter. When an individual commits crimes on behalf of a legal entity, it must be possible to prosecute and sanction them both ....

The Convention requires States to ensure that legal persons held liable in accordance with article 26 are subject to effective, proportionate and dissuasive criminal or non-criminal sanctions, including monetary sanctions (art. 26, para. 4).

This specific provision complements the more general requirement of article 30, paragraph 1, that sanctions must take into account the gravity of the offence. Given that the investigation and prosecution of crimes of corruption can be quite lengthy, States with a legal system providing for statutes of limitation must ensure that the limitation periods for the offences covered by the Convention are comparatively long (see also art. 29).

The most frequently used sanction is a fine, which is sometimes characterized as criminal, sometimes as non-criminal and sometimes as a hybrid. Other sanctions include exclusion from contracting with the Government (for example public procurement, aid procurement and export credit financing), forfeiture, confiscation, restitution, debarment or closing down of legal entities. In addition, States may wish to consider non- monetary sanctions available in some jurisdictions, such as withdrawal of certain advantages, suspension of certain rights, prohibition of certain activities, publication of the judgment, the appointment of a trustee, the requirement to establish an effective internal compliance programme and the direct regulation of corporate structures.

The obligation to ensure that legal persons are subject to appropriate sanctions requires that these be provided for by legislation and should not limit or infringe on existing judicial independence or discretion with respect to sentencing.

OECD Convention

Article 2 of the OECD Convention states:

- Each Party shall take such measures as may be necessary, in accordance with its legal principles, to establish the liability of legal persons for the bribery of a foreign public official.

The clause "in accordance with its legal principles" reflects the Convention's goal of functional equivalency, meaning that State Parties are required to sanction the bribery of foreign public officials in the same manner that they would sanction other offences committed by corporations, without mandating changes in the fundamental principles of their respective legal systems.62 In this regard, the Commentaries on the Convention state that if the concept of criminal responsibility of legal persons is not recognized in a nation's legal system, that nation is not required to establish it. Furthermore, Article 3(2) requires that if criminal liability for legal persons is not available, State Parties shall ensure that legal persons are subject to "effective, proportionate and dissuasive non-criminal sanctions, including monetary sanctions, for bribery of foreign public officials." This wording is very similar to the requirements regarding the sanctioning of legal persons later adopted in UNCAC. Pursuant to Article 3(4), State Parties shall also consider the imposition of additional civil or administrative sanctions, such as exclusion from participation in public procurement processes, exclusion from entitlement to certain benefits or a judicial winding-up order. These and other civil remedies are discussed in Chapter 7, Sections 7 to 10.

In 2009, the OECD Council adopted the 2009 Recommendation for Further Combatting Bribery and Annex I, which stated that member parties to the convention should not treat prosecution of natural persons as a prerequisite to also prosecuting the corporation, and secondly it provided guidance on different methods for attributing liability to the company based on the actions or inactions of natural persons associated with the company.

Pieth notes that the OECD Working Group on Bribery has been reluctant to give directives on which sanctions it feels meet the standard of "effective, proportionate and dissuasive."63 Upon reviewing the Working Group on Bribery's Phase One evaluation of Japan (where it considered the sanctions available in Japan to be insufficient), Pieth argues that two principles are discernible:

By virtue of this finding, the WGB [Working Group on Bribery] established two principles: first, that sanctions against corporations must be sufficiently 'tough' to have an impact on large multinational corporations, second, that according to the concept of functional equivalence a trade-off is possible between two theoretically quite different instruments, i.e. the corporate fine and the forfeiture/confiscation of illicit profits (Article 3(3) of the Convention).

Pieth goes on to address how the different concepts of corporate criminal liability compare to the standard of effective, proportionate and dissuasive sanctions:

- With respect to those countries which have implemented corporate criminal liability, the application of a mere identification model, imputing only offences of the most senior management to corporations and also frequently refusing a concept of 'aggregate knowledge', would in our view fail to meet the requirements of 'effective, proportionate and dissuasive sanctions'.

As will be noted below, the above comments are relevant to the UK. They were also applicable to Canada before the 2004 legislative changes which provided a broader definition of corporate liability. Pieth then adds:

- On the other hand, the terms of Articles 2 and 3 of the Convention would be met by countries whose liability concept includes lack of due diligence by senior management, allowing junior agents to engage in bribery.

According to this view, the many State Parties that rely on the identification theory to trigger liability of corporate entities are failing to meet their full OECD Convention obligations.

Overview of Corporate Liability in the 41 State Parties to the OECD Anti-Bribery Convention

The OECD's Working Group on Bribery (WGB) has conducted a comparative study on liability of legal persons in the 41 Parties to the OECD Anti-Bribery Convention. In December 2016, the WGB released its final stocktaking report.

The report notes the vast global expansion of liability for "legal persons" that has taken place since the Convention's adoption in 1997:

- After the adoption of the Convention, many Parties initiated law- making events relevant for LP [legal person] liability and foreign bribery. These included:
  - — Creation of LP liability frameworks for foreign bribery in the absence of prior legal traditions. Based on information provided in the WGB's monitoring reports, it appears that 16 Parties (39%) took steps to create LP liability systems apparently without any previous experience before the adoption of the Convention: Austria, Belgium, Bulgaria, Chile, Colombia, Czech Republic, Estonia, Greece, Hungary, Italy, Latvia, Luxembourg, Russian Federation, Slovenia, Spain, and Switzerland.
  - — Adaptation or application of LP liability systems that existed in some form before the Convention to cover foreign bribery. In addition, 24 Parties (59%) adapted or applied pre-existing systems for LP liability to foreign bribery while implementing the Convention: Australia, Brazil, Canada, Denmark, Finland, France, Germany, Iceland, Ireland, Israel, Japan, Korea, Mexico, Netherlands, New Zealand, Norway, Poland, Portugal, Slovak Republic, South Africa, Sweden, Turkey, United Kingdom and the United States.

- A multi-stage process of refining legal approaches to LP liability. Twenty-one countries (51%) have two or more entries in the timeline after the 1997 adoption of the Convention: Australia, Brazil, Canada, Colombia, Estonia, France, Germany, Greece, Hungary, Latvia, Mexico, New Zealand, Norway, Poland, Portugal, Slovak Republic, Spain, Sweden, Switzerland, Turkey and the United States. These multiple entries suggest that the creation of an LP liability regime may be, for many countries, an ongoing search for an appropriate fit with the local legal system through experimentation and adaptation as they apply their laws. [footnotes omitted]

In regard to each OECD country, the report examines nine distinct aspects of the legal test or standard for liability of legal persons as well as three aspects of sanctions for legal persons found liable. Some of these features of legal person liability from the report are summarized below. As might be expected, there is significant variance in these features of legal person liability.

Sources of Liability for Legal Persons

According to the report:

- 73% of Parties have liability for legal persons in statutes, while 27% have liability in case law (e.g., common law).
- 48% have legal liability in statutes other than their general penal law (whether or not there are also provisions in their general penal law).
- 24% have bribery-specific legislation dealing with liability for legal persons.

Three Standards for Imputing Legal Liability

The report states:

- Based on WGB reports, it would appear that at least 38 countries (93%) can hold legal persons liable when a person with the highest level of managerial authority commits the offence. At least 31 countries (76%) can also hold them liable if a person with such authority directs or authorises the offence. Finally, at least 29 Parties (71%) can hold companies liable if an officer or other manager fails to prevent the offence "through a failure to supervise ... or ... a failure to implement adequate controls."

Circumstances under Which a Natural Person's Acts Will Be Attributed to a Legal Person

Some countries require multiple circumstances (i.e., a cumulative approach) while other countries only require one of several factors (an alternative approach). The report notes in part:

- A second complexity shown in Table 5 is that some countries impose different conditions as a function of the level of authority or role that the natural person offender has in relation to the legal person. At least ten Parties (24%) have conditions that depend on whether or not the natural person who engages in bribery has managerial authority within the legal person. In contrast, 29 Parties (71%) appear to apply the same conditions to attribute the acts of any relevant natural person to the legal person, without regard to the level of authority that the relevant person has.

In footnotes 38 and 39, the report states:

- It should be noted, however, that this number may simply reflect the fact that it is not yet clear how a legal person would be held liable for an offence committed by a lower-level employee given the absence of case law in some jurisdictions. ... As shown in Table 5 below, some of the countries that require that the offence has been committed with the intent to benefit the legal person include: Austria (offence committed "for the benefit of entity"); Canada ("with the intent ... to benefit" the LP); Chile ("for the benefit" of the LP); Germany (offence must have violated the "duties incumbent on the legal person" or either "enriched"—or have been "intended" to enrich—the LP); Mexico (the offence for the "benefit" of the LP); and the United States ("for the benefit" of the LP).

For the more detailed conditions (e.g., benefit or interest, within the scope of duties), the frequency is as follows:

- Twenty-seven Parties (66%) will consider whether the acts of a relevant natural person were committed for the legal person's benefit or interest;
- Twenty-one Parties (51%) will consider whether the acts of a relevant natural person were committed as a result of a failure to supervise;
- Fourteen (34%) will consider whether the acts of a relevant natural person were committed in the legal person's name or on its behalf;
- Twelve (29%) will consider whether the acts of a relevant natural person were committed within the scope of the natural person's duties or authority; and
- Twelve Parties (29%) will consider whether the acts of a relevant natural person were related to the legal person's activity. [footnotes omitted]

Liability of Legal Persons for Acts of Intermediaries

Intermediaries can be "related" (i.e., subsidiaries or individual entities within a corporate group) or unrelated (i.e., third-party agents, consultants or contractors). The law on liability of legal persons for acts of intermediaries varies significantly depending on the existence of various circumstances. The report studies each country on the basis of various circumstances. In respect to related intermediaries, the report states:

> Some of the more noteworthy models of liability for related entities are:
>
> - **In the spirit of the organisation:** According to the WGB report, Dutch law enforcement officials indicated that the Netherlands can prosecute a parent company for an offence committed by its subsidiary if the parent entity "knew about the illegal acts of the subsidiary or if the act was carried out 'in the spirit of the legal entity'". According to Dutch authorities, an act performed "in the spirit of the entity" could include acts "useful for the legal person in the business conducted by the legal person" as well as acts resulting from behaviours that were either "accepted or used to be accepted ... by the legal person".
> - **"On behalf of":** In some countries, a parent company can be liable for the acts of its subsidiary, if the subsidiary is an "agent" or otherwise acting on its behalf. According to Norwegian officials and other panellists at the WGB's on-site visit, Norway can hold the parent liable whenever the subsidiary acts "on behalf of" the parent. In the United States, "a parent may be liable for its subsidiary's conduct under traditional agency principles", whenever it has sufficient "control", whether formally or in fact, over the subsidiary's operations or conduct. Whenever such an "agency relationship" arises, the "subsidiary's actions and knowledge" can trigger criminal or other liability for the parent company.
> - **"For the benefit of":** According to Slovenia, a parent company can be held liable if it "benefited from the bribe given by subsidiary". Such approaches potentially go beyond the "agency" model to encompass wrongdoing that objectively benefits a parent company, even though the subsidiary that committed the offence may not be controlled by, or otherwise acting for, the parent company at the time of the offence.
> - **Corporate Groups:** Brazil's corporate liability regime notably holds "parent, controlled or affiliated companies ... jointly liable for the perpetration of acts" covered by the law. Perhaps in recognition of the broad scope of this liability, Brazil limits such liability to "applicable fines" and the "full compensation" for damages caused. [footnotes omitted]

In regard to unrelated intermediaries the report notes:

> - Table 9 explores whether and how the Parties can hold legal persons liable for the acts of unaffiliated business partners or other third parties. It shows that at least 31 countries (76%) have laws that would allow them to hold

companies liable for the unlawful acts of unrelated intermediaries under certain conditions.

- The most common reason identified by the WGB for holding a legal person liable for an offence committed by an unrelated entity or third party agent is that the legal person in fact participated in, or directed, the unlawful act. Based on WGB findings and supplemental information provided by the Parties, this was true in 27 countries (66%).
- Agency principles provided the second most frequent ground for imposing liability on a legal person for the acts of its unrelated business partners. At least seven countries (17%) can hold a legal person liable for bribery committed by a third party authorised to act on the legal person's behalf. These are Denmark, Estonia, Iceland, Korea, Slovenia, Turkey and the United States.
- At least 10 countries (24%) can hold a legal person liable on a theory other than complicity or agency. For example, the WGB found that at least one country, Portugal, can impose liability on a legal person that ratifies or approves the unlawful conduct of an unrelated intermediary after the fact. One other country, Canada, provided supplemental information indicating that it can also hold an LP liable on this basis. Examples of other techniques for holding legal persons liable for the unlawful acts of their business partners, include:
    - **Associated persons**: The Section 7 of the United Kingdom's Bribery Act 2010 makes certain companies liable for the acts of any "associated" person who "performs services" for them. Section 8(2) of the UK Bribery Act specifies that "the capacity in which [the associated person] performs services for or on behalf of [the legal person] does not matter".
    - **Consortium or Joint Venture Members:** Brazil's corporate liability regime holds companies that are members of a consortium liable for the unlawful acts committed by other consortium member "within the scope of their respective consortium agreement". As with its rules for attributing liability within corporate groups, Brazil limits liability for consortium members to "applicable fines" and the "full compensation" for damages caused. Poland has a similar provision holding a legal person liable for the acts of its joint venture partners, provided that the legal person had "knowledge" of the act or "consents" to it.
    - **Negligence offence:** Parties have widely different approaches to determining whether the requisite "fault" or "intent" (often referred to as dol in civil law traditions or as the mens rea element in the common

law world) has been established within the company-intermediary relationship. Some countries have attempted to side-step the difficulty of proving intent by holding legal persons liable for negligence. For example, Sweden has enacted a "negligent financing" offence, whereby a legal person can be sanctioned for providing money in a "grossly negligent" manner to an intermediary who then uses it for bribery. [footnotes omitted]

Successor Liability

The report explains the importance of robust successor liability principles to the effective enforcement and sanctioning of corruption offences:

- In a corporate law context, when a legal person merges with or acquires another entity, the successor or acquiring legal person can, in certain circumstances, assume the predecessor entity's liabilities. Successor liability in the context of foreign bribery refers to whether and under what conditions LP liability for the offence is affected by changes in company identity and ownership. Without it, a legal person may avoid liability by reorganising or otherwise altering its corporate identity. In some legal systems, however, successor liability is viewed as problematic in the criminal law context because it is viewed as conflicting with the fundamental notion that no one can be punished for the act of another. [footnotes omitted]

Neither the OECD Anti-Bribery Convention, nor the 2009 Recommendation, specifically refer to successor liability. The report also notes:

- Among the Parties, at least 18 countries (44%) have some form of successor liability for foreign bribery or other criminal offences.
- Table 10 also reports the types of transactions or reorganizations that can trigger successor liability, including name change or reincorporation (at least 12 countries, or 29%), merger/acquisition (at least 16 countries, or 39%), division or divestiture (at least 11 countries, or 27%) and dissolution (7 countries, or 17%).
- A striking feature of Table 10 is the large number of unknowns indicated by question marks.
- Although the issue has not been fully explored in the WGB reports, some of the Parties' legal frameworks and practices concerning successor liability deserve special attention:
    - **Comprehensive statutory frameworks:** In some countries, the legislature has clearly adopted a set of provisions that comprehensively address successor liability. ... Other countries, such as the United States rely on well-established jurisprudence or other legal principles to ensure successor liability.

- **Limits on sanctions:** Brazil limits the type sanctions that may be imposed on successor companies to the payment of fines and compensation for damage. ... The WGB expressed concern that limiting the ability to confiscate the profits of foreign bribery from successor companies "deprives the administration of one of the most serious deterrents to foreign bribery".
- **Mechanisms to prevent the extinction of a legal person:** ... For instance, under Belgium's 1999 Act establishing LP liability, a judge may, after finding "serious indications of guilt on the part of a legal person", impose a provisional measure to suspend "any proceedings to dissolve or wind up the legal entity" or block any transfers of assets that "could result in the legal entity becoming insolvent." [footnotes omitted]

Jurisdiction over Legal Persons and their Nationality

Both of these topics are analyzed in the report. That analysis is included in Chapter 3, Section 1.

US Law

Under the US common law doctrine of respondeat superior, a corporation will be vicariously liable for acts of its employees that violate the FCPA if the employee was acting within the scope of his or her authority and, at least in part, for the benefit of the company. Under this principle, even low-level employees acting in contravention of an express direction not to bribe a foreign official may still trigger liability for the corporation. The term "scope of authority" means within the course of the employee's ordinary duties. Tarun explains:

> For example, an international salesman agreeing to bribe a foreign official in order to obtain or retain business will be deemed to be acting within the scope of his authority. The focus is on the function delegated to the agent or employee and whether the conduct falls within that general function. So long as the agent or employee's acts are consistent with his general employment function, his employer may be held liable for those acts, even if they were contrary to express corporate policy. [footnotes omitted]

In addition, "the benefit of the corporation" need not be the sole motivating factor behind the employee's decision to offer a bribe: "So long as the motive includes a direct or ancillary benefit to the corporation—either realized or unrealized—a corporation will be accountable for the agent or employee's acts."

Corporate Criminal Liability under the *FCPA* Arising from the Acts of Foreign Subsidiaries

According to Tarun, whether US corporations are directly liable for the acts of their foreign subsidiaries is somewhat uncertain. He states:

- While the legislative history and one case indicate that foreign subsidiaries of US companies acting on their own and not as agents of a US parent are not subject to the anti-bribery provisions ... the Resource Guide to the US FCPA states that there are two ways in which a parent company can be liable for bribes paid by a subsidiary:
  - First, a parent may have participated sufficiently in the activity to be directly liable for the conduct – as, for example when it directed its subsidiary's misconduct or otherwise directly participated in the bribe scheme. Second, a parent may be held liable for its subsidiary's conduct under traditional agency principles.

According to the Resource Guide, control over the subsidiary, both general and in terms of the specific transaction, is the key factor in determining whether an agency relationship exists. If the relationship exists, the subsidiary's actions and knowledge are imputed to the parent.

Tarun states that although the FCPA does not specifically address liability arising from the behaviour of foreign subsidiaries, there are "at least five" bases in American law under which a parent corporation could be liable for acts of bribery undertaken by its foreign subsidiaries:

- First, a US company may be liable for bribery under agency principles if it had knowledge of or was willfully blind to the misconduct of its subsidiary. Second, a US parent corporation that authorizes, directs, or controls the wayward acts of a foreign subsidiary may be liable. Third a US company may be held liable under principles of respondeat superior where its corporate veil can be pierced. Fourth, a US Company that takes actions abroad in furtherance of a bribery scheme may be found liable under the Act's 1998 alternative theory of nationality jurisdiction. Fifth, foreign subsidiaries may be liable if any act in furtherance of an illegal bribe took place in the United States territory.

In addition, under the accounting provisions of the FCPA, if the records of the parent and the subsidiary are consolidated for the purposes of filing documents pursuant to the SEC's mandatory reporting requirements, a parent company may be liable for the accounting violations of a foreign subsidiary.

Successor Liability

After a merger or acquisition, the successor company assumes the predecessor company's liabilities, including those arising under the FCPA. No liability will be created where there was none before, however; for example, if the predecessor was outside FCPA jurisdiction, it will not be retroactively subject to the FCPA after acquisition. Generally, the DOJ will only pursue FCPA actions against successor companies in extreme, egregious scenarios, such as the continuation of violations by the successor company.

UK Law

According to the traditional principles of corporate criminal liability in the UK, corporations, partnerships and unincorporated bodies may be held criminally liable for offences under section 1, 2 and 6 of the Bribery Act.82 Under UK law, a corporation is its own legal entity with its own legal personality. This means that the corporation, separately from the natural persons who perform the activities of the corporation, can be involved in a corrupt transaction. The corporation may be involved in corrupt transactions either as an offender or as a victim. A corporation can be convicted of common law and statutory offences, including offences which require mens rea.

There are a few ways in which a corporation may be held criminally liable in the UK. If the offence is strict liability and requires no mens rea, there is no problem attributing liability to a corporation. A corporation can also be held vicariously liable for the acts of its employees or agents in situations where a natural person would also be vicariously liable, for example, where a statute imposes vicarious liability. This means that the acts and state of mind of employees or agents are attributed to the corporate body.

For offences that require mens rea and do not allow vicarious liability, corporate liability depends on the identification principle. If the offence is committed by an officer who is senior enough to be part of the directing mind and will of the company, and if the offence was committed within the scope of the offender's authority as a corporate officer, the offender's acts and state of mind will be deemed those of the company itself. The corporation can be convicted of an offence without a natural person being prosecuted for that offence. The identification principle is used to determine corporate liability for offences under sections 1, 2 and 6 of the Bribery Act as well as the false accounting offences under the Theft Act.

Because of the need to find subjective fault (mens rea) in one of the company's directing minds, the identification doctrine is often ineffective in establishing corporate liability. Firstly, identifying the directing minds of a large multinational corporation can be a challenge. Even when the directing minds can be identified, attributing fault to senior officers presents difficulties. Ashworth explains that the doctrine "allows large companies to disassociate themselves from the conduct of their local managers, and thus to avoid criminal liability. Moreover, where a large national or multi-national company is prosecuted, the identification principle requires the prosecution to establish that one of the directors or top managers had the required knowledge or culpability. Managers at such a high level tend to focus on broader policy issues, not working practices." As a result, in cases of bribery committed by a foreign agent in a foreign country to secure business for a company, it can be very difficult to prove that a senior officer of that company was the directing mind behind the bribery offence. The identification doctrine also fails to establish liability for corporate culture, which can develop independently from senior officers at the highest levels. Further, English law does not allow aggregation of the states of mind of more than one person in the corporation in order to satisfy mens rea requirements. Thus, historically it was very difficult for corporations to be convicted of bribery offences. Indeed, Maton says "there has never been a successful prosecution in England of a company for bribery."

The difficulty of attributing liability to corporations, especially large multinational corporations, prompted criticism in Phase 1 and Phase 2 Evaluations of the UK by the OECD Working Group. The UK has addressed the difficulties of the identification doctrine by creating offences that impose a duty on companies, for example, in the Corporate Manslaughter and Corporate Homicide Act of 2007. The imposition of a corporate duty bypasses the difficulty of establishing culpability on the part of a controlling mind in the company. Section 7 of the Bribery Act is another example of this form of corporate liability.

Bribery Act Section 7

Section 7 creates a new strict liability offence of failure of a commercial organization to prevent bribery. It is triggered when a person associated with a "relevant commercial organization" (bodies corporate or partnerships) bribes another person for the benefit of the commercial organization. A conviction under section 7 does not require a conviction for a "Corporate Attribution and the Directing Mind and Will" (2011) 127 Law Q Rev 239 suggests the wider Meridian test is not always applied.

A codified defence to the charge exists. The organization is exonerated if it can prove, on a balance of probabilities, that notwithstanding the actions of the associated person, it had adequate procedures in place to prevent such persons from engaging in bribery.

Section 7 defines the scope of this new offence in the following words:

- A relevant commercial organisation ("C") is guilty of an offence under this section if a person ("A") associated with C bribes another person intending—
  - to obtain or retain business for C, or
  - to obtain or retain an advantage in the conduct of business for C.

Under section 7, a commercial organization may be found guilty of an offence if anyone associated with the company's business participates in bribery, unless the organization has adequate procedures in place to prevent the bribery. The offence can be made out even if the controlling minds of the organization were completely unaware of the bribery. To be "associated" with the organization, person A must be a "person who performs services for or on behalf of" the organization. The capacity in which he or she performs these services does not matter; for example, person A may be an employee, agent or subsidiary, and there need not be a formal contract or in fact any degree of control. Person A does not need to have a close connection with the UK and may be an individual, a body corporate or a partnership. If person A is a subsidiary, the parent company will only be liable if the subsidiary acts in the parent's interest. If the subsidiary bribes in its own interests, the parent will not be liable, even if the subsidiary is wholly owned by that parent.

The phrase "bribes another person" means that person A is or would be guilty of an offence under sections 1 or 6, whether prosecuted or not, or would be guilty of such an offence if section 12(2)(c) and (4) dealing with jurisdiction to prosecute were omitted. Furthermore, Sections 12(2)(c) and 12(4) deal with the "close connection to the UK"; therefore persons associated with commercial organisations can be found to be "bribing another person" for the purposes of the organisation failing to prevent bribery, even if the activity took place outside of the UK and the individual had no close connection with the UK, so long as the organisation fell within the definition of a commercial organisation.

the person will be deemed to have committed the offence if his or her conduct amounted to aiding, abetting, counselling or procuring the offence.[90]

Section 7 applies to "relevant commercial organisations," that is, companies incorporated in the UK or partnerships formed in the UK, as well as to bodies corporate and partnerships incorporated or formed anywhere and carrying on a business or part of a business in the UK. As Gentle notes, the careful drafting of "carries on a business," rather than simply "carries on business", is reflective of the wide jurisdiction of the offence. The mere business presence of an overseas entity in the UK, irrespective of whether business is actually carried out in the UK, is enough to fulfill the jurisdictional requirements of the offence. That being said, the Government intends a "common sense approach" and has suggested that organizations without a "demonstrable business presence in the United Kingdom" will not be caught by this section.

It should be noted that the Bribery Act contains no provision specifically insulating person A from secondary liability in respect to the offence under section 7 (in contrast to, for example, the offence in the UK of corporate manslaughter).93 However, person A is already guilty of the intentional offence of bribery under sections 1 or 6, so it would be somewhat pointless to also charge or convict person A of the strict liability offence under section 7 where person A's conduct of aiding and abetting the section 7 offence is exactly the same conduct that constitutes the section 1 or section 6 offence.

Section 7(2) states that a full defence to the charge is available if the company can prove on a balance of probabilities that it had adequate procedures in place and followed those procedures at the time the bribery occurred in order to prevent associated persons from engaging in bribery. For more information on the adequate procedures defence, refer to Section 2.4.3(i) of Chapter 2.

According to Wells, the significance of this new offence to UK law "cannot be over emphasized." 94 The provision places important obligations on companies to proactively prevent corruption within their organization. Wells views the provision as key to ensuring corporate accountability for bribery. However, the OECD Working Group on Bribery's Phase 3 Report (March 2012) notes that the section 7 offence does not completely eliminate the limitations of the UK's narrow identification doctrine. 95 If the "associated person" is a subsidiary or another company, the identification doctrine is still necessary to determine whether the associated person committed bribery.

The provision has also received criticism for being overly broad. Jordan, a Senior Investigations Counsel with the Foreign Corrupt Practices Unit of the US SEC, believes the "provision is both revolutionary and dangerous."96 Bean and MacGuidwin refer to it as "by far the most outrageously overreaching aspect of the Act."97 They question the usefulness of the "adequate procedures" defence, since the occurrence of bribery indicates that the procedures in place were not sufficient to prevent the instance of bribery. In the Ministry of Justice's Guidance document, the Ministry listed six principles that should inform a corporate compliance program, but these principles are fairly general and are not binding on a court. These principles of good corporate compliance programs are discussed in Chapter 8 of this book.

In December 2016, Sweett Group PLC pleaded guilty to failing to prevent an act of bribery committed by its subsidiary, Cyril Sweett Interntional Limited, in order to secure a contract with Al Ain Ahlia Insurance Company (AAAI) for the building of the Rotana Hotel in Abu Dhabi. 98 In February 2016, Sweett Group PLC was sentenced and ordered to pay £2.25 million, thus becoming the first company to be fined under section 7 of the Bribery Act.99 The SFO's successful prosecution of Sweett Group speaks to the importance of implementing an adequate anti-corruption compliance program.

Notably, the US also considered codifying this type of compliance defence but ultimately rejected this approach. Instead, the US FCPA places positive obligations on companies to make and keep accurate books and records and to maintain a system of internal accounting controls. In Skinnider's paper, "Corruption in Canada: Reviewing Practices from Abroad to Improve Our Response," the compliance defence is described as follows:

3. The Affirmative Compliance Defences

The compliance defence provides that corporations will not be held vicariously liable for a violation of the foreign corruption act by its employees or agents if the company established procedures reasonably designed to prevent and detect such violations by employees and agents. Generally this refers to employees and not officers or directors. Such a defence is an affirmative defence for corporations faced with possible criminal charges if the corporation can present "good faith efforts" to achieve compliance with the laws, usually demonstrated by corporate compliance programmes. This defence recognises that despite best efforts and with the utmost diligence, corporations can still find themselves the subject of criminal prosecutions. [footnotes omitted]

Canadian Law

Pursuant to section 2 of CFPOA, the offence provisions apply to "persons," as defined in section 2 of the Criminal Code. Section 2 of the Criminal Code states that "person" includes an organization, which is defined as:

- a public body, body corporate, society, company, firm, partnership, trade union or municipality, or
- an association of persons that
  - is created for a common purpose,
  - has an operational structure, and
  - holds itself out to the public as an association of persons.

Therefore, companies and other organizations are considered "persons" under CFPOA and the Criminal Code and may be prosecuted for CFPOA and Criminal Code offences. It should also be noted that by knowingly engaging in corruption offences on three or more occasions, companies meet the definition of "criminal organization" under section 467.1, and can therefore be prosecuted for the additional criminal organization offences in the Criminal Code. Notably, the broad definition of "organization" extends liability to types of organizations that do not have the status of legal persons in the same way that corporations do.

Prior to 2004, corporate criminal liability was based on the common law principle of the directing mind. In 2003, the Canadian Government amended the Criminal Code and replaced the common law "directing minds" doctrine with a statutory scheme for corporate criminal liability. This new statutory scheme uses a much broader and more flexible definition of which officials in a corporation are to be "identified" as the corporation in respect to their acts, omissions and states of mind. Via section 34(2) of the federal Interpretation Act, the new Criminal Code corporate liability scheme also applies to CFPOA offences. Section 22.1 of the Criminal Code widens the scope of corporate criminal liability in the context of criminal and penal negligence offences, and section 22.2 provides the test for other mens rea-based offences. Section 22.2 is the relevant section of the Criminal Code for determining corporate liability for offences under the CFPOA since those offences require the prosecutor to prove subjective fault. It reads as follows:

- In respect of an offence that requires the prosecution to prove fault— other than negligence—an organization is a party to the offence if, with the intent at least in part to benefit the organization, one of its senior officers
  - acting within the scope of their authority, is a party to the offence;
  - having the mental state required to be a party to the offence and acting within the scope of their authority, directs the work of other representatives of the organization so that they do the act or make the omission specified in the offence; or
  - knowing that a representative of the organization is or is about to be a party to the offence, does not take all reasonable measures to stop them from being a party to the offence.

This statutory scheme for corporate liability for crimes which require subjective fault still relies on the identification theory. However, the common law concept of "directing minds" has been replaced with the broader concept of "senior officers." A "senior officer" is defined in the Criminal Code as follows:

- a representative who plays an important role in the establishment of an organization's policies or is responsible for managing an important aspect of the organization's activities and, in the case of a body corporate, includes a director, its chief executive officer and its chief financial officer.

"Representative" is defined to mean "a director, partner, employee, member, agent or contractor of the organization."

The term "senior officer" is broader than the common law directing minds concept as it includes persons who are responsible for managing an important aspect of the company's activities. Under the old test, in order for a person to be considered a directing mind, he or she had to be more than a manager of an important aspect of the company's activities; he or she also had to have the authority to design or implement corporate policy. In practice, this made establishing corporate criminal liability very difficult.

In the new definition of "senior officer," the terms "managing" and "an important aspect of the organization's activities" require further definition. So far, there have been very few cases that have interpreted these key parts of the definition of "senior officer. In R v Metron Construction Corporation, the Ontario Court of Appeal imposed a fine of $750,000 on the accused corporation for criminal negligence causing death contrary to section 221 of the Criminal Code. The negligence charge arose out of a workplace accident caused primarily by serious negligence on the part of the site supervisor and the foreman. The foreman died in the accident along with three other workers. Metron Construction plead guilty to one count of criminal negligence causing death under section 221 of the Criminal Code. No doubt the guilty plea was premised on the conclusion that if they disputed criminal liability at trial, they would be convicted on the basis of the new test for criminal liability under section 22.1 and the new duty in section 217.1 of the Criminal Code, which requires persons who have the authority to direct the work of others "to take all reasonable steps to prevent bodily harm" to those persons. In a subsequent trial, the site supervisor was found guilty of four counts of criminal negligence causing death. As noted, had Metron plead not guilty, undoubtedly the court would have held that the site supervisor was a "senior officer" and therefore the senior officer's criminal negligence was also Metron's criminal negligence. Under the narrower "directing minds" test applied in Canada before the 2004 amendments, it is highly unlikely that the site supervisor would have been held to be a directing mind of Metron since he had not been delegated "governing executive authority" over a part of the company business. As Warning, Edwards and Todd note, the case demonstrates how sections 22.1 and 22.2 of the Criminal Code expand the criminal liability of corporations in Canada to include criminal conduct by employees who are not in an executive management position but nevertheless hold a significant amount of "localized responsibility" within the corporation. As a result, if a company delegates responsibility to a foreign agent to engage in an important aspect of the company's business, the agent is likely to be deemed a senior officer and his or her bribery could be imputed to the company, even if no one else in the company knew the foreign agent was bribing officials.

In R c Pétroles Global Inc.,108 the accused company was convicted of price-fixing under the federal Competition Act. The company operated 317 gas stations in Ontario, Quebec and New Brunswick. A regional manager (Payette) managed over 200 gas stations in Quebec and New Brunswick and six subordinate territory managers who were responsible for their portion of those 200 stations. The regional manager and two of the territorial managers were involved in the price fixing. At the preliminary inquiry, the judge held that all three were "senior officers" on the ground that each of them managed an "important aspect of the company's activities."110 At trial, Justice Toth found that the regional manager was definitely a senior officer and therefore his actions and state of mind were the actions and state of mind of the company. Justice Toth held that it was therefore unnecessary to decide whether the two territorial managers were also "senior officers" and he expressly declined to rule on that issue. Justice Toth did note that the definition of senior officer involves a functional analysis that goes beyond the mere title "manager." The management under consideration must involve an important aspect of the company's activities.

Under section 22.2(a), quoted above, a corporation may be criminally liable if a senior officer acting within the scope of his or her authority is a party to a CFPOA offence (this would include situations where the senior officer is a party to an offence by virtue of aiding or abetting another in the commission of an offence). In addition, the acts of the senior officer must have been done with the intention, at least in part, of benefiting the corporation. Section 22.2(b), quoted above, does not appear to expand the liability of corporations beyond the combined effect of section 22.2(a) and the common law doctrine of innocent agents.111

Section 22.2(c), however, does significantly expand the law. Under the common law directing minds doctrine, it was not clear to what extent, if any, a company could be held liable for its omission to take action to prevent bribery. However, this is no longer the case under section 22.2(c). A senior officer's failure to take reasonable steps to stop an employee's offence can now attach liability to the corporation for that offence. Under the Canadian criminal law, citizens are not guilty of an offence for failing to try to stop it or failing to report it, unless the law places a specific duty on specific people in specific circumstances to take reasonable steps to stop the commission of the crime. Section 22.2(c) places obligations on company managers and other senior officers to take all reasonable measures to stop others connected with the organization from being parties to an offence when they are aware that an offence is occurring or is about to occur. This requires a significant level of cooperation among senior officers and encourages timely reporting of any violations. As Macpherson notes, if a senior officer of one department became aware that a representative reporting to another department intended to offer a bribe to a foreign public official, the fact that the senior officer might have no managerial powers within that department is irrelevant; the corporation will be criminally liable unless the senior officer takes all reasonable measures to stop the bribery.112 Macpherson suggests that reporting up the chain of command, rather than requiring outside reporting to police, should satisfy the "all reasonable measures" requirement; otherwise some senior officers may be placed in conflicts of interest. However, whether the law requires external reporting is not clear.113 When determining whether a senior officer took all reasonable measures, courts will also likely consider factors relevant to the due diligence defence, such as industry standards and risk management techniques.

Unlike section 7 of the UK Bribery Act, section 22.2(c) stops short of prescribing positive obligations to prevent wrongdoing on behalf of company representatives. Section 22.2(c) is only implicated when a senior officer "knows" the representative is or is about to become a party to an offence or when the senior officer is willfully blind to this. It does not include instances when a senior officer is recklessly or negligently unaware that bribery or false accounting is taking place within the corporation.

PARTY OR ACCOMPLICE LIABILITY

In most legal systems, the person who gives a bribe and the person who receives a bribe are referred to as the principal offenders. But most legal systems also criminalize the conduct of persons who aid (assist), abet (encourage) or counsel (solicit, incite or procure) the principal offender in the commission of the offence. These persons are referred to as parties, accomplices or secondary parties to an offence. In the US, the UK and Canada, these secondary parties are deemed guilty of the same offence as the principal offender. They are also liable for the same punishments as the principal offender. The actual sentence imposed will depend on the degree of involvement and the degree of responsibility of each offender. Some civil law countries treat secondary parties differently. German law, for instance, punishes a person who incites an offence (a solicitor) in the same way as it punishes a perpetrator of the offence if he or she intentionally induces the perpetrator to commit the offence. A person who intentionally assists the principal (a facilitator) in the commission of the offence is criminally liable, but his or her sentence will be less severe than that of a principal.115 While virtually all countries criminalize some form of accomplice liability, there are both significant and subtle differences between legal systems with respect to accomplice liability.

UNCAC

UNCAC requires State Parties to criminalize acts of secondary participation in the offences set out in UNCAC in accordance with the State Party's domestic criminal law. Party liability is addressed in Article 27(1), which states:

- Each State Party shall adopt such legislative and other measures as may be necessary to establish as a criminal offence, in accordance with its domestic law, participation in any capacity such as an accomplice, assistant or instigator in an offence established in accordance with this Convention.

Note that Article 27(1) is a mandatory requirement for state parties and that it requires criminalization of "participation in any capacity."

OECD Convention

Similarly, the OECD Convention mandates that those who are complicit in the act of bribing a foreign public official must be held liable. Article 1(2) requires that each State Party take necessary measures "to establish that complicity in, including incitement, aiding and abetting, or authorization of an act of bribery of a foreign public official shall be a criminal offence."

US Law

Under section 2 of US Federal Criminal Law (18 USC. § 2), an individual, corporation or other legal entity who "aids, abets, counsels, commands, induces or procures" the commission of an offense or "willfully causes an act to be done which if directly performed by him or another would be an offense" is guilty of that offence and "is punishable as a principal." In this sense, the liability of the aider, abettor, etc., is derivative—it is based on the offense committed by the principal offender. The aider, abettor, etc., is sometimes referred to as a secondary party to distinguish him or her from the principal offender; but, in law the principal offender and the secondary offender are guilty of the same offence. Section 2 of the US Code applies to all federal offenses including the bribery offences in the FCPA. For further discussion of corporations as principal offender or aider, abettor or counsellor, see Section 2.5.

While accomplice liability is usually based on acts, an omission to act may actually assist or encourage the commission of an offence. In the US, there is generally no accomplice liability for omissions to act (e.g., failure to report or stop an act of bribery) unless the law has placed a specific legal duty on that person to act. Accomplice liability in the US also extends in general to ancillary offenses which are a natural and probable consequence of committing the principal offense. If A agrees to assist P to commit bribery and as part of the bribery scheme P threatens V with violence, then A is also liable for the offense of making threats of violence, if such threats were a natural and probable consequence of carrying out the bribery scheme. For a detailed analysis of party liability in the US, see LaFave's book Substantive Criminal Law.

UK Law

Section 8 of the Accessories and Abettors Act 1861, as amended by the Criminal Law Act 1977, provides that anyone "who aids, abets, counsels or procures" the commission of any indictable UK offence is liable and punishable for that offence as a principal offender. Therefore, anyone who, by an act or omission of a legal duty, assists or encourages the commission of an offence under the Bribery Act will be punished in the same way as the principal offender. The accessory must intend to assist the principal offender and must have knowledge of the essential elements of the principal offender's offence. Voluntary attendance at the scene of the crime and a failure to stop the crime are not necessarily sufficient to constitute an act of assistance.

English criminal law also extends liability to all persons who belong to a common unlawful purpose (sometimes called a joint venture) for further offences that are committed by one member of that group in carrying out the common unlawful purpose, provided these further offences are a reasonably foreseeable consequence of carrying out the unlawful purpose. Thus if A, B and C have a common unlawful purpose to bribe a foreign minister in hopes of obtaining a government contract and A, in carrying out the common purpose, forges an official document, then B and C are guilty of forgery if that forgery was a reasonably foreseeable consequence of carrying out the bribery scheme. This form of liability is sometimes referred to as joint enterprise liability or parasitic liability.

A secondary party can be convicted even if the principal is acquitted, provided there is admissible evidence at the secondary party's trial to establish that the offence was committed and that the accused assisted or encouraged the commission of the offence. However, if the secondary party withdraws unequivocally from the common purpose and communicates this in time, he or she will have a defence (in contrast to conspiracy, which offers no defence for withdrawal from an agreement) to any offences committed after the withdrawal by other members of the common purpose.

Pursuant to section 14, the Bribery Act also establishes liability for senior company officers, such as directors, managers, company secretaries or those purporting to act in such a capacity, who "consent or connive" in the commission of a Bribery Act offence under sections 1, 2 or 6 by a legal entity (see Chapter 2, Section 2.4.2(iv)). It has been suggested that the concept of "consent and connivance" is wider and more flexible than accomplice liability.120 The concept does not necessarily require that aid be given intentionally; it could also criminalize reckless behaviour. It likely also captures instances where a senior officer knows the bribery offence is occurring, but does nothing to stop it even if the senior officer did not actually aid or encourage the offence's commission. Senior officers can also face party liability if they consent or connive in the commission of false accounting provisions under the Theft Act.

Canadian Law

The CFPOA does not explicitly mention secondary parties to the indictable offence of bribery of foreign public officials. However, via section 34(2) of the federal Interpretation Act,121 all the provisions of the Criminal Code that relate to indictable offences also apply to bribery of foreign public officials.122 Sections 21 and 22 of the Criminal Code address secondary party liability. Section 21(1) of the Criminal Code criminalizes the actions (or omissions of legal duties) of anyone who aids in the commission of an offence or abets any person in committing an offence. Pursuant to section 21(1), aiders, abettors and principal offenders who actually commit the offence are all guilty of the same offence and subject to the same penalties set out for that offence. As well, pursuant to section 21(2), when two or more people form a common unlawful purpose to commit an offence and during the course of that unlawful purpose one of them commits an ancillary offence, they are all parties to that offence if they knew or ought to have known that the commission of the ancillary offence was a probable consequence of carrying out the common unlawful purpose. A corporation or other organization can also be a member of a conspiracy if the requirements of sections 22.1 or 22.2 of the Criminal Code are met (further discussed in Section 2.7 above).

Section 22(1) of the Criminal Code makes those who counsel an offence liable for that offence if that offence is committed. If the offence is counselled but not committed, the counsellor is liable for a separate inchoate offence of incitement under section 464 of the Criminal Code; that offence is subject to the same punishment as an attempt to commit the offence that was counselled. Section 22(2) creates party liability for the counsellor for all reasonably foreseeable ancillary offences committed by the person counselled. For a more detailed analysis of party liability, see a standard Canadian criminal law textbook.

INCHOATE OFFENCES

Certain offences are described as inchoate (or uncompleted) crimes, as opposed to "full or complete crimes." The major inchoate crimes are attempt and conspiracy. Many common law legal systems (including the UK and Canada) also criminalize the inchoate offence of counselling an offence which is not committed (sometimes termed incitement). Although referred to as inchoate or incomplete, these offences are nonetheless distinct crimes on their own. Generally, common law states are more willing to punish inchoate crimes than civil law countries. Sweden, for example only punishes attempts for certain crimes, attempted bribery not being one of them.124 In this section, the UNCAC and OECD provisions on each of these three forms of inchoate offences will be examined, followed by a description of how the law in the US, UK and Canada deals with each offence.

Attempts

Countries around the world treat attempts to commit an offence in different ways. Some countries, such as Japan and Korea, do not criminalize attempts at all. In countries that do punish attempts, there is general agreement that the criminal law should not punish criminal thoughts alone; attempts are not committed until the offender engages in some acts for the purpose of committing the crime. But do all acts engaged in for the purpose of committing the offence in question constitute the offence of an attempt? In some countries, certain preliminary acts are classified as mere acts of preparation rather than an attempt, but at a certain point, acts will cross the line from preparation to attempt. Most common and civil law countries do not punish preparatory acts until they have reached the threshold of an "attempt." However, there are some European states that do consider preparatory acts in respect to at least some criminal offences to be a crime. These countries include the Czech Republic (section 8 of the Criminal Code), Poland (Article 16 of the Criminal Code) and Russia (section 66 of the Criminal Code).

In practice, the distinction between mere preparatory acts and actual attempts is often difficult to draw, and the line between them is unclear in many states. Germany, France and a number of other European countries consider the point at which preparation becomes an attempt to be "with the act which immediately precedes the execution of the full offence."125 In other words, attempted offences are not committed until the offender is very close to executing or completing the full offence. On the other hand, in many common law countries, including the UK, the US and Canada, the threshold of an attempt is reached earlier, before the perpetrator has reached the "last act" stage. Matis characterizes the English criminal law approach as a "midway course" between the point of mere preparation and the last act stage. In the US, the Model Penal Code suggests that an attempt begins when the offender has taken "a substantial step" towards the commission of the substantive offence. The point at which countries draw the line between an act of preparation and an attempt is often influenced by the rationale which that country relies upon in criminalizing an attempt. There are three possible rationales:

- **Prevention:** If there is no offence until the crime is committed (therefore removing police power to intervene before the crime is committed), crime prevention would be thwarted and harm would unnecessarily be caused to victims.
- **Moral fault:** People who attempt to commit crimes demonstrate a criminal disposition and deserve to be punished. Their state of mind is as morally blameworthy as persons who are successful in completing the crime.
- **Deterrence:** Punishing attempts may be necessary to deter others who may be contemplating the commission of a similar crime.

The law of attempts also raises the issue of whether voluntary withdrawal from an attempt forms a defence. Withdrawal, or voluntary desistance, refers to instances where the perpetrator has reached the stage of attempt, but has a change of heart before the full offence is completed. France, Germany and Norway accept a defence of voluntary withdrawal, while other countries like Australia have rejected this notion.

UNCAC

In consideration of the different approaches to the criminalization of attempts among the international community, UNCAC does not impose mandatory obligations on states to criminalize attempts or other types of preparatory actions in regard to most corruption- related offences. Article 27(2) provides a State Party "may" create an offence of attempted bribery. Article 27(3) provides that a State Party "may" create an offence for engaging in preparatory acts to commit bribery. Articles 27(2) and (3) state:

- Each State Party may adopt such legislative and other measures as may be necessary to establish as a criminal offence, in accordance with its domestic law, any attempt to commit an offence established in accordance with this Convention.
- Each State Party may adopt such legislative and other measures as may be necessary to establish as a criminal offence, in accordance with its domestic law, the preparation for an offence established in accordance with this Convention.

It is interesting to note that UNCAC is more prescriptive with regard to money laundering. Article 23(1) provides that State Parties "shall, subject to the basic concepts of its legal system ... establish criminal offences" in respect to "attempts to commit" any of the money laundering offences listed in Article 23.

OECD Convention

The OECD Convention also respects the fact that countries take different approaches to the criminalization of inchoate offences. Article 1(2) states that an "[a]ttempt ... to bribe a foreign public official shall be a criminal offence to the same extent as an attempt ... to bribe a public official is an offence" in one's own country. The Commentaries on the OECD Convention accompanying the Convention clarify that:

> The offences set out in paragraph 2 are understood in terms of their normal content in national legal systems. Accordingly, if authorisation, incitement, or one of the other listed acts, which does not lead to further action, is not itself punishable under a Party's legal system, then the Party would not be required to make it punishable with respect to bribery of a foreign public official.

Consequently, the OECD Working Group on Bribery does not look unfavourably on the legal systems of states that do not punish attempted bribery, such as Sweden, Japan and Korea.129 It is also worth noting that the offence of attempted bribery of a foreign official would likely only cover a narrow ambit of behaviour, since offering or promising a bribe to a foreign public official is treated as part of the offence of bribery under the OECD Convention. Zerbes notes that in some countries the offer to bribe is considered complete before the offer reaches the foreign public official: "A mere attempt to commit bribery is not envisaged by the FCPA, nor by Belgian, Finnish, French, Hungarian, or Spanish law, given the fact that they all regard the full offence as having been committed when someone seeks to induce a public servant."

The Convention also does not address other points of difference among states, such as how severely attempts are punished or whether attempts to commit offences that are factually impossible are criminalized.

US Law

Most state penal codes and the US Model Penal Code have a provision in their general part which makes it an offense to attempt any offense. Some state penal codes and the US Code only penalize attempts within the context of specific offenses.132 In US law, a key point is whether the conduct of the accused has gone beyond mere acts of preparation and entered the realm of attempts. The details of the US law of attempts can be found in any standard American textbook of criminal law.133 Voluntary abandonment of an attempt (i.e., the plan to commit an offense) is recognized as a defense under the Model Penal Code and under many state penal codes.134 Because the offense of bribery is broadly stated in section 78dd-1, it is not generally necessary to resort to attempted bribery. In section 78dd-1, bribery includes not only the completed offense "of paying the bribe and receiving the benefit," but also the "uncompleted" offenses of "offering, authorizing or promising" to pay a bribe, even if nothing further happens in regard to the actual payment of the bribe. Thus, attempts to bribe a foreign official will be caught in the full offense of bribery as defined in section 78dd-1.

UK Law

Under section 1 of the Criminal Attempts Act 1981, it is an offence to attempt to commit any offences that are indictable in England and Wales. Section 1(4) stipulates that it is not an offence to attempt to commit conspiracy or to attempt to aid, abet or counsel a substantive offence. Under section 1(1), a person is guilty of attempting to commit an offence if, with the intention of committing an applicable offence, "a person does an act which is more than merely preparatory to the commission of the offence." Once a person's actions have reached the stage of attempting an offence, the attempt is complete. It is not a defence if the perpetrator voluntarily withdraws from the attempt, although voluntary desistance may be evidence that the accused never really had the requisite intent to commit the substantive offence to begin with. 135 Historically, UK courts applied the "last step" test (i.e., to be classified as an attempt the accused's conduct must have reached the last step before completion of the full offence). More recent case law suggests that the offender does not need to have commenced the last act before the completion of the substantive offence, but the precise line between merely preparatory acts and actual attempts is still unclear. As with US law, the law of attempts is not frequently resorted to for Bribery Act offences since the offences of bribery in that Act involve not only giving or receiving a bribe, but also offering to give or promising to give, or requesting or agreeing to receive, a bribe.

Canadian Law

Section 34(2) of the federal Interpretation Act states that all the provisions of the Criminal Code that relate to indictable offences also apply to the offence provisions of other federal statutes. 136 Therefore, although not explicitly noted in CFPOA, the three major inchoate offences in Canada (counselling a crime not committed, attempt and conspiracy) apply to CFPOA offences of bribing a foreign public official and falsifying books and records. These inchoate offences also apply to domestic corruption offences, which are found in the Criminal Code.

Pursuant to section 24(1) of the Canadian Criminal Code, anyone who, with the intention to commit an offence, "does or omits to do anything for the purpose of carrying out his intention is guilty of an attempt to commit the offence whether or not it was possible under the circumstances to commit the offence." However, section 24(2) clarifies that mere preparation to commit an offence is not considered an attempt.

Like other legal systems, Canadian courts have struggled with the distinction between preparatory acts and attempts. In the 1986 Supreme Court of Canada decision in R v Deutsch, the Court held that there is no general rule for distinguishing between preparation and an attempt and that the distinction should be left to the common sense of the trial judge.137 Writing for the majority, Justice Le Dain went on to state:

- In my opinion the distinction between preparation and attempt is essentially a qualitative one, involving the relationship between the nature and quality of the act in question and the nature of the complete offence, although consideration must necessarily be given, in making that qualitative distinction, to the relative proximity of the act in question to what would have been the completed offence, in terms of time, location and acts under the control of the accused remaining to be accomplished.

The Court's failure to express a clear test to determine whether particular acts fulfill the actus reus requirement of an attempt offence remains troubling to some commentators, who argue that criminal law principles demand that a more clear formulation of the actus reus of attempt offences be available to the public.139 The issue of whether voluntary withdrawal is a defence to an attempt charge has not been fully considered in Canada.

The maximum penalty under section 463 of the Criminal Code for attempts to commit indictable offences other than those punishable by life in prison is half the maximum penalty that would have been available had the attempt succeeded.

Conspiracy

The offence of conspiracy involves at its core an agreement between two or more persons to commit an offence. Many civil law countries only criminalize conspiracy to commit a limited number of very serious crimes, which generally do not include bribery. Most common law countries criminalize conspiracy to commit a broader range of offences, including the offence of bribery. Unlike the law of attempts, conspirators may be convicted when no concrete steps beyond reaching the agreement have been taken. The criminalization of conspiracy is more controversial than the criminalization of attempts. Conspiracy occurs well before an attempt to commit an offence, and its criminalization can lead to a form of collective guilt that may unfairly punish individuals for the wrongdoing of others. In the past, the criminalization of conspiracy has also been used to suppress political dissent. However, the availability of an offence of conspiracy to commit corruption offences allows enforcement agencies to arrest perpetrators before harm has occurred and can be an effective weapon against organized crime.

UNCAC

While Article 27 of UNCAC specifically references the adoption of provisions criminalizing parties to bribery and attempts to commit bribery, UNCAC is silent on conspiracy to commit bribery. However, Article 23 states that "subject to the basic concepts of its legal system, State Parties shall establish a criminal offence for conspiracy to commit" any of the money laundering offences in Article 23.

OECD Convention

As with attempts, rather than mandating a globally consistent approach, Article 1(2) focuses on consistency within the domestic context when dealing with criminalization of conspiracy. A conspiracy or an attempt to bribe a foreign official must be penalized in the same way (if any) as conspiracies or attempts to bribe domestic public officials.

US Law

The US criminalizes conspiracies to bribe foreign public officials. Charges under the FCPA will often be accompanied by a charge under the federal general conspiracy statute (18 USC § 371), which makes it a crime to conspire to commit an offense against the US or to conspire to defraud the US. The applicable punishment is either a fine or a prison term of up to five years (unless the object of the conspiracy is a misdemeanor offense, in which case the punishment shall not exceed the maximum punishment for that offense). The elements of the offense of conspiracy to commit bribery can be found in Tarun's book The Foreign Corrupt Practices Act Handbook.143 He lists the four elements of a federal conspiracy as follows:

- An agreement by two or more persons,
- To commit the unlawful object of the conspiracy,
- With knowledge of the conspiracy and with actual participation in the conspiracy, and
- The commission of an overt act in furtherance of the conspiracy by at least one co- conspirator.

It is important to note that the conspiracy offense is not complete until one of the co- conspirators commits an overt act in furtherance of the conspiracy. This does not have to be a criminal act in its own right, but can be a non-criminal preparatory act, such as opening a bank account that is to be used as a part of the bribery scheme. By contrast, the offence of conspiracy in the UK and Canada does not require any overt acts in furtherance of the conspiracy. The law of conspiracy in the US is set out in detail in LaFave's book Substantive Criminal Law.

Tarun notes that charging individuals or corporations with both a general conspiracy offence and a substantive FCPA offence offers several advantages to the prosecution. In this regard, he states:

- First, the ongoing nature of conspiracy lends itself to expansive drafting, particularly in temporal terms. Conspiracies frequently are alleged to have continued for years and occasionally decades. Second, the breadth and vagueness of a conspiracy count allow the admission of much proof that might otherwise be inadmissible. Third, a conspiracy count enables the government to broadly join persons and allegations. A conspiracy can allege an agreement to defraud multiple entities, individuals, and companies or both the government (e.g., the Securities and Exchange Commission) and private entities and individuals. Fourth evidentiary rules with respect to co- conspirator declarations enlarge the admissibility of often-damaging statements in conspiracy trials [Under the US Federal Rules of Evidence, out of court statements made by a co-conspirator in furtherance of the conspiracy may be admitted against the accused]. Fifth, because the conspiracy is a continuing crime, its five-year statute of limitations does not begin to run until either the conspiracy's objectives are met, the conspiracy is abandoned, its members affirmatively withdraw, or the last overt act committed in furtherance of the conspiracy occurs. [footnotes omitted]

UK Law

For the purposes of most corruption-related offences, the old common law offence of conspiracy has been replaced with the Criminal Law Act 1977. 146 Section 1(1) of the Act provides that a person is liable for conspiring to commit an offence if that person agrees with at least one other person to pursue a course of conduct that, if carried out according to plan, would necessarily involve the commission of any offence. The key element is the agreement. Evidence of negotiations without proof of an agreement is insufficient. To be convicted, the defendant must have intended to enter the agreement, intended that the purpose of the agreement be carried out, and had knowledge of the relevant circumstances. Recklessness rather than actual knowledge of these circumstances is insufficient. If a defendant withdraws from a conspiracy immediately after entering the agreement, this does not provide a defence, but may be used to mitigate the sentence. A company may be a party to a conspiracy if an officer forming part of its directing mind enters the agreement on the company's behalf.

The courts discourage the charging of both conspiracy and the substantive crime that the parties conspired to commit due to the length and complexity of resulting trials and the unfairness of convicting accused persons for two separate crimes for what constitutes one continuous transaction. However, charging both offences can provide the prosecution with evidentiary advantages.

English courts will have jurisdiction over a conspiracy offence if the agreement is made in England or Wales to commit an offence abroad or if an agreement was made abroad to commit an offence in England or Wales, regardless of an absence of acts done in furtherance of the agreement in England or Wales.

Canadian Law

In R v Karigar, the court noted that section 3 of the CPFOA incorporates the idea of conspiracy. As stated by the court, "a conspiracy or agreement to bribe foreign public officials is a violation of the Act. ... the use of the term 'agrees' imports the concept of conspiracy." The court further elaborated that the agreement need not be between the giver and receiver of the bribe. Even if the word "agrees" in section 3 of the CFPOA does not import the concept of conspiracy, the Criminal Code provisions on conspiracy also apply to the bribery offences in the CFPOA.155 Conspiracy to commit an indictable offence is set out under section 465(1)(c) of the Criminal Code as follows:

- every one who conspires with any one to commit an indictable offence ... is guilty of an indictable offence and liable to the same punishment as that to which an accused who is guilty of that offence would, on conviction, be liable.

The essence of the offence consists of an agreement between two or more persons to commit an indictable offence. There must be a common agreement between the parties to work together to commit the offence(s). Unlike the US conspiracy offence, there is no requirement that one of the co-conspirators take any action in furtherance of the conspiracy. The offence is complete the moment the agreement is reached. Like in the US, hearsay evidence spoken by a co-conspirator is admissible against the other conspirators, although there must be independent evidence of a conspiracy before this information may be used in court. Because of this permissive evidence rule, the conspiracy charge is sometimes referred to as "the prosecutor's darling." The criminalization of conspiracy is generally justified by the principle that two people with a plan to commit an offence are more dangerous than one person plotting alone. This justification has been questioned, and numerous commentators and organizations have called on the Canadian government to narrow the offence of conspiracy.

Canadian courts have territorial jurisdiction over defendants who conspire in Canada to commit an act abroad that constitutes an offence both in Canada and the foreign country. Further, Canada will have jurisdiction if the defendant conspires elsewhere to commit any act in Canada that is an offence in Canada.

Incitement (or Solicitation)

Inciting or counselling an offence that is later committed by the person who was counselled makes the incitor or counsellor a party to, and therefore guilty of, the offence committed. But suppose a person incites or counsels another person to commit an offence, but that other person does not commit it. The incitor or counsellor cannot be a party to the offence counselled because that offence was never committed and his or her acts of counselling or inciting are too preliminary to convict the person of an attempt to commit the offence. Some countries have created a separate inchoate offence for counselling an offence that is not committed, which is called incitement in the UK and Canada and solicitation in the US.

UNCAC and the OECD Convention

The inchoate offence of incitement is not specifically mentioned in either UNCAC or the OECD Convention. But there is no pressing need for this type of separate inchoate offence, since the definition of bribery under both conventions includes conduct such as "requesting a bribe," regardless of whether the bribe is paid, or "offering a bribe," regardless of whether the bribe is accepted or not.

US Law

The inchoate offence of incitement (which includes counselling, encouraging, instigating or soliciting) is referred to as the offence of solicitation in the US. The elements of this inchoate offence can be found in a standard American textbook on criminal law.159 However, because of the expanded definition of the offense of bribery in section 78 dd-1, there is little or no need to use the offence of solicitation in respect to bribery offenses.

UK Law

In the UK, the common law offence of incitement was recognized by at least 1769. It has now been replaced by section 44 of the Serious Crimes Act 2007. Under this section, those that intentionally commit acts that are capable of encouraging or assisting in the commission of an offence are themselves committing an offence, regardless of whether the substantive offence is carried out and regardless of whether their acts actually encourage or assist the principal offender. In order for the offence to be made out, the person doing the encouraging or assisting (D1) must intend to assist or encourage the substantive offence, or must believe that the substantive offence will be committed and that their acts will encourage or assist its commission. Section 65 clarifies that acts reducing the risk of criminal proceedings for the principal offender are considered to be capable of assisting or encouraging the commission of an offence.

English courts have jurisdiction if the defendant knew or believed that the substantive offence would be committed in England or Wales, regardless of where the acts of encouragement or assistance took place. English courts also have jurisdiction if the encouragement or assistance took place in England or Wales, but the defendant knew or believed the substantive offence would take place abroad so long as the defendant knew the offence was illegal both in the UK and in the country of the substantive offence.

Canadian Law

A person who counsels another person to commit an offence that is later committed is considered a party to that offence (section 22 of the Criminal Code). However, a person who counsels another to commit an offence that is not committed is guilty of a different offence that is sometimes referred to as the offence of incitement. Section 464 of the Criminal Code states:

> ◉ 464 Except where otherwise expressly provided by law, the following provisions apply in respect of persons who counsel other persons to commit offences, namely,
>
> - every one who counsels another person to commit an indictable offence is, if the offence is not committed, guilty of an indictable offence and liable to the same punishment to which a person who attempts to commit that offence is liable; and
> - every one who counsels another person to commit an offence punishable on summary conviction is, if the offence is not committed, guilty of an offence punishable on summary conviction.

The term "counselling" is wide and, pursuant to section 22(3) of the Criminal Code, "includes procuring, soliciting or inciting." The mens rea of the offence requires an intention that the counselled offence be committed or recklessness in the sense of a conscious disregard for a substantial and unjustified risk that the offence counselled was likely to be committed. The offence of incitement under section 464 has not been used in Canada so far to prosecute a person who counsels bribery that was not actually committed. It could have been used in the prosecution of Wallace and three other Canadians in respect to the alleged bribe offer in the Padma River Bridge project in Bangladesh (see Section 1.1 of Chapter 1).

CHAPTER-4

MONEY LAUNDERING

INTRODUCTION TO MONEY LAUNDERING

The term "money laundering" describes a range of practices used to disguise the source of illicit profits and integrate them into the legitimate economy. Simply put, money laundering means 'washing' dirty money so that it appears clean. Corrupt officials and other criminals use money laundering techniques to hide the true sources of their income. This allows them to avoid detection by law enforcement and to spend their profits freely. Money laundering in some form is an essential part of most illicit enterprises, although methods vary widely. Large drug-trafficking organizations and corrupt public officials use complex, multi-jurisdictional layering schemes; small-time criminals use simpler strategies.

As Baker points out in a 2013 article, all the illicit funds in the global economy flow through similar channels. Drug smugglers, tax evaders and corrupt officials use their money for different ends and acquire it by different means. Nonetheless, Baker notes:

- All three forms of illicit money – corrupt, criminal, and commercial – use this structure, originally developed in the West originally for the purpose of moving flight capital and tax evading money across borders. In the 1960s and 1970s drug dealers stepped into these same channels to move their illicit money across borders. In the 1980s and 1990s, seeing how easy it was for the drug dealers to do it, other kinds of racketeers stepped into these same structures to move their illicit money across borders. In the 1990s and in the early years of this new century, again seeing how easy it was for drug dealers and racketeers, terrorist financiers also stepped into these same channels to move their illicit money across borders. Drug dealers, criminal syndicate heads, and terrorist masterminds have not invented any new ways of shifting illicit money across borders. They merely utilize the mechanisms we originally created to move corrupt and commercially tax evading money across borders.

Therefore, suppressing money laundering through a variety of anti-money-laundering (AML) schemes is essential to combating terrorist financing, organized crime and corruption. What Baker calls the "global shadow financial system" is integral to a broad range of corrupt and criminal activities worldwide.2 Indeed, as Beare notes, while the 1931 arrest, conviction and downfall of Al Capone is often dismissed as being "merely for tax evasion," his undoing was in fact due to a failure to launder illicit money adequately.

Because the purpose of money laundering is to conceal the source of illicit funds, it is inherently difficult to measure its global scope. In a recent article, McCarthy summarizes some of the more common estimates:

- The IMF and the World Bank, for example, have estimated that some 2-4 per cent of the world's GDP stems from illicit sources. Agarwal and Agarwal (2004; 2006), using regression analysis and forecasts, suggest an even higher level of 5-6 per cent. At this rate somewhere between $2.0-2.5 trillion should flow through the money laundering market on an annual basis. Walker (1999, 2004, 2007) however, claims that this is too low a figure and, using input-output and gravity models, proposes that the true amount is more like $3 trillion per annum. Each estimate is subject to some criticism (cf. Reuter 2007), and are variously said to be overblown – either by media hype, or measurement errors – by as much as +/- 20 per cent (Schneider, 2008). Despite all this the consensus remains that the market for money laundering is a significant one.

Despite the wide range of estimates, there is a degree of consensus among researchers. No one has an accurate estimate, but everyone agrees that a large amount of money is being laundered every year.

THE ESSENTIAL ELEMENTS OF MONEY LAUNDERING

There are many ways to launder money. Most scholars break laundering schemes into three stages to make it easier to compare, contrast and analyze different methods. These three stages are:

1. **Placement:** illicit funds are used to make a purchase in the legitimate economy;
2. **Layering:** through repeated transactions, the source of the funds is concealed; and
3. **Integration:** the funds are fully and untraceably integrated into the economy.

Regardless of how a money laundering scheme works, it can be broken into these three stages. The "layering" stage, in which the source of the funds is concealed, is where most of the activity occurs in any given scheme. In small-scale schemes, the layering process may be quite simple. In large, complex laundering schemes, it may involve hundreds of transactions in multiple jurisdictions.

A useful and easily readable description of the basic concepts of money laundering and its prevention can be found in the Global Organization of Parliamentarians Against Corruption (GOPAC)'s 2011 guide, the Anti-Money Laundering Action Guide for Parliamentarians. 5 GOPAC is a non-profit organization made up of current or former legislators from around the globe. The organization is dedicated to promoting accountability and good governance in national parliaments in order to combat corruption.

THE MOST COMMON METHODS OF MONEY LAUNDERING

As noted above, the term "money laundering" encompasses a wide variety of different schemes used by everyone from small-time drug dealers to corrupt heads of state. As Beare notes, "[i]t is impossible to identify all the laundering possibilities - from cults to marathons and beyond," noting in the 1990s the Solar Templar doomsday cult was accused of being a front for laundering, and the Los Angeles Marathon Corporation was convicted of money laundering. Methods of money laundering can be as simple as small businesses dealing in cash using illicit cash to generate greater profits or as complex as international schemes using methods of concealing funds including offshore laundering havens, shell companies and wire transfers.6 Beare identifies four typologies of money laundering schemes. Simple-limited schemes launder relatively small volumes of illicit proceeds through small cash-based businesses such as bars and vending machine companies. Simple-unlimited schemes can launder large amounts of money with few transactions utilizing big-budget companies with unclear resources, materials and service costs. Serial-domestic schemes use numerous financial transactions, moving funds through a network of transactions that involve multiple banks. Serial-international schemes use multiple transactions and international services, often returning funds into big banks in North America and Europe. Both serial domestic and serial-international schemes can use professionals such as lawyers and accountants.7 The Liberty Reserve Global takedown demonstrates complex schemes used by money launderers. Liberty Reserve offered a digital currency service based in Costa Rica. The DOJ created a diagram of the complexity of the investigation, which involved 17 countries and 36 mutual legal assistance treaty (MLAT) requests in 15 countries for execution of search warrants, wiretap authorizations, freezing or seizing assets, all of which culminated in 5 arrests.

This chapter focuses on money laundering in the context of corruption. While a great deal of global AML efforts are directed towards controlling organized crime and preventing terrorist financing, those topics are beyond the scope of this book. The following excerpt from "Laundering the Proceeds of Corruption," a 2011 report produced by the Financial Action Task Force (FATF), describes the most common money-laundering methods used by corrupt officials.9 The FATF is an inter-governmental policy group composed of 34 nations, including the US, the UK and Canada, which sets standards in the form of the FATF 40 Recommendations, promotes procedures for combatting money laundering and evaluates member states' performance.

BEGINNING OF EXCERPT

An Analysis of the Most Common Methods Used to Launder the Proceeds of Grand Corruption

- Laundering of corruption proceeds can take a variety of forms, depending on the nature of the corrupt act. In the grand corruption context, the most prevalent forms of proceeds are those arising from 1) bribe-taking or kickbacks; 2) extortion; 3) self- dealing and conflict of interest; and 4) embezzlement from the country's treasury by a variety of fraudulent means. Understanding the typical methods by which PEPs ["politically exposed persons" – a technical term for public officials in the AML context] unlawfully obtain proceeds assists in understanding how those funds could be laundered.
- In bribery, money flows from a private entity, generally speaking, to a PEP or associate in exchange for the grant of some sort of government concession: a contract for goods or services, for example, or the right to extract resources from the state. The proceeds of the bribery flow from the bribe giver to the corrupt PEP or an associate, possibly through a shell company or trust in which the PEP is the beneficial owner; it may never touch the home country of the corrupt PEP. A good example of this is found in the Bangkok film festival case, in which two promoters were able to bribe certain Thai officials to obtain the rights to sponsor and manage a government-funded film festival in Thailand.10 The bribes were paid simply by means of the wire transfer of funds from US-based accounts, where the promoters were located, into offshore accounts in third countries maintained by family members of the PEP. The bribes never passed through Thailand, although that was the locus of the corrupt activity.
- However, as noted later in the section on the use of cash, sometimes funds are retained in the country where the corruption takes place. For example, Joseph Estrada, then the President of the Philippines, often received cash or check payments from gambling operators in exchange for their protection from arrest or law enforcement activities. This money was simply deposited

into domestic accounts in the name of a fictional person or in corporate vehicles established by Estrada's attorney, and then used for a variety of expenses. 11 Likewise, in the case of the bribery of US Congressman Randall Cunningham, who was a senior legislator with significant control over military expenditures, a military contractor bribed him both by checks to a corporation controlled by Cunningham, but also by agreeing to purchase real estate owned by Cunningham at a vastly inflated price.12

- Proceeds are also generated through extortion schemes. In such schemes, funds are passed from the victim to the PEP. This can be done within the country or elsewhere. Pavel Lazarenko, former Prime Minister of Ukraine, regularly required entities that wished to do business in Ukraine to split equally the profits of the enterprise with him in exchange for his influence in making the business successful. These businesses would transfer a share of ownership to Lazarenko associates or family members, and money would be wired from the victim companies to offshore accounts controlled by Lazarenko.[13]
- Self-dealing occurs when a PEP has a financial interest in an entity which does business with the state. The PEP is able to use his official position to ensure that the state does business with the entity, thereby enriching the PEP. A US Senate report noted a situation in which one West African PEP was responsible for selling the right to harvest timber from public lands, while at the same time owning the same company that had been awarded those rights.14 In such situations, money would flow from the affected country's accounts or central bank to accounts owned by the corporation or entity owned or controlled by the PEP.
- Finally, embezzlement schemes are used in a number of corruption cases. Money flows can occur in a number of ways, using a variety of methods. In the case involving former governor of Plateau state in Nigeria, Joshua Dariye, for example, a grant for environmental contracts was made from the federal government to the State, and the money was deposited into a bank account established by the State. Dariye used his influence to cause the bank to issue a bank draft creditable to an account at a different Nigerian bank that Dariye had established under an alias about ten months previously.15 In the case involving Sani Abacha, then the President of Nigeria, Abacha directed his national security advisor to create and present false funding requests, which Abacha authorised. Cash "in truckloads" was taken out of the central bank to settle some of these requests. The national security advisor then laundered the proceeds through domestic banks or Nigerian and foreign businessmen to offshore accounts held by family members.

- Thus, it would appear that all stages of the money laundering process – placement, layering, and integration – are present in the laundering of proceeds regardless of the manner of corruption. The specific methods by which the funds are actually laundered are discussed below.

END OF EXCERPT

Use of Corporate Vehicles and Trusts

BEGINNING OF EXCERPT

- The project team's review of the case studies showed that every examined case featured the use of corporate vehicles, trusts, or non-profit entities of some type. That this is the case should perhaps not be surprising; corporate vehicles and trusts have long been identified by FATF as posing a risk for money laundering generally, and are addressed in Recommendations 33 and 34. 17 WGTYP [Working Group on Typologies] long ago noted in its 1996-1997 Report on Money Laundering Typologies of the common use of shell corporations, and the advantages they provide in concealing the identity of the beneficial owner and the difficulty for law enforcement to access records.
- WGTYP issued a report detailing the risks of misuse of corporate vehicles and trusts in October 2006.18 The intervening ten years changed little. As that report noted, "[o]f particular concern is the ease with which corporate vehicles can be created and dissolved in some jurisdictions, which allows these vehicles to be...misused by those involved in financial crime to conceal the sources of funds and their ownership of the corporate vehicles." This point was again made more recently in FATF's 2010 typology, Money Laundering Using Trust and Company Service Providers.19
- These typologies, as well as other publically available information, set forth the money laundering risks that corporate vehicles and trusts present, regardless of the predicate crime. Features of corporate vehicles that enhance the risk of money laundering include:
    - the ease with which corporate vehicles can be created and dissolved in some jurisdictions;
    - that a vehicle can be created as part of a series of multi-jurisdictional structures, in which a corporation in one jurisdiction is owned by one or more other corporations or trusts in other jurisdictions;
    - the use of specialised intermediaries and professionals to conceal true ownership;
    - the ease in which nominees may be used to disguise ownership, and corporations;

- and other vehicles whose only purpose is to disguise the beneficial owner of the underlying asset.

- Moreover, each jurisdiction has its own set of requirements regarding identification of the beneficial owner and the circumstances under which that information may be accessed. As discussions within the FATF regarding clarification of the standards related to beneficial ownership have demonstrated, few jurisdictions collect beneficial ownership information at the time of company formation, increasing the challenges of international cooperation. Each of these features has the effect of making it more difficult for financial institutions, regulators, and law enforcement to obtain information that would allow for an accurate understanding of the ownership and control of the assets involved and the purposes for which specific financial transactions are conducted. Some vehicles are even designed to protect against asset confiscation; certain trusts, for example, require the trustee to transfer assets upon receiving notice of a law enforcement or regulatory inquiry.

- The ease by which an individual can obtain a corporate vehicle is highlighted by J.C. Sharman's recently-published foray into purchasing shell corporations. Sharman, a professor at Griffith University in Brisbane, Australia, noted that of 45 service providers he was able to contact, 17 of them were willing to form the company with only a credit card and mailing address (to receive the documents). 22 Sharman acknowledged that the relatively small sample size of his study "necessitates a degree of modesty about the findings," and that obtaining a bank account for the corporations without divulging an identity would be more difficult. Nevertheless, as he notes, "If one law-abiding individual with a modest budget can establish anonymous companies and bank accounts via the Internet using relatively high-profile corporate service providers, how much simpler is it likely to be for criminals, who are not bound by any of these restrictions, to replicate this feat?"

- In the corruption context, it is easy to understand why a corrupt PEP may wish to use a corporate vehicle. In some jurisdictions, PEPs are subject to public asset disclosure requirements, rules regarding engaging in outside transactions to prevent self-dealing and conflicts of interest, and a host of other codes of conduct, and ethical prohibitions.23 Specific investigative bodies and watchdog groups may exist to guard against corruption, and in many countries a robust media is able to publicise missteps by public officials. Some countries have effectively implemented FATF Recommendation 6 [now Recommendation 12], and require financial institutions to conduct enhanced due diligence for those customers who are foreign PEPs. PEPs have their career and reputation at stake if found to be in possession of unexplained wealth. In this environment, corrupt PEPs have a greater need than others to ensure that specific criminal assets cannot be identified with or traced back to them. Corporate vehicles thus provide one of the most effective ways to separate the origin of the illegal funds from the fact that the PEP controls it.

- One example of this comes from the case of Augusto Pinochet, the former President of Chile. Pinochet was assisted by his US-based bank (and its U.K. branch) in setting up corporate vehicles in order to both hide his assets and shield them from the reach of asset freezing and confiscation or civil recovery orders. Specifically, Pinochet was able to set up offshore shell corporations and a trust in 1996 and 1998, even after a Spanish magistrate had filed a detailed indictment against Pinochet for crimes against humanity and issued world-wide freezing orders. 24 These corporations, established in jurisdictions that at the time had weak AML controls, were listed as the nominal owners of the US bank accounts and other investment vehicles that benefited Pinochet and his family. The bank's KYC documentation listed only the corporations, not Pinochet, as the owners of the accounts, despite the fact that the bank knew that Pinochet was the beneficial owner (since the bank itself had set up the corporations). The bank has since been convicted of AML-related criminal charges.
- According to the case study of Vladimiro Montesinos, Peruvian President Fujimori's security advisor, he used shell corporations very effectively to disguise and move money illegally obtained through defence contracts with the Peruvian government.25 Such a scheme, involving several corporate vehicles in a number of jurisdictions with each vehicle holding bank accounts in yet other jurisdictions, is designed to frustrate any financial institution, regulator or government investigator attempting to unravel the scheme.

END OF EXCERPT

Use of Gatekeepers

BEGINNING OF EXCERPT

- Gatekeepers were significantly represented in the cases within the project team inventory. "Gatekeepers are, essentially, individuals that 'protect the gates to the financial system' through which potential users of the system, including launderers, must pass in order to be successful." The issue of gatekeepers has been addressed by FATF on several occasions, including WGTYP's 2003- 2004 Report, which concluded:

- Increasingly, money launderers seek out the advice or services of specialised professionals to help facilitate their financial operations. This trend toward the involvement of various legal and financial experts, or gatekeepers, in money laundering schemes has been documented previously by the FATF and appears to continue today. The work undertaken during this year's exercise confirmed and expanded the FATF's understanding of specific characteristics of this sector and what makes it vulnerable to money laundering. The most significant cases each involve schemes of notable sophistication, which were possible only as a result of the assistance of skilled professionals to set up corporate structures to disguise the source and ownership of the money.

- In 2010, FATF published its Global Money Laundering and Terrorist Financing Threat Assessment, which described gatekeepers as a "common element" in complex money laundering schemes. The report noted that gatekeepers' skills are important in creating legal structures that could be used to launder money and for their ability to manage and perform transactions efficiently and to avoid detection. Recommendation 12 [now Recommendation 22] acknowledges the role that such gatekeepers can play by recommending that such individuals engage in due diligence and record keeping when engaged in certain activities.

- The review of the cases illustrates the variety of ways in which gatekeepers, in particular lawyers, are used to launder the proceeds of corruption. They have been used to create corporate vehicles, open bank accounts, transfer proceeds, purchase property, courier cash, and take other means to bypass AML controls. In addition, lawyers have subsequently used rules of attorney-client privilege to shield the identity of corrupt PEPs.

- West African PEPs: In four separate case studies of West African PEPs and their families, the US Senate discovered that lawyers were used to create corporate vehicles, open bank accounts and purchase property with the express purpose of bypassing AML controls set up to screen for PEPs.27 For example, the son of the President of one West African nation, who himself was a minister within the government, wished to purchase real estate and aircraft within the United States. To do so, a lawyer for the PEP opened bank accounts there. However, because of US banking rules requiring enhanced level of due diligence for funds moving through those accounts, several US banks closed the accounts on the belief that they were being used to conduct suspicious transactions. In response, the lawyers for the PEP would deposit incoming funds into attorney-client or law office accounts, and then transfer the money into newly-created accounts for the PEP. Due to the fact that the lawyer's accounts were not subject to the same enhanced due diligence as the PEP, the lawyer was able to circumvent the enhanced AML/CFT measures. Ultimately, at least two banks were able to identify the fact that the attorney's accounts were being utilised in this manner and closed the attorney accounts, but not before hundreds of thousands of dollars had passed through.

- Duvalier case: Haitian government assets diverted by Jean-Claude Duvalier were likewise disguised by the use of lawyers as intermediaries, who would hold accounts for the Duvalier family. This, according to the UK court that examined the matter, had the added advantage of the use of professional secrecy to avoid identifying the client.28 The court opinion identified numerous accounts held by law firms for Duvalier and his family, both in the UK and in Jersey. The use of professional secrecy was used to attempt to prevent an inquiry into the nature of the funds.
- Chiluba case: Similarly, in a civil recovery suit instituted in the UK against the former President of Zambia, the court, in its factual findings, described in great detail the use of certain lawyers and law firms to distribute and disguise money embezzled from the coffers of the Zambian government.29 Special corporate vehicles had been set up, purportedly for use by the country's security services, and government funds were transferred to accounts held by those entities. Thereafter, millions of dollars were transferred to the client accounts of certain law firms, from which the lawyers would then make certain disbursals upon instructions from complicit PEPs. These disbursals were to other accounts located both in Zambia and in other countries, as well as payments for personal expenses and asset acquisitions for the government officials and their families. As the Court noted in its opinion, "There is no reason for his client account to be used for any genuine currency transactions. This is ... money which has been traced back to [the Zambian Ministry of Finance]. It is a classic example of washing money through [the attorney's] client account to hide its origins and to clothe it with an aura of respectability."
- The court also noted an instance in which the PEP's lawyer withdrew GBP 30 000 – an amount that vastly exceeded the President's annual salary – and delivered it personally to the President. Moving the money through the lawyer's accounts disguised the fact that the money originated from government accounts, and further hampered the ability to trace the proceeds. The court noted that the lawyers involved did not make any efforts to determine the source or the purpose of the money: "Yet [the lawyer] made no enquiry as to how the President could simply take such a

large amount of money. An honest solicitor would not participate in such a transaction without a full understanding of its nature so that he could be satisfied it was lawful. [The lawyer] did not so satisfy himself because he was unwilling to ask the question because he was afraid of the answer." Additionally, the lawyers involved formed foreign shell corporations, which were then used to purchase properties with government money for the benefit of corrupt officials.

END OF EXCERPT

Use of Domestic Financial Institutions

BEINNING OF EXCERPT

- Much of the focus on PEPs to date has been to ensure that foreign PEPs are subject to enhanced due diligence regarding the source of funds deposited into financial institutions – in other words, measures to prevent corrupt PEPs from laundering their proceeds in foreign bank accounts. For example, the Third EU Directive requires enhanced due diligence only for foreign PEPs. The UNCAC, however, does not distinguish between foreign PEPs and those prominent political figures within the institution's own country. The World Bank policy paper on PEPs notes that many financial institutions do not distinguish between foreign and domestic PEPs.30
- The Interpretive Note to Recommendation 6 encourages jurisdictions to extend its EDD requirements to domestic PEPs as well. Recently the FATF has discussed the degree to which domestic PEPs should be subject to enhanced due diligence, and in addressing the issue, has recommended that domestic PEPs continue to be considered on a risk-based approach, and that foreign PEPs continue to receive enhanced due diligence.31
- Some typology exercises the project team reviewed have concluded that domestic PEPs may present a significant risk for corruption-related money laundering. Professor Jason Sharman, in summarizing the ADB/OECD paper on PEPs, characterised the notion that domestic PEPs do not present a threat of money laundering as a "myth." 32 The project team's analysis of the case study inventory found that PEPs are not only using foreign financial institutions to transfer and hide the proceeds of corruption. PEPs are also using domestic financial institutions to launder funds.
- Perhaps the most obvious example of this involves President Joseph Estrada of the Philippines, who was convicted in his country of the crime of plunder. The court's ruling in that case noted that a significant portion of the money that Estrada collected as a result of kickbacks from illegal gambling and tobacco excise taxes ultimately ended up at a bank account

in the Philippines in the name of an alias, Jose Velarde. The court noted that Estrada used the account and would simply sign Velarde's name to deposit slips, oftentimes in the presence of bank personnel. Money that went through that account was used for various asset purchases, including real estate for the benefit of Estrada.

- The US Senate, in its 2010 investigation of the use of US banks to launder corruption proceeds, described in two different reports the banking and asset purchase activities of the President of a West African oil producing country as well as that of his son, who was also a high-level government official. The son, for example, in purchasing in cash a house in the United States for USD 30 million, wire transferred money, in six different USD 6 million tranches, from a personal bank account he held in his own country, through an account in France and then to the United States. The son had an official government monthly salary of approximately USD 6 000.
- The case involving assets stolen by Joshua Chibi Dariye also highlight the use of domestic accounts in at least the initial stages of a more complex scheme. Dariye, the Governor of Plateau State in the Federal Republic of Nigeria from May 1999 through May 2007, embezzled money belonging to the state in several ways. Checks issued from the central bank of Nigeria to Plateau State for ecological works were received by Dariye and, rather than being deposited into a government account, were instead diverted to an account in Nigeria Dariye had established using an alias. The money was then transferred to accounts held in Dariye's own name in the UK. Likewise, Dariye purchased real estate by diverting money destined for a Plateau State account into an account in Nigeria in the name of a corporation he controlled. That corporation, in turn, transferred money to UK accounts in the corporation's name to effectuate the real estate purchase.
- Raul Salinas, the brother of the President of Mexico, likewise was able to move money out of his home country by using the Mexican branch of a US-based international bank. A US-based bank official introduced Salinas' then-fiancée to a bank official at the Mexico City branch of the bank. The fiancée, using an alias, would deliver cashier's checks to the branch, where they were converted to dollars and wired to US accounts.
- PEPs need accounts in their own country in which to fund their lifestyles, and there have been examples in which the PEP, after secreting money overseas, then moved the money back to his home country. The US Senate, in its 2004 investigation of corruption-related money laundering, provided one such example. Augusto Pinochet of Chile, notwithstanding a modest official government salary, was able to secret millions of dollars in UK and

US accounts, often through the use of aliases and family members. In 1998 a Spanish investigating magistrate instituted worldwide asset freeze orders as a result of an investigation into Pinochet's role in human rights abuses and other crimes and was subsequently facing charges in Spain and Chile. Pinochet was able however, to purchase USD 1.9 million in cashier's checks (in USD 50 000 increments) from his account in the US, which he was thus able to cash using banks in Chile.

- That corrupt PEPs would seek to move money outside of their home jurisdiction is at the root of Recommendation 6, requiring enhanced due diligence for foreign PEPs. An examination of the corruption case studies revealed that in nearly every case foreign bank accounts were being used in part of the scheme. Beginning with one of the earliest cases, Marcos of the Philippines, through the significant and egregious activity of Sani Abacha and a number of Nigerian governors, and most recently with the US Senate's study of three West African heads of state, corrupt PEPs nearly universally attempt to move their money outside of their home country. This money is typically moved from developing countries to financial institutions in developed countries or those with a stable climate for investment.
- Of course, corruption is not restricted to developing countries. The project team analyzed the Nino Rovelli judicial corruption matter, for example. 37 There, approximately USD 575 million was paid out to individuals as a result of bribes paid to judicial officials in Italy. The money ultimately was moved and disguised in a series of financial transactions involving accounts and corporate vehicles in the United States, British Virgin Islands, Singapore, Cook Islands and Costa Rica. Likewise, the developing world's financial systems may well be used to hide money. In the Titan Corporation bribery case for example, bribes from a US corporation to the President of Benin, intended to secure government contracts in telecommunications, was moved, in cash, directly to Benin.
- The reason for this preference is obvious. Foreign accounts hold the advantage of being harder to investigate for the victim country, are perceived of as more stable and safer, and are more easily accessed than accounts held in the PEPs home country. Moreover, a PEP can "stack" foreign jurisdictions: a bank account in one country could be owned by a corporation in another jurisdiction, which is in turn owned by a trust in a third jurisdiction. Each additional country multiplies the complexity of the investigation, reduces the chances of a successful result, and extends the time needed to complete the investigation.

END OF EXCERPT

Use of Nominees

BEGINNING OF EXCERPT

- The use of associates or nominees – trusted associates or family members, but not necessarily the lawyers and accountants described in the gatekeepers section – to assist the PEP in disguising and moving the proceeds of corruption was common in the inventory of cases. FATF has documented the use of such nominees previously. The WGTYP annual report for 2003-2004 noted at paragraph 78:
    - PEPs, given the often high visibility of their office both inside and outside their country, very frequently use middlemen or other intermediaries to conduct financial business on their behalf. It is not unusual therefore for close associates, friends and family of a PEP to conduct individual transactions or else hold or move assets in their own name on behalf the PEP. This use of middlemen is not necessarily an indicator by itself of illegal activity, as frequently such intermediaries are also used when the business or proceeds of the PEP are entirely legitimate. In any case, however, the use of middlemen to shelter or insulate the PEP from unwanted attention can also serve as an obstacle to customer due diligence that should be performed for every customer. A further obstacle may be involved when the person acting on behalf of the PEP or the PEP him or herself has some sort of special status such as, for example, diplomatic immunity.
- A typical use of nominees can be found in the case of Arnoldo Aleman. Aleman was able to siphon government funds through a non-profit institution known as the Nicaraguan Democratic Foundation (FDN), an entity incorporated by Aleman's wife in Panama. In addition, Aleman and his wife set up both front companies and non-profit organisations to funnel money through. Lastly, Aleman was able to defraud the government in the sale of telecommunications frequency to a private entity, using companies set up by advisors to Aleman. Aleman was also assisted in his efforts to steal and subsequently move money through the active participation of Byron Jerez, the country's tax commissioner at the time.
- The scheme set up by a high level PEP in a Central American country likewise depended on the assistance of both family members as well as other associates to succeed. The PEP would divert money that was intended to be paid to the country's treasury through a series of financial transactions, which would then ultimately end up in foreign bank accounts in the name of the PEP's former wife and daughter.

END OF EXCERPT

Use of Cash

BEGINNING OF EXCERPT

- The use of cash, and its placement into the financial system, has long been identified as a method for the laundering of proceeds of crime. Indeed, when the FATF 40 Recommendations were first issued in 1990, the focus of many of its preventative measures was on detecting money laundering at the cash proceeds stage. The anonymous nature of cash, with its lack of paper trail, is attractive and may outweigh other negatives. Some of the predicate crimes, such as drug trafficking, are historically cash businesses. Indeed, even for crimes that do not generate cash requiring placement into the financial system, WGTYP has noted (Report on Money Laundering Typologies, 2000-2001) some laundering schemes in which the proceeds are converted back to cash in order to break the paper trail.
- While smaller-scale, endemic corruption (in which money is provided to lower- or mid-level government officials in order to act or refrain from acting in their official capacity), would be expected to generate cash in need of placement, the grand corruption cases would not be expected to have significant amounts of cash. A cash payment to a PEP would break the chain of bank records, of course, but it would require the PEP to run the gauntlet of AML/CFT controls designed to combat placement of illegally-derived cash into the system. This would include the possibility that the PEP's transactions (as well as those for his family and close associates) are subject to enhanced due diligence in accordance with Recommendation 6. In each case in which the PEP receives the cash, he must engage in a calculus to determine whether the risks associated with placement – including the possibility of EDD as a result of his PEP status – outweigh the benefits of having broken the chain. It appears that in a significant number of cases, the corrupt PEP wants the cash and, moreover is able to place the cash without attracting undue attention.
- The US Senate's investigation of corruption-related money laundering identified the President of one oil rich West African country, for which a US bank accepted nearly USD 13 million in cash deposits over a three-year period into accounts controlled by the President or his wife. The report noted that some of these deposits were for a million dollars at a time, and the currency was in shrink-wrap packaging. The report could identify no legitimate source for such currency. This same bank also provided USD 1.9 million in cashier checks to a PEP from a South American country, using the maiden name of the wife of the PEP as the payee. These cashiers' checks were ultimately cashed in the PEP's home country. The bank involved was

fined and criminally prosecuted for these violations and ultimately was closed as a result.

- The Zambian asset recovery lawsuit, noted above, also highlights the use of cash. As part of the scheme, the president of Zambia directed his UK-based lawyer to withdraw GBP 30 000 in cash from accounts containing diverted government money and deliver it to him personally. There were also other significant cash payments, including a USD 250 000 payment made from a diverted account to the Zambian Ambassador to the United States, which he then took in a suitcase to Switzerland and gave to the head of the Zambian security service, and hundreds of thousands of dollars in cash used to purchase property in the UK and elsewhere. The court found that there was no legitimate purpose for the large cash withdrawals.
- Other case studies have shown the presence of significant amounts of unexplained cash. Diepreye Alamieyeseigha, for example, was found to have over GBP 1 000 000 in his apartment in the UK at the time of his arrest, notwithstanding the fact that as governor of Bayelsa State in Nigeria, his salary was a fraction of that. Another governor of a Nigerian state around that time, Joshua Chibi Dariye, previously discussed, was found to have deposited into his UK accounts in excess of GBP 480 000 during a four and a half year period. According to a US Senate report on the matter, immediately after Sani Abacha's death in 1998, his wife was stopped at a Lagos airport with 38 suitcases full of cash, and his son was found with USD 100 million in cash. According to the World Bank study he was able to place significant amounts of cash in the financial system by using associates. Lastly, Montesinos used cash couriers to transfer funds from Switzerland to Mexico and Bolivia.
- PEPs have an advantage not usually available to the general public: the use (and abuse) of the so-called "diplomatic pouch." Intended to protect free communication between diplomats and their foreign missions, a diplomatic bag is protected from search or seizure by the 1961 Convention on Diplomatic Relations.43 A diplomatic bag may only be used for official materials and, while the Convention protects it from search, it does not relieve the carrier of adherence to the laws of the host nation, including cross-border currency reporting requirements.
- Such was the situation that the US Senate uncovered in its report on the financial affairs of one West African PEP. His daughter, who was in graduate school in the United States, asked her US bank to count certain cash she had stored in her safe deposit box. The bank found USD 1 million in cash, in USD 100 bills, wrapped in plastic. When asked about the source of the

money, the daughter replied that her father, the PEP, provided her the cash when he came into the United States, and that he often brought cash into the United States. The PEP had never declared his transport of the cash, as he was required to do by US law.

END OF EXCERPT

INTERNATIONAL STANDARDS FOR PREVENTION AND CRIMINALIZATION OF MONEY LAUNDERING

UNCAC

As discussed in previous chapters, UNCAC is the most extensive and most widely ratified international convention addressing corruption. In addition to prohibiting bribery and other forms of corruption, the drafters of UNCAC recognized that effective anti-money laundering strategies are an important factor in preventing and detecting large-scale corruption. Like other forms of corruption, the transnational nature of money laundering necessitates international cooperation and consistent standards in anti-money laundering efforts. UNCAC therefore addresses money laundering in both Chapter II (Preventative Measures) and in Chapter III (Criminalization and Law Enforcement). Article 14 sets out standards for State Parties to follow in developing anti-money laundering measures, while Article 23 of UNCAC criminalizes the laundering of the proceeds of corruption. A more comprehensive overview of the anti-money laundering provisions of UNCAC can be found in Carr and Goldby's paper, "The UN Anti-Corruption Convention and Money Laundering."

Article 23 is ambitious in scope. It criminalizes the actions of those involved in money laundering in a number of different capacities. Unlike some of the other criminalization provisions of UNCAC, the criminalization of money laundering under Article 23 is mandatory, although the provision may be adapted if necessary to conform to the "fundamental principles" of the State Party's domestic law. Article 23 provides as follows:

Article 23. Laundering of proceeds of crime

1. Each State Party shall adopt, in accordance with fundamental principles of its domestic law, such legislative and other measures as may be necessary to establish as criminal offences, when committed intentionally:
    a. (i) The conversion or transfer of property, knowing that such property is the proceeds of crime, for the purpose of concealing or disguising the illicit origin of the property or of helping any person who is involved in the commission of the predicate offence to evade the legal consequences of his or her action;

- (ii) The concealment or disguise of the true nature, source, location, disposition, movement or ownership of or rights with respect to property, knowing that such property is the proceeds of crime;

b. Subject to the basic concepts of its legal system:

   i. The acquisition, possession or use of property, knowing, at the time of receipt, that such property is the proceeds of crime;

   ii. Participation in, association with or conspiracy to commit, attempts to commit and aiding, abetting, facilitating and counselling the commission of any of the offences established in accordance with this article.

The following excerpt from the Legislative Guide for the Implementation of the United Nations Convention against Corruption provides guidance on Article 23 to legislators tasked with incorporating Article 23 into a state's domestic legislation:

BEGINNING OF EXCERPT

Money-laundering

Article 23 requires the establishment of offences related to the laundering of proceeds of crime, in accordance with fundamental principles of domestic law. The related Convention articles addressing measures aimed at the prevention of money- laundering were discussed in the previous chapter.

In the context of globalization, criminals take advantage of easier capital movement, advances in technology and increases in the mobility of people and commodities, as well as the significant diversity of legal provisions in various jurisdictions. As a result, assets can be transferred instantly from place to place through both formal and informal channels. Through exploitation of existing legal asymmetries, funds may appear finally as legitimate assets available in any part of the world.

Confronting corruption effectively requires measures aimed at eliminating the financial or other benefits that motivate public officials to act improperly. Beyond this, combating money-laundering also helps to preserve the integrity of financial institutions, both formal and informal, and to protect the smooth operation of the international financial system as a whole.

As noted in the previous chapter, this goal can only be achieved through international and cooperative efforts. It is essential that States and regions try to make their approaches, standards and legal systems related to this offence compatible, so that they can cooperate with one another in controlling the international laundering of criminal proceeds. Jurisdictions with weak or no control mechanisms render the work of money launderers easier. Thus, the Convention against Corruption seeks to provide a minimum standard for all States.

The Convention against Corruption specifically recognizes the link between corrupt practices and money-laundering and builds on earlier and parallel national, regional and international initiatives in that regard. Those initiatives addressed the issue through a combination of repressive and preventive measures and the Convention follows the same pattern (see also chap. II of the present guide).

One of the most important of the previous initiatives related to the Organized Crime Convention, which mandated the establishment of the offence of money-laundering for additional predicate offences, including corruption of public officials, and encouraged States to widen the range of predicate offences beyond the minimum requirements.

"Predicate offence" is defined as "any offence as a result of which proceeds have been generated that may become the subject of an offence as defined in article 23 of this Convention" (art. 2, subpara. (h)).

As a result of all these initiatives, many States already have money laundering laws. Nevertheless, such laws may be limited in scope and may not cover a wide range of predicate offences. Article 23 requires that the list of predicate offences include the widest possible range and at a minimum the offences established in accordance with the Convention against Corruption.

The provisions of the Convention against Corruption addressing the seizure, freezing and confiscation of proceeds (see art. 31) and the recovery of assets (see chap. V of the Convention and, especially, art. 57) include important related measures. States should review the provisions they already have in place to counter money- laundering in order to ensure compliance with these articles and those dealing with international cooperation (chap. IV). States undertaking such a review may wish to use the opportunity to implement the obligations they assume under other regional or international instruments and initiatives currently in place.

Article 23 requires that States parties establish the four offences related to money- laundering described in the following paragraphs:

Conversion or transfer of proceeds of crime

The first offence is the conversion or transfer of property, knowing that such property is the proceeds of crime, for the purpose of concealing or disguising the illicit origin of the property or of helping any person who is involved in the commission of the predicate offence to evade the legal consequences of his or her action (art. 23, para. 1 (a) (i)).

The term "conversion or transfer" includes instances in which financial assets are converted from one form or type to another, for example, by using illicitly generated cash to purchase precious metals or real estate or the sale of illicitly acquired real estate, as well as instances in which the same assets are moved from one place or jurisdiction to another or from one bank account to another.

The term "proceeds of crime" means "any property derived from or obtained, directly or indirectly, through the commission of an offence" (art. 2, subpara. (e)).

With respect to the mental or subjective elements required, the conversion or transfer must be intentional, the accused must have knowledge at the time of conversion or transfer that the assets are criminal proceeds and the act or acts must be done for the purpose of either concealing or disguising their criminal origin, for example by helping to prevent their discovery, or helping a person evade criminal liability for the crime that generated the proceeds.

As noted in article 28 of the Convention against Corruption, knowledge, intent or purpose may be inferred from objective factual circumstances.

Concealment or disguise of proceeds of crime

The second money-laundering offence is the concealment or disguise of the nature, source, location, disposition, movement or ownership of or rights with respect to property, knowing that such property is the proceeds of crime (art. 23, para. 1 (a) (ii)).

The elements of this offence are quite broad, including the concealment or disguise of almost any aspect of or information about property.

Here, with respect to the mental or subjective elements required, the concealment or disguise must be intentional and the accused must have knowledge that the property constitutes the proceeds of crime at the time of the act. This mental state is less stringent than for the offence set forth in article 23, subparagraph 1 (a) (i). Accordingly, drafters should not require proof that the purpose of the concealment or disguise is to frustrate the tracing of the asset or to conceal its true origin.

The next two offences related to money-laundering are mandatory, subject to the basic concepts of the legal system of each State party.

Acquisition, possession or use of proceeds of crime

The third offence is the acquisition, possession or use of proceeds of crime knowing, at the time of receipt, that such property is the proceeds of crime (art. 23, para. 1 (b) (i)).

This is the mirror image of the offences under article 23, paragraph 1 (a)(i) and (ii), in that, while those provisions impose liability on the providers of illicit proceeds, this paragraph imposes liability on recipients who acquire, possess or use the property.

The mental or subjective elements are the same as for the offence under article 23, paragraph 1 (a) (ii): there must be intent to acquire, possess or use, and the accused must have knowledge, at the time this occurred, that the property was the proceeds of crime. No particular purpose for the acts is required.

(i) Participation in, association with or conspiracy to commit, attempts to commit and aiding, abetting, facilitating and counselling the commission of any of the foregoing offences

The fourth set of offences involves the participation in, association with or conspiracy to commit, attempts to commit and aiding, abetting, facilitating and counselling the commission of any of the offences mandated by the article (art. 23, para. 1 (b) (ii)).

These terms are not defined in the Convention against Corruption, allowing for certain flexibility in domestic legislation. States parties should refer to the manner in which such ancillary offences are otherwise structured in their domestic system and ensure that they apply to the other offences established pursuant to article 23.

[Note – see Chapter 3, Sections 3 and 4, for a discussion on inchoate crimes and secondary liability.]

The knowledge, intent or purpose, as required for these offences, may be inferred from objective factual circumstances (art. 28). National drafters could see that their evidentiary provisions enable such inference with respect to the mental state, rather than requiring direct evidence, such as a confession, before the mental state is deemed proven.

Under article 23, States parties must apply these offences to proceeds generated by "the widest range of predicate offences" (art. 23, para. 2 (a)).

At a minimum, these must include a "comprehensive range of criminal offences established in accordance with this Convention" (art. 23, para. 2 (b)). For this purpose, "predicate offences shall include offences committed both within and outside the jurisdiction of the State party in question. However, offences committed outside the jurisdiction of a State party shall constitute predicate offences only when the relevant conduct is a criminal offence under the domestic law of the State where it is committed and would be a criminal offence under the domestic law of the State party implementing or applying this article had it been committed there" (art. 23, para. 2 (c)). So, dual criminality is necessary for offences committed in a different national jurisdiction to be considered as predicate offences.

Many States already have laws on money-laundering, but there are many variations in the definition of predicate offences. Some States limit the predicate offences to trafficking in drugs or to trafficking in drugs and a few other crimes. Other States have an exhaustive list of predicate offences set forth in their legislation. Still other States define predicate offences generically as including all crimes, or all serious crimes, or all crimes subject to a defined penalty threshold.

An interpretative note for the Convention against Corruption states that "money- laundering offences established in accordance with this article are understood to be independent and autonomous offences and that a prior conviction for the predicate offence is not necessary to establish the illicit nature or origin of the assets laundered. The illicit nature or origin of the assets and, in accordance with article 28, any knowledge, intent or purpose may be established during the course of the money- laundering prosecution and may be inferred from objective factual circumstances" (A/58/422/Add.1, para. 32).

The constitutions or fundamental legal principles of some States do not permit the prosecution and punishment of an offender for both the predicate offence and the laundering of proceeds from that offence. The Convention acknowledges this issue and, only in such cases, allows for the non-application of the money-laundering offences to those who committed the predicate offence (art. 23, para. 2 (e)).

END OF EXCERPT

Article 14 – Measures to Prevent Money-Laundering

As mentioned above, in addition to mandating the criminalization of money laundering, UNCAC also requires state parties to take measures to establish a regulatory regime intended to prevent money laundering. The relevant article is Article 14, which is reproduced below:

Article 14. Measures to prevent money-laundering

1. Each State Party shall:
    a. Institute a comprehensive domestic regulatory and supervisory regime for banks and non-bank financial institutions, including natural or legal persons that provide formal or informal services for the transmission of money or value and, where appropriate, other bodies particularly susceptible to money-laundering, within its competence, in order to deter and detect all forms of money- laundering, which regime shall emphasize requirements for customer and, where appropriate, beneficial owner identification, record-keeping and the reporting of suspicious transactions;
    b. Without prejudice to article 46 of this Convention, ensure that administrative, regulatory, law enforcement and other authorities dedicated to combating money-laundering (including, where appropriate under domestic law, judicial authorities) have the ability to cooperate and exchange information at the national and international levels within

the conditions prescribed by its domestic law and, to that end, shall consider the establishment of a financial intelligence unit to serve as a national centre for the collection, analysis and dissemination of information regarding potential money-laundering.

2. States Parties shall consider implementing feasible measures to detect and monitor the movement of cash and appropriate negotiable instruments across their borders, subject to safeguards to ensure proper use of information and without impeding in any way the movement of legitimate capital. Such measures may include a requirement that individuals and businesses report the cross-border transfer of substantial quantities of cash and appropriate negotiable instruments.
3. States Parties shall consider implementing appropriate and feasible measures to require financial institutions, including money remitters:
   a. To include on forms for the electronic transfer of funds and related messages accurate and meaningful information on the originator;
   b. To maintain such information throughout the payment chain; and
   c. To apply enhanced scrutiny to transfers of funds that do not contain complete information on the originator.
4. In establishing a domestic regulatory and supervisory regime under the terms of this article, and without prejudice to any other article of this Convention, States Parties are called upon to use as a guideline the relevant initiatives of regional, interregional and multilateral organizations against money-laundering.
5. States Parties shall endeavour to develop and promote global, regional, subregional and bilateral cooperation among judicial, law enforcement and financial regulatory authorities in order to combat money-laundering.

Carr and Goldby note that Article 14(1) requires states to implement a regulatory and supervisory regime that monitors both formal and informal methods of transferring money in order to combat money laundering. 47 They state that "[t] he system known as Hawala (in India) or Fie Ch'ieu (in China) is typically used by migrant workers to transfer small amounts of money to relatives in villages lacking bank accounts or access to banks, but can also be abused by criminals." 48 Although Carr and Goldby welcome this inclusion of informal networks of money transfer into supervisory regimes, they argue that "much research still needs to be done in order to design an effective regime for the regulation and supervision of such informal networks."

Article 14 of UNCAC also requires states to develop comprehensive anti-money laundering regimes. Although not expressly mandated, there is a strong suggestion by UNCAC that states look to international standard setting bodies, such as the FATF, when designing anti- money laundering frameworks. Therefore, although the FATF recommendations are not themselves binding international law, in addition to their independent ability to set standards through peer pressure, they are given some degree of legal recognition under UNCAC.

The following excerpt from the UNCAC Legislative Guide summarizes and explains the various mandated and recommended actions that, pursuant to Article 14, State Parties are to follow:

BEGINNING OF EXCERPT

Summary of Main Requirements

- Article 14 contains two mandatory requirements:
  a. To establish a comprehensive domestic regulatory and supervisory regime to deter money-laundering (para. 1 (a));
  b. To ensure that agencies involved in combating money-laundering have the ability to cooperate and exchange information at the national and international levels (para. 1 (b)).
- In addition, pursuant to article 14 States must consider:
  a. Establishing an FIU (para. 1 (b));
  b. Implementing measures to monitor cash movements across their borders (para. 2);
  c. Implementing measures to require financial institutions to collect information on originators of electronic fund transfers, maintain information on the entire payment chain and scrutinize fund transfers with incomplete information on the originator (para. 3);
  d. Developing and promoting global, regional and bilateral cooperation among relevant agencies to combat money-laundering (para. 5).

Mandatory requirements: obligation to take legislative or other measures

Regulatory and supervisory regime

Article 14, paragraph 1 (a), requires that States parties establish a regulatory and supervisory regime within their competence in order to prevent and detect money-laundering activities. This regime must be comprehensive, but the precise nature and particular elements of the regime are left to States, provided that they require, at a minimum, banks and non-bank financial institutions to ensure:

- Effective customer identification;
- Accurate record-keeping;
- A mechanism for the reporting of suspicious transactions.

The requirements extend to banks, non-bank financial institutions (e.g. insurance companies and securities firms) and, where appropriate, other bodies that are especially susceptible to money-laundering (art. 14, para. 1 (a)). The interpretative notes add that other bodies may be understood to include intermediaries, which in some jurisdictions may include stockbrokering firms, other securities dealers, currency exchange bureaux or currency brokers (A/58/422/Add.1, para. 18). An addition to the equivalent provisions in the Organized Crime Convention is that financial institutions include "natural or legal persons that provide formal or informal services for the transmission of money or value" (art. 14, para. 1 (a)). This is a reference to concerns about both formal remitters and informal value-transfer systems, such as the hawala networks that originated in South Asia and have become global in recent decades. These channels offer valuable services to expatriates and their families, but are also vulnerable to abuse by criminals, including corrupt public officials.

Thus, this regime should apply not only to banking institutions, but also to areas of commerce where high turnover and large volumes make money-laundering likely. Previous experience shows that money-laundering activities have taken place in the real estate sector and in the trade of commodities, such as gold, precious stones and tobacco.

In many forums, the list of institutions is being expanded beyond financial institutions to include businesses and professions related to real estate and commodities. For example, recommendation 12 of the FATF Forty Recommendations extends, when certain conditions are met, the requirements of customer due diligence and record-keeping to casinos, real estate agents, dealers in precious metals and stones, lawyers, notaries, other independent legal professionals and accountants and trust and company service providers. Similar requirements are set forth in article 1 of Directive 2005/60/EC adopted by the European Parliament and the Council of the European Union on 26 October 2005.

More recently, increased attention has been focused on money service businesses and informal value-transfer systems, such as hawala and hundi. In a growing number of jurisdictions, these are also subject to a regulatory regime for the purposes of detecting money-laundering, terrorist financing or other offences.

Customer identification entails requirements that holders of accounts in financial institutions and all parties to financial transactions be identified and documented. Records should contain sufficient information to identify all parties and the nature of the transaction, identify specific assets and the amounts or values involved, and permit the tracing of the source and destination of all funds or other assets.

The requirement for record-keeping means that client and transaction records should be kept for a specified minimum period of time. For example, under the FATF Forty Recommendations, at least five years is recommended, while for States parties to the International Convention for the Suppression of the Financing of Terrorism, retention of records for five years is mandatory.

Suspicious transactions are to be notified to the FIU or other designated agency. Criteria for identifying suspicious transactions should be developed and periodically reviewed in consultation with experts knowledgeable about new methods or networks used by money launderers.

The interpretative notes indicate that the words "suspicious transactions" may be understood to include unusual transactions that, by reason of their amount, characteristics and frequency, are inconsistent with the customer's business activity, exceed the normally accepted parameters of the market or have no clear legal basis and could constitute or be connected with unlawful activities in general (A/58/422/Add.1, para. 19). The International Convention for the Suppression of the Financing of Terrorism defines suspicious transactions as all complex, unusually large transactions and unusual patterns of transactions, which have no apparent economic or obviously lawful purpose (General Assembly resolution 54/109, annex, art. 18, para. 1 (b) (iii)).

The powers to be granted to regulators and staff of the FIU to inspect records and to compel the assistance of record keepers in locating the records must also be defined. As some of these records may be covered by confidentiality requirements and banking secrecy laws that prohibit their disclosure, provisions freeing financial institutions from complying with such requirements and laws may be considered. Drafters should also ensure that the inspection and disclosure requirements are written in such a way as to protect financial institutions against civil and other claims for disclosing client records to regulators and FIUs.

The implementation of such measures is likely to require legislation. In particular, the requirement that financial institutions must disclose suspicious transactions and the protection of those who make disclosures in good faith will require legislation to override banking secrecy laws (see also paras. 1-3 of art. 52, on the prevention and detection of transfers of proceeds of crime).

Domestic and international cooperation

Coordination of efforts and international cooperation is as central to the problem of money-laundering as it is to the other offences covered by the Convention against Corruption. Beyond the general measures and processes such as extradition, mutual legal assistance, joint investigations and asset recovery (which are covered in detail in the sections on international cooperation in chapter IV and asset recovery in chapter V, below), the Convention seeks to strengthen such coordination and cooperation.

Article 14, paragraph 1 (b), requires that administrative, regulatory, law enforcement and other domestic authorities in charge of the efforts against money- laundering are able to cooperate at both the national and international level. This includes the exchange of information within the conditions prescribed by their domestic law. This must be done without limiting or detracting from (or in the words of the Convention, "without prejudice to") the requirements generated by article 46 (Mutual legal assistance).

In order for cooperation to be possible, domestic capabilities must be developed for the identification, collection and interpretation of all relevant information. Essentially, three types of entity may be part of a strategy to combat money-laundering and could, thus, be considered by States:

a. Regulatory agencies responsible for the oversight of financial institutions, such as banks or insurance entities, with powers to inspect financial institutions and enforce regulatory requirements through the imposition of regulatory or administrative remedies or sanctions;
b. Law enforcement agencies responsible for conducting criminal investigations, with investigative powers and powers to arrest and detain suspected offenders and that are subject to judicial or other safeguards;
c. FIUs, which are not required under the Convention, whose powers are usually limited to receiving reports of suspicious transactions, analysing them and disseminating information to prosecution agencies, although some such units have wider powers (see more on FIUs in sect. V.E, below).

The authority of each entity to cooperate with national bodies and with other similar agencies in other States is usually specified in the relevant legislation. If States do have such entities, legislation may be needed to amend existing mandates and the division of labour among these entities, in accordance with each State's constitutional or other principles and the specificities of its financial services sector.

Some of these measures may constitute a strong challenge for countries in which the financial sector is not heavily regulated and the necessary legislation and administrative infrastructure may have to be created. It is essential to note, however, that the relevance and utility of these arrangements are not limited to the control of money-laundering, but also to corruption. They also strengthen confidence in the financial infrastructure, which is instrumental to sustainable social and economic development.

The remaining provisions of this article are also closely connected to domestic and international cooperation, and are examined below, as they are not mandatory under the Convention.

Optional requirements: obligation to consider

a. Financial intelligence units

Article 14, paragraph 1 (b), requires States parties to consider the establishment of FIUs to serve as a national centre for the collection, analysis and dissemination of information regarding potential money-laundering. Since the 1990s, many States have established such units as part of their regulatory police or other authorities. There is a wide range of structure, responsibilities, functions and departmental affiliation or independence for such units. According to the interpretative notes, the call for the establishment of an FIU is intended for cases where such a mechanism does not yet exist (A/58/422/Add.1, para. 20).

The Egmont Group (an informal association of FIUs) has defined such units as a central, national agency responsible for receiving (and, as permitted, requesting), analysing and disseminating to the competent authorities, disclosures of financial information (a) concerning suspected proceeds of crime; or (b) required by national legislation or regulation; in order to counter money laundering.

The Convention does not require that an FIU be established by law, but legislation may still be required to institute the obligation to report suspicious transactions to such a unit and to protect financial institutions that disclose such information in good faith (see also art. 58, on FIUs). In practice, the vast majority of FIUs are established by law. If it is decided to draft such legislation, States may wish to consider including the following elements:

a. Specification of the institutions that are subject to the obligation to report suspicious transactions and definition of the information to be reported to the unit;

b. Legislation defining the powers under which the unit can compel the assistance of reporting institutions to follow up on incomplete or inadequate reports;

c. Authorization for the unit to disseminate information to law enforcement agencies when it has evidence warranting prosecution and authority for the unit to communicate financial intelligence information to foreign agencies, under certain conditions;

d. Protection of the confidentiality of information received by the unit, establishing limits on the uses to which it may be put and shielding the unit from further disclosure;

e. Definition of the reporting arrangements for the unit and its relationship with other Government agencies, including law enforcement agencies and financial regulators. States may already have money-laundering controls in place that can be expanded or modified to conform to the requirements of article 14 relating to money-laundering and those of article 31 relating to freezing, confiscation, seizure, disposal of proceeds, as well as provisions on asset recovery, as necessary.

It is worth noting that actions taken to conform to article 14 may also bring States into conformity with other conventions and initiatives, such as Security Council resolution 1373 (2001), the International Convention for the Suppression of the Financing of Terrorism, the Organized Crime Convention and the FATF Nine Special Recommendations on Terrorist Financing.

Further information about various options that can be included in laws, regulations and procedures to combat money-laundering can be obtained from the Anti-Money-Laundering Unit of the United Nations Office on Drugs and Crime.

(b) Other measures

As part of the effort to develop the capacity to provide effective international cooperation, States are required to consider the introduction of feasible measures aimed at monitoring the cross-border movement of cash and other monetary instruments (art. 14, para. 2). The goal of such measures would be to allow States to detect and monitor the movement of cash and appropriate negotiable instruments across their borders, subject to safeguards to ensure proper use of information and without impeding in any way the movement of legitimate capital. Such measures may include a requirement that individuals and businesses report the cross-border transfer of substantial quantities of cash appropriate negotiable instruments. Generally, structures based on monitoring or surveillance will require legal powers giving inspectors or investigators access to information on cross-border transactions, in particular in cases where criminal behaviour is suspected.

Article 14, paragraph 3, contains provisions going beyond the Organized Crime Convention. It requires that States consider the implementation of measures obliging financial institutions, including money remitters:

a. To include on forms for the electronic transfer of funds and related messages accurate and meaningful information on the originator;

b. To maintain such information throughout the payment chain; and

c. To apply enhanced scrutiny to transfers of funds that do not contain complete information on the originator.

The concern is essentially about the identification of remitters and beneficiaries on the one hand and the traceability of the transaction on the other. There are no exact estimates on the extent of funds transferred across national borders, especially with respect to informal remitters, who are popular in many countries. Given that they range in the tens of billions of United States dollars, however, it is an area of regulatory concern.

As mentioned above, the Convention against Corruption builds on parallel international initiatives to combat money-laundering. In establishing a domestic regulatory and supervisory regime, States parties are called upon to use as a guideline the relevant initiatives of regional, interregional and multilateral organizations against money-laundering (art. 14, para. 4). An interpretative note states that during the negotiations, the words "relevant initiatives of regional, interregional and multilateral organizations" were understood to refer in particular to the Forty Recommendations and the Eight52 Special Recommendations of the FATF, as revised in 2003 and 2001, respectively, and, in addition, to other existing initiatives of regional, interregional and multilateral organizations against money-laundering, such as the Caribbean Financial Action Task Force, the Commonwealth, the Council of Europe, the Eastern and Southern African Anti-Money-Laundering Group, the European Union, the Financial Action Task Force of South America against Money Laundering and the Organization of American States" (A/58/422/Add.1, para. 21).

Ultimately, States are free to determine the best way to implement article 14. However, the development of a relationship with one of the organizations working to combat money-laundering would be important for effective implementation.

In implementing article 14, paragraph 4, States may wish to consider some specific elements relative to the measures that the comprehensive regulatory regime must include. The Forty Recommendations are useful in this regard, as are model regulations that have been prepared by the United Nations Office on Drugs and Crime and the Organization of American States (see sect. II.G (Information resources) at the end of this chapter of the guide).

168. Furthermore, paragraph 5 of article 14 requires that States endeavour to develop and promote global, regional, subregional and bilateral cooperation among judicial, law enforcement and financial regulatory authorities in order to combat money- laundering.

END OF EXCERPT

OECD Anti-Bribery Convention

The OECD Convention does not deal extensively with money laundering, but it does touch on the issue in articles 7 and 8, which are reproduced below:

- Article 7: Money Laundering

Each Party which has made bribery of its own public official a predicate offence for the purpose of the application of its money laundering legislation shall do so on the same terms for the bribery of a foreign public official, without regard to the place where the bribery occurred.

- Article 8: Accounting

  In order to combat bribery of foreign public officials effectively, each Party shall take such measures as may be necessary, within the framework of its laws and regulations regarding the maintenance of books and records, financial statement disclosures, and accounting and auditing standards, to prohibit the establishment of off-the-books accounts, the making of off-the- books or inadequately identified transactions, the recording of non-existent expenditures, the entry of liabilities with incorrect identification of their object, as well as the use of false documents, by companies subject to those laws and regulations, for the purpose of bribing foreign public officials or of hiding such bribery.

Each Party shall provide effective, proportionate and dissuasive civil, administrative or criminal penalties for such omissions and falsifications in respect of the books, records, accounts and financial statements of such companies.

The OECD website notes that "The Financial Action Task Force (FATF) is the international standard setter in the development and promotion of national and international policies to combat money laundering and terrorist financing" [emphasis in original] and that "[t]he OECD's work on tax crime and money laundering is designed to complement that carried out by FATF."54 The FATF recommendations, which are covered in the following section, provide a more comprehensive treatment of money laundering and the measures that states can take to combat it.

FATF Recommendations

As already noted, the Financial Action Task Force (FATF) is a governmental policy group composed of 34 nations including the US, UK and Canada. The latest version of the FATF Recommendations was released in 2012. There are 40 recommendations in this new version, which merged the original 40 recommendations (issued in 1996) with nine additional 2003 recommendations (on countering terrorism financing). The recommendations can be found at: <http://www.fatf-gafi.org/topics/fatfrecommendations/documents/fatf- recommendations.html>. The Recommendations also include interpretive notes. The following excerpt from Paul Allan Schott's Reference Guide to Anti-Money Laundering and Combating the Financing of Terrorism, 2nd ed (World Bank, 2006) provides a general introduction to the FATF and the Recommendations. This excerpt is based on the 2003 version of the Forty Recommendations, but this does not affect the validity of the general comments set out below.

BEGINNING OF EXCERPT

[Chapter III: International Standard Setters, pp. III-7 to III-12]

Formed in 1989 by the G-7 countries, the Financial Action Task Force on Money Laundering (FATF) is an intergovernmental body whose purpose is to develop and promote an international response to combat money laundering. In October of 2001, FATF expanded its mission to include combating the financing of terrorism.

FATF is a policy-making body, which brings together legal, financial and law enforcement experts to achieve national legislation and regulatory AML and CFT reforms. Currently, its membership consists of 31 [now 34] countries and territories and two regional organizations.58 In addition, FATF works in collaboration with a number of international bodies59 and organizations. 60 These entities have observer status with FATF, which does not entitle them to vote, but otherwise permits full participation in plenary sessions and working groups.

FATF's three primary functions with regard to money laundering are:

1. monitoring members' progress in implementing anti-money laundering measures;
2. reviewing and reporting on laundering trends, techniques and counter-measures; and
3. promoting the adoption and implementation of FATF anti-money laundering standards globally.

1. The Forty Recommendations

FATF has adopted a set of 40 recommendations, The Forty Recommendations on Money Laundering (The Forty Recommendations), which constitute a comprehensive framework for AML and are designed for universal application by countries throughout the world. The Forty Recommendations set out principles for action; they permit a country flexibility in implementing the principles according to the country's own particular circumstances and constitutional requirements. Although not binding as law upon a country, The Forty Recommendations have been widely endorsed by the international community and relevant organizations as the international standard for AML.

The Forty Recommendations are actually mandates for action by a country if that country wants to be viewed by the international community as meeting international standards. The individual recommendations are discussed in detail throughout this Reference Guide and, particularly in Chapters V, VI, VII, and VIII.

The Forty Recommendations were initially issued in 1990 and have been revised in 1996 and 2003 to take account of new developments in money laundering and to reflect developing best practices internationally. [The current version of the Forty Recommendations was revised in 2012.]

Monitoring Members Progress

Monitoring the progress of members to comply with the requirements of The Forty Recommendations is facilitated by a two-stage process: self assessments and mutual evaluations. In the self-assessment stage, each member responds to a standard questionnaire, on an annual basis, regarding its implementation of The Forty Recommendations. In the mutual evaluation stage, each member is examined and assessed by experts from other member countries.

In the event that a country is unwilling to take appropriate steps to achieve compliance with The Forty Recommendations, FATF recommends that all financial institutions give special attention to business relations and transactions with persons, including companies and financial institutions, from such non-compliant countries and, where appropriate, report questionable transactions, i.e., those that have no apparent economic or visible lawful purpose, to competent authorities.62 Ultimately, if a member country does not take steps to achieve compliance, membership in the organization can be suspended. There is, however, the process of peer pressure before these sanctions are enforced.

Reporting on Money Laundering Trends and Techniques

One of FATF's functions is to review and report on money laundering trends, techniques and methods (also referred to as typologies). To accomplish this aspect of its mission, FATF issues annual reports on developments in money laundering through its Typologies Report. These reports are very useful for all countries, not just FATF members, to keep current with new techniques or trends to launder money and for other developments in this area.

The NCCT List

One of FATF's objectives is to promote the adoption of international AML/CFT standards for all countries. Thus, its mission extends beyond its own membership, although FATF can only sanction its member countries and territories. Thus, in order to encourage all countries to adopt measures to prevent, detect and prosecute money launderers, i.e., to implement The Forty Recommendations, FATF has adopted a process of identifying those jurisdictions that serve as obstacles to international cooperation in this area. The process uses 25 criteria, which are consistent with The Forty Recommendations, to identify such non-cooperative countries and territories (NCCT's) and place them on a publicly available list.

[In response to criticisms levied against the use of the NCCT list, the last country on the NCCT list was removed in 2006, and no new states have been reviewed by the FATF under the NCCT criteria since 2001. Many felt that the NCCT focused attention unfairly on smaller, less powerful nations while ignoring the failings of more powerful countries such as the United States. Since it is no longer relevant, the remainder of the section on the NCCT list has not been included in this excerpt. However, the FATF has continued to issue public statements on high-risk and non-compliant countries. This list presently includes Iran, the Democratic People's Republic of Korea and Algeria. It is available at: http://www.fatf-gafi.org/topics/high- riskandnon-cooperativejurisdictions/]

Terrorist Financing

FATF also focuses its expertise on the world-wide effort to combat terrorist financing. To accomplish this expanded mission FATF has adopted nine Special Recommendations on Terrorist Financing (Special Recommendations). As part of this effort, FATF members use a self-assessment questionnaire of their country's actions to come into compliance with the Special Recommendations. FATF is continuing to develop guidance on techniques and mechanisms used in the financing of terrorism.

END OF EXCERPT

The FATF prepares guidance and best practices documents to assist states in implementing the Recommendations. Seven such documents have been published since the latest version of the Recommendations was released in 2012. They are available on the FATF website: <http://www.fatf-gafi.org/documents/guidance/>.

STATE-LEVEL AML REGIMES: US, UK AND CANADA

Introduction to the Essential Elements of AML Regimes

While the FATF Recommendations provide a global standard for AML measures, these recommendations must be put into place at the state level to be effective. The global effectiveness of the AML regime depends on a degree of standardization, but each state must also create a regime that fits within its domestic legal framework and policy goals. As a result, despite many shared elements, there is significant variation between different state- level AML regimes.

The overall goal of state-level AML regimes is to allow centralized monitoring of the financial sector. The set of laws and policies contained in the FATF Recommendations is intended to enable sweeping state surveillance and intelligence gathering across the financial sector. Data concerning suspicious transactions is transmitted to a central organization for analysis and selected information is then passed to law enforcement agencies for investigation. In general, the goal is to create a system in which suspicious transactions or patterns of transactions are promptly detected and thoroughly investigated, preventing the abuse of financial institutions by organized crime and corrupt officials.

There are three principal elements in a state-level AML regime, each of which is dealt with in a separate section below. The first element is a Financial Intelligence Unit (FIU). FIUs are central, national-level organizations that collect and analyze information concerning suspicious transactions reported by financial institutions. They pass selected information along to the appropriate law enforcement agencies for investigation.

The second element of a state-level AML regime is sweeping regulation of the financial sector, which requires financial institutions to report information to the FIU. There are three basic aspects of this regulatory framework. The first is customer due diligence measures (CDD), which require financial institutions to collect identifying information from each of their customers. The second is record keeping requirements, which require financial institutions to retain all information collected for at least five years. The final aspect is transaction reporting requirements, which require financial institutions to report certain transactions to their respective FIUs.

The third element of a state-level AML regime is the creation of tools that law enforcement agencies can use to effectively prosecute money launderers once their activities are detected. These include the creation of stand-alone criminal offences for money laundering to enable prosecution of launderers. In theory, the three elements discussed above should create a state-level regime in which money laundering can be effectively combated through cooperation between the financial sector, the FIU and law enforcement agencies.

While the three elements described above are present in all state-level AML regimes that conform to the FATF recommendations, how each is put into place varies considerably from country to country. The following section surveys the state-level AML regimes in the US, Canada and the UK, comparing and contrasting the different approaches taken in each jurisdiction. Each subsection begins by reproducing the appropriate FATF recommendation, and then briefly discusses how the recommendation has been enacted by each of the three governments.67

Financial Intelligence Units

FATF Recommendations

Recommendation 29 of the FATF requires that each member state create a financial intelligence unit (FIU) as part of its AML regime. These FIUs cooperate internationally through their membership in the Egmont Group, an informal network whose membership currently includes 139 state-level FIUs. The Egmont

Group's website, <http://www.egmontgroup.org/>, provides a library of research reports produced by the organization as well as sanitized cases from member FIUs.

The full text of Recommendation 29 is reproduced below:

29. Financial intelligence units

Countries should establish a financial intelligence unit (FIU) that serves as a national centre for the receipt and analysis of: (a) suspicious transaction reports; and (b) other information relevant to money laundering, associated predicate offences and terrorist financing, and for the dissemination of the results of that analysis. The FIU should be able to obtain additional information from reporting entities, and should have access on a timely basis to the financial, administrative and law enforcement information that it requires to undertake its functions properly.

There is considerable scope available to states in implementing this recommendation. All that is strictly required is the creation of a central organization that collects and analyzes reports of suspicious transactions and "other information." Some states have chosen to create FIUs with a broad range of powers, while others have taken a more minimal approach. Furthermore, there is nothing in the recommendation to indicate how the FIU should relate to other government agencies, or who it should report to. States have made different choices in this regard as well. The following section briefly discusses and compares the FIUs created by the UK, the US and Canada respectively.

The US FIU is known as the Financial Crimes Enforcement Network (FinCEN).68 Canada, displaying US influence, chose the name Financial Transactions and Reports Analysis Centre of Canada (FINTRAC).69 The UK, taking a more prosaic approach, named its FIU the UK Financial Intelligence Unit (UKFIU). 70 FinCEN and FINTRAC are independent organizations that report through the financial arms of their respective states. FinCEN reports to the Secretary of the Treasury 71 and FINTRAC to the Minister of Finance. 72 In contrast, UKFIU is situated within the law enforcement apparatus of the UK (in an indication of this embedded role, the organization does not have its own website). It forms part of the National Crime Agency (NCA). The NCA website describes its function as follows:

- The NCA has a wide remit. We tackle serious and organised crime, strengthen our borders, fight fraud and cyber crime, an d protect children and young people from sexual abuse and exploitation. We provide leadership in these areas through our organised crime, border policing, economic crime and CEOP commands, the National Cyber Crime Unit and specialist capability teams. The NCA works closely with partners to deliver operational results. We have an international role to cut serious and organised crime impacting on the UK through our network of international liaison officers.

Had the US and Canada taken a similar approach, their FIUs would have been created as specialist bodies within the Federal Bureau of Investigation (FBI) and Royal Canadian Mounted Police (RCMP). Instead, FINCEN and FINTRAC have considerably more autonomy from law enforcement than UKFIU, as well as broader powers.

US

Established under the *Bank Secrecy Act,* FINCEN performs a variety of functions, covering data gathering, regulation, research and analysis. Its website describes the organization's powers as follows:

- Congress has given FinCEN certain duties and responsibilities for the central collection, analysis, and dissemination of data reported under FinCEN's regulations and other related data in support of government and financial industry partners at the Federal, State, local, and international levels. To fulfill its responsibilities toward the detection and deterrence of financial crime, FinCEN:
  - Issues and interprets regulations authorized by statute;
  - Supports and enforces compliance with those regulations;
  - Supports, coordinates, and analyzes data regarding compliance examination functions delegated to other Federal regulators;
  - Manages the collection, processing, storage, dissemination, and protection of data filed under FinCEN's reporting requirements;
  - Maintains a government-wide access service to FinCEN's data, and networks users with overlapping interests;
  - Supports law enforcement investigations and prosecutions;
  - Synthesizes data to recommend internal and external allocation of resources to areas of greatest financial crime risk;
  - Shares information and coordinates with foreign financial intelligence unit (FIU) counterparts on AML/CFT efforts; and
  - Conducts analysis to support policymakers; law enforcement, regulatory, and intelligence agencies; FIUs; and the financial industry.74

Under the Bank Secrecy Act (BSA), FinCEN can bring enforcement actions for BSA violations.75 For example, in May 2015, a FinCEN enforcement action led to the imposition of a $700,000 fine on a virtual currency exchange company that lacked an AML program.76 In June 2015, FinCEN fined a casino in the Northern Mariana Islands $75 million for its failure to institute an AML program, hire compliance staff and create procedures for detecting suspicious transactions.77 In July 2015, FinCEN imposed "special measure five" on Tanzania-based FBME Bank Ltd, meaning US financial institutions are barred from "opening or maintaining correspondent accounts or payable through accounts for or on behalf of FBME."78 FinCEN alleges that FBME is being used to facilitate money laundering and that high-risk shell companies are among its customers.79 The bank expressed outrage at the ban and claimed it did not receive adequate notice, although FinCEN issued a notice in July 2014 warning that FBME was a primary money laundering concern and could be subject to a final ban. 80 For a full list of FinCEN enforcement actions see: <https://www.fincen.gov/news-room/enforcement-actions>.

UK

The UK's FIU responsibilities were transferred from the Serious Organized Crime Agency to the National Crime Agency (NCA) in 2013 with the passing of the Crime and Courts Act. In contrast to FinCEN, the UKFIU page on the NCA website states simply: "The UK Financial Intelligence Unit (UKFIU) receives, analyses and distributes financial intelligence gathered from Suspicious Activity Reports (SARs)."81 While FinCEN and FINTRAC also handle SARs, which will be discussed in more detail in the following section, they also do a great deal more. UKFIUs mandate is narrower, likely due to its integration within the state's law enforcement apparatus. FinCEN and FINTRAC have broader mandates and greater organizational independence.

Canada

Similarly to its US counterpart, FINTRAC's description of its function is comprehensive, covering data gathering, analysis and research. The organization's website states that:

- Our mandate is to facilitate the detection, prevention and deterrence of money laundering and the financing of terrorist activities, while ensuring the protection of personal information under our control. We fulfill our mandate through the following activities:
    - Receiving financial transaction reports and voluntary information on money laundering and terrorist financing in accordance with the legislation and regulations and safeguarding personal information under our control;
    - Ensuring compliance of reporting entities with the legislation and regulations;
    - Producing financial intelligence relevant to money laundering, terrorist activity financing and threats to the security of Canada investigations;
    - Researching and analyzing data from a variety of information sources that shed light on trends and patterns in money laundering and terrorist financing;

- Maintaining a registry of money services businesses in Canada;
- Enhancing public awareness and understanding of money laundering and terrorist activity financing.

FINTRAC is authorized by legislation to provide information to foreign FIUs, and also receives information from FIUs and law enforcement agencies in other jurisdictions (23-34).

FINTRAC has broad powers to search without warrant, investigate and report to police authorities. Normal criminal law protections do not apply. For example, FINTRAC can enter any premises without a warrant unless the premises are a dwelling.84 Terence D. Hall notes that "[t]here is a tension between the values placed on privacy and the protection of personal information and the public policy goals of deterring criminal activity and the financing of terrorism by requiring the collection and disclosure of personal and proprietary information." In 2013, Canada's Privacy Commissioner audited FINTRAC, reporting that FINTRAC "continues to receive and retain personal information not directly related to its mandate."

Regulation of Financial Institutions and Professionals

Customer Due Diligence

FATF Recommendation 10 deals with customer due diligence (CDD) measures. The essence of CDD is requiring financial institutions to ascertain whom they are dealing with for each major transaction. The full text of the recommendation is reproduced below.

Customer due diligence

BEGINNING OF EXCERPT

Financial institutions should be prohibited from keeping anonymous accounts or accounts in obviously fictitious names.

Financial institutions should be required to undertake customer due diligence (CDD) measures when:

i. establishing business relations;

ii. carrying out occasional transactions: (i) above the applicable designated threshold (USD/EUR 15,000); or (ii) that are wire transfers in the circumstances covered by the Interpretive Note to Recommendation 16;

iii. there is a suspicion of money laundering or terrorist financing; or

iv. the financial institution has doubts about the veracity or adequacy of previously obtained customer identification data.

The principle that financial institutions should conduct CDD should be set out in law. Each country may determine how it imposes specific CDD obligations, either through law or enforceable means.

The CDD measures to be taken are as follows:

a. Identifying the customer and verifying that customer's identity using reliable, independent source documents, data or information.

b. Identifying the beneficial owner, and taking reasonable measures to verify the identity of the beneficial owner, such that the financial institution is satisfied that it knows who the beneficial owner is. For legal persons and arrangements this should include financial institutions understanding the ownership and control structure of the customer.

c. Understanding and, as appropriate, obtaining information on the purpose and intended nature of the business relationship.

d. Conducting ongoing due diligence on the business relationship and scrutiny of transactions undertaken throughout the course of that relationship to ensure that the transactions being conducted are consistent with the institution's knowledge of the customer, their business and risk profile, including, where necessary, the source of funds.

Financial institutions should be required to apply each of the CDD measures under (a) to (d) above, but should determine the extent of such measures using a risk-based approach (RBA) in accordance with the Interpretive Notes to this Recommendation and to Recommendation 1.

Financial institutions should be required to verify the identity of the customer and beneficial owner before or during the course of establishing a business relationship or conducting transactions for occasional customers. Countries may permit financial institutions to complete the verification as soon as reasonably practicable following the establishment of the relationship, where the money laundering and terrorist financing risks are effectively managed and where this is essential not to interrupt the normal conduct of business.

Where the financial institution is unable to comply with the applicable requirements under paragraphs (a) to (d) above (subject to appropriate modification of the extent of the measures on a risk-based approach), it should be required not to open the account, commence business relations or perform the transaction; or should be required to terminate the business relationship; and should consider making a suspicious transactions report in relation to the customer.

These requirements should apply to all new customers, although financial institutions should also apply this Recommendation to existing customers on the basis of materiality and risk, and should conduct due diligence on such existing relationships at appropriate times.

END OF EXCERPT

As discussed in the first section of this chapter, PEPs launder large amounts of misappropriated government funds and bribes every year. Because of the particular risks associated with PEPs, FATF Recommendation 12, set out below, requires enhanced due diligence when dealing with them as customers:

BEGINNING OF EXCERPT

Politically exposed persons

Financial institutions should be required, in relation to foreign politically exposed persons (PEPs) (whether as customer or beneficial owner), in addition to performing normal customer due diligence measures, to:

a. have appropriate risk-management systems to determine whether the customer or the beneficial owner is a politically exposed person;

b. obtain senior management approval for establishing (or continuing, for existing customers) such business relationships;

c. take reasonable measures to establish the source of wealth and source of funds; and

d. conduct enhanced ongoing monitoring of the business relationship.

Financial institutions should be required to take reasonable measures to determine whether a customer or beneficial owner is a domestic PEP or a person who is or has been entrusted with a prominent function by an international organisation. In cases of a higher risk business relationship with such persons, financial institutions should be required to apply the measures referred to in paragraphs (b), (c) and (d).

END OF EXCERPT

Both the UK and Canada have created comprehensive regulatory frameworks to implement the above recommendations. 87 Both countries require financial institutions to collect and record personal information about their customers. As suggested by the FATF, both also require banks to conduct ongoing monitoring of the customer relationship and to take steps to identify the beneficial owners of customers that are organizations. Finally, both Canada and the UK require financial institutions to take steps to determine if their customers are PEPs and require enhanced due diligence in such cases. The PEP concept has been criticized by some for its vagueness. Different definitions are used internationally, and challenges arise in determining who fits each definition. Financial institutions must choose where to draw the line, which is often far from clear cut.

At present, the US CDD regime is somewhat weaker. US regulations require financial institutions to set up a Customer Identification Program (CIP) to determine the identity of each customer. However, there are no specific requirements to identify beneficial ownership or conduct ongoing monitoring of the customer relationship. FINCEN is moving to address these weaknesses in the near future. A proposal for new regulations incorporating these elements was released in 2014.91 The US does require enhanced CDD in the case of correspondent accounts created by US banks for non-US persons. These measures include a requirement to determine beneficial ownership of any organizations involved and to determine whether the account holder is a Senior Foreign Political Figure (the US statutory language, roughly equivalent to PEP).

Transaction Reporting

FATF Recommendation 20 requires states to create legal requirements for financial institutions to report any suspicious transactions to their respective FIUs:

- 20. Reporting of suspicious transactions
- If a financial institution suspects or has reasonable grounds to suspect that funds are the proceeds of a criminal activity, or are related to terrorist financing, it should be required, by law, to report promptly its suspicions to the financial intelligence unit (FIU).

Canada, the US and the UK follow this recommendation, requiring that all suspicious transactions be reported to their FIUs by financial institutions. However, there are some significant variations between the different reporting regimes. The UK only requires that all suspicious transactions be reported to UKFIU. 93 The US and Canada have similar requirements, but both countries also require that all transactions over $10,000 be reported to their respective FIUs.95 Canada requires anyone, including members of the public, who imports or exports cash or monetary instruments with a value of $10,000 or more to report the transaction to a customs officer. Reports are then passed on to FINTRAC.

The UK has taken a strict risk-based approach to transaction reporting, while Canada and the US have supplemented this with threshold-based reporting requirements. However, this should not be taken to mean that the UK's regime is weaker. Their reporting requirements are backed up with harsh sanctions for failure to report suspicious transactions. Failure to disclose can result in up to five years imprisonment or a fine, or both. While the UK has taken a slightly different approach, it is not a more lenient one, and this "fear factor" has led to a dramatic increase in SAR submissions. However, critics claim that the high cost of compliance with the UK's SAR regime is disproportionate to its effectiveness.

Record-Keeping

The final piece of the regulatory regime proposed by the FATF Recommendations is the requirement for financial institutions to retain transaction records and customer information for at least five years. This requirement is set out in Recommendation 11:

11. Record-keeping

Financial institutions should be required to maintain, for at least five years, all necessary records on transactions, both domestic and international, to enable them to comply swiftly with information requests from the competent authorities. Such records must be sufficient to permit reconstruction of individual transactions (including the amounts and types of currency involved, if any) so as to provide, if necessary, evidence for prosecution of criminal activity.

Financial institutions should be required to keep all records obtained through CDD measures (e.g. copies or records of official identification documents like passports, identity cards, driving licences or similar documents), account files and business correspondence, including the results of any analysis undertaken (e.g. inquiries to establish the background and purpose of complex, unusual large transactions), for at least five years after the business relationship is ended, or after the date of the occasional transaction.

Financial institutions should be required by law to maintain records on transactions and information obtained through the CDD measures.

The CDD information and the transaction records should be available to domestic competent authorities upon appropriate authority.

The US, UK and Canada all require financial institutions to store records for five years in accordance with Recommendation 11. While the information stored in these records will vary slightly based on differences in their respective CDD regimes, there are no significant variations with regard to the record-keeping requirements themselves.

Money Laundering Offences

FATF Recommendations and UNCAC

FATF Recommendation 3 requires states to create offences to directly criminalize money laundering. The recommendation is reproduced below, along with an interpretive note. FATF Recommendation 3 on money laundering was produced in the original 2003 FATF Forty Recommendations. Recommendation 3 was drafted on the basis of two existing UN Conventions: the 1998 Narcotic Drugs and Psychotropic Substances Convention and the 2000 Transnational Organized Crime Convention. The money laundering provisions in those two conventions are now consolidated in the money laundering provisions in UNCAC. FATF Recommendation 3 provides:

Money laundering offence

Countries should criminalise money laundering on the basis of the Vienna Convention and the Palermo Convention. Countries should apply the crime of money laundering to all serious offences, with a view to including the widest range of predicate offences.

Interpretive Note to Recommendation 3 (Money Laundering Offence)

1. Countries should criminalise money laundering on the basis of the United Nations Convention against Illicit Traffic in Narcotic Drugs and Psychotropic Substances, 1988 (the Vienna Convention) and the United Nations Convention against Transnational Organized Crime, 2000 (the Palermo Convention) [and now in accordance with Articles 14 and 23 of UNCAC (2005), which are discussed in detail in Sections 4.1.1 and 4.1.2 of this Chapter].
2. Countries should apply the crime of money laundering to all serious offences, with a view to including the widest range of predicate offences. Predicate offences may be described by reference to all offences; or to a threshold linked either to a category of serious offences; or to the penalty of imprisonment applicable to the predicate offence (threshold approach); or to a list of predicate offences; or a combination of these approaches.
5. Predicate offences for money laundering should extend to conduct that occurred in another country, which constitutes an offence in that country, and which would have constituted a predicate offence had it occurred domestically. Countries may provide that the only prerequisite is that the conduct would have constituted a predicate offence, had it occurred domestically.
6. Countries may provide that the offence of money laundering does not apply to persons who committed the predicate offence, where this is required by fundamental principles of their domestic law.

The US, the UK and Canada all have money laundering offences that generally comply with FATF and UNCAC requirements. However, there are significant differences between the three countries' provisions. Canada and the US define money laundering as the use of the proceeds of a list of specified offences ("predicate offences"). The UK takes a more inclusive approach. Under its regime, virtually all profit-driven crime can lead to money laundering charges.

US

In the United States, money laundering is primarily enforced at the federal level. Thirty-six states have money laundering offences. Where money laundering is criminalized at the state level, federal and state authorities work closely together. Approximately 2,500 natural and legal persons are charged with federal money laundering offences each year, resulting in over 1,200 convictions. In 2014, a total of 3,369 money laundering charges were laid and 1,967 convictions registered (the greater number of charges accounted for by the fact that a person may be charged with multiple counts of various money laundering offences).

The two primary money laundering offences are 18 USC 1956: Money Laundering (proceeds laundering) and 18 US 1957: Money Laundering (transactional). Respectively, charges for these offences were laid 1,895 and 517 times in 2014, accounting for 72% of all money laundering charges in United States. Other money laundering related charges are USC 1952: Interstate & foreign travel/ transportation, including of proceeds, in aid of racketeering enterprises, 18 USC 1962: Receiving or deriving income from racketeering activities (RICO) and 31 USC 5332: Bulk cash smuggling.

The relevant provisions of 18 USC 1956 and 18 USC 1957 are reproduced below:

- 18 U.S. Code s.1956 – Laundering of monetary instruments
  a. (1) Whoever, knowing that the property involved in a financial transaction represents the proceeds of some form of unlawful activity, conducts or attempts to conduct such a financial transaction which in fact involves the proceeds of specified unlawful activity—
     A. (i) with the intent to promote the carrying on of specified unlawful activity; or

        (ii) with intent to engage in conduct constituting a violation of section 7201 or 7206 of the Internal Revenue Code of 1986; or
     B. knowing that the transaction is designed in whole or in part—

        (i) to conceal or disguise the nature, the location, the source, the ownership, or the control of the proceeds of specified unlawful activity; or

        (ii) to avoid a transaction reporting requirement under State or Federal law,

shall be sentenced to a fine of not more than $500,000 or twice the value of the property involved in the transaction, whichever is greater, or imprisonment for not more than twenty years, or both. For purposes of this paragraph, a financial transaction shall be considered to be one involving the proceeds of specified unlawful activity if it is part of a set of parallel or dependent transactions, any one of which involves the proceeds of specified unlawful activity, and all of which are part of a single plan or arrangement.

2. Whoever transports, transmits, or transfers, or attempts to transport, transmit, or transfer a monetary instrument or funds from a place in the United States to or through a place outside the United States or to a place in the United States from or through a place outside the United States—
    A. with the intent to promote the carrying on of specified unlawful activity; or
    B. knowing that the monetary instrument or funds involved in the transportation, transmission, or transfer represent the proceeds of some form of unlawful activity and knowing that such transportation, transmission, or transfer is designed in whole or in part—
        i. to conceal or disguise the nature, the location, the source, the ownership, or the control of the proceeds of specified unlawful activity; or
        ii. to avoid a transaction reporting requirement under State or Federal law,

shall be sentenced to a fine of not more than $500,000 or twice the value of the monetary instrument or funds involved in the transportation, transmission, or transfer, whichever is greater, or imprisonment for not more than twenty years, or both. For the purpose of the offense described in subparagraph (B), the defendant's knowledge may be established by proof that a law enforcement officer represented the matter specified in subparagraph (B) as true, and the defendant's subsequent statements or actions indicate that the defendant believed such representations to be true.

3. Whoever, with the intent—
    A. to promote the carrying on of specified unlawful activity;
    B. to conceal or disguise the nature, location, source, ownership, or control of property believed to be the proceeds of specified unlawful activity; or
    C. to avoid a transaction reporting requirement under State or Federal law,

conducts or attempts to conduct a financial transaction involving property represented to be the proceeds of specified unlawful activity, or property used to conduct or facilitate specified unlawful activity, shall be fined under this title or imprisoned for not more than 20 years, or both. For purposes of this paragraph and paragraph (2), the term "represented" means any representation made by a law enforcement officer or by another person at the direction of, or with the approval of, a Federal official authorized to investigate or prosecute violations of this section. [Emphasis added. The remainder of the section has not been included.]

18 U.S. Code s.1957 – Engaging in monetary transactions in property derived from specified unlawful activity

a. Whoever, in any of the circumstances set forth in subsection (d), knowingly engages or attempts to engage in a monetary transaction in criminally derived property of a value greater than $10,000 and is derived from specified unlawful activity, shall be punished as provided in subsection (b).
b. (1) Except as provided in paragraph (2), the punishment for an offense under this section is a fine under title 18, United States Code, or imprisonment for not more than ten years or both. If the offense involves a pre-retail medical product (as defined in section 670) the punishment for the offense shall be the same as the punishment for an offense under section 670 unless the punishment under this subsection is greater.

   (2) The court may impose an alternate fine to that imposable under paragraph (1) of not more than twice the amount of the criminally derived property involved in the transaction.
c. In a prosecution for an offense under this section, the Government is not required to prove the defendant knew that the offense from which the criminally derived property was derived was specified unlawful activity.
d. The circumstances referred to in subsection (a) are—
   1. that the offense under this section takes place in the United States or in the special maritime and territorial jurisdiction of the United States; or
   2. that the offense under this section takes place outside the United States and such special jurisdiction, but the defendant is a United States person (as defined in section 3077 of this title, but excluding the class described in paragraph (2)(D) of such section).
e. Violations of this section may be investigated by such components of the Department of Justice as the Attorney General may direct, and by such components of the Department of the Treasury as the Secretary of the Treasury may direct, as appropriate, and, with respect to offenses over which the Department of Homeland Security has jurisdiction, by such components of the Department of Homeland Security as the Secretary of Homeland Security may direct, and, with respect to offenses over which the United States Postal Service has jurisdiction, by the Postal Service. Such authority of the Secretary of the Treasury, the Secretary of Homeland Security, and the Postal Service shall be exercised in accordance with an agreement which shall be entered into by the Secretary of the Treasury, the Secretary of Homeland Security, the Postal Service, and the Attorney General.

f. As used in this section—

1. the term "monetary transaction" means the deposit, withdrawal, transfer, or exchange, in or affecting interstate or foreign commerce, of funds or a monetary instrument (as defined in section 1956 of this title) by, through, or to a financial institution (as defined in section 1956 of this title), including any transaction that would be a financial transaction under section 1956 of this title, but such term does not include any transaction necessary to preserve a person's right to representation as guaranteed by the sixth amendment to the Constitution;
2. the term "criminally derived property" means any property constituting, or derived from, proceeds obtained from a criminal offense; and
3. the terms "specified unlawful activity" and "proceeds" shall have the meaning given those terms in section 1956 of this title. [Emphasis added]

While the US statutory provisions are longer and more complex than their Canadian equivalents (discussed below), their overall effect is similar. Only the proceeds of certain crimes ("specified unlawful activity") can give rise to a money laundering charge. The term "specified unlawful activity" is defined in 18 USC 1956(c)(7), and provides a long list of offenses that encompasses most serious crimes and includes violations of the *Foreign Corrupt Practices Act*. To be convicted, the accused must have known that the property in question was derived from unlawful activity of some kind. The two US provisions excerpted above include a variety of different uses that can give rise to a money laundering conviction, including attempting to avoid transaction reporting requirements and promoting the carrying on of a specified unlawful activity (funding further crimes). However, the overall effect is that money laundering consists of using the proceeds of certain defined crimes in certain defined ways.

Sentences for money laundering offenses are often lengthy and can reach a life term. From 2010-2015, prison sentences greater than 61 months (5 years) were imposed in 40% of convictions, while non-custodial sentences were used in only 15% of convictions. The table below outlines the sentences given in US federal money laundering cases from 2010-2014.

Table 4.1 Sentencing for Money Laundering Convictions (FY2010-FY2014)

Offense	# of Defendants	Not imprisoned	1-12 Months	13-14 Months	25-36 Months	37-60 Months	61+ Months	Life
18 USC 1956	5076	784	341	520	456	823	2106	46
18 USC 1957	1253	174	81	145	112	249	486	6

Source: *US Mutual Evaluation Report (FATF, 2016) at 74.*

UK

In the UK, money laundering is criminalized by sections 327-329 of the Proceeds of Crime Act, 2002 (POCA). Those provisions provide as follows:

Concealing etc

- A person commits an offence if he—
  - conceals criminal property;
  - disguises criminal property;
  - converts criminal property;
  - transfers criminal property;
  - removes criminal property from England and Wales or from Scotland or from Northern Ireland.
- But a person does not commit such an offence if—
  - he makes an authorised disclosure under section 338 and (if the disclosure is made before he does the act mentioned in subsection (1)) he has the appropriate consent;
  - he intended to make such a disclosure but had a reasonable excuse for not doing so;
  - the act he does is done in carrying out a function he has relating to the enforcement of any provision of this Act or of any other enactment relating to criminal conduct or benefit from criminal conduct.
- Concealing or disguising criminal property includes concealing or disguising its nature, source, location, disposition, movement or ownership or any rights with respect to it.

Arrangements

- A person commits an offence if he enters into or becomes concerned in an arrangement which he knows or suspects facilitates (by whatever means) the acquisition, retention, use or control of criminal property by or on behalf of another person.
- But a person does not commit such an offence if—
  - he makes an authorised disclosure under section 338 and (if the disclosure is made before he does the act mentioned in subsection (1)) he has the appropriate consent;
  - he intended to make such a disclosure but had a reasonable excuse for not doing so;
  - the act he does is done in carrying out a function he has relating to the enforcement of any provision of this Act or of any other enactment relating to criminal conduct or benefit from criminal conduct.

[The meaning of "suspicion" in section 328 has been the subject of some debate due to its subjectivity. The case law has indicated a preference for the "more than fanciful possibility" test. It should also be noted that "arrangement" does not include legal proceedings.]

Acquisition, use and possession

- A person commits an offence if he—
  - acquires criminal property;
  - uses criminal property;
  - has possession of criminal property.
- But a person does not commit such an offence if—
  - he makes an authorised disclosure under section 338 and (if the disclosure is made before he does the act mentioned in subsection (1)) he has the appropriate consent;
  - he intended to make such a disclosure but had a reasonable excuse for not doing so;
  - he acquired or used or had possession of the property for adequate consideration;
  - the act he does is done in carrying out a function he has relating to the enforcement of any provision of this Act or of any other enactment relating to criminal conduct or benefit from criminal conduct.
- For the purposes of this section—
  - a person acquires property for inadequate consideration if the value of the consideration is significantly less than the value of the property;
  - a person uses or has possession of property for inadequate consideration if the value of the consideration is significantly less than the value of the use or possession;
  - the provision by a person of goods or services which he knows or suspects may help another to carry out criminal conduct is not consideration.

As the above provisions make clear, the UK's domestic AML offences encompass a considerably larger range of acts than their equivalents in the US and Canada.

Section 340(3) of the POCA defines criminal property broadly. Property is criminal property if:

a. it constitutes a person's benefit from criminal conduct or it represents such a benefit (in whole or part and whether directly or indirectly), and

b. the alleged offender knows or suspects that it constitutes or represents such a benefit.

The person benefitting from criminal conduct need not commit the criminal act. The definition also includes property from anywhere in the world.

In the UK, unlike Canada and the US, there is no defined set of predicate offences for money laundering. There is also no need, under some of the provisions above, for any intent to conceal the source of the funds. The use or possession of the proceeds of any crime whatsoever can be prosecuted as money laundering. Under this regime, stealing and selling bicycles can give rise to money laundering charges. There is a requirement that the accused know that the proceeds in question were derived from criminal activity and a statutory defence if the accused reported the act as a suspicious transaction. Nonetheless, far more criminal activity is captured by this regime than in either the US or Canada.

Section 333 of the POCA also creates an offence of "tipping off." The offence is committed where a person in the regulated sector tells a customer or third person that a money laundering investigation is underway or under consideration and where this disclosure is likely to be prejudicial.

Sentencing guidelines for money laundering offences came into force October 1, 2014. For more information see Chapter 7, Section 5.

Canada

Money laundering laws in Canada were first enacted in 1989 and were subsequently amended in 1997, 2001 and 2005. The current money laundering offences are set out in sections 462.31(1) and 354(1) of the Criminal Code, which state:

- Laundering proceeds of crime
    - 462.31(1) Every one commits an offence who uses, transfers the possession of, sends or delivers to any person or place, transports, transmits, alters, disposes of or otherwise deals with, in any manner and by any means, any property or any proceeds of any property with intent to conceal or convert that property or those proceeds, knowing or believing that all or a part of that property or of those proceeds was obtained or derived directly or indirectly as a result of
        a. the commission in Canada of a designated offence; or
        b. an act or omission anywhere that, if it had occurred in Canada, would have constituted a designated offence.
- Possession of property obtained by crime
    - 354(1) Every one commits an offence who has in his possession any property or thing or any proceeds of any property or thing knowing that all or part of the property or thing or of the proceeds was obtained by or derived directly or indirectly from

- the commission in Canada of an offence punishable by indictment; or
- an act or omission anywhere that, if it had occurred in Canada, would have constituted an offence punishable by indictment [Emphasis added].

There are three important aspects to section 462.31. First, it applies only to the proceeds of "designated offences." The term "designated offence" is defined in section 462.3 of the Criminal Code as an offence that may be prosecuted as an indictable offence under Canadian legislation, unless is it expressly excluded by regulation. This means violations of the Corruption of Foreign Public Officials Act or bribery offences in the Criminal Code are included as designated offences. Second, while the range of actions that can constitute the actus reus of the offence is broad, there must be intent to conceal on the part of the accused. Finally, the accused must know or believe that the property or proceeds were derived from the commission of an indictable offence. An offence under section 462.31 is punishable by up to ten years imprisonment. Section 354(1) does not require any intent to conceal the source of the property or proceeds, but it requires specific knowledge that the property was derived from an indictable offence. Therefore, only certain uses of the proceeds of relatively serious crimes will be caught by these provisions.

Money laundering charges are typically laid along with a predicate offence such as bribery or drug trafficking. From 2010 to 2014, 1,800 money laundering charges were laid in 1,027 cases involving one or more counts of money laundering along with other offences. Prosecuting the money laundering is typically not prioritized in these circumstances. The tables below, reproduced from FATF's 2016 mutual evaluation of Canada, show that while the conviction rate for these cases was 59.6%, the money laundering charge led to a conviction only 9.4% of the time.105 Conversely, the money laundering charge was stayed 14.6% of the time and withdrawn 72.7% of the time. In FATF's mutual evaluation of Canada, discussed in greater detail in Section 6.3.3 of this chapter, it is explained that insufficient evidence, avoidance of over-charging, plea bargaining, and length of proceedings in money laundering cases were some of the reasons why this is done.106 Given the principle of totality in sentencing, pursuing a money laundering charge when there is already a conviction for the predicate offence may not greatly increase the sentence, and therefore prosecutors may believe their resources are better directed at crafting a plea bargain or focusing on the predicate offence.

Table 4.2 Results of ML-Related Cases

	2010	2011	2012	2013	2014	total	%
Guilty	82	108	140	136	146	612	59.6%
Acquitted	2	0	0	4	7	13	1.3%

	2010	2011	2012	2013	2014	total	%
Stayed	8	12	15	26	18	79	7.7%
Withdrawn	49	63	74	64	53	303	29.5%
Other decisions	0	0	12	4	4	20	1.9%
Total	141	183	241	234	228	1027	100%

Source: *Statistics Canada's Integrated Criminal Court Survey (ICCS) as cited in Canada Mutual Evaluation Report (FATF, 2016) at 52.*

Table 4.3 Results of ML-Charges

	2010	2011	2012	2013	2014	total	%
Guilty	38	21	35	31	44	169	9.4%
Acquitted	5	1	8	6	9	29	1.6%
Stayed	17	26	144	45	31	263	14.6%
Withdrawn	132	190	366	327	294	1309	72.7%
Other decisions	2	2	14	7	5	30	1.7%
Total	194	240	567	416	383	1800	100%

Source: *Statistics Canada's Integrated Criminal Court Survey (ICCS) as cited in Canada Mutual Evaluation Report (FATF, 2016) at 52.*

Conviction rates for money laundering were higher in cases where that is the only charge laid. In a limited sample size of 35 single-charge money laundering cases from 2010 to 2014, 12 resulted in convictions, a 34.3% rate. Stays were imposed 14.3% of the time, a comparable proportion as when money laundering is charged with other offences, while withdrawals were far less frequent, occurring 40% of the time, compared to 72.7% when money laundering is charged alongside other offences.

Sentencing for money laundering ranges from non-custodial sentences to penitentary terms. FATF suggests sanctions imposed in Canada for money launderers are low and not dissuasive enough. In 145 sentencing cases where money laundering was the most serious offence, nearly half received no prison time, and only 11% received over 2 years' incarceration.

Table 4.4 Sanctions in ML Cases where ML was the Most Serious Offence, from 2010 to 2014

	Number	Percentage
Custodial Sentence	**80**	**55.2%**
• Less than 12 months	47	32.4%
• 12 to 24 months	17	11.7%

• More than 24 months	16	11.0%
Conditional sentence, probation, fine, restitution	65	44.8%
Total	**145**	**100.0%**

Note. There are other undisclosed cases where the ML offence runs concurrently with another MSO. Source: Canada Mutual Evaluation Report (FATF, 2016) at 54.

The Role of Legal Professionals

FATF Recommendations

FATF Recommendations 22 and 23 state that lawyers should be required to engage in CDD measures when performing transactions for clients and to report suspicious transactions. Many members of the legal profession and legal organizations such as the Canadian Bar Association have strongly opposed the inclusion of lawyers in these reporting regulations.108 The interpretive note to Recommendation 23, reproduced below, modifies FATF's position somewhat:

- Interpretive Note to Recommendation 23 (DNFBPS [designated non-financial businesses and professions] – Other Measures)
    - Lawyers, notaries, other independent legal professionals, and accountants acting as independent legal professionals, are not required to report suspicious transactions if the relevant information was obtained in circumstances where they are subject to professional secrecy or legal professional privilege.
    - It is for each country to determine the matters that would fall under legal professional privilege or professional secrecy. This would normally cover information lawyers, notaries or other independent legal professionals receive from or obtain through one of their clients: in the course of ascertaining the legal position of their client, or (b) in performing their task of defending or representing that client in, or concerning judicial, administrative, arbitration or mediation proceedings.
    - Countries may allow lawyers, notaries, other independent legal professionals and accountants to send their STR [suspicious transaction report] to their appropriate self-regulatory organisations, provided that there are appropriate forms of cooperation between these organisations and the FIU.
    - Where lawyers, notaries, other independent legal professionals and accountants acting as independent legal professionals seek to dissuade a client from engaging in illegal activity, this does not amount to tipping-off.

In this interpretive note, the FATF clarifies that its recommendations are tempered by the requirements of legal privilege and confidentiality, and leaves it in the hands of member states to decide how to implement an AML regime that respects those duties. Lawyers in the US, the UK and Canada are subject to different degrees of regulation. This variation is a function of a number of factors, principally legislative policy, the power of the bar and the constitutional structure of the country in question. For instance, after the government of Canada attempted to impose stringent regulations on the legal profession, the Federation of Law Societies successfully challenged these measures on constitutional grounds (further discussed at Section 5.5.4). In the UK, on the other hand, lawyers have been less successful in staving off state regulation of their practice.

There are two principal ways that lawyers must deal with state-level AML regimes. The first is regulation. Similarly to financial institutions, lawyers in some countries are subject to reporting, record-keeping and CDD requirements. The second is direct criminal liability. In some countries, AML laws are drafted in such a way that lawyers must be extremely careful to avoid prosecution for careless handling of funds or lack of due diligence in the ordinary course of their practice.

US

To date, the US has not taken serious steps to regulate lawyers as part of their AML regime. According to an article on the International Bar Association's Anti-Money-Laundering Forum:

- the American legal system regards legal professional privilege as fundamental to the lawyer-client relationship. Therefore, it is disinclined towards modifying its current anti-money laundering legislation to include professionals such as lawyers. Trust and confidence are considered as keystone principles to the legal professional relationship. They would be eroded indefinitely, if lawyers were required to reveal information relating to the client to third parties, based upon mere suspicions. A client must feel free to seek legal assistance and be able to communicate with his legal representative fully and frankly.

US lawyers are not subject to any mandatory reporting requirements, with one exception. They are required to report any cash transaction greater than $10,000 to the IRS.110 Other than that, their work is outside the US AML regime.

US lawyers are also not likely to be caught by the country's anti-money laundering offenses in the ordinary course of their work. As discussed in Section 5.4, the US money-laundering offenses require that the accused have actual knowledge that the funds in question were derived from criminal activity. While some courts have held that willful blindness is sufficient to make out this element of the offence, it is still unlikely that a lawyer who was not knowingly complicit in a money laundering scheme could be successfully prosecuted.

UK

Lawyers in the UK are in an unenviable position relative to their North American colleagues. They face significant potential criminal liability under section 328 of the POCA, even in the ordinary course of their practice. Section 328 targets those who assist in the layering and integration stages of the money laundering process. The Crown is required to establish that the accused entered into or became concerned in an arrangement that they knew or suspected "facilitates (by whatever means) the acquisition, retention, use or control of criminal property by or on behalf of another person." This provision is intended to catch financial advisors, accountants, lawyers and other professionals who assist in a money laundering scheme.

Section 328 is broad enough that even careless lawyers can be prosecuted. For example, in R v Duff, a solicitor was sentenced to six months imprisonment because he suspected that his client's funds had been criminally derived, but did not report his suspicions.112 This came to light some years later when his client was arrested for cocaine smuggling.113 There are statutory defences to a section 328 charge, but they require the accused either to have reported their suspicions or to have a reasonable excuse for their failure to do so. This regime forces lawyers to report any suspicions or face criminal charges.

The UK courts have limited the scope of section 328 somewhat. In the 2005 case of Bowman v Fels, the English Court of Appeal held that section 328 does not apply to lawyers involved in ordinary litigation or other dispute resolution processes who, as a result of the privileged information they receive, come to suspect that the property at issue is criminal property. The case involved a family law dispute. The claimant, Ms. Bowman, sought recognition of a proprietary interest in the defendant's home based on the doctrine of constructive trust. The claimant and the defendant had previously both lived in the house together in a common- law relationship. During the course of preparing for litigation, the claimant's solicitors began to suspect that the house may have been criminal property and became concerned that if they did not disclose their suspicions to the authorities that they would be held liable under section 328 for participating in an arrangement to aid their client in acquiring an interest in criminal property. The Court in Bowman clarified that the solicitors were in no such danger. Section 328 does not override the concept of legal privilege and therefore would not have applied to the acts of the solicitors of the claimant or the defendant.

However, the Court in Bowman did not address the position of lawyers who assist clients in matters not involving litigation. Therefore, the potential liability of lawyers acting in a transactional context remains uncertain.

Canada

The Canadian government has tried unsuccessfully to subject lawyers to reporting and CDD requirements much like those imposed on financial institutions. When they were promulgated, the Proceeds of Crime (Money Laundering) and Terrorist Financing Act and Regulations applied to lawyers. They imposed reporting and CDD requirements and allowed searches of law offices and seizure of evidence. The application of the Act and Regulations to lawyers was challenged by the Federation of Law Societies on constitutional grounds. In a 2015 ruling, the Supreme Court upheld the Federation's position and read down the relevant provisions to effectively exclude lawyers from the Act and Regulations. The Federation has created model rules to deal with money laundering, which have been adopted by the provincial law societies. The Federation's model rule on cash transactions states that "[a] lawyer shall not receive or accept from a person, cash in an aggregate amount of $7,500 or more Canadian dollars in respect of any one client matter or transaction." The B.C. Law Society Rule 3-59 also adopts the $7,500 cash rule. However, these rules are less comprehensive and generally impose less stringent requirements than the government's Regulations. The federal legislation and regulations require that financial institutions and other professionals, such as accountants or investment brokers, report all transactions of $10,000 or more to FINTRAC. On the other hand, lawyers need not report cash transactions to anyone. The law societies take the position that when a cheque or electronic bank transfer of $10,000 or more is received by a law firm, that money has already been subjected to the automatic FINTRAC reporting requirement (for $10,000 or more) at the point of deposit of that money with a financial institution.

As in the US, Canadian lawyers are unlikely to be prosecuted for money laundering offences unless they deliberately facilitate a money laundering scheme. As discussed in Section 5.4.4, the Canadian offences require that the accused have actual knowledge that the funds in question were obtained through the commission of an indictable offence. Willful blindness, but not subjective recklessness, will normally suffice as actual knowledge. Section 462.31(1) of the Criminal Code also requires some intent to conceal the source of the funds. Mere careless conduct on the part of a lawyer is unlikely to make out the offence.

EVALUATING THE EFFECTIVENESS OF AML REGIMES

Introduction

This section discusses tools for evaluating the success or failure of state-level AML regimes and introduces the two most common international evaluators, the Basel Institute on Governance and the FATF. It describes both the Basel AML Index and the FATF mutual evaluation process and briefly summarizes how the US, the UK and Canada performed on each of these evaluations. It then excerpts a critical evaluation from the Canadian Senate and discusses some of the systemic barriers to creating effective state-level AML regimes.

The Basel AML Index

Since 2012, the Basel Institute on Governance has produced an annual index on anti-money laundering.121 The Basel AML Index provides a useful tool for assessing and comparing the risk of money laundering in different countries worldwide and for observing over time changes to that risk within a given country.

The index is a composite weighting of the average of 14 indicators, relying on data provided by groups such as FATF, Transparency International and the World Bank.122 For the 2016 report, data was available for 149 countries who were given a score from 0 (lowest risk) to 10 (highest risk).

Factors weighed in the total score are:

- 65% - Money Laundering/Terrorist Financing Risk
- 15% - Financial Transparency & Standards
- 10% - Corruption Risk
- 5% - Public Transparency & Accountability
- 5% - Political Risk124

Table 4.5 A sample of 20 countries and their scores and rankings from the 2016 Basel Index.

Country	Overall Score (0-10)	Rank (1-149)
Iran	8.61	1
Afghanistan	8.51	2
Panama	7.09	25
Nigeria	6.97	32
Brazil	6.23	56
Russia	6.22	58
Guatemala	5.97	66
Luxembourg	5.89	70
Japan	5.76	76
India	5.69	78
Switzerland	5.46	88
Italy	5.36	90
Germany	5.33	92

Country	Overall Score (0-10)	Rank (1-149)
United States	5.17	97
Taiwan, China	5.12	99
France	5.03	103
Canada	5.00	105
South Africa	4.86	117
United Kingdom	4.77	121
Finland	3.05	149

It is important to note that the Index measures risk of money laundering and terrorist financing. In practice, factors relating to a country's financial sector and economy are important considerations for money launderers and can contribute significantly to the volume of laundering in any given country. For example, the US ranks 97th of 149 countries, meaning there are approximately 50 countries which have a lower risk for money laundering. However, that US ranking does not mean that all the countries which were ranked as lower money laundering risks are doing more, or are more effective, in trying to control and prevent money laundering. In practice, the majority of international money launderers choose not to operate in small, isolated economies. One study found that nearly half of the world's money laundering originates in the US, due in part to the dominance of US dollars in global markets and transactions.

FATF Mutual Evaluations

FATF assesses compliance with its AML recommendations through a process of mutual evaluation. For the first three rounds of evaluation, countries were assessed on their technical compliance with the FATF recommendations. However, a new methodology was developed in 2013 to evaluate the effectiveness of AML regimes. This methodology is used in the ongoing fourth round of FATF evaluations, which began in mid-2014. So far, only Australia, Belgium, Ethiopia, Norway and Spain have undergone this revised evaluation process. The calendar of fourth round evaluations can be seen at: <http://www.fatf- gafi.org/media/fatf/documents/assessments/Global-assessment-calendar.pdf>.

Evaluations are carried out by teams of experts, described by FATF as follows:

- An assessment team will usually consist of 4 expert assessors (comprising at least one legal, financial and law enforcement expert), principally drawn from FATF members, and will also include members of the FATF secretariat. Depending on the country and the money laundering and terrorist financing risks, additional assessors or assessors with specific expertise may also be required.

Prior to 2014, countries were assigned a rating for compliance with each FATF recommendation. Possible ratings were C (compliant), LC (largely compliant), PC (partially compliant) or NC (non-compliant). After an evaluation, a country may be required to report back to the FATF at intervals to describe its progress in addressing any shortcomings identified by the evaluation team.

The US, UK and Canada have not yet undergone evaluations under the 2013 methodology and the third round of evaluations ended before the new FATF recommendations were released in 2012. Only Canada has undergone a follow-up report since 2012. Care must be exercised in using the FATF evaluations as a basis for comparing AML regimes in the US, UK, Canada and elsewhere. Also, the process for conducting mutual evaluations and the FATF Recommendations themselves have changed significantly over the past ten years. The mutual evaluations and follow-up reports on each member state were prepared at different times, and may not be directly comparable. The mutual evaluations are intended as a tool to assist countries to improve their AML regimes and to allow the FATF to exert peer pressure on reluctant countries. The evaluations are not a global comparative survey for scholarly analysis.

Nonetheless, the FATF mutual evaluation process provides the best primary data on global AML efforts and is an important source for surveys by other organisations, including the Basel Institute. The following sections summarize the most recent evaluations of the AML regimes in the US, the UK and Canada, focusing on any key weaknesses identified.

US

The United States had a FATF mutual evaluation in 2016, which like the previous evaluation in 2006 was generally positive. The United States has significant exposure to potential money laundering due to the global dominance of the US dollar. The US was one of the first countries to place significant focus on money laundering and has a developed anti-money laundering system.

Of FATF's 40 recommendations, the US was found compliant with 11, largely compliant with 20, partially compliant with 6 and non-compliant with 3. The non-compliances related to lacking trans-parency of beneficial ownership and the regulation of designated non- financial businesses and professions including lawyers, accountants and real estate agents.

Mutual legal assistance from the US was positive. From 2009 to 2014, the US received 1,541 requests from MLA relating to money laundering, terrorist financing or asset forfeiture and recovery and granted the request in 1,062 of those cases.

Table 4.6 Response to Incoming MLA Requests

Response to incoming MLA requests	ML	TF	Asset Forfeiture
Granted	568	53	501
Deined (gronds include lack of evidence, assitance not legally available, and other process reason)	64	3	72
ML and asset forfeiture cases: Other reason for not executing request (includes unable to located evidence, and other non- process reasons)	150	N/A	102
TF cases: Other reason for not executing request (includes no response from requestor, unable to locate evidence, and withdrawn	N/A	14	N/A
Inexecutable under U.S law	4	0	10
Total number of MLA requests related to ML, TF & asset forfeiture	786	70	685

***Source:** US Mutual Evaluation Report (FATF, 2016) at 164.*

In the same years, 21 requests to extradite a money laundering suspect were made, resulting in 10 extraditions. Contested extraditions took an average of one year to resolve.

Table 4.7 Response to Incoming Extradition Requests

Response to incoming extradition requests	ML	TF
Granted	10	0
Denied	3	0
Other (includes cases withdrawn, fugitive not located, fugitive located in another country or fugitive arrested in requesting country)	6	0
Inexecutable under U.S law	2	0
Total number of MLA requests related to ML, TF	21	0

***Source:** US Mutual Evaluation Report (FATF, 2016), at 165.*

One beneficial aspect of the US system is the assigning of an attorney to US embassies in specific countries to assist in mutual legal assistance and extradition requests.

Recommendations made in the FATF mutual evaluation include ensuring beneficial ownership information is required to be obtained at the federal level as well as assessing and addressing exposure to the risk of money laundering by non-financial businesses and professions such as lawyers, accountants and real estate agents.

UK

The last mutual evaluation of the UK took place in 2007. Overall, the assessment team concluded that the country's AML regime was effective. As the executive summary notes:

- The UK has a comprehensive legal structure to combat money laundering and terrorist financing. The money laundering offence is broad, fully covering the elements of the Vienna and Palermo Conventions, and the number of prosecutions and convictions is increasing. The terrorist financing offence is also broad. The introduction of the Proceeds of Crime Act 2002 (POCA) has had a significant and positive impact on the UK's ability to restrain, confiscate and recover proceeds of crime. The UK has also established an effective terrorist asset freezing regime. Overall, the UK FIU appears to be a generally effective FIU. The UK has designated a number of competent authorities to investigate and prosecute money laundering offences. Measures for domestic and international co- operation are generally comprehensive as well.

However, the report noted that a key weakness in the regime was its failure to comply fully with Recommendation 5 (customer due diligence, which is now Recommendation 10 in the 2012 Recommendations).

A follow-up report produced in 2009 describes the steps the UK had taken to address the deficiencies identified in the 2007 report. It concludes that:

- The UK has taken substantive action towards improving compliance with Recommendation 5, and nearly all of the deficiencies identified in the MER [mutual evaluation report] relating to the customer due diligence (CDD) framework have been addressed by the Money Laundering Regulations 2007. Although a few shortcomings remain, the UK has taken sufficient action to bring its compliance to a level essentially equivalent to LC [largely compliant].

The UK has recently introduced a beneficial ownership law that requires disclosure in a publicly accessible registry of the beneficial ownership of companies and trusts. That law will greatly aid in the identification of money launderers. Mandatory disclosure of beneficial ownership is discussed more fully in Chapter 5, Section 5.2.2.

Canada

Canada had a FATF mutual evaluation in 2016, and that evaluation noted significant progress since the previous evaluation in 2007. The FATF report noted overall that "Canada has a strong framework to fight ML and TF, which relies on a comprehensive set of laws and regulations, as well as a range of competent authorities." Of the 40 FATF recommendations, Canada was found compliant with 11, largely compliant with 18, partially compliant with 6 and non-compliant with 5. The non-compliant ratings resulted from the anti-money laundering legal obligations being inoperative in respect to lawyers, inadequate beneficial ownership laws (discussed in Chapter 5, Section 5.2.2 of this book) and failing to meet the standards for foreign politically exposed persons.137 The latter concern was addressed through amended regulations to the Proceeds of Crime (Money Laundering) and Terrorist Financing Act in July 2016.

The evaluation states that most high-risk areas are governed by Canada's AML/CTF framework, but finds that the exemption of legal counsel, law firms and Quebec notaries is a "significant loophole" in Canada's framework.138 This has a trickle-down effect throughout the AML/CTF regime. As the evaluation notes "[i]n light of these professionals' key gatekeeper role, in particular in high-risk sectors and activities such as real-estate transactions and the formation of corporations and trusts, this constitutes a serious impediment to Canada's efforts to fight ML."

The evaluation suggests that law enforcement results are not commensurate with Canada's money laundering risk and that asset recovery appears low. The report notes that some provinces appear more effective in asset recovery, citing Quebec as an example. As discussed in Chapter 6, Section 3.1.2, Quebec is the only province to have a dedicated, multi- governmental anti-corruption agency.

As discussed in Section 5.4.4 of this chapter, the evaluation is also critical of the prosecution of money laundering cases, finding that there is a high percentage of withdrawals and stays of proceedings and that sanctions in money laundering cases are not sufficiently dissuasive.

The evaluation commended Canada's mutual legal assistance system. From 2008 to 2015, Canada received 383 mutual legal assistance requests for money laundering offences. Canada provided assistance in 253 of these requests, while 17 were withdrawn, 36 abandoned and 7 refused. Feedback from 46 counties found that assistance provided by Canada is of good quality.

Canada is also cooperative with extradition requests, although the process can be lengthy. From 2008 to 2015, Canada received 92 requests for extradition in money laundering cases, 77 of which came from the US. These resulted in 48 persons being extradited and 13 subject to other measures such as deportation or voluntary return.143 As noted in Section 6.3.1 of this chapter, contested extradition from the US in money laundering cases is resolved in one year on average. The extradition process from Canada is lengthier, with 53% of cases taking 18 months to 5 years to complete, 28% from 3 to 5 years and 4% over 5 years.

Recommendations stemming from the mutual evaluation included mitigating the risks posed by the exclusion of lawyers, law firms and Quebec notaries from the

MLTF Act, engaging prosecutors at earlier stages in money laundering cases and ensuring asset recovery is pursued as a policy objective.

Other Evaluations

As the previous two sections demonstrate, both the FATF and the Basel Institute are relatively positive about the performance of the US, the UK and Canada. However, in the case of the Basel Index this is a relative measure – it simply shows that many other countries in the world are doing worse in reducing or controlling their risk of money laundering. In the case of the FATF mutual evaluations, most of the focus is on implementation of the Recommendations. However, in some cases, even complete compliance with the FATF Recommendations may not produce an effective AML regime in practice. Some commentators have produced more critical reviews of the AML regimes discussed above.

The excerpt below is from a 2013 Canadian Senate report entitled "Follow the Money: Is Canada Making Progress in Combatting Money Laundering and Terrorist Financing? Not Really." 147 This Report was completed pursuant to section 72 of the PCMLTFA, which mandates that a Parliamentary Committee review the act every five years. As the title of the report suggests, the Senate committee found that there is little evidence that the PCMLTFA, FINTRAC and the rest of Canada's anti-money laundering regime is effective at reducing or prosecuting money laundering. The Report goes on to suggest eighteen recommendations for reform. The following excerpt (pages 5-7) provides an overview of the Committee's findings and recommendations:

BEGINNING OF EXCERPT

The Impact

Recognizing that Canada's anti-money laundering and anti-terrorist financing legislation has had incremental changes over the past 11 years, the Committee believes that it is appropriate to examine the extent to which Canada's Regime is effective in detecting and deterring the laundering of money and the financing of terrorist activities, and contributes to the successful investigation and prosecution of those who are involved in these criminal activities. The Committee is interested in the responses to several questions:

- Have the scope and magnitude of money laundering and terrorist financing in Canada diminished over time?
- Are the time, money and other resources dedicated to addressing these activities having sufficient "results?" and
- What changes are needed to bring about better "results?"

Throughout the hearings, the Committee questioned witnesses about the scope and magnitude of money laundering and terrorist financing in Canada. While the Committee learned that FINTRAC has a solid reputation internationally, witnesses shared only limited and imprecise information about the extent to which the Regime meets its objective of detecting and deterring money laundering and terrorist financing. The Committee believes that there continues to be a clear need for legislation to combat money laundering and terrorist financing in Canada.

The Committee feels that there is a lack of clear and compelling evidence that Canada's Regime is leading to the detection and deterrence of money laundering and terrorist financing, as well as contributing to law enforcement investigations and a significant rate of successful prosecutions. It is possible that some witnesses were unable to share confidential information in a public meeting. It is also possible that information about the success or failure of the Regime is not being collected. In any event, the Committee feels that the current Regime is not working as effectively as it should, given the time, money and other resources that are being committed by reporting entities, a variety of federal departments and agencies, other partners and taxpayers.

Given that multinational financial institutions have recently been implicated in money laundering and terrorist financing, the Committee is concerned about non-compliance with the Act by reporting entities. While the majority of non-compliance charges laid in Canada are in relation to cross-border reporting offences, the Committee is aware of the July 2012 report by the United States (U.S.) Senate Permanent Subcommittee on Investigations of the U.S. Senate Committee on Homeland Security and Governmental Affairs, entitled U.S. Vulnerabilities to Money Laundering, Drugs, and Terrorist Financing: HSBC Case History, in relation to HSBC and money laundering using international wire transfers. [In 2013, HSBC paid $1.9 billion to settle money laundering charges filed by the US Department of Justice.] The U.S. Senate Committee made several recommendations designed to strengthen anti-money laundering and anti-terrorist financing controls, particularly in relation to large, multinational financial institutions with affiliates in jurisdictions that are considered to be at high risk of being targeted by money launderers and those who finance terrorism. As financial institutions play a critical role in preventing illicit money from entering the financial system, the Committee feels that FINTRAC must be vigilant in ensuring that Canada's reporting entities comply with their obligations under the Act.

The Committee believes that an approach involving incremental legislative and regulatory changes must end. Consequently, ongoing efforts are needed to ensure that the resources committed to detecting, deterring, investigating and prosecuting money laundering and terrorist financing offences have the best "results" in the least costly, burdensome and intrusive manner. While it is virtually impossible to eliminate the illegal activities that lead to the need to launder money, a continuation of the current incremental approach – which appears to involve changes to fill gaps by adding reporting entities and to meet evolving FATF recommendations that may or may not have relevance for Canada – is not the solution that Canada needs at this time.

Having conducted a comprehensive study, the Committee's view is that the Act should be amended to address three issues:

- the existence of a structure for Canada's Regime that leads to increased performance in relation to the detection, deterrence, investigation and prosecution of money laundering and terrorist financing;
- the existence of information-sharing arrangements that ensure that suitable information is being collected and shared with the right people at the appropriate time, bearing in mind the need to protect the personal information of Canadians; and
- the existence of a scope and focus for the Regime that is properly directed to ensuring that individuals and businesses report the required information to the appropriate entity in an expedient manner.

The time for incremental change to the Regime has ended. The time for examination of fundamental issues has arrived.

END OF EXCERPT

Some commentators criticize the high costs of AML measures for businesses and society and question whether these costs are worth the potentially negligible benefits of AML regimes.149 See, for example, Michael Levi & Peter Reuter, "Money Laundering" (2006) 32:1 Crime and Justice.

Barriers to Creating Effective AML Measures

There are a variety of reasons why it is difficult to create effective AML measures. First, there are the difficulties posed by the lack of information available to legislators at the national and international level. There is no accurate estimate of the global scope of money laundering or its extent in any particular country. This makes it difficult to evaluate the success of any particular AML measure, since we cannot accurately measure the impact of any such measure. The secrecy surrounding government and FIU information also poses a challenge to those researching the effectiveness of AML measures.

Investigation of money laundering also presents many problems, such as the morass of data and the length of time between a corrupt act and its discovery.151 A further difficulty is that a successful AML regime relies heavily on the cooperation of the financial sector, which may have much more money to gain by facilitating money laundering than stopping it. As Beare and Schneider note in their 2007 book Money Laundering in Canada:

- The rhetoric of financial institutions come across as if all of the objectives of the banks are equal: profit, risk management, customer satisfaction, and a sense of societal/corporate responsibility towards the reduction of money laundering. In reality, these goals are often seen to be contradictory and are not given equal attention. As we have noted, a focus on profitability runs throughout the banking sector. Picking up on the 'what gets measured and gets rewarded, gets done' line of reasoning (Bogach and Gordon, 2000), it is important to consider the reward system within those institutions that have claimed to implement sound voluntary codes, especially where those codes might work against other rewarded objectives. During the US Senate's 1999 review of the operations of private banking, one bank official stated that 'no- one took the "know-your-customer" policies seriously until bonuses were threatened.' The internal study of bank defalcations [failure to repay loans] within Canadian financial institutions revealed a maze of individual, departmental, and branch incentives that were offered based on performance. These individual and group rewards were so coveted that they were seen to be partially responsible for overzealous banking decisions (e.g., unwise loans and credit lines). Peer pressure from group incentives was particularly powerful. Hence any policy that resulted in the loss of customers – especially customers with large amounts of money – operated against the current reward structure. Banks are organized around the concept of attracting funds, and few banks reward those who turn money away.

Gordon further criticizes this reliance on the private sector to report transactions and keep records. He calls for a greater role for the public sector and FIUs in AML efforts.153 The recent movement to require public disclosure of the beneficial owners of shell companies and trusts is discussed in Chapter 5, Section 5.2.2 of this book.

Fletcher and Hermann outline several other challenges for AML regimes. 154 Political immunity of high-level politicians may block prosecution of money laundering offences. Corrupt officials may also use AML measures to freeze funds of their opponents and can frustrate the efforts of law enforcement in other countries to gather evidence against themselves or their government. Bank secrecy laws continue to pose a challenge to AML efforts, although strict secrecy has been relaxed due to FATF blacklisting and increased international pressure since September 11, 2001. Finally, Fletcher and Hermann note that the creation of FIUs is expensive for developing countries, and the effectiveness of FIUs has been questioned in less advanced, cash-oriented economies.

www.ingramcontent.com/pod-product-compliance
Lightning Source LLC
LaVergne TN
LVHW062115200926
848484LV00007B/1674
9781787151369